EARLY FIREARMS OF GREAT BRITAIN AND IRELAND

from the collection of Clay P. Bedford

EARLY FIREARMS

OF GREAT BRITAIN AND IRELAND FROM

THE COLLECTION OF CLAY P. BEDFORD

The Metropolitan Museum of Art

Distributed by New York Graphic Society, Greenwich, Connecticut

Designed by Peter Oldenburg
Printed by Reehl Litho, Inc.
Copyright © 1971 by The Metropolitan Museum of Art
All rights reserved

Library of Congress catalog card number   77-178856
Paperbound, International Standard Book Number   0-87099-113-2
Clothbound, International Standard Book Number   0-87099-112-4

CONTENTS

INTRODUCTION

The first mention of a handgun in England is found in a writ dated 7th November 1388. However, from extant examples, one could begin the study of English hand firearms with Henry VIII. Before Henry's invasion of France in 1513, John de Castro, a merchant of Spain, was commissioned to supply eighty handguns, each complete with powder horn, for which he was paid six shillings a gun. In a royal proclamation of 1544, concerning firearms for military use as well as for hunting, Henry considered it expedient to have "some number of his subjects skilled and exercised in the feat of shooting in handguns and hagbusshes, as well for the defence of the realm against enemies," and stated that he would give "licence and liberty to all and singular his majesty's subjects born within his grace's dominions being of age of sixteen and upwards that they and every of them from henceforth may lawfully shoot in handguns and hagbusshes without incurring forfeiture loss or damage for the same." However, it was still forbidden to shoot game in the neighborhood of any of the King's palaces, and in any other place without the license of the owner of the ground. The earliest breechloading handguns appear to be the two made for Henry VIII now in the Tower of London. The original locks, evidently wheel-locks, are missing from both. One of the guns has the initials HR and the date 1537 on the finely chased and gilt barrel; on the breech block is stamped WH over a fleur-de-lis. This may be the mark of William Hunt, who was appointed Keeper of the King's Handguns and Demi-Hawks in 1538. In the inventory of 1547 of arms and armor at the Tower are listed 6700 "demi-hakes or hand-gonnes," also 275 "shorte gonnes for horsemen, w^h cases of lether furnyshed w^h hornes and purses." Leaving aside military firearms, there is clear evidence that fine firearms were being made in London early in the 17th century. Enriched fowling pieces were sent in 1614 as a gift from James I to Philip III of Spain, the remnants of which are still in the Royal Armory in Madrid. It is probable that these arquebuses were made by the London craftsman Stephen Russell. Russell's name occurs in the accounts of the Exchequer as receiving payment for "rich damasked pieces" and "rich white pieces" with cases, flasks, and molds. In London the Worshipful Company of Gunmakers was first established in 1637, the gunmakers having previously belonged to the Company of Workmen Armourers. This incorporation and the ultimate adoption of a proofmark (interlaced letters GP crowned used in conjunction with the view mark V crowned) of the Gunmakers' Company was the beginning of the compulsory proof of firearms in England. English firearms antedating 1700 are extraordinarily rare.

This exhibition covers about three centuries and deals primarily with civilian firearms. With the excepton of two Elizabethan pieces, a matchlock musket of about 1580 (no. 102) and a snaphance carbine of about 1600 (no. 103), and a James I dog-lock musket of about 1610 (no. 104), the earliest date from the English Civil War and Commonwealth periods (1642-60). Beginning about 1680 is a remarkable group of gentleman's holster pistols with steel or silver mounts. In the early part of the 17th century, when journeys were made on horseback, long holster pistols were common. Throughout the 18th century, when private coaches and public stages ran between the more important towns, shorter pistols became fashionable. There were no railways or police, and when traveling more than a few miles, it was usual to go armed. The dueling pistol was a highly developed weapon, and England, more than any other country, was responsible for its design. It had refinements such as accurate sights, quick-firing locks with adjustable hair triggers, heavy barrels to prevent flinching, and specially fitted stocks for natural balance. The wooden case with accessories was introduced to house the dueling pistol.

Firearms with unusual structural features, seldom found outside museums or collections of experienced collectors, are included in this exhibition. Early breechloaders are well represented by ingenious inventions, although none were entirely successful, since it was not possible to make a practical breechloader with the use of loose powder. Safety devices designed to prevent the accidental discharge of loaded weapons were among the most important mechanical improvements. An early safety is the steel or battery in the snaphance, as it can be kept away from the pan until ready to discharge. The dog lock, a safety of English origin early in the 17th century, was widely used on New England muskets.

The ballistics of firearms antedating 1700 were primitive; the bores were large, over $\frac{1}{2}$ inch, imparting to the flight of the ball a high trajectory; the effective range was rarely over fifty yards, at which distance, however, the striking force was terrific. Little attention seems to have been paid to the importance of maintaining a meticulously clean bore: the composition and efficiency of black powder varied hopelessly; guns became fouled, hot, and useless after the first few shots. Except in unusual cases, guns were clumsy to handle, and the gunlocks were of such uncertain performance that wing shooting was almost impossible.

Sporting and custom-built officer's firearms form the heart of the exhibition. By the early 1700s in England, shooting birds on the wing was beginning to become popular. *The Sportsmen's Directory* (1792) recorded that "the art of shooting flying is arrived at tolerable perfection." Great lovers of the chase were often great patrons of the arts. For this reason a craftsman was apt to take special care in making his patron's gun an object of beauty as well as of precision. During all the British Colonial wars, many of the officers carried non-military weapons, that is, sporting arms, generally ornamented, which had been acquired before the call to service. The flintlock gun was brought to its highest perfection by Joseph (1795-1835) and John Manton (1780-1834), Henry Nock (1772-1804), Durs Egg

(1785-1834), and James Purdey, Sr. (1784-1863); the work of these masters is well represented in the exhibition. These pieces are reminders that the lock, stock, and barrel of the modern gun are simply the perfection of ideas that are centuries old. The early English firearms are appreciated for the proven strength of the metal used in the barrels, the reliability of performance of the locks, the excellent quality of workmanship, and their attractive finished appearance. It is hoped that the visitor to this exhibition will not look upon them merely as weapons, but rather as objects that required consummate skill on the part of the artists who made them. Moreover, a sportsman would naturally take excellent care of his firearms, so that they would perform efficiently in the field, and this accounts for the fine condition of most of those exhibited.

It should be recalled that the famous British gunmakers who turned out sporting guns also worked for the government by private contract, although mainly in a supervisory capacity. The fine rifled sporting gun was a superior weapon, and it was from private customers, rather than from government departments, that gunmakers received their incentive toward technical improvements. During the period 1805-35, British gunmakers made contributions, many of which are included in the exhibition, that revolutionized the art. In studying the mechanisms represented, one sees the gunmakers' ingenuity in solving these intricate problems; in studying the ornament, how skillfully the design was adopted to structural features—often an ornamental scroll served the additional purpose of giving strength to the delicate reverse-curved hammer.

The reliability of the firearm was determined by the lock, and this, the most delicate mechanism of the piece, was also the most developed. The cock was strongly sprung and its action made short and sharp; a bridle from the pan to the steel screw appeared late in the 17th century (see no. 12); the friction of the mainspring with the tumbler of the lock was eliminated by a link between them; a roller and bridge were fitted to the steel spring, thus smoothing the forward movement of the pan cover when the flint struck the steel; a pivoted segment known as the "detent" was applied to the side of the tumbler to prevent the sear from catching in the half-cock notch when the lock was fired; waterproof pans were developed.

The performance of the firearm depended upon the quality of the barrel. A historic patent, No. 1598, was issued to Henry Nock on April 25, 1787, whereby the touchhole was pierced into a chamber in the center of the breech plug, enabling the priming powder to ignite the middle of the charge in the barrel. In 1806 J. Jones patented an improved method of manufacturing gun barrels. He made the barrels by twisting a skelp with beveled edges around a mandril, so that the edges overlapped each other, and then welding together the edges of the skelp. Once introduced, the manufacture of twisted barrels increased rapidly in importance. In fact, the principles of welding and forging iron and steel to give both practical and aesthetic results had been in use for centuries. The best double-barrels were welded together, not merely juxtaposed and bound. A late development was the method of hooking the barrel to the false breech, which facilitated the removal of the barrel for cleaning or storing. The last barrel maker of note was William Fullerd of Clerkenwell, a man of high reputation for all kinds of sporting barrels (see no. 131).

The exhibition presents firearms made by about 125 leading British and Irish gunmakers during a period when they were world renowned for their skill. Most of the pieces were made in London. However, some of the finest work was done by provincial gunmakers. Doncaster, Oxford, Rochester, Salisbury, Warwick, Whitehaven, and Windsor are represented by firearms of exceptional quality. The exhibition also includes many fine firearms, especially in the two-, three-, and four-barrel types, that were made in Birmingham, sometimes completely finished there but sold through a dealer in London with the dealer's trade name and the London Gunmakers' proofmarks. The Birmingham Proof Company was formed in 1813; its proofmark comprises the letters BPC below the crown and crossed scepters. Twenty-seven of the English items have silversmiths' marks, all but two of which have been identified.

Ireland and Scotland are each represented by six gunmakers. The Rigby family, active in Dublin since 1735, is represented by four percussion-cap firearms. One of these (no. 213) made by William and John Rigby has an ingenious lock that has a hammer with a revolving turret head arranged over a group of four nipples; as the hammer was cocked, the striker moved round to each nipple in turn. The latest firearm in the exhibition (no. 101) is a cased double-barreled centerfire cartridge rifle made by Alexander Henry in Edinburgh in 1875, a Christmas present from Queen Victoria to her personal attendant John Brown.

In preparing the catalogue, care was taken to date the pieces accurately. The dating is based on the style and decorative and structural features of each firearm. When it bears the gunmaker's name, dates of his activities are known; when the original owner's name is engraved on the firearm or when the original owner has been identified from a crest on the escutcheon, this is often an aid in establishing a date. There are a score of such instances in the exhibition, and of special interest are nos. 91 and 94-96, which bear the crest of the dukes of Bedford. Silver mounts made after the Silver Act of 1738 are often marked with a date letter, which is usually accurate within a year or two of the making of the piece. Firearms were often numbered in sequence, hence the dates of serial numbers on pieces in the exhibition were identified from records of the gunmakers; some military firearms are dated on the lock plate and also bear the contractor's name (see Group 9, Military Pistols); dates are also determined from patent numbers such as those appearing on nos. 101, 125, 132, 140, 141, and 185; a few other pieces are dated (see nos. 40, 41, and 80).

The efficient assistance of the staff of The Metropolitan Museum of Art in the preparation of the catalogue and the installation of the exhibition is gratefully acknowledged. The photographs were taken by Richard Dietrich of Phoenix, Arizona, with the exception of the cover illustrations by William F. Pons, manager of the Museum Photo Studio. Too numerous to mention individually are the collectors and curators who aided in the formation of the collection. We must, however, mention W. Keith Neal, Claude Blair, Peter Dale, and Geoffrey Jenkinson, among the English students, and also Leon Jackson of Dallas, Texas, who assisted in the interpretation of the firearms. Due to the limitation of time, it was not practical to complete some of the research that was initiated. John F. Hayward, formerly in charge of Arms and Armour at the Victoria and Albert Museum, and Howard Blackmore, of the Armouries at the Tower of London, made significant contributions to the catalogue. To all the above specialists, the writers extend their appreciation.

CLAY P. BEDFORD

STEPHEN V. GRANCSAY,
Curator Emeritus, Arms and Armor,
The Metropolitan Museum of Art

1

CIVIL WAR AND COMMONWEALTH PISTOLS

The earliest English pistols have locks with a sear that moves horizontally, passing through the lock plate and engaging the tail of the cock when the piece is cocked. The same principle is used in the Dutch snaphance, which derives from the wheel lock. Wheel-lock pistols became a favorite weapon for cavalry by the middle of the 16th century, but no wheel-lock firearm of undoubted English make has yet been identified. However, wheel-lock pistols are shown in the engraved plates to Captain John Cruso's *Militarie Instructions for the Cavallrie*, published in Cambridge in 1632.

A feature of the early English locks on nos. 2–5 is the dog catch that engages on the projecting tail of the cock and serves as a safety catch. Nos. 3–5 have rifled barrels; they are among the earliest rifled pistols of English workmanship. The first patent for rifled barrels was granted in London in 1635 to Arnold Rotsipen, presumably a German immigrant. The inventor claimed "to rifle, cutt out and screwe barrels, as wide or as close, or as deepe or as shallowe, as shall be required, and with great ease."

The plain pistols that comprise this group are today much scarcer than the later pistols with engraved and chased steel or silver mounts, which have always been appreciated for their beauty of ornament.

1. Flintlock Pistol (Bedford 1521)

Barrel, brass, octagonal. Lock plate, flat faced, filed with faceted edge; lock with horizontally acting sear, internal steel spring; cock with rounded face, faceted steel. Walnut full stock with fishtail butt; brass furniture; three side nails; button trigger, no trigger guard.

Apparently the earliest-known English flintlock of this construction, the pistol may be seen as a development between the English lock pistol of 1630–35 in the William G. Renwick collection, Tucson (Lenk, *The Flintlock*, pl. 4, no. 1) and the holster pistol of 1640–45 in the Mark Dinely collection, Berwick St. John, England (Hayward, *The Art of the Gunmaker*, vol. I, pl. 52 a).

About 1640
Overall length 11½ in.; barrel 6⁷⁄₁₆ in.
Caliber .55 (28 gauge). Weight 1 lb.

2. Dog-lock Pistol (Bedford 709)

Barrel in two stages, molded girdle between, octagonal changing to polygonal at breech, forward stage round. Lock plate, flat faced, engraved with conventional flowers and inscribed H. BARNE, with horizontally operating sear, internal steel spring, dog safety catch engaging between half and full cock, loop-neck cock, faceted steel. Stock, solid ebony, carved with conventional leaves, silver butt cap lacking; acorn-shaped trigger, no trigger guard; no proofmarks.

Harman Barne, an immigrant of Dutch or German origin, was gunmaker to Prince Rupert (1619–82), Count Palatine of the Rhine and nephew of Charles I. The prince was a general of the Royalist armies during the Civil War and returned to England in 1660 as Admiral of Charles II's fleet. Barne's activity as a gunmaker to the Royalists caused him trouble during the Commonwealth (1649–60), and in 1650 he was imprisoned and then released on condition that he leave London. He nevertheless remained. In 1657 he was admitted to the Gunmakers' Company. In 1660 he successfully petitioned Charles II for the appointment of Royal Handgun Maker. He died the following year shortly after being appointed to the Court, that is, the governing body, of the Gunmakers' Company. He is best known for his horseman's rifled pistols with turnoff barrels.

Harman Barne, London, about 1640
Overall length 11⅛ in.; barrel 6¼ in.
Caliber .45 (48 gauge). Weight ½ lb.
Literature: George, *English Pistols and Revolvers*, p. 14, pl. III, 5; Hayward, *The Art of the Gunmaker*, vol. I, pp. 212–217.

3. Rifled Dog-lock Pistol (Bedford 1175)

Barrel in two stages separated by faceted girdle, breech octagonal changing to polygonal, engraved with tulips and overlapping leaves, forward stage round, engraved with conventional foliage at girdle and muzzle, rifled with eight grooves; London proofmarks at breech. Lock plate engraved with tulips, cock with monster; horizontally acting sear, dog safety catch. Rosewood (Brazil wood) full stock with silver butt cap pierced

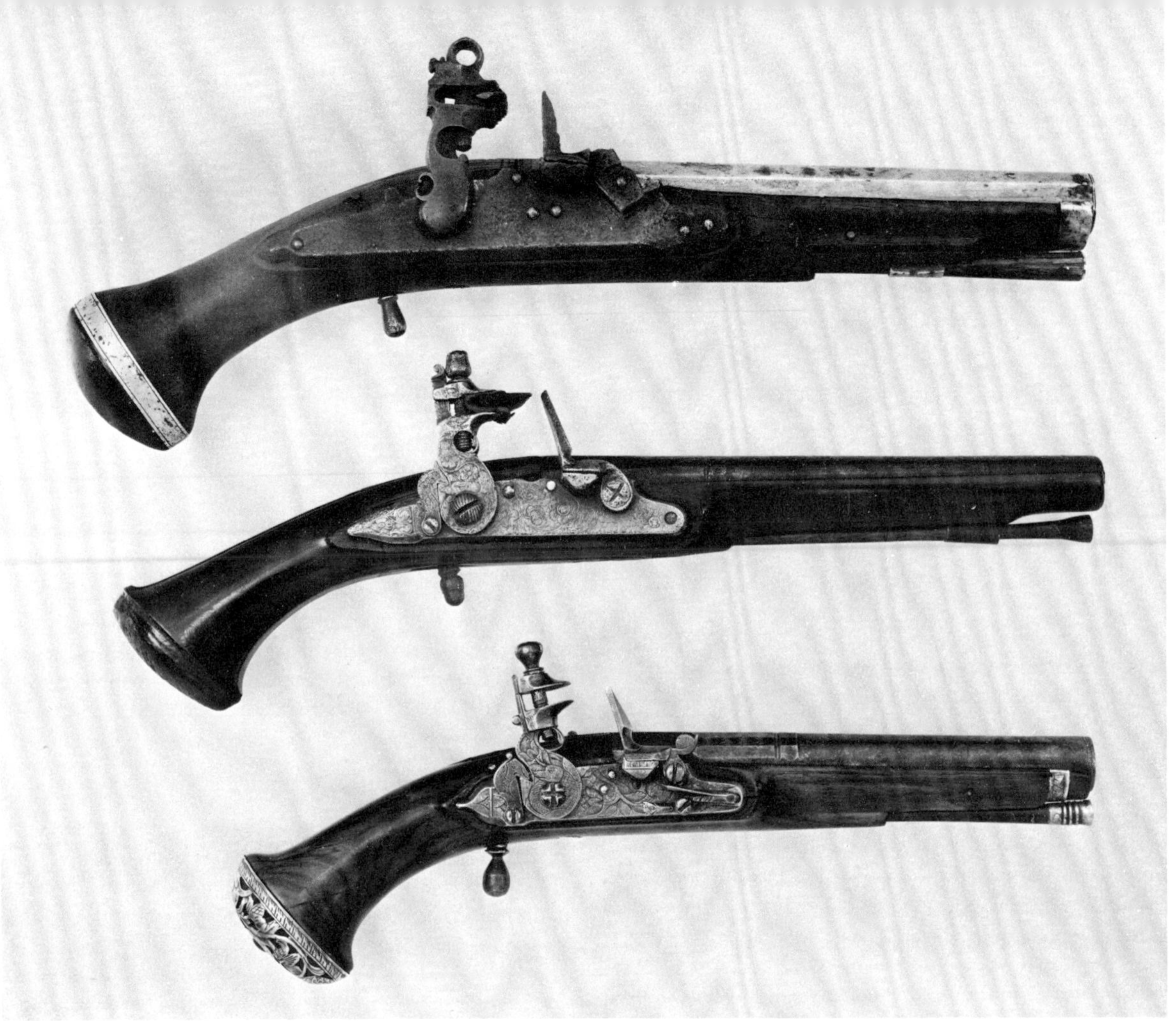

1

4

2

3

5

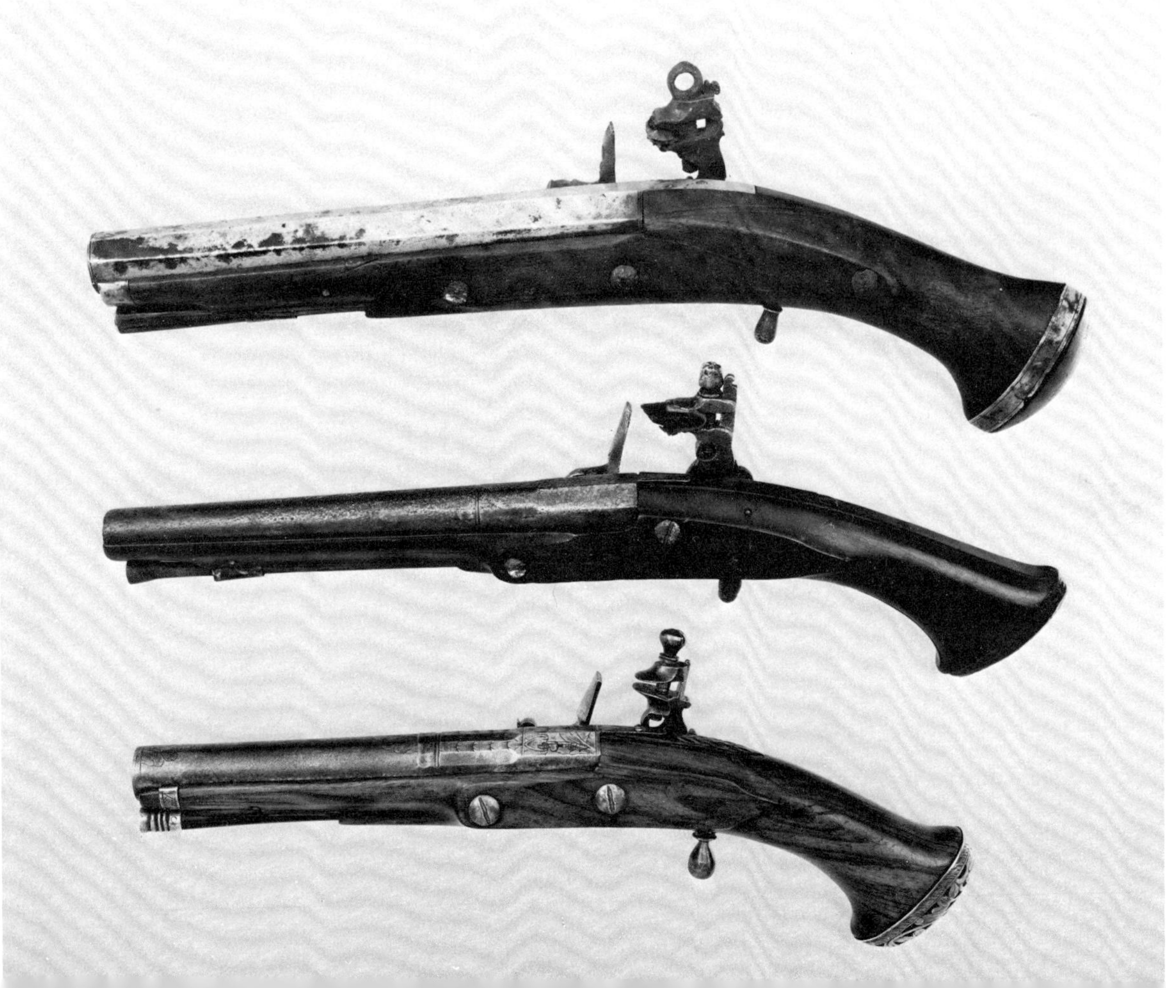

1

4

2

5

3

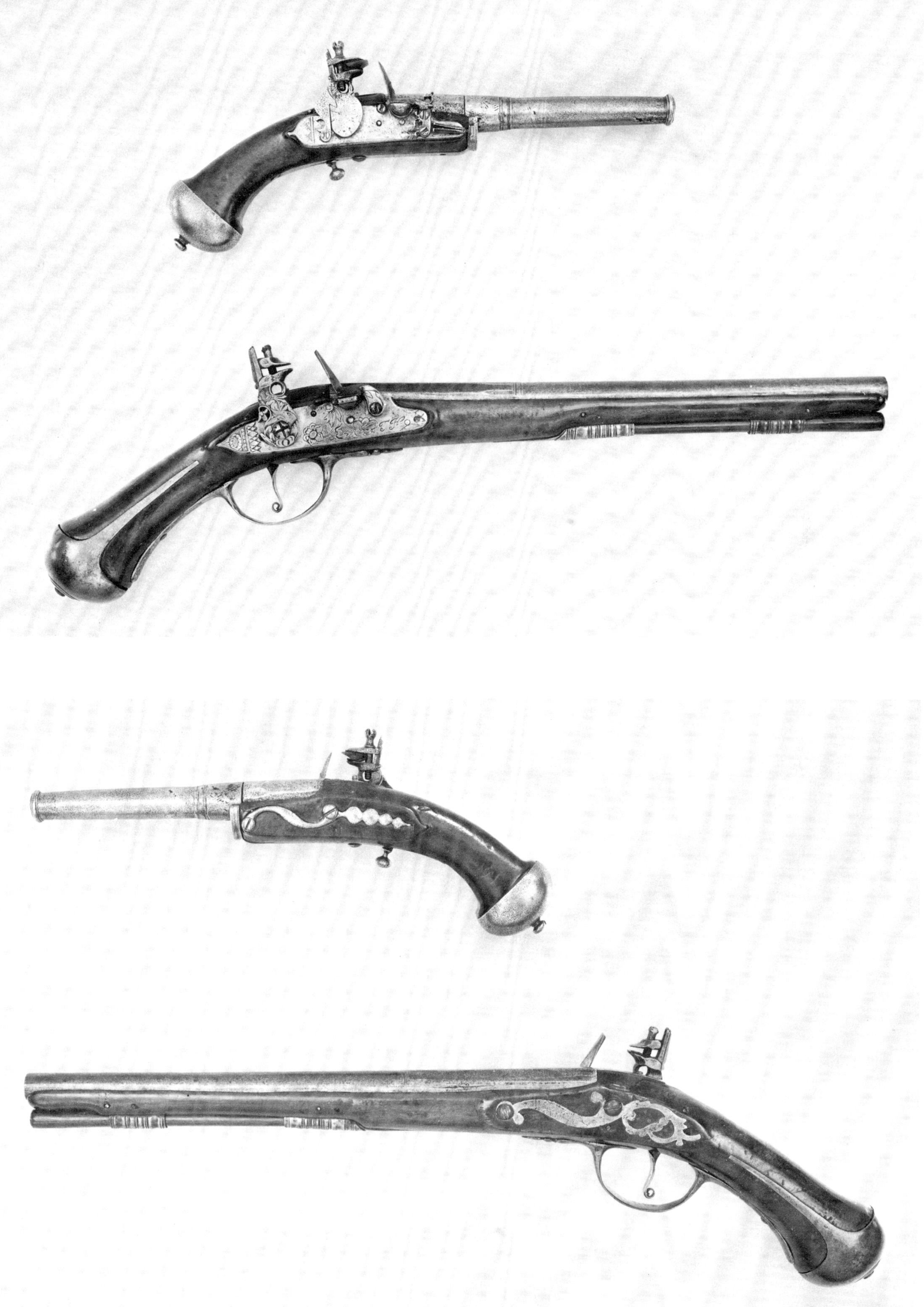

and engraved with conventional flowers; button trigger, no trigger guard.

This pistol is in exceptional condition considering its early date. For a pair of English pistols of similar form from Newburgh Priory, Yorkshire, by tradition Oliver Cromwell's, see Hayward, "English Pistols of the XVII Century," p. 5.

About 1650
Overall length 9¾ in.; barrel 5⅜ in.
Caliber .46 (48 gauge). Weight ½ lb.

4. Rifled Dog-lock Pistol (Bedford 1078)

One of a pair. Turnoff barrel rifled with eight grooves, in two stages, separated by molded girdle, breech octagonal changing to polygonal, forward stage round, molded muzzle ring. Lock plate, flat faced, engraved with tulips; horizontally acting sear, dog safety catch, steel and feather-spring screws joined by bridle. Walnut half stock with steel furniture, oval butt cap, reverse-curved side plate with rattail extension.

This type of rifled pistol, usually of larger dimensions, was much used during the Civil War and Commonwealth periods (1642–60).

About 1650
Overall length 12 in.; barrel 6½ in.
Caliber .45 (48 gauge). Weight 1¼ lb.

5. Rifled Dog-lock Pistol (Bedford 1146)

Barrel rifled with eight grooves, in two stages, molded girdle between, breech octagonal changing to polygonal, forward stage round. Lock of early construction with horizontally operating sear, dog safety catch; lock plate, flat faced, engraved with gunmaker's initials TH and conventional flowers; loop cock engraved with monster; faceted steel, internal steel spring. Walnut full stock; plain steel furniture; spurred pommel; flat, pierced ribbon side plate with two side nails; two baluster ramrod pipes; plain ramrod.

The construction and shape of the lock, and the presence of a dog safety catch as well, are typical of mid-17th-century English firearms.

About 1650
Overall length 20 in.; barrel 13 in.
Caliber .55 (28 gauge). Weight 1¾ lb.

2

SINGLE-BARRELED HOLSTER FLINTLOCK PISTOLS

The thirty-four pistols in this group cover approximately the period 1680–1840. Many of the finest pistols of decorative merit in the exhibition are included here. All, except the latest, have full stocks, and all, save one percussion cap, are flintlocks. The barrels are secured by two transverse pins, except for nos. 35–39, in which they are secured by slides. The early pistols (1680–1700) have decorative figured stocks of burl-walnut with steel, silver, or brass furniture, engraved and chased; the later silver-mounted pistols (1700–86) have straight-grained walnut stocks. Much of the silver furniture is stamped with identifiable silversmith's initials, and also a date letter. A number have an escutcheon engraved with the crest of the original owner.

Gunmakers, proud of their reputations, signed their pieces. The thirty-four signed pieces represent the work of twenty-nine, most of them prominent London gunmakers, though Birmingham, Doncaster, Dublin, Oxford, and Rochester makers are also represented. Many of them were masters of the Gunmakers' Company, which received its charter in 1637.

Portability was a feature that encouraged mounted men to carry pistols. By the time of the English Civil War, cavalrymen carried a pair as well as a sword. They fired at close range without slackening speed and went in with the sword. Pistol fire was also used in pursuit.

6. Holster Pistol (Bedford 1193)

One of a pair. Barrel in three stages separated by molded girdles, engraved over breech with Roman warrior and trophy of arms, forward stages engraved with scrolling foliage; London proofmarks and gunmaker's mark on facet at breech, partly obliterated; two barrel pins; barrel tang engraved and secured by plain screw. Lock plate engraved with man attacking dog, and cherub within foliage; pan integral with lock plate; swan-neck cock; feather spring. Barrel and lock both inscribed C. WARREN. Figured burl-wood stock carved with raised border at barrel tang; steel furniture; pommel, with spurs, has butt cap chased with grotesque mask; dragon side plate has two side nails; escutcheon with acanthus finials; trigger guard has vase-and-acorn finial; ramrod with disk finial passes through two baluster pipes.

Charles Warren was admitted freeman of the Gunmakers' Company in 1684.

Charles Warren, London, about 1680
Overall length 16½ in.; barrel 10 in.
Caliber .56 (28 gauge). Weight 1¾ lb.

7. Holster Pistol (Bedford 711)

One of a pair. Barrel in three stages separated by molded girdles, rear stage octagonal developing into polygonal with alternate facets fluted, forward stages round; engraved strawberry foliage on breech; iron blade front sight; London proofmarks. Lock plate engraved with strawberry foliage terminating in dragon head. Barrel and lock plate inscribed I. DAFTE. Burl-wood stock carved with scrolls; steel furniture; pommel, with spurs, engraved with strawberry foliage and half figure on each side; serpentine side plate; openwork escutcheon chased with mask; trigger guard has vase-and-plant finial.

John Dafte was admitted freeman of the London Gunmakers' Company in 1668 and was master in 1694–95.

John Dafte, London, about 1680
Overall length 18¼ in.; barrel 11¹¹⁄₁₆ in.
Caliber .61 (20 gauge). Weight 2¼ lb.
Literature: George, *English Pistols and Revolvers*, p. 31, pl. 4, nos. 3–4.

8. Holster Pistol (Bedford 1189)

One of a pair. The side plate only of companion pistol, presumably destroyed, is in Victoria and Albert Museum. Barrel, blued, in three stages separated by molded girdles, rear stage octagonal developing into polygonal, forward stages round; engraved foliate scrolls at breech. Lock plate engraved with strawberry foliage, winged cherub, faun's head, and name MATHIAS. Figured burl-wood stock, carved with raised borders; steel furniture; pommel engraved with scrolls, has butt cap chased with lion mask in high relief; side plate flat, pierced, engraved with scolls, half figure, and chimerical heads; escutcheon is pierced plate engraved with foliation, bird heads, bust of warrior, and fool's mask; trigger guard has vase-and-plant finial.

The absence of the London proofmark suggests that this pistol was made by a provincial. The lock plate and furniture are engraved in the manner of Claude and

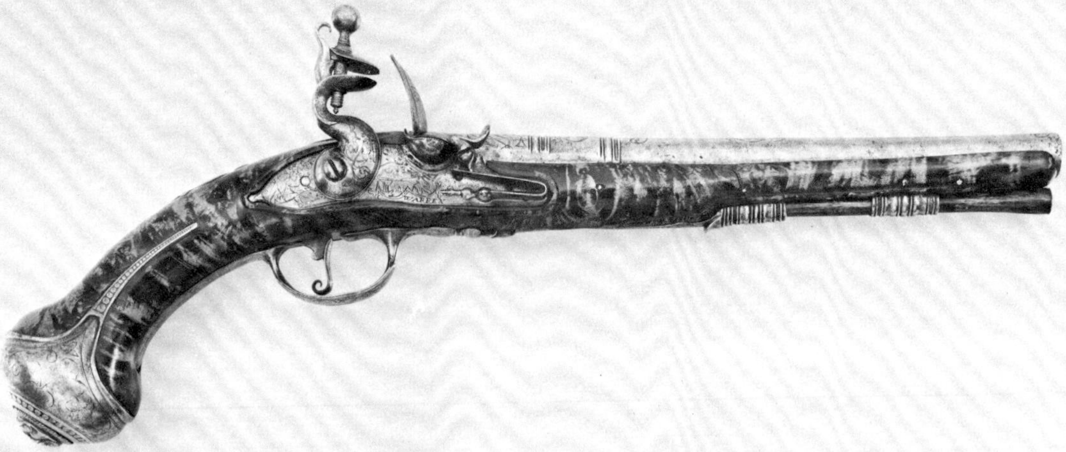

6

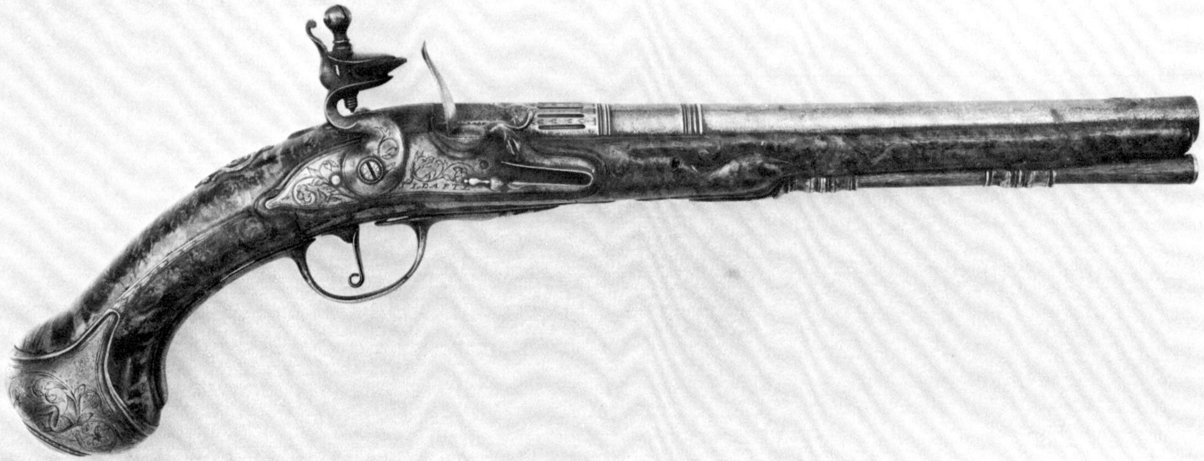

7

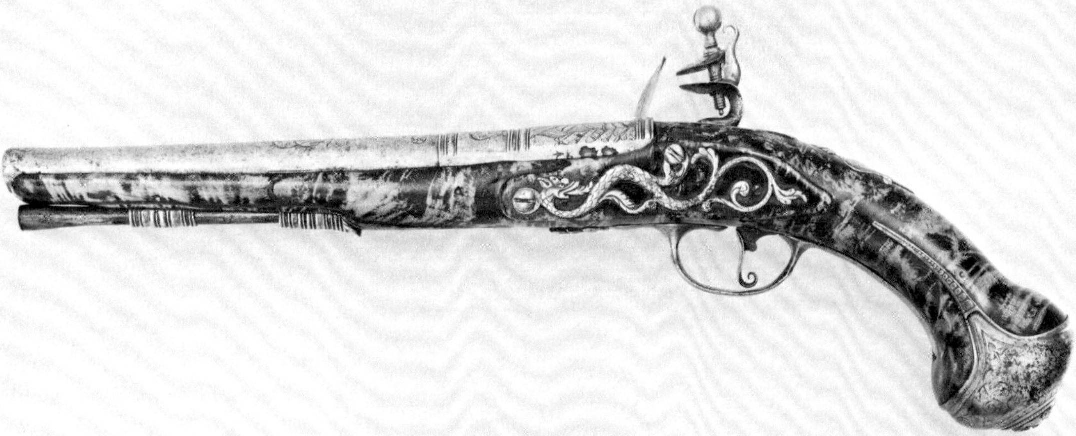

6

7

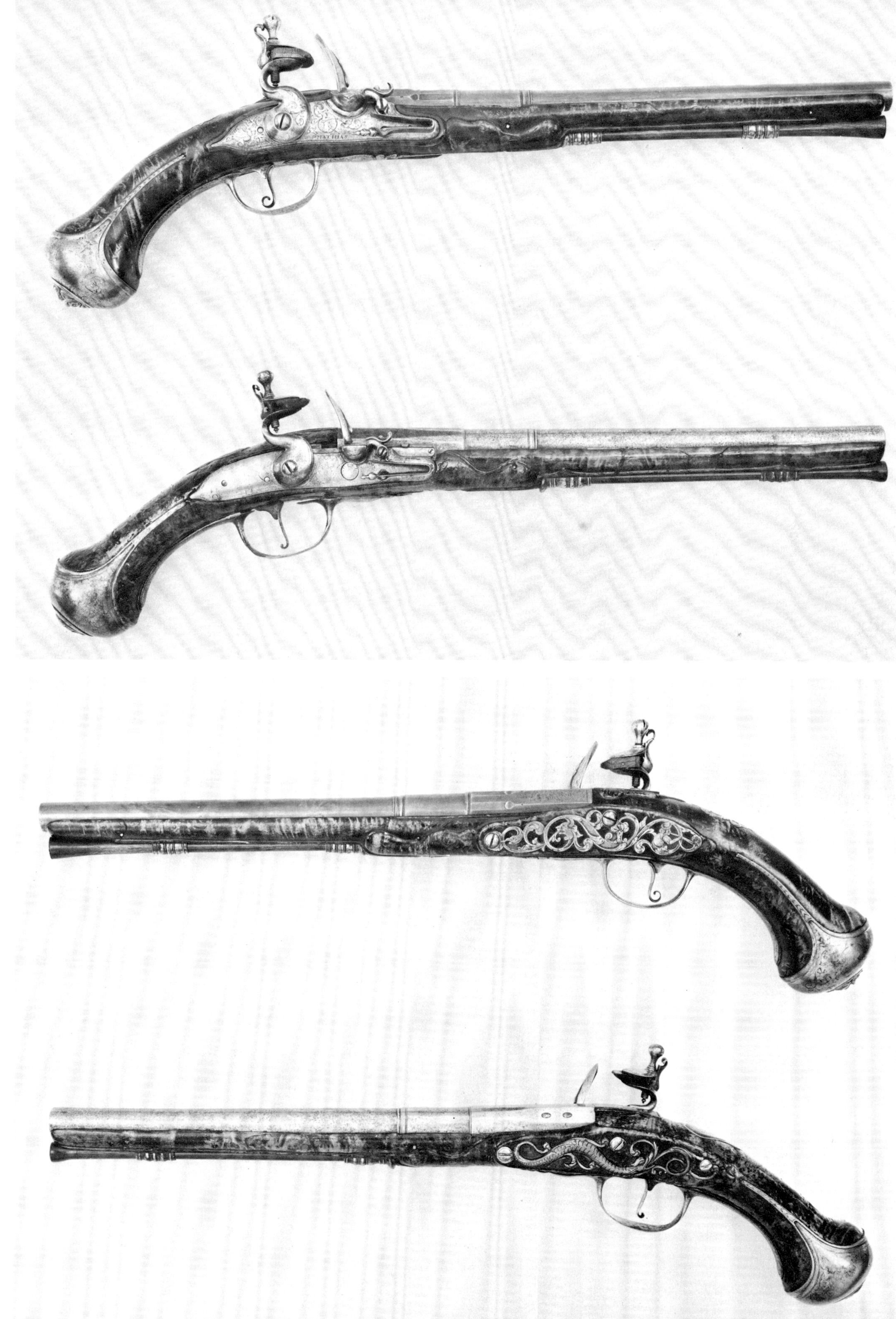

8

9

8

9

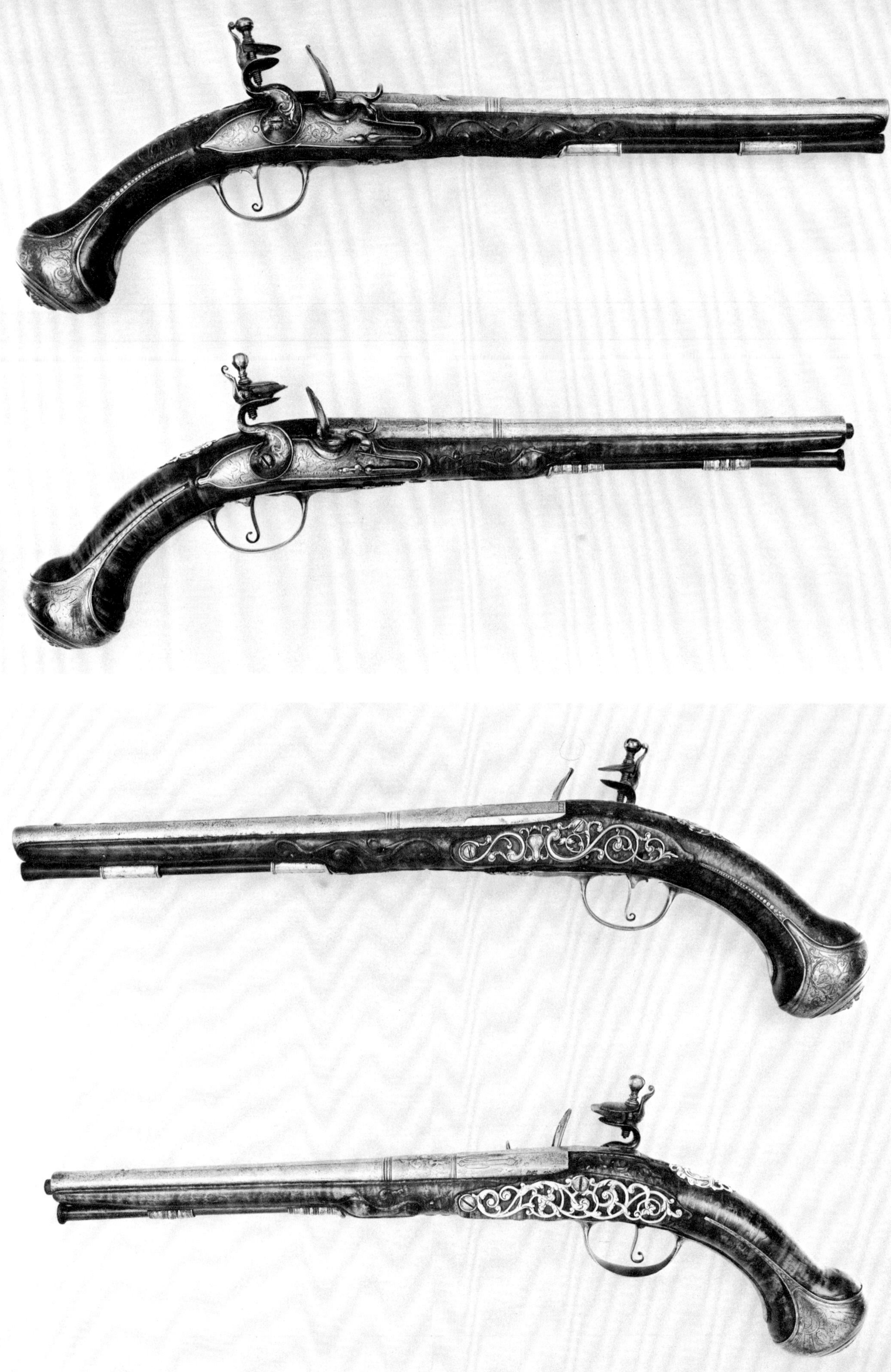

10

11

Jacques Simonin, whose designs were first published in Paris in 1684.

> Mathias, about 1680
> Overall length 20 in.; barrel 13¼ in.
> Caliber .66 (16 gauge). Weight 2¼ lb.
> Literature: Hayward, *The Art of the Gunmaker*, vol. II, p. 329, pl. 19 b.

Andrew Dolep, London, about 1685
Overall length 19¾ in.; barrel 13 in.
Caliber .61 (21 gauge). Weight 2¼ lb.
Literature: Baxter, *Superimposed Load Firearms*, pp. 123–125, pls. 71, 71a; Blackmore, *Guns and Rifles of the World*, figs. 195–196; Hayward, *The Art of the Gunmaker*, vol. II, pp. 60–62; Hayward, "The Firearms Collection of the Armeria Reale, Turin," p. 126, fig. 29 b.

9. Two-shot Superimposed-load Pistol (Bedford 895)

Barrel in three stages, with molded rings between, rear stage faceted, forward two stages round; left breech facet stamped with London proofmarks; two vents, forward one two inches from end of breech. Lock has two pans, lower one integral with lock plate; priming powder placed in upper pan and moves in longitudinal depressed track that leads to front vent; front vent and track have longitudinal hinged cover; upper pan cover released by spring with discoid button below pan and slides toward butt, the reverse of normal; second vent and pan in normal position, second charge fired here. Burl-walnut stock; steel furniture; oval pommel and butt cap chased with lion head in relief; serpentine side plate; inverted-pear-shaped escutcheon; trigger guard with vase finial.

Andrew Dolep, described as a Dutchman and naturalized in 1691, was one of the most gifted London gunmakers during the last quarter of the 17th century. He first applied for admission to the Gunmakers' Company in 1681, but was not admitted until 1686, when he was gunmaker to the Earl of Dartmouth, Master General of the Ordnance. He supplied a fine set of firearms for Ferdinando de' Medici (1663–1713), the eldest son of Grand Duke Cosimo III of Tuscany, including a gun with superimposed load of the same system as no. 9, inscribed DOLEP LONDINI FECIT, now in the Armeria Reale, Turin (no. T 105). Dolep, still working in 1711, died in 1713.

10. Holster Pistol (Bedford 1299)

One of a pair. Barrel in two stages with molded girdle between, engraved and chased with foliate scrolls over breech; sighting rib and iron blade front sight. Lock plate engraved with winged figures terminating in scrolls; cock and steel chased. Figured burl-wood stock, carved with scrolls; steel furniture; pommel engraved with winged figures, and butt cap chased with mask; side plate pierced and chased with foliate

10

11

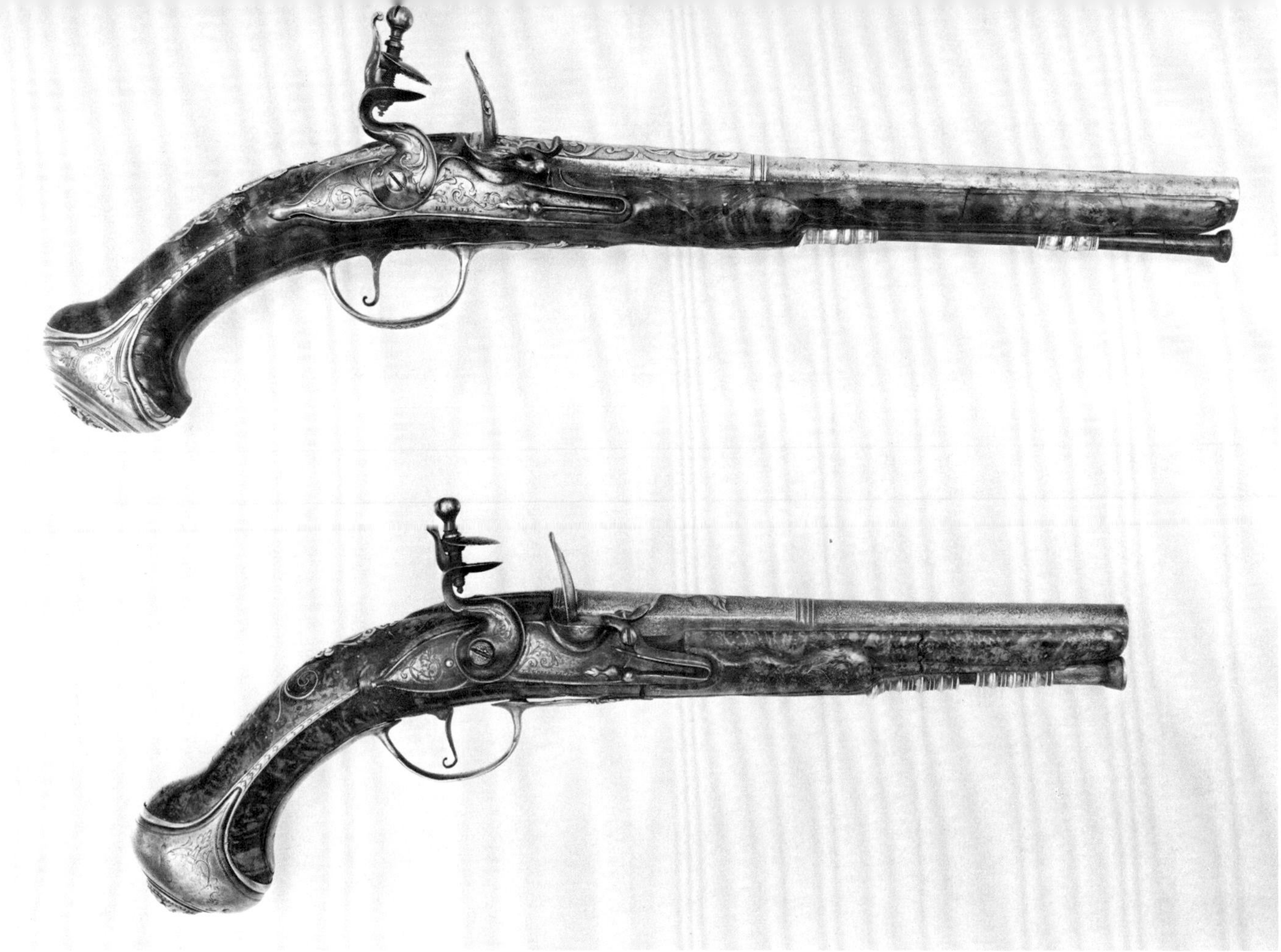

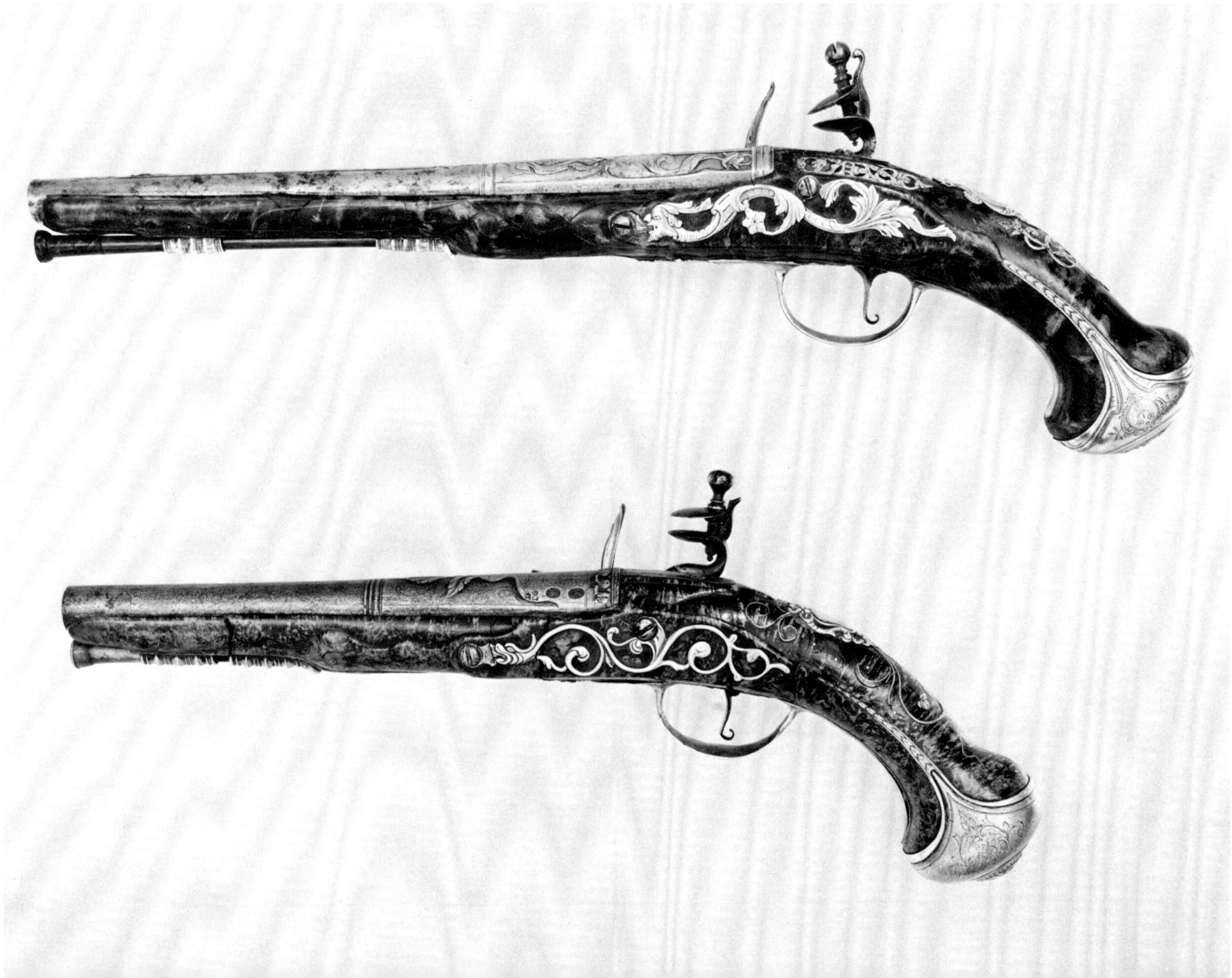

12

scrolls; escutcheon with framed blank area in center surmounted by ducal coronet, flanked by harpies, with mask at base.

13

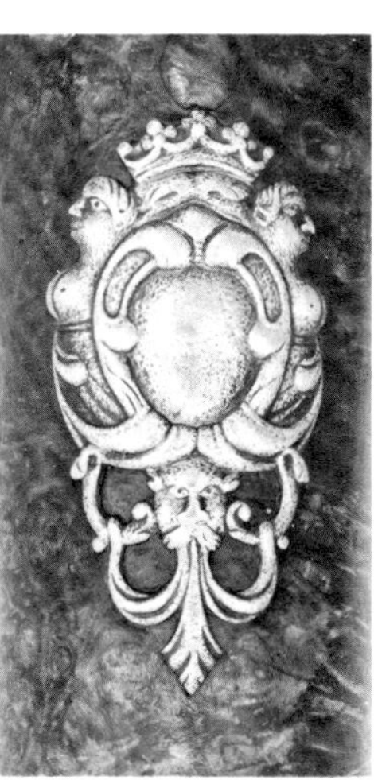

James Ermendinger, an immigrant, became gunmaker to Prince Rupert. He was admitted to the Gunmakers' Company in 1682 and was naturalized in 1689. The motifs on the furniture of no. 10 are almost exact copies from the pattern books of the Paris engravers Claude and Jacques Simonin.

James Ermendinger, London, about 1690
Overall length 19¹³⁄₁₆ in.; barrel 13 in.
Caliber .61 (20 gauge). Weight 2¼ lb.

11. Holster Pistol (Bedford 1547)

Barrel in three stages with molded girdles between, octagonal changing to fluted polygonal at breech, second stage round chased with mask in relief, forward stage round; silver bead front sight. Lock plate with rounded face engraved with trophies of arms and inscribed ERMENDINGER; cock and steel chased with scrolls. Figured burl-wood stock carved with foliate scrolls and raised borders; furniture of polished steel, except side plate and escutcheon, which are of silver; pommel engraved with busts of Roman warriors and trophies of arms; butt cap chased in relief with faun's mask; side plate pierced and chased with leafy scrolls enclosing grotesque head; silver escutcheon is of same design as steel escutcheon on no. 10, its engraved crest effaced; trigger guard has vase-and-plant finial.

James Ermendinger, London, about 1690
Overall length 19¼ in.; barrel 12³⁄₁₆ in.
Caliber .61 (20 gauge). Weight 2¼ lb.

12. Holster Pistol (Bedford 1509)

One of a pair, unusually fine in workmanship. Barrel in two stages with molded girdle between, chased scrollwork over breech enclosing heraldic cartouche; muzzle area chased with long ribbon on which is inscribed HENRY ELLIS IN DONCASTER; barrel tang engraved with bird; sighting rib and silver blade front sight. Lock plate engraved with scrolls and name H. ELLIS; cock and steel chased with foliation; bridle from pan to steel screw. Figured burl-wood stock; silver furniture; butt cap chased in relief with mask; undulating side plate chased with foliation and human-mask finial. Crest of Bagshaw family (London, Derby, Essex) engraved on barrel, escutcheon, and either side of pommel.

12

13

The design of the furniture is based on the pattern book of the Paris engraver Claude Simonin. A pair of flintlock holster pistols with silver furniture, the barrels

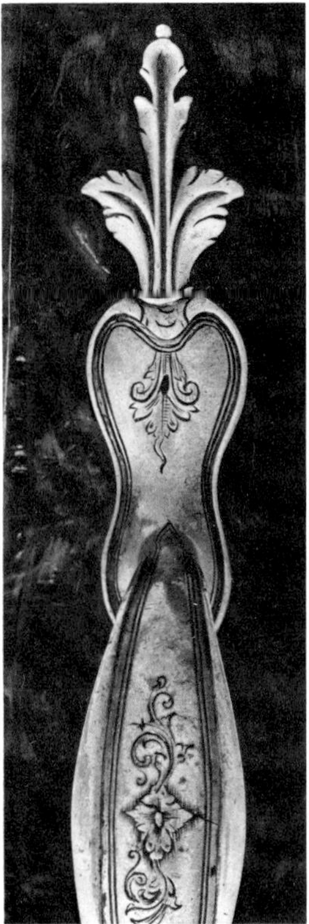

signed HENRY ELLIS IN DONCASTER FECIT, is in the Mark Dinely collection, Berwick St. John, England; their cartouches enclose the crest of Stones of Mosborough, County Derby, and their escutcheons are engraved with the full Stones arms (Hayward, *The Art of the Gunmaker*, pl. 16 b-c). A pair of pocket pistols by Ellis are in the Scott Collection, Glasgow Art Gallery.

Henry Ellis, Doncaster, Yorkshire, about 1690
Overall length 18¾ in.; barrel 12 in.
Caliber .60 (22 gauge). Weight 2¼ lb.

13. Holster Pistol   (Bedford 1250)

Barrel in two stages, molded girdle between, chased over breech with leaf, forward stage round; barrel about three inches shorter than it was originally; stamped with London proofmarks and gunmaker's mark TG crowned. Lock plate engraved with scrolls terminating in monster. Barrel and lock plate inscribed T. GREEN FECIT. Figured burl-walnut stock carved with raised borders and inlaid with scrolling silver wire ending in flower heads; silver furniture bearing silversmith's mark BV (William Bull; entered at Goldsmiths' Hall, 1697); pommel has butt cap chased in relief with mask and is struck with three marks; escutcheon with

blank shield surmounted by mask and bordered with scrolls; trigger guard has vase-and-plant finial and bears three marks, including date letter for 1699, the earliest silver date letter recorded on an English firearm.

The escutcheon is the same as on nos. 14 and 21.

Thomas Green, who worked in the Minories, was admitted freeman of the Gunmakers' Company in 1693 and was master in 1720. Also by Green are a musket with dog lock, lock plate engraved by T. Green, barrel bearing the maker's mark, in the Tower Armouries, London (XII.81), and a holster flintlock pistol illustrated in Glendenning, *British Pistols and Guns*, pl. 3.

Thomas Green, London, 1699
Overall length 15⅝ in.; barrel 9 in.
Caliber .66 (16 gauge). Weight 2¼ lb.

14. Holster Pistol (Bedford 808)

One of a pair; the companion pistol has been re-stocked. Barrel chased with scrolls at breech; sighting rib inscribed WORNALL LONDINI and engraved with figure of Fame blowing trumpet; iron bead front sight. Lock plate inscribed with name WORNALL and engraved with scrolling foliage enclosing winged figure and fly. Burl-walnut stock carved with raised borders, forward three inches restored; silver furniture engraved with strawberry foliage enclosing monsters; pommel engraved with repeated acanthus-leaf motif that frames

grotesque-mask butt cap; escutcheon the same as on no. 13. The furniture, not marked, is attributed to William Bull, whose mark appears on the similar mounts of nos. 19 and 21.

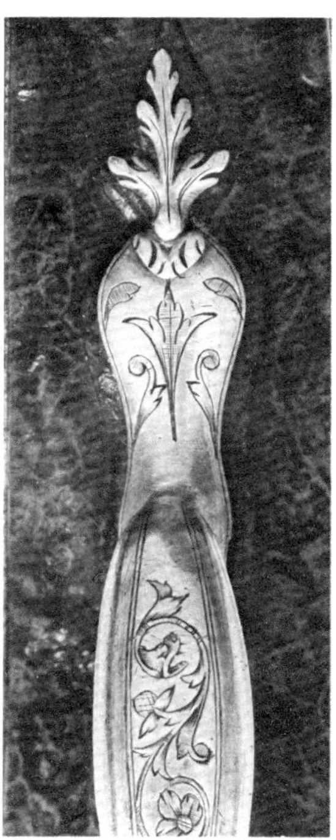

Edward Wornall was a maker of gun barrels who worked in London about 1690–1705. In the Victoria and Albert Museum is a flintlock pocket pistol of about 1690 (M.185–1928) signed WORNALL LONDINI (Blair, *Pistols of the World*, fig. 297).

Edward Wornall, London, about 1700
Overall length 19½ in.; barrel 12¾ in.
Caliber .56 (28 gauge). Weight 2½ lb.

15. Holster Pistol (Bedford 1523)

Barrel in two stages with molded girdle between, of circular section, engraved over breech with scrolling foliage. Lock plate with rounded face, filed with raised edges, is lightly engraved with foliage, and within a cartouche name and place: J. NICHOLES OXON. Figured burl-wood stock has raised borders; gilt-brass furniture; pommel engraved with vine leaves and butt cap chased with mask; pierced dragon side plate; es-

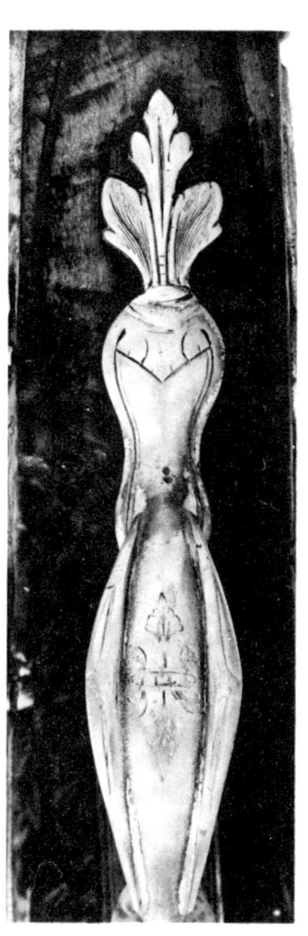

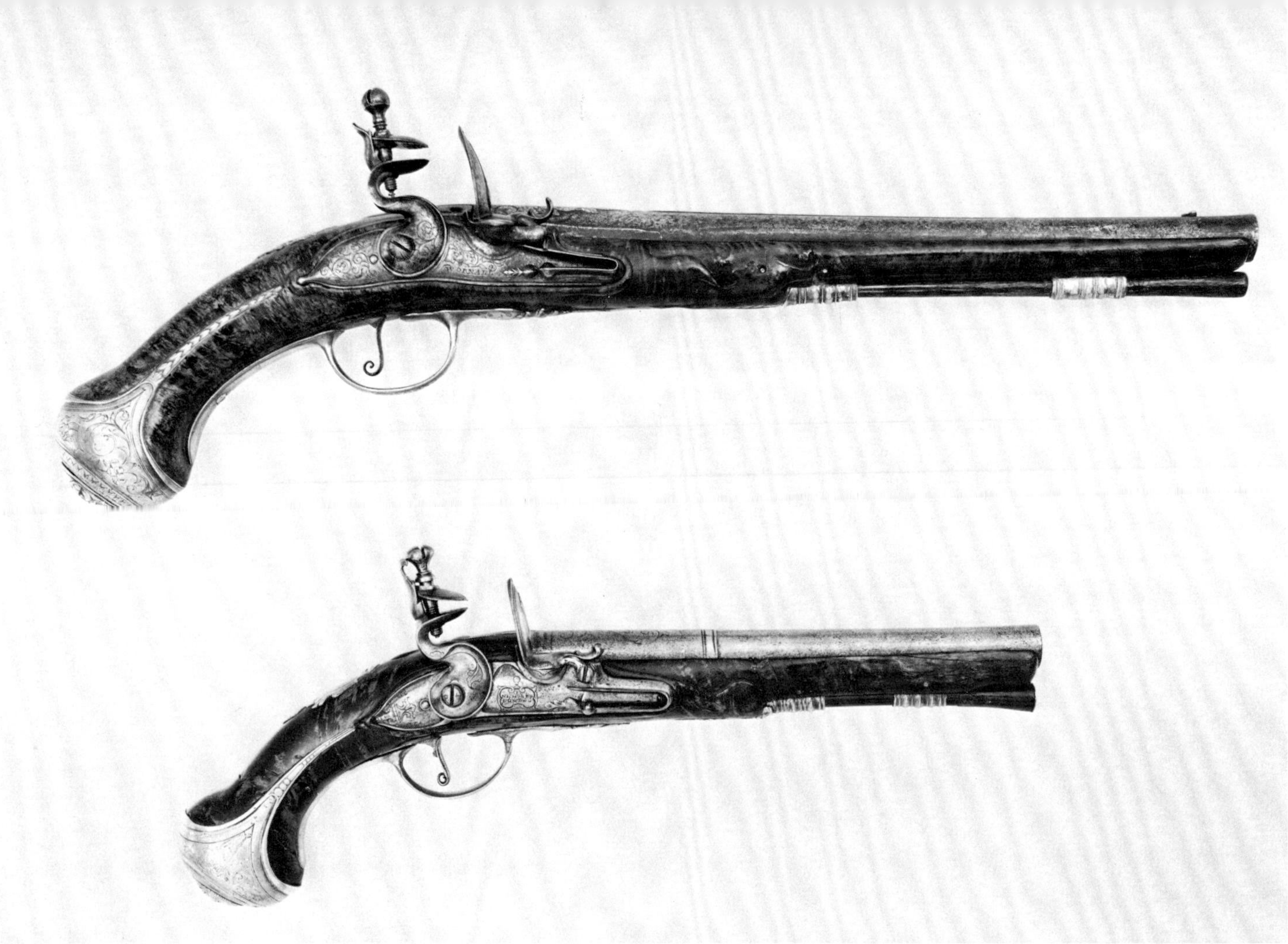

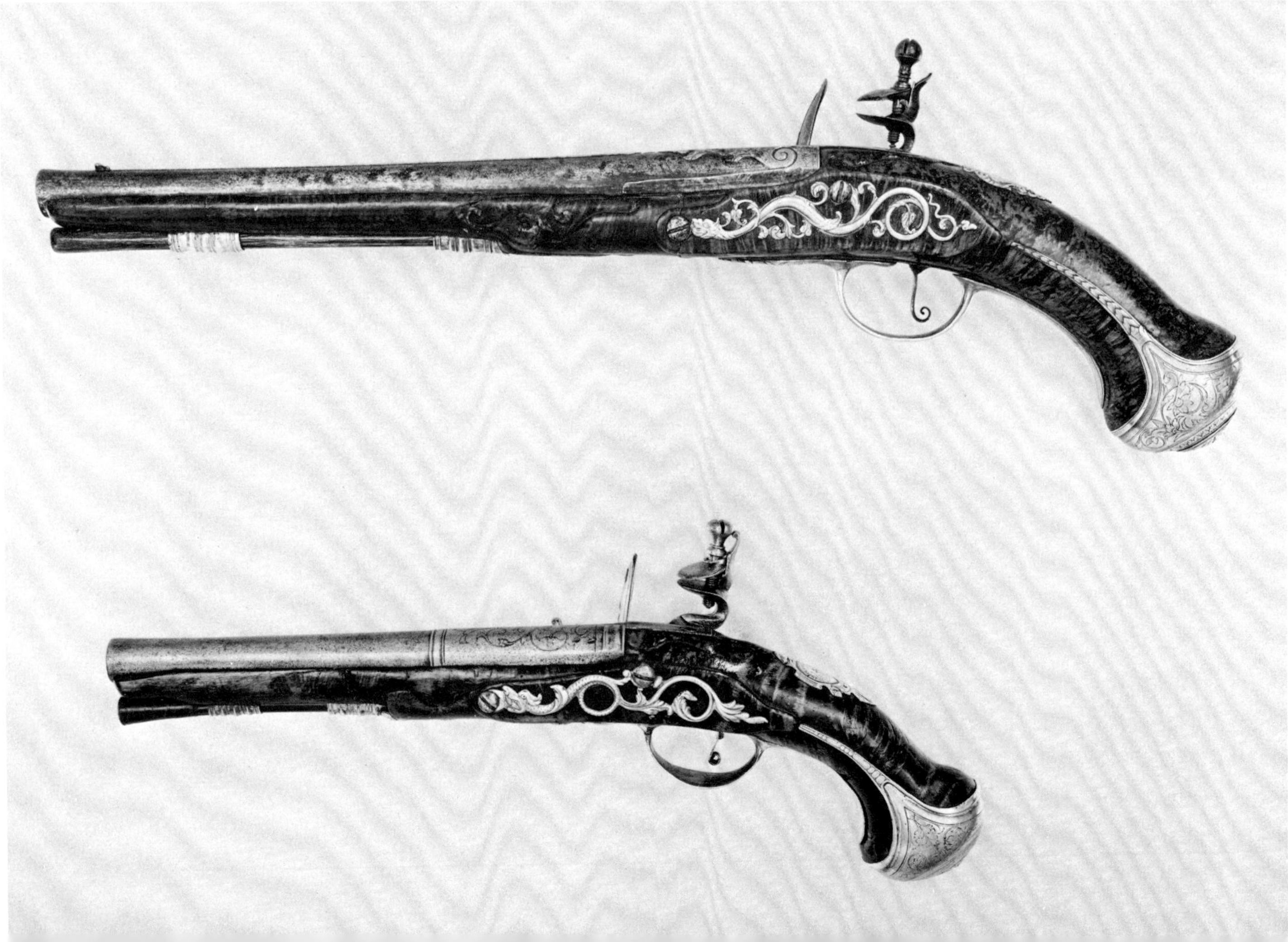

cutcheon engraved with crest (cross between two wings surmounted by motto IN CRUCE GLORIOR) of Sir Robert Pye, a parliamentarian who died in 1701; trigger guard has vase-and-plant finial; ramrod retains iron worm.

J. Nicholes, Oxford, about 1700–10
Overall length 14½ in.; barrel 8½ in.
Caliber .64 (18 gauge). Weight 1¾ lb.

Armourer to George I. He died in 1741. This pistol is one of his earliest known productions.

Lewis Barbar, London, about 1700
Overall length 19⅛ in.; barrel 12¼ in.
Caliber .64 (18 gauge). Weight 2½ lb.
Literature: Hayward, *The Art of the Gunmaker*, vol. II, pp. 80–81, pl. 20 a.

16. Pair of Holster Pistols   (Bedford 1041)

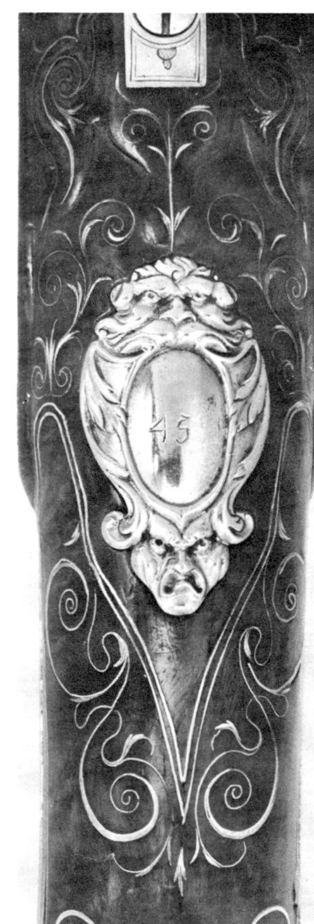

Barrel in two stages, leafy molded girdle between, chased with leafy scrolls at breech and engraved with Roman warrior's bust; above girdle, arms of George Ludwig, duke of Hesse-Darmstadt (1669–1705), an officer under William II of England, who may have presented the pair of pistols to him, are engraved within collar of the Golden Fleece; at breech are stamped three unidentified marks; iron blade front sight. Lock plate chased with grotesque mask and engraved with trophy of arms and scrolling foliage; cock and steel are chased with scrolls. Both barrel and lock plate inscribed BARBAR LONDINI. Straight-grained walnut stock inlaid with silver wire scrolls; highly polished steel furniture; pommel engraved with scrolling foliage and chimerical heads, and butt cap chased in relief with faun's mask; side plate pierced and chased with scrolls and bird heads; escutcheon chased with foliation and different masks at base and apex, and incised with inventory number 45; trigger guard has vase-and-plant finial.

Lewis Barbar was of French birth. He was naturalized in England in 1700 and elected master of the Gunmakers' Company in 1717 and 1727. One of the best makers of his time, he was appointed Gentleman

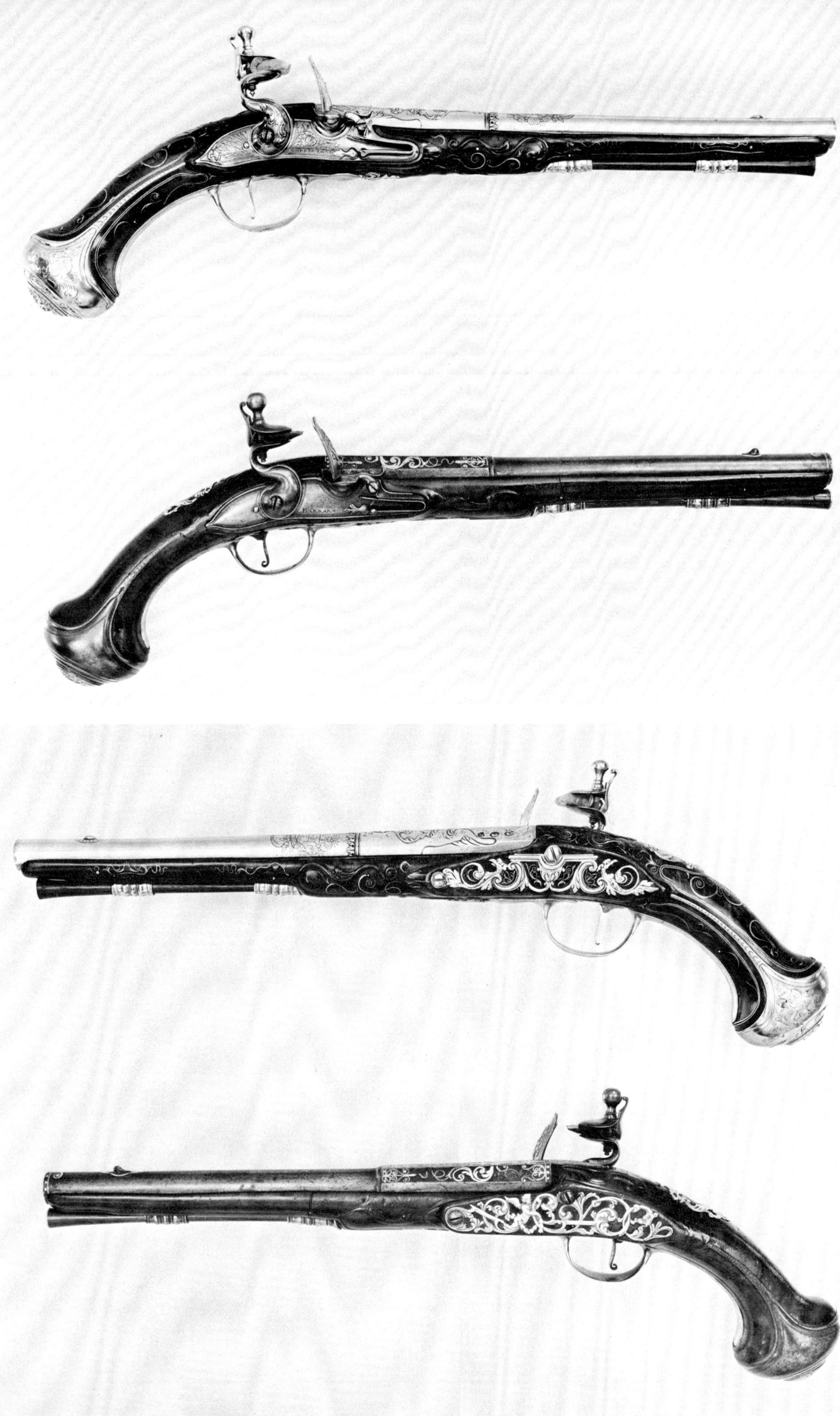

17. Holster Pistol   (Bedford 1031)

Barrel, blued, divided in two stages with molded girdle between; forward stage round, with gold damascening around muzzle; octagonal breech damascened in gold with foliation and name BARBAR; stamped with London proofmarks and gunmaker's mark LB; iron bead front sight within gold damascened border. Lock plate, rounded, bordered by engraved lines; steel is chased with leaf pattern. Walnut stock carved to outline mounts with some leaf ornament around barrel tang; steel and silver furniture; pommel of steel with engraved borders has cap of silver cast and chased with bust of Hercules

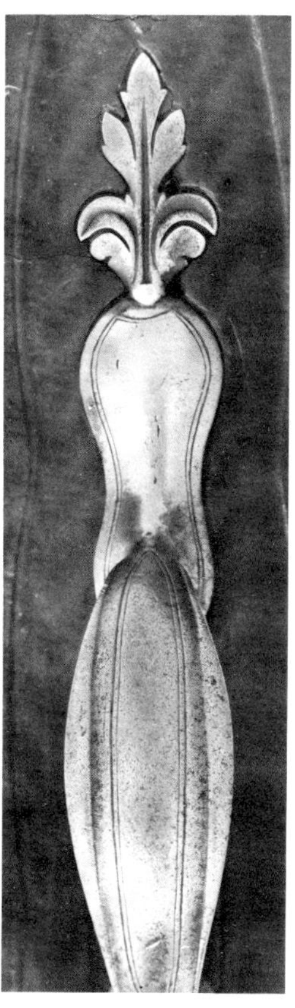

wearing lion's skin within beaded border; side plate of silver pierced and chased with cherub within scrolling foliage with dragon's heads; blank silver escutcheon surmounted by crown, with scrolls at sides and lion's head at base; trigger guard of steel has vase-and-plant finial.

Lewis Barbar, London, about 1710
Overall length 18⅝ in.; barrel 12 in.
Caliber .70 (14 gauge). Weight 2¼ lb.

18. Holster Pistol   (Bedford 1024)

One of a pair. Barrel, round, in three stages separated by molded girdles, engraved with conventional foliage over breech, in front of which is engraved LONDINI; stamped with London proofmarks and gunmaker's mark IW surmounted by star. Lock plate, flat faced, inscribed J. WILLOWES FECIT, has engraved borders and grotesque mask at tail; cock engraved with scrolls; steel and pan are faceted. Walnut stock carved to outline mounts and with foliage around barrel tang; brass furniture; pommel has engraved borders and foliage, and chased flower butt cap; foliate serpentine side plate cast and chased in relief; blank escutcheon; trigger guard with vase-and-flower finial; ramrod has iron worm.

John Willowes was admitted freeman of the Gunmakers' Company in 1701.

John Willowes, London, about 1710–15
Overall length 16³⁄₁₆ in.; barrel 9⅝ in.
Caliber .65 (17 gauge). Weight 2 lb.

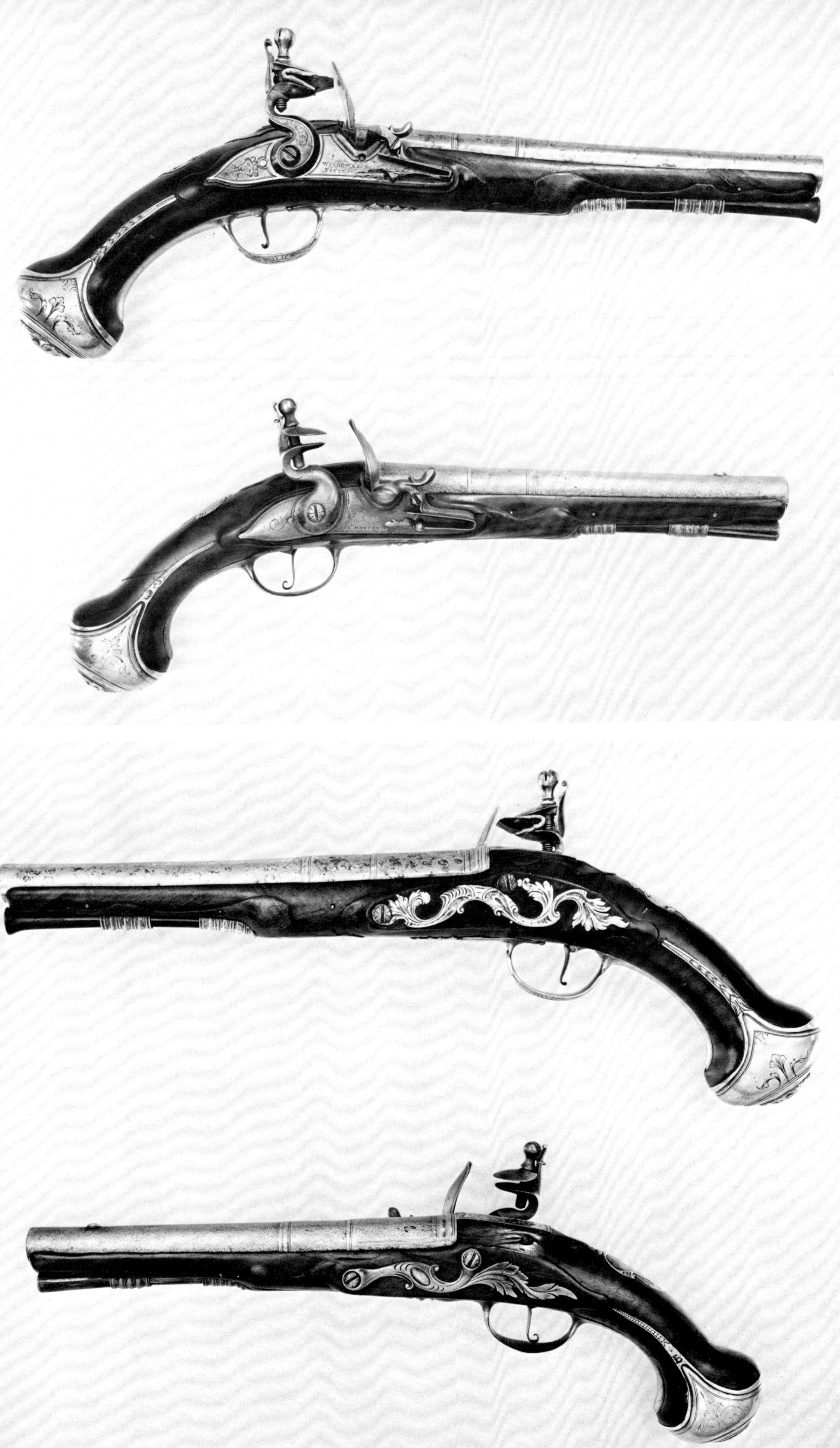

18

19

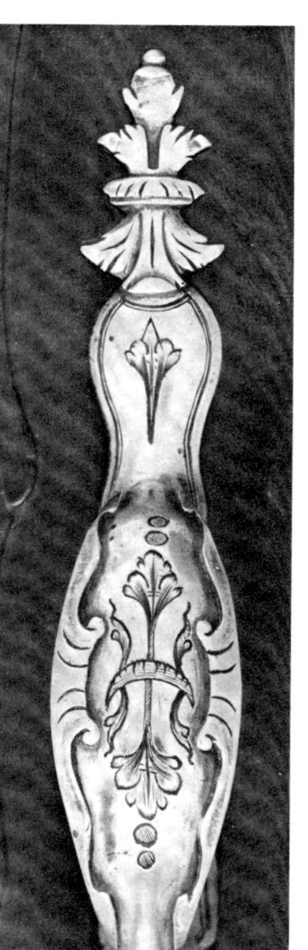

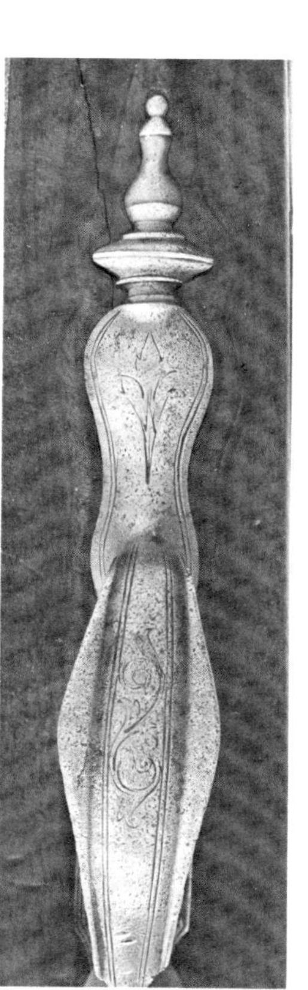

18

19

19. Holster Pistol (Bedford 1183)

Barrel, round, stamped with London proofmarks and divided into three stages, separated by molded girdles; iron blade front sight. Lock plate with rounded face, lightly engraved with scrolls and inscribed ROBT. HARVEY. Walnut stock carved to outline mounts; steel furniture, except for silver spurred pommel with grotesque-mask butt cap; London date letter for 1712 and silversmith's mark BV (William Bull) are struck on spurs; serpentine side plate chased with foliation; blank escutcheon in form of covered vase with foliate motif at base; trigger guard has covered-vase finial.

Robert Harvey was admitted freeman of the Gunmakers' Company in 1702 and was master in 1725.
Robert Harvey, London, 1712
Overall length 14¾ in.; barrel 8⅝ in.
Caliber .67 (16 gauge). Weight 1¾ lb.

20. Holster Pistol (Bedford 879)

One of a pair. Barrel in two stages, molded girdle between, chased at breech with leafy cartouche enclosing name R. ROWLAND and LONDINI, forward stage

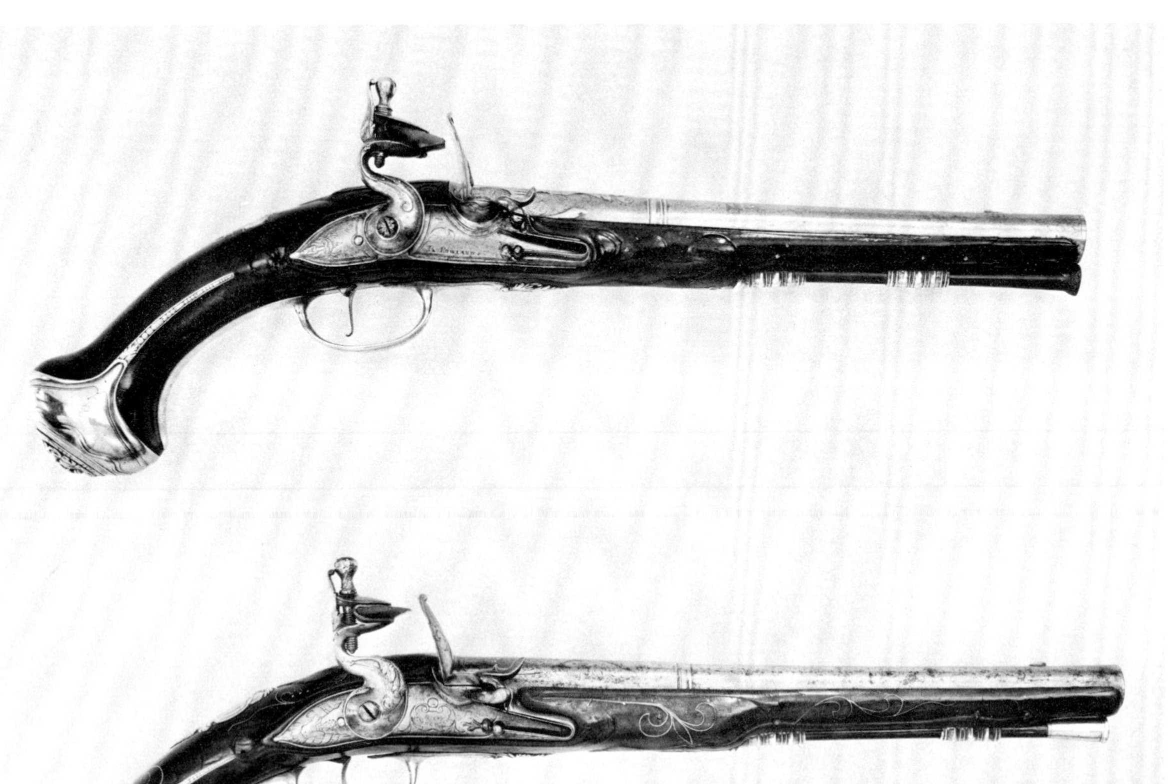

20

21

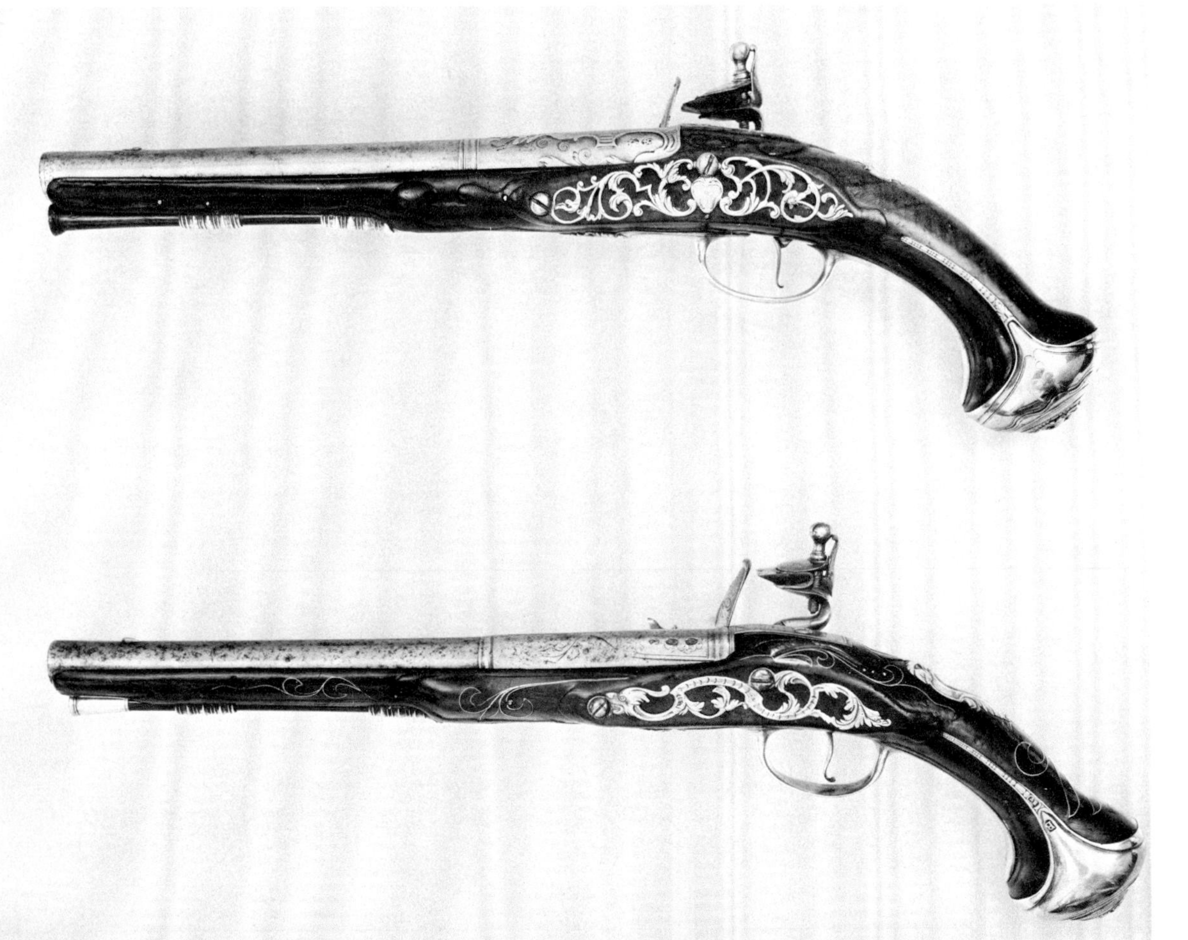

20

21

round, engraved ring of foliage at muzzle; London proof-marks at breech; rear V-sight, bead front sight; barrel tang has foliate motifs engraved and chased in relief. Lock plate with rounded face engraved with faun's mask, foliage, and name R. ROWLAND; lock plate, cock, and steel filed with raised borders; cock has descent arrest; feather spring. Walnut stock carved with raised borders around mounts; silver furniture; spurred pommel with grotesque-mask cap within wavy-edged cartouche; pierced foliate side plate; blank escutcheon surmounted by mask; trigger guard engraved with devil's mask.

Robert Rowland was admitted freeman of the Gunmakers' Company in 1715. He was presumably a descendant of Henry Rowland, who was the first master of the Gunmakers' Company, in 1637–38.

Robert Rowland, London, about 1715–20
Overall length 16¾ in.; barrel 10⁵⁄₁₆ in.
Caliber .67 (16 gauge). Weight 2 lb.
Literature: Blair, *Pistols of the World*, pls. 250–251.

21. Holster Pistol (Bedford 880)

Barrel in two stages, separated by molded girdle, breech chased and engraved with foliage, forward stage of circular section; at breech are stamped London proofmarks and gunmaker's initials RS; iron bead front sight. Lock plate, round-faced, filed with raised edges and engraved with baroque cartouche enclosing name RICH. SINCKLER, tail engraved with trophy of arms; cock and steel chased with foliage; bridle between pan and pan-cover screw, pivot peg inserted from reverse side. Walnut stock, carved to outline mounts and with foliage around barrel tang, is inlaid with scrolling silver wire; silver furniture; spurred pommel, cap chased in relief with grotesque mask within engraved borders; pommel stamped with figure of Britannia, lion's head erased, date letter for 1717, and silversmith's mark BV

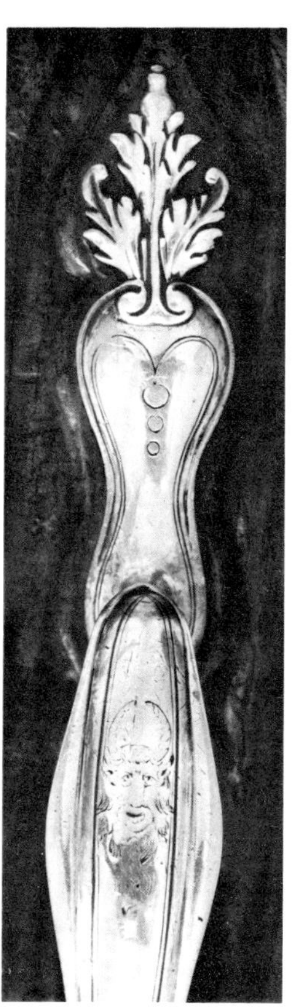

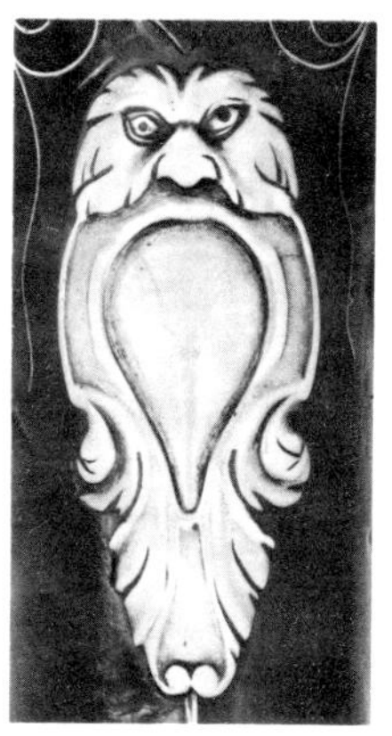

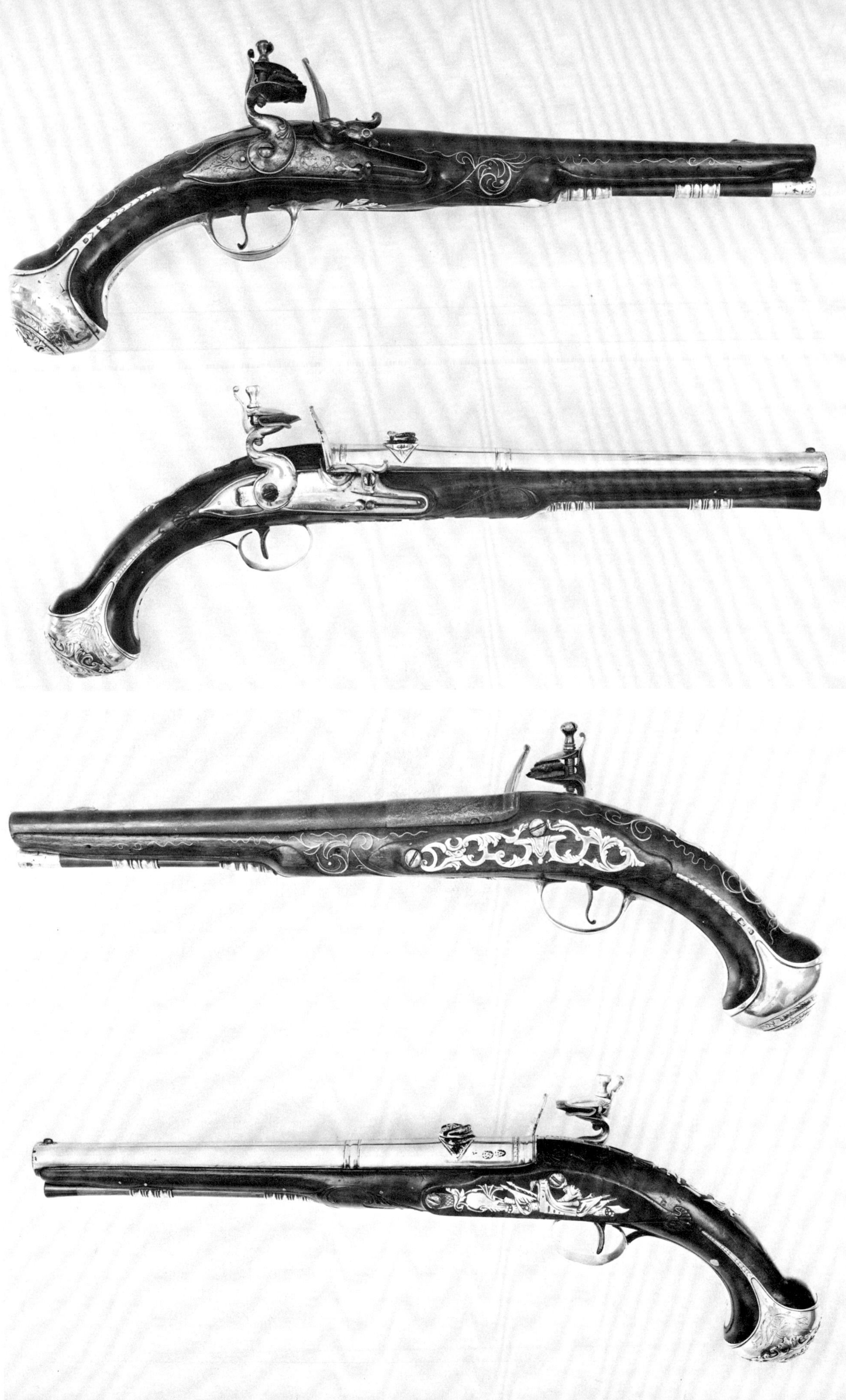

22

23

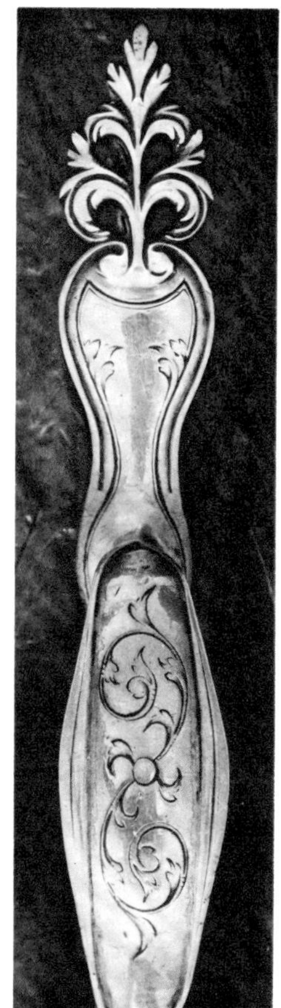

22

faun within engraved leafy borders; pierced foliate side plate; blank escutcheon; trigger-guard finial in form of leaf; silver ramrod head.

Richard Sinckler, London, 1720
Overall length 17¾ in.; barrel 11 1/16 in.
Caliber .63 (18 gauge). Weight 2⅜ lb.

23. Rifled Breech-loading Holster Pistol
(Bedford 1202)

Rifled barrel in two stages with molded girdle between; screw plug over breech for loading ball; London proofmarks; iron blade front sight; hinged silvered-iron leaf rear sight with three apertures folds into depression and blends into barrel tang; slot cut in loading plug could also serve as rear sight. Both barrel and lock plate inscribed R. ROWLAND; lock plate filed with raised edges; bolt safety. Walnut stock carved with

(William Bull); serpentine pierced side plate with dragon's-head terminal; blank escutcheon surmounted by mask and bordered with scrolls; trigger guard engraved with foliage and terminating in pierced leaf; two baluster ramrod sockets; whalebone ramrod with silver tubular finial.

Richard Sinckler was admitted freeman of the Gunmakers' Company in 1713.

Richard Sinckler, London, 1717
Overall length 17½ in.; barrel 11 in.
Caliber .67 (16 gauge). Weight 2 lb.

23

22. Holster Pistol (Bedford 1168)

Barrel, cylindrical, in three stages separated by molded girdles; London proofmarks; silver blade front sight. Lock plate with rounded surface and raised edges, inscribed R. SINCKLER on ribbon terminating in dragon's head; between pan and pan-cover screw is bridle, as on no. 21, also by Sinckler. Walnut stock, carved to outline mounts and with foliage around barrel tang, inlaid with scrolling silver wire; silver furniture bearing Britannia standard hallmark for 1720 and silversmith's mark IH; spurred pommel terminates in relief mask of

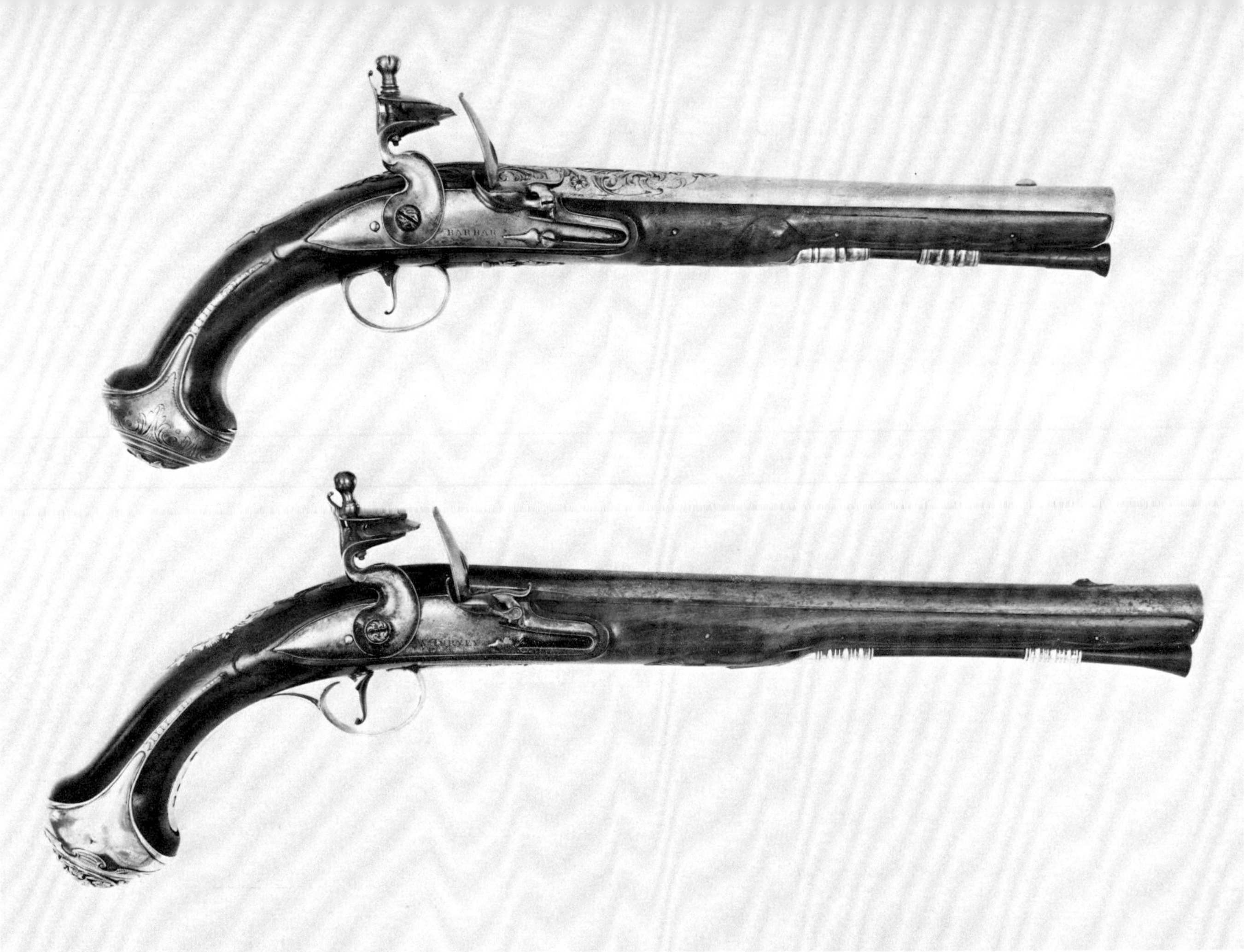

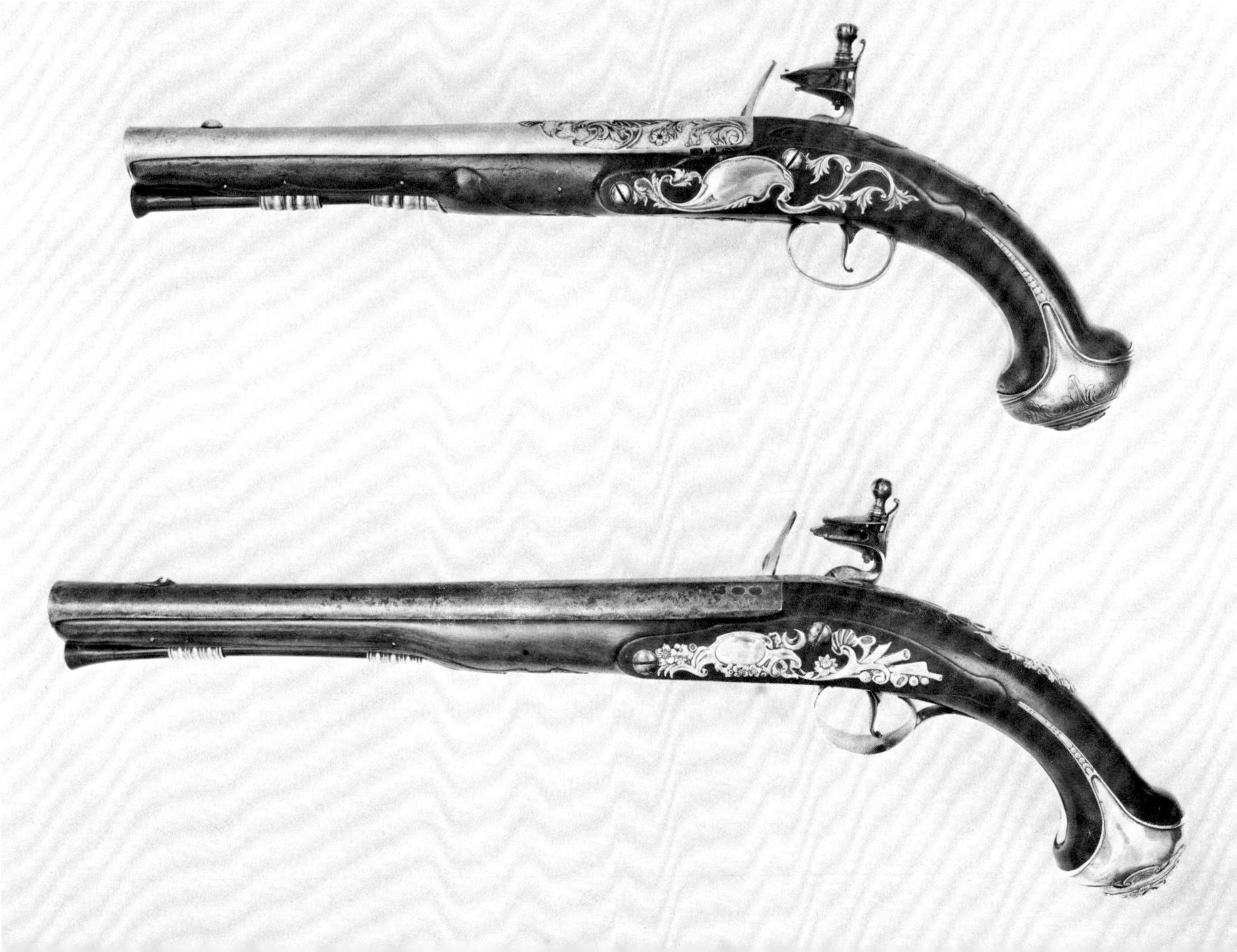

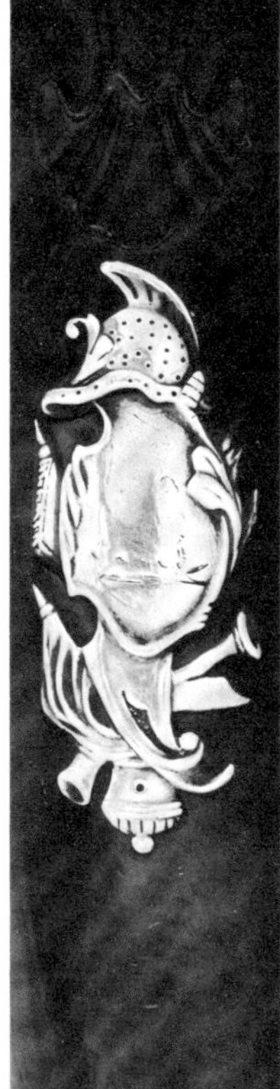

graved with conventional leaves; cap chased with eight-petaled flower; pierced side plate encloses rococo cartouche; symmetrical blank escutcheon chased with acanthus leaves and conventionalized shell motif at top; trigger guard has pedestal-and-plant finial; pins secure barrel and two baluster ramrod pipes; ramrod with steel disk finial and, at opposite end, iron spiral worm.

Lewis Barbar, London, about 1740–45
Overall length 16½ in.; barrel 10 in.
Caliber .67 (16 gauge). Weight 2 lb.

shells, foliage, and four-petaled flower; silver furniture; spurred pommel engraved with trophies, and cast and chased with lion's mask within leafy cartouche; side plate and escutcheon in form of trophy of arms; trigger-guard tang stamped with leopard crowned, lion passant, and date letter for 1741.

This is the earliest holster pistol with bolt safety in the exhibition. Made about 1720, the pistol was restocked and provided with an aperture sight in or after 1741. The walnut stock, in excellent condition, is unusually fine in workmanship. The silver furniture is of exceptional quality; unfortunately the silversmith has not struck his mark. The silvering of lock and barrel appears to have been done within the recent past.

Robert Rowland, London, about 1720
Overall length 17½ in.; barrel 11 in.
Caliber .66 (16 gauge). Weight 2 lb.

24. Holster Pistol (Bedford 1191)

Barrel, round in section, breech chased with panel of symmetrical foliage and flowers against gold matted ground, name BARBAR in rectangular panel in center; London proofmarks; iron blade front sight. Lock plate with rounded face and raised edges inscribed BARBAR; bridle connects pan with steel. Walnut stock carved with shells and scrolls; steel furniture; spurred pommel en-

25. Holster Pistol (Bedford 1207)

One of a pair. Barrel, blued, of circular section, except for top facet, which is engraved W. TURVEY LONDON and terminates in engraved shell; at breech on left side of barrel are London proofmarks and gun-maker's mark, WT surmounted by fleur-de-lis; silver blade front sight with leaf-shaped base. Lock plate, round faced, cut with raised edges and inscribed W. TURVEY; steel has vertical ridge in middle; pan with flash fence and bridle extending to pan-cover screw. Walnut stock carved with shells behind barrel tang and rear ramrod pipe; silver furniture; spurred pommel chased with strapwork cartouche bordering pommel cap

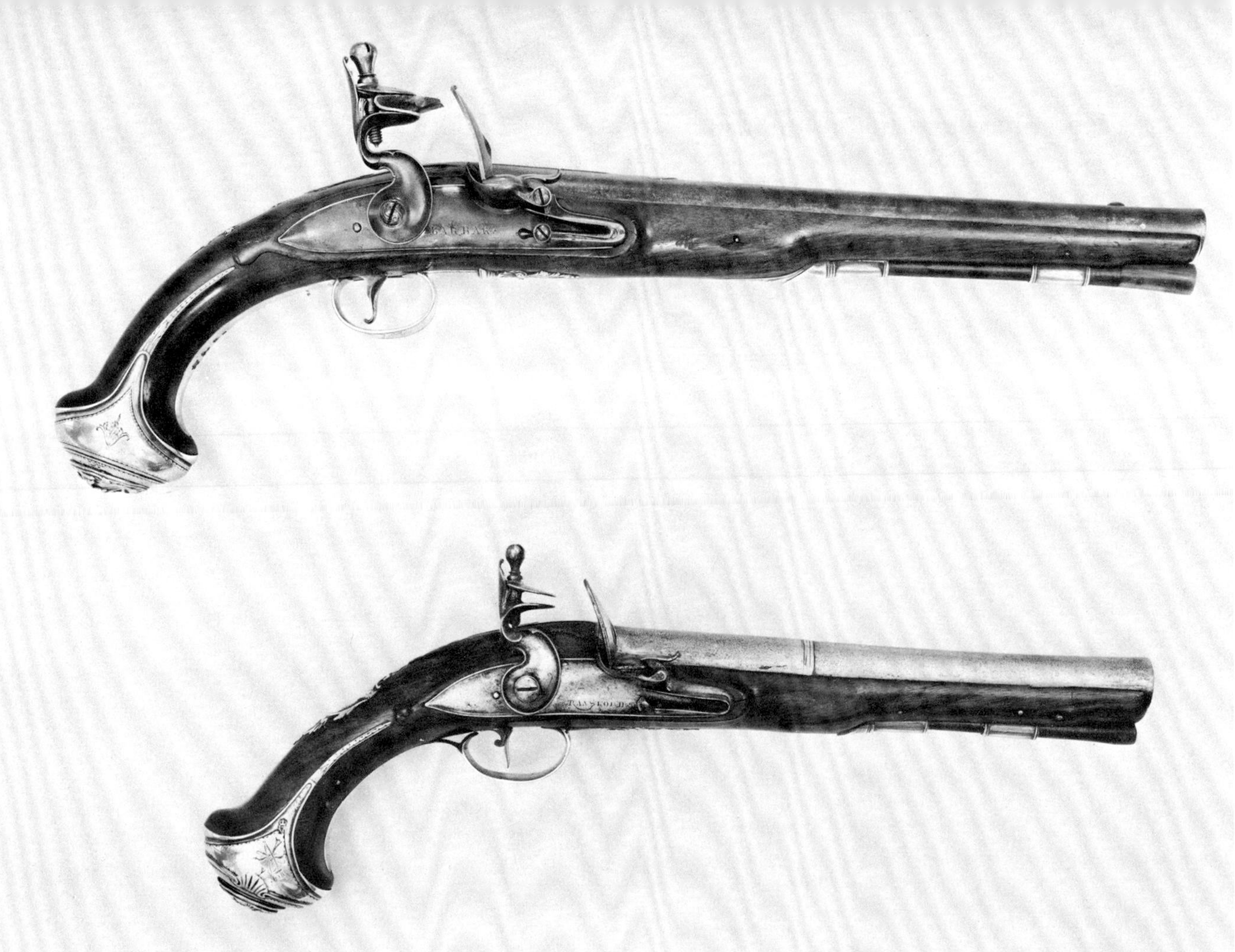

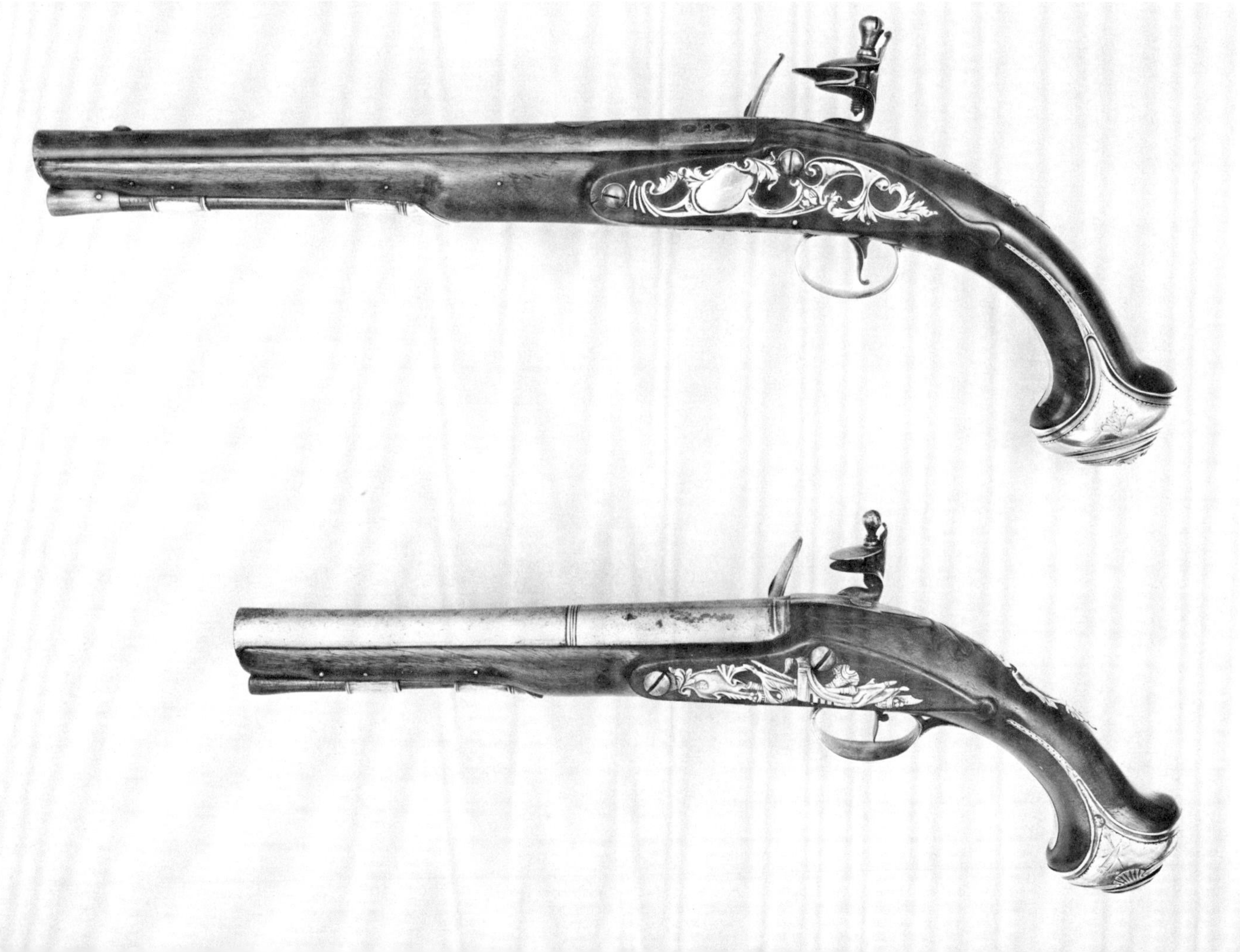

26

27

26. Holster Pistol   (Bedford 1528)

One of a pair. Barrel, of circular section, retains much of original browning; top facet over breech inscribed BARBAR; adjacent are London proofmarks between which are initials IB (James Barbar); silver blade front sight. Lock plate, round faced, filed with raised edges and inscribed BARBAR; steel has vertical ridge down center; bridle between pan and pan-cover screw. Walnut stock carved to outline mounts and with shell behind barrel tang; spurred pommel with engraved borders, cap chased with faun's mask in high relief; side plate pierced and chased with rococo scrolls enclosing oval escutcheon; symmetrical escutcheon surmounted by shell and engraved with crest; mound surmounted by sun in splendor; trigger guard has shell-and-foliation finial and is stamped with four marks: initials IB (James Brooker) in rectangle, crowned lion head, lion passant, and date letter for 1748; two ramrod pipes and ramrod with horn finial.

James Barbar, son of Lewis Barbar, was an apprentice to his father and in 1722 was made freeman of the Gunmakers' Company, of which in 1742 he was

26

chased in relief with flower surrounded by smaller flowers; pierced and chased side plate composed of asymmetrical cartouche with flowers and trophy of arms; escutcheon surmounted by crescent and bordered by trophies of arms, central oval panel engraved with goat's crest of dukes of Bedford, surmounted by ducal coronet; silver trigger guard has pedestal-and-shell finial; on trigger-guard tang are date letter for 1744, silversmith's mark JA (Jeremiah Ashley), lion passant, and leopard head crowned.

William Turvey, son of Edward Turvey, was admitted freeman of the Gunmakers' Company in 1711 and was master in 1733. The two Turveys were among the best London gunmakers of the first half of the 18th century.

William Turvey, London, 1744
Overall length 18 in.; barrel $11^{13}/_{16}$ in.
Caliber .71 (13 gauge). Weight $2\frac{1}{4}$ lb.

27

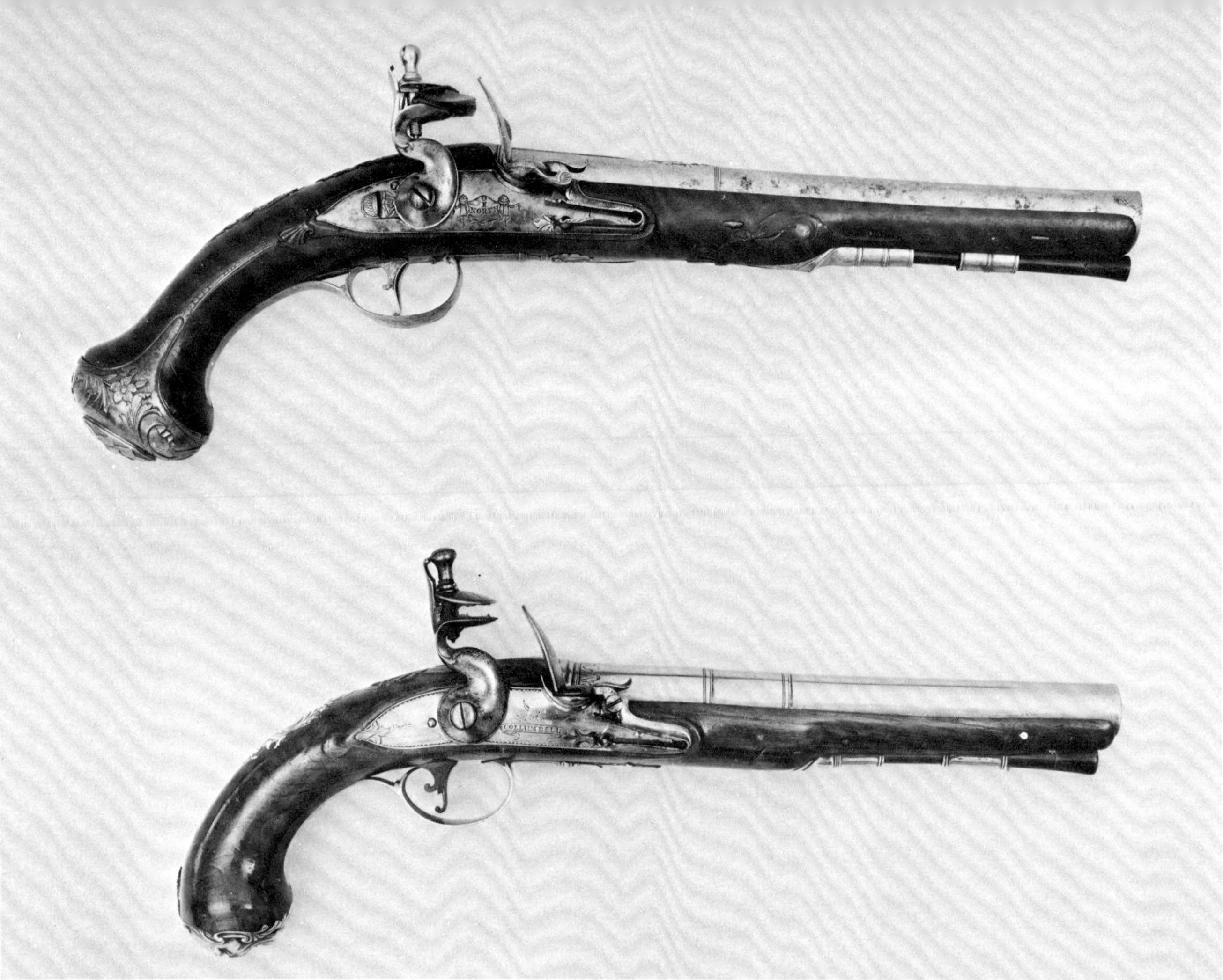

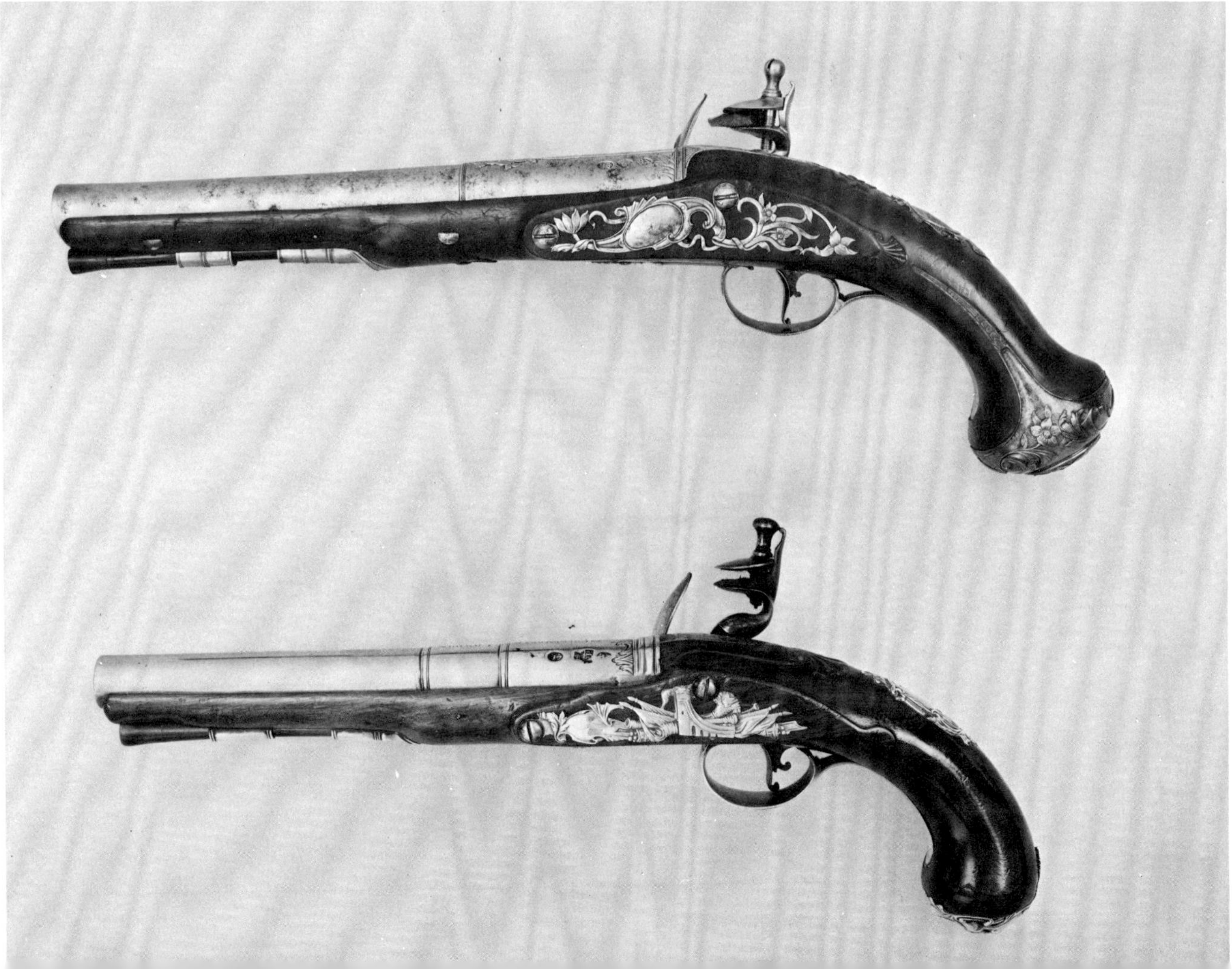

upper ramrod pipe and the escutcheon, are struck with the Dublin hallmark. Michael Ransford worked in Dublin from about 1735 until his death in 1757.

> Michael Ransford, Dublin, about 1745
> Overall length 14⅛ in.; barrel 8¼ in.
> Caliber .69 (14 gauge). Weight 1½ lb.
> Literature: Blackmore, *Royal Sporting Guns at Windsor*, p. 55, pl. 11; Christie's sale, June 10, 1969, lot 191.

master. Like his father, he was appointed Gentleman Armourer to the king, in his case, George II. A pair of pistols identical to no. 26 and its mate, also by James Barbar, with silver mounts bearing the date letter for 1757, is illustrated in Hayward, "English Flint-lock Pistols from 1740 to 1760," p. 154. The goldsmith's mark IB, entered at Goldsmiths' Hall in 1734, is attributed to James Brooker.

> James Barbar, London, 1748
> Overall length 17⅛ in.; barrel 10⅞ in.
> Caliber .62 (20 gauge). Weight 2 lb.

27. Holster Pistol (Bedford 1265)

One of a pair. Barrel in two stages, both of circular section, separated by engraved girdle; rear sight cut in ring around breech. Lock plate, round faced, filed with raised edges; bridle between pan and pan-cover screw. Walnut stock, carved with asymmetrical foliage behind barrel tang; silver furniture; spurred silver pommel with engraved borders, cap has grotesque mask in relief surrounded by oval cartouche composed of shells and scrolls; side plate chased with trophies of arms; symmetrical escutcheon, shell at top, grotesque mask at base, engraved with crest: armored hand holding dagger and rising from ducal coronet; trigger-guard finial is asymmetrical leaf.

All the silver mounts of this pistol, except for the

28. Holster Pistol (Bedford 1252)

Barrel in two stages, separated by molded girdle; breech stage chased in relief with leaf-and-flower design, top facet inscribed E. NORTH LONDON; barrel tang channeled to serve as rear sight. Lock plate with rounded face, filed with raised edges, inscribed on swag of drapery with maker's name E. NORTH; cock has descent arrest; bolt safety engages at half cock; feather spring; vent unlined; flash fence integral with pan; bridle between pan and pan-cover screw; steel has vertical ridge. Walnut stock carved with naturalistic flowers around barrel tang, and with shell motif adjacent to rear ramrod pipe, lock plate, and side plate; steel furniture with same motifs; spurred pommel chased with flowers and leaves, pommel cap with flower head; side

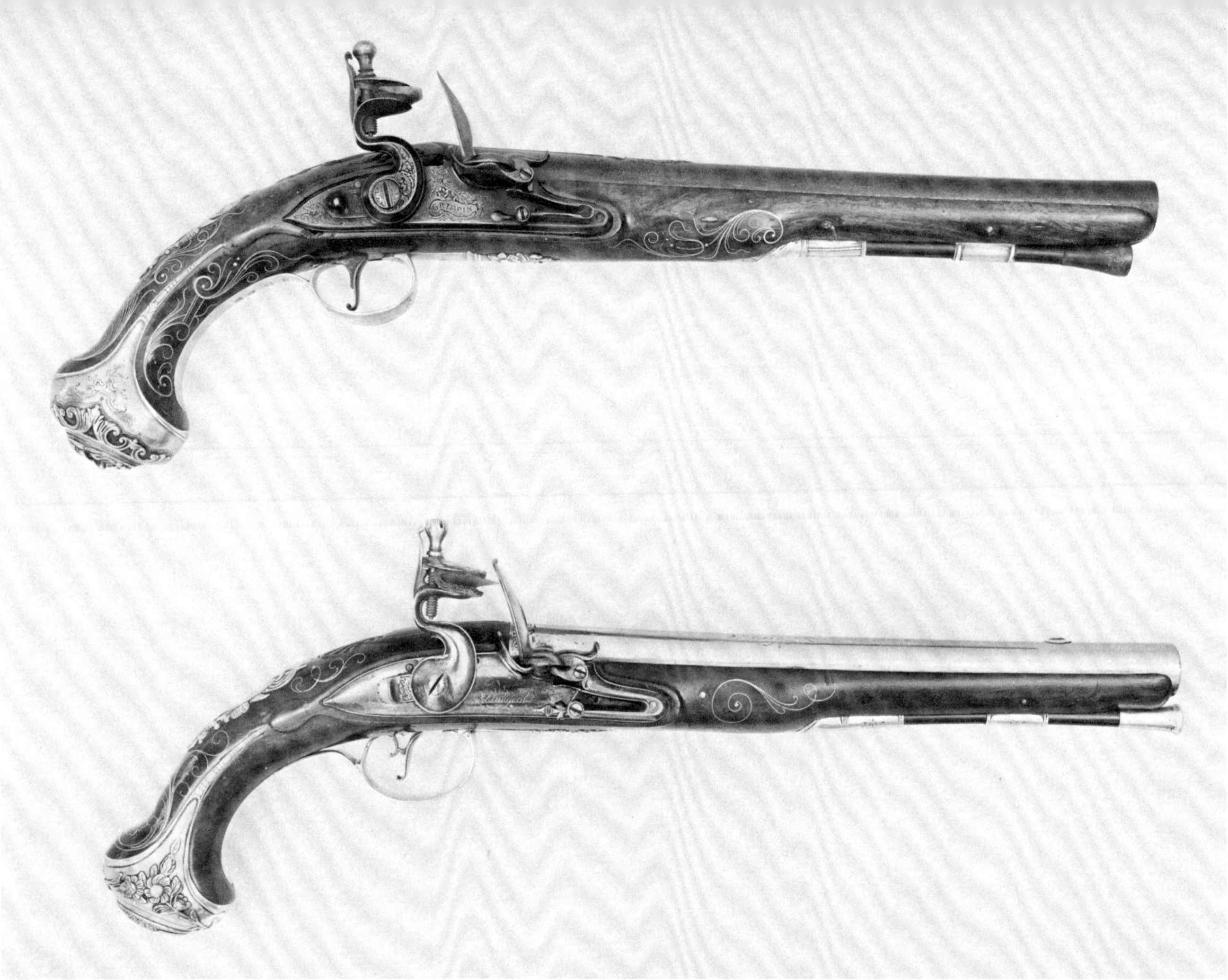

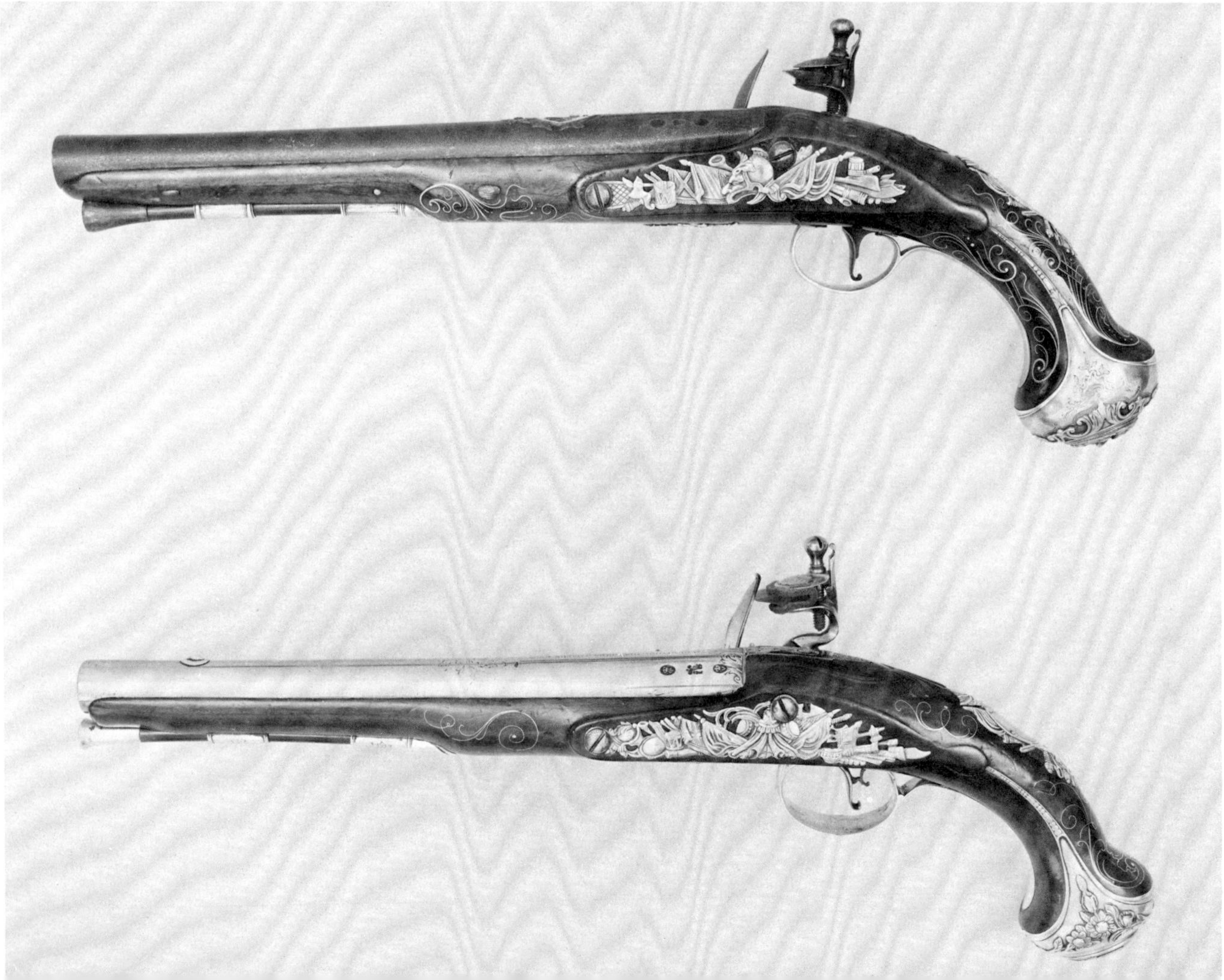

plate pierced with floral scrolls enclosing oval escutcheon; blank asymmetrical escutcheon bordered by scrolls and flowers; trigger guard, engraved with foliation, has pedestal-and-shell finial.

Edward North submitted his proof piece for approval and was admitted freeman of the Gunmakers' Company in 1729; he was master in 1753 and 1758.

Edward North, London, about 1750–60
Overall length 14⅝ in.; barrel 9 in.
Caliber .68 (15 gauge). Weight 1½ lb.

29. Holster Pistol (Bedford 884)

One of a pair. Barrel, brass, of circular section, in three stages, molded rings between, engraved with conventional foliage around breech; inscribed COLLUM-BELL LONDON at breech, where also are London proofmarks between which is gunmaker's mark, initials PH crowned. Lock plate, round faced, of silver with engraved borders, name COLLUMBELL inscribed on ribbon; cock with descent arrest and feather spring of steel; pan has integral flash fence. Walnut stock carved with rococo shell behind barrel tang; silver furniture; grotesque-mask butt cap; side plate and escutcheon decorated with trophies of arms; trigger guard, engraved with flower, has pedestal-and-vase finial; marks on trigger-guard tang: date letter for 1757, leopard head crowned, lion passant, JA (Jeremiah Ashley).

David Collumbell, who worked in London from about 1735 to 1765, was one of the leading gunmakers of his time. He was not a member of the Gunmakers' Company.

David Collumbell, London, 1757
Overall length 13 in.; barrel 8¹⁄₁₆ in.
Caliber .64 (18 gauge). Weight 1½ lb.

30. Holster Pistol (Bedford 1082)

One of a pair. Barrel of circular section, browned, faceted on top at breech and inscribed in gold GRIFFIN LONDON; in front of signature are chased shell on gold ground and six-petaled flower; adjacent to signature are London proofmarks and barrelsmith's mark F crowned for foreigner, one not a member of Gunmakers' Company. Lock plate, flat faced, inscribed GRIFFIN, filed with beveled edges, engraved with flower sprays; safety bolt engaging at half cock; roller bearing on end of pan cover; gold-lined vent; priming pan has flash fence below which is crescentic water-drain slit. Walnut stock carved with shell behind barrel tang and inlaid with scrolling silver wire; silver furniture bears marks: JA (Jeremiah Ashley), lion passant, lion head crowned, and date letter for 1762; spurred pommel engraved with rococo scrolls; cap chased with faun's mask in relief within border of scrolls; trophies of arms decorate side plate and escutcheon, latter engraved with crest: eagle

31. Holster Pistol   (Bedford 1160)

One of a pair. Barrel, brass, of circular section, faceted on top at breech and inscribed BUMFORD MINORIES LONDON, in front of which is engraved foliate motif; near breech, barrel is stamped with London proofmarks between which is gunmaker's mark initials IB surmounted by fleur-de-lis; silver bead front sight. Lock plate, round faced, inscribed BUMFORD; cock has descent arrest; safety bolt engages cock at half cock; gold-lined vent and pan; flash fence integral with pan; bridle between pan and pan-cover screw; water drain at base of flash fence; feather spring. Walnut stock carved with shell behind barrel tang and inlaid with scrolling silver wire; oval butt cap, with spurs, has frame chased in relief with flowers and ribbons; in center is flower motif chased in relief; side

with wings displayed and owner's initials WG; trigger-guard finial is leaf and flower; ramrod with horn finial has spiral worm on opposite end.

Chiseled decoration against a gold ground, though usual on the Continent in the mid-18th century, occurs on English firearms of the highest quality only. For information on Joseph Griffin, see no. 63.

Joseph Griffin, London, 1762
Overall length 16½ in.; barrel 10½ in.
Caliber .70 (14 gauge). Weight 2 lb.

plate and blank escutcheon are chased with trophies, latter surmounted by helmet; trigger-guard finial is pedestal surmounted by shell and flowers; trigger-guard tang stamped with date letter for 1767, lion head crowned, lion passant, and silversmith's mark, partly erased, but apparently IK (John King).

John Bumford submitted his proof piece in 1742 and was admitted freeman of the Gunmakers' Company; he was master in 1751 and 1756. His mark is no. 58 on the Gunmakers' Company mark plate. The Minories was a center of London gunmaking in the late 18th century.

John Bumford, London, 1767
Overall length 15⅞ in.; barrel 10 in.
Caliber .63 (17 gauge). Weight 2¼ lb.

32. Holster Pistol (Bedford 1574)

One of a pair. Barrel, blued, of Spanish form, engraved with husk trails over breech; Tower private proofmark; rear sight on false breech; silver blade front sight; gold-lined vent. Lock plate, flat faced, inscribed GRICE and etched with trophy of arms and flowers; link between steel and feather spring; bridle between pan and pan-cover screw. Walnut stock inlaid with scrolling silver wire and with shell behind barrel tang; silver furniture with silversmith's mark of Moses Brent and London hallmark for 1781; spurred pommel, cap chased with trophy of arms framed by shells and scrolls; side

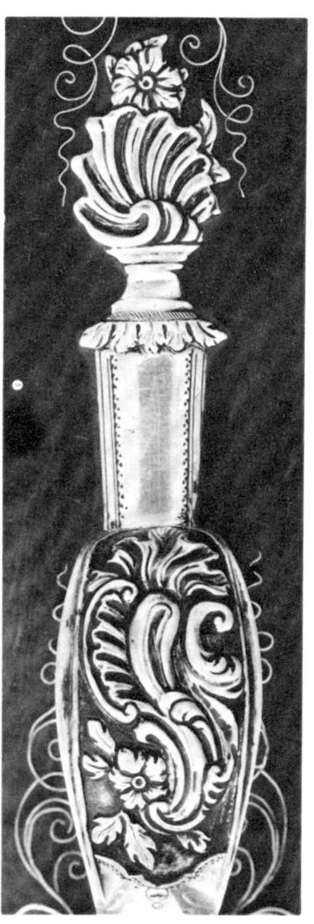

plate pierced and chased with trophy of arms; trigger guard chased with rococo scrolls; whalebone ramrod

with silver head.

Joseph Grice belonged to a Birmingham family of gunmakers, but he presumably had a finishing workshop in London. In addition to making special firearms, Grice was a government contractor who supplied regulation military arms.

Joseph Grice, London, 1781
Overall length 16¼ in.; barrel 10⅛ in.
Caliber .63 (17 gauge). Weight 2 lb.

33. Holster Pistol (Bedford 1508)

One of a pair. Barrel of Spanish form, blued surface, inlaid with gold ribbon on top facet of breech, inscribed with maker's address ROYAL EXCHANGE LONDON; gold-lined vent; silver blade front sight. Lock plate, flat faced, etched and engraved with rococo scrolls, signed BENNETT on inlaid gold oval plaque; roller bearing between steel and feather spring; bridle between pan and pan-cover screw; gold-lined pan, safety catch locking pan cover. Walnut stock carved with shell behind barrel tang; silver furniture with London hallmark for 1781 and mark of silversmith Moses Brent; spurred pommel engraved with trails of husks, cap chased in high relief with flower head; pierced floral side plate; rococo escutcheon.

Moses Brent was a principal supplier of silver furni-

ture to the London gunmakers' trade. His mark was first entered at Goldsmiths' Hall in 1775, when has was

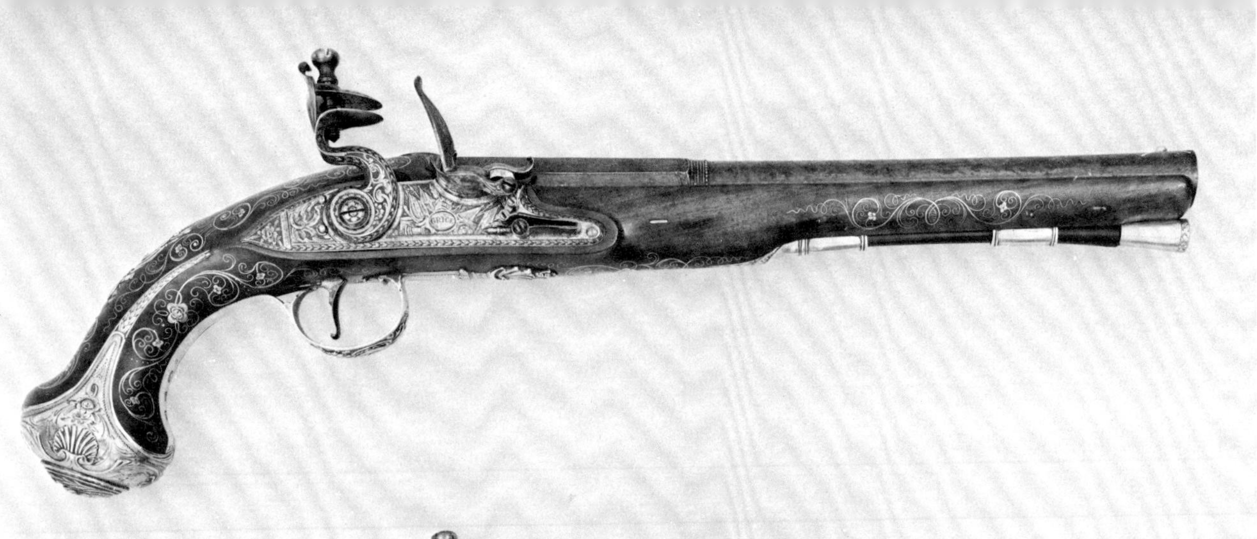

32

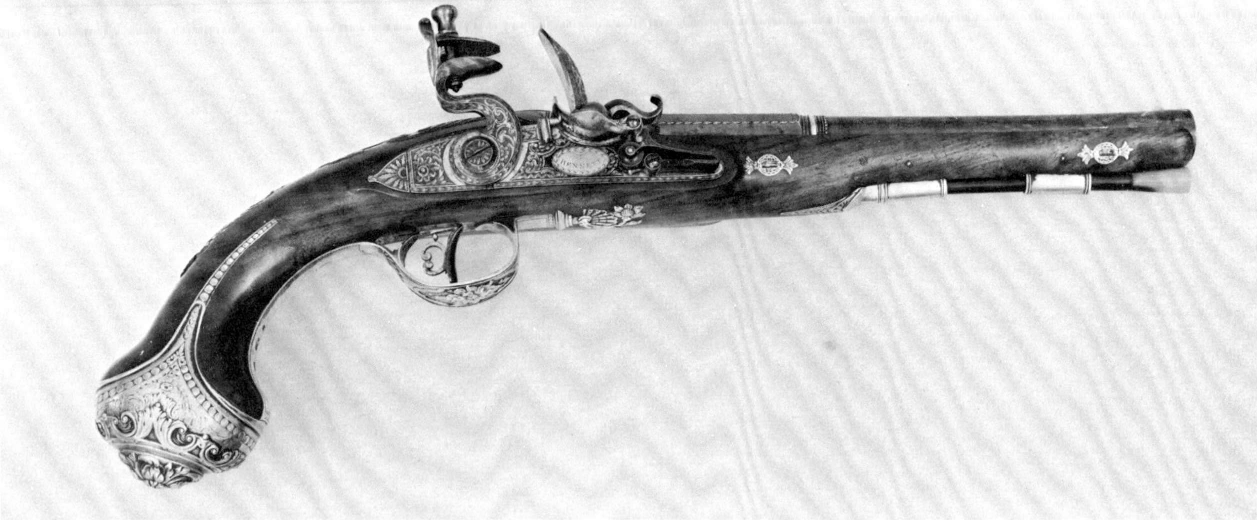

33

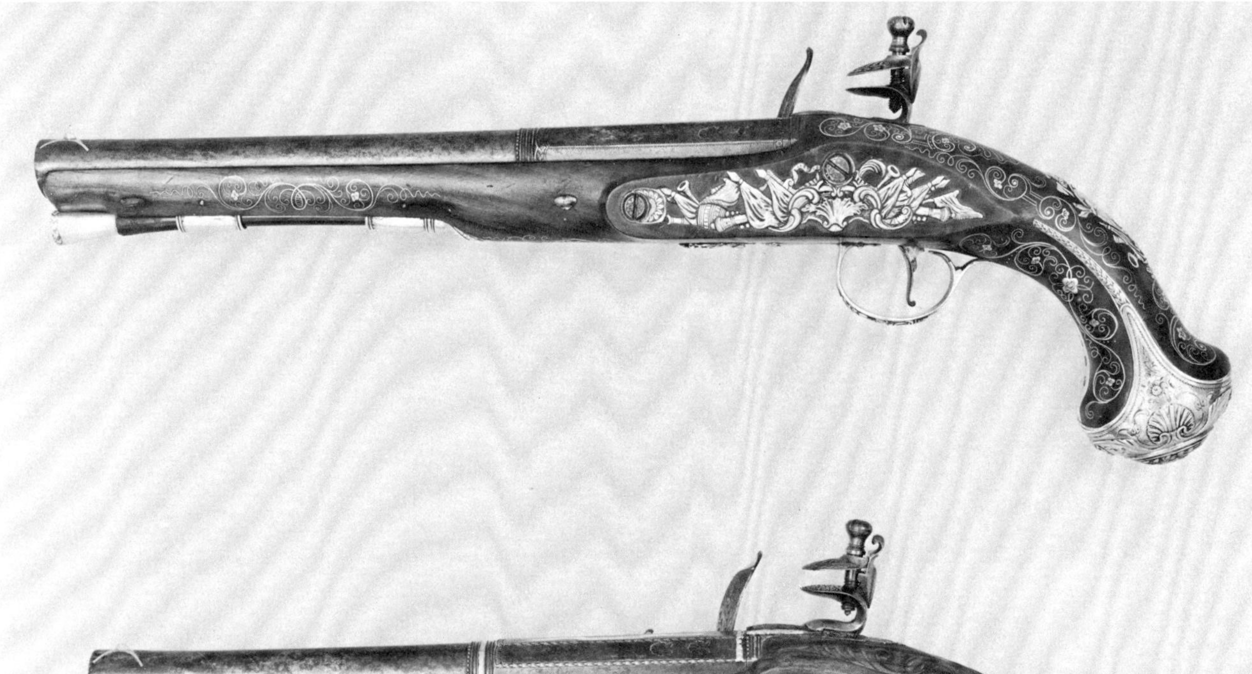

32

33

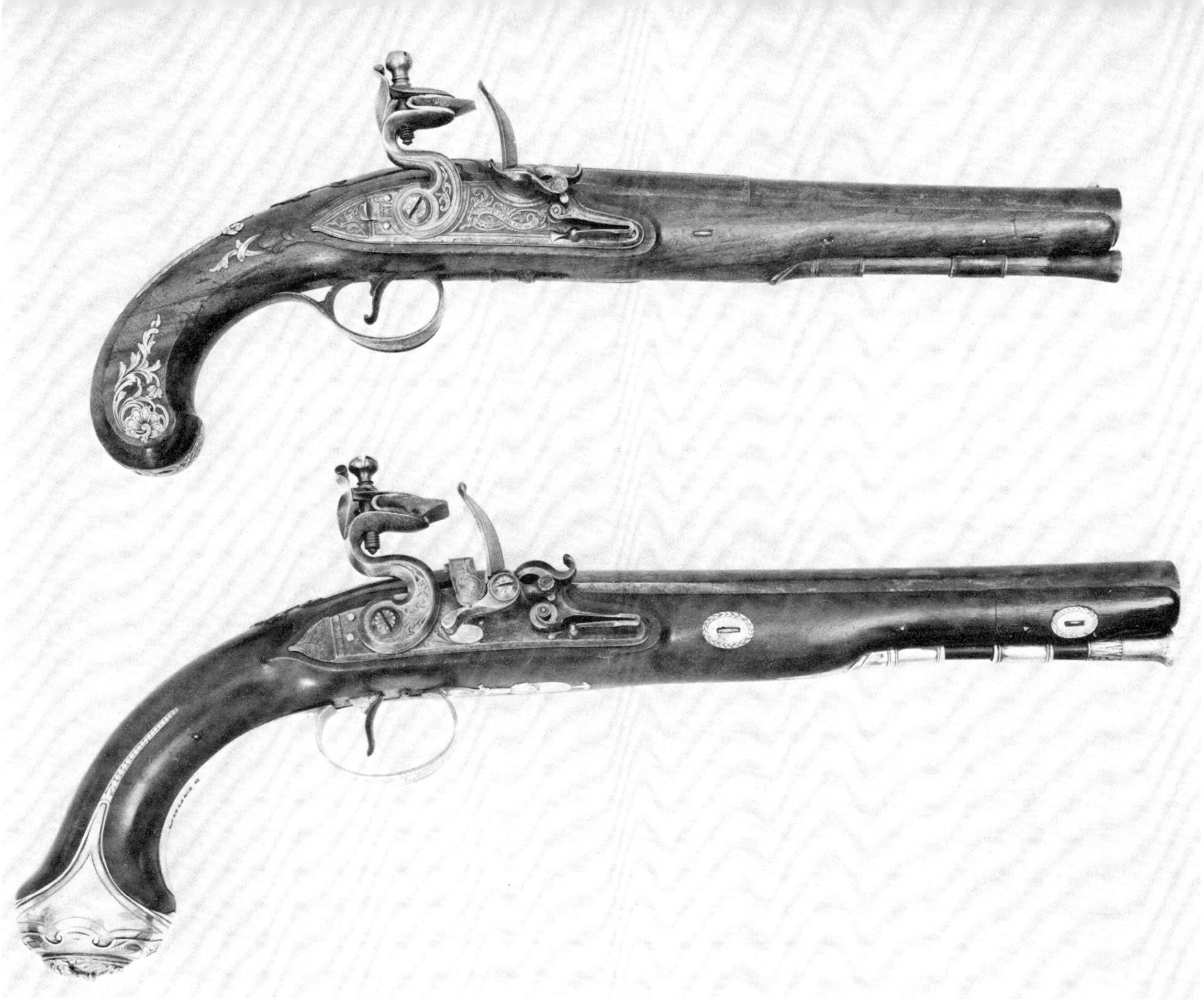

34

35

34

35

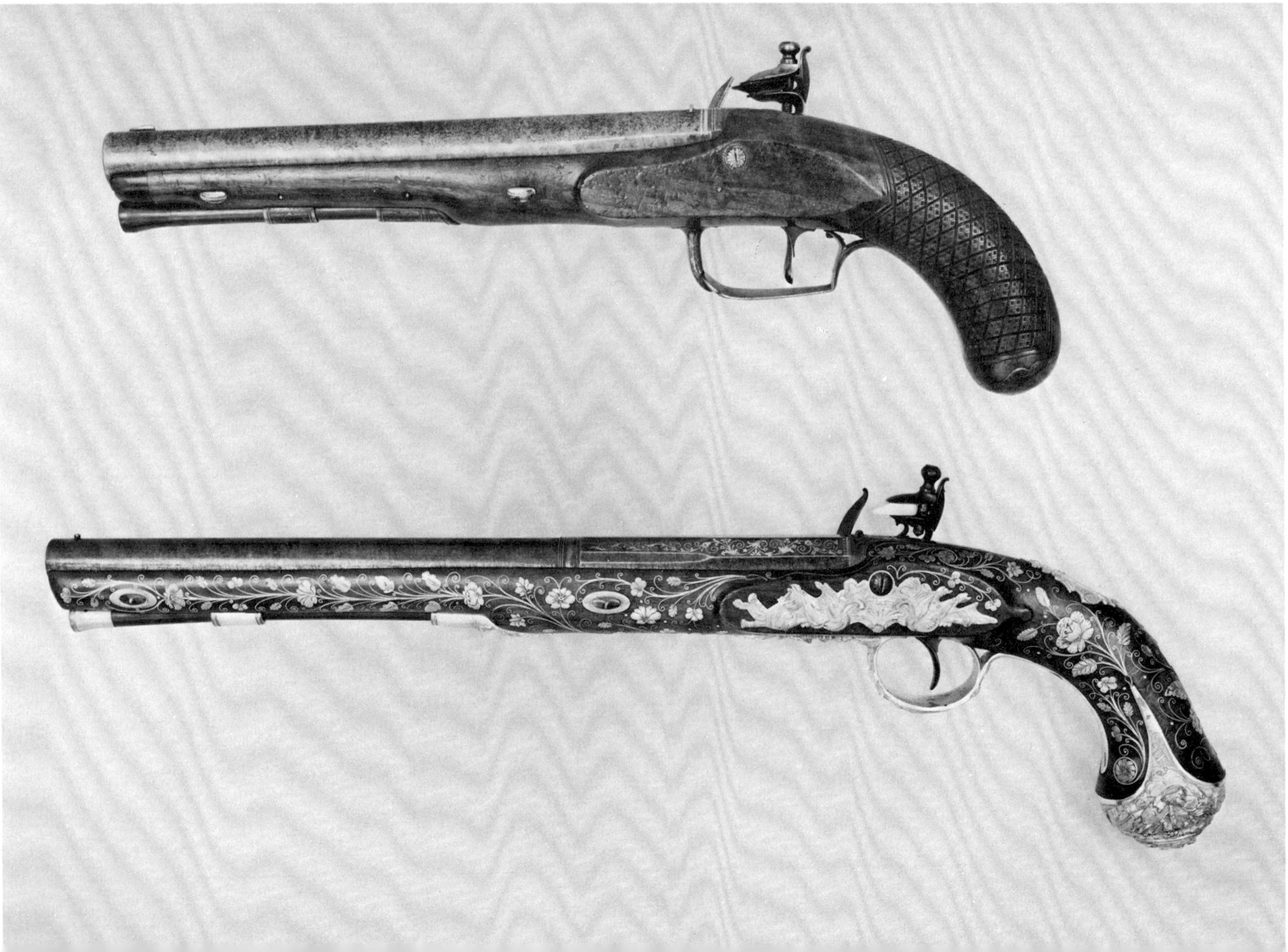

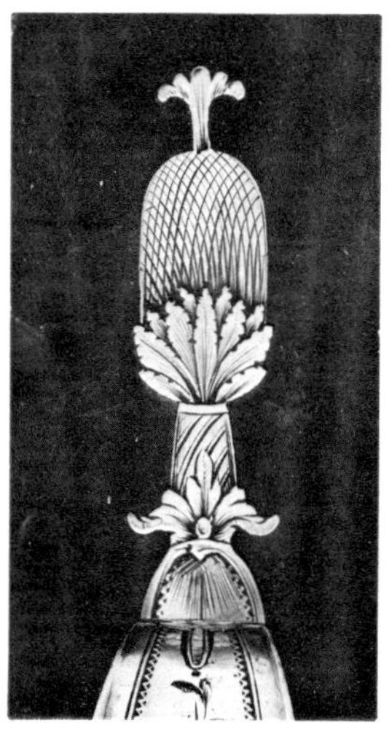

working at Hinde Court, Noble Street. He moved to the Hatton Garden area in 1800, and his last mark was registered from Leather Lane in 1817. John Bennett was a sword cutler and goldsmith as well as a gunmaker.

John Bennett, London, 1781
Overall length 15¼ in.; barrel 8¾ in.
Caliber .60 (20 gauge). Weight 1¾ lb.

34. Holster Pistol (Bedford 1077)

One of a pair. Barrel, blued, in two stages, both of circular section with flat, tapering top strap extending full length; top strap at breech inscribed J. PROBIN and engraved with conventional foliation; rear sight in false breech; silver bead front sight; no proofmarks. Lock plate, flat faced, etched and engraved with rococo scrolls framing inscription J. PROBIN; roller bearing between steel and feather spring; bridle from pan to pan-cover screw; gold-lined vent; bolt safety. Walnut stock carved with shell behind false breech; profuse inlay of cut silver sheet engraved with interlaced ribbons, trails of bushes, and rococo scrolls; side plate of similar design; trigger guard of iron terminates in acorn; two iron ramrod pipes.

The butt has a form corresponding to that of early dueling pistols.

John Probin, Birmingham, about 1780–85
Overall length 15 in.; barrel 9 in.
Caliber .62 (20 gauge). Weight 1½ lb.

35. Magazine-primed Dueling Pistol (Bedford 724)

Stub barrel, faceted, with flattened top inscribed JOVER & SON LONDON; left side facet stamped with London proofmarks between which are initials WI (William Jover); two gold transverse lines at breech; two barrel slides with engraved silver slots. Lock plate

with flat face and filed beveled edges has gold oval plaque engraved JOVER; priming magazine operated by pushing forward cam on end of pan; cock and lock-plate tail engraved with rococo scrolls; roller bearing on feather spring; bridle from pan to pan-cover screw; vent and pan are gold lined; hair trigger and detent. Walnut stock carved with rococo shell behind barrel tang; silver furniture; spurred pommel with engraved borders, cap is faun's mask chased in relief, surrounded by cartouche of scrolling strapwork; oval escutcheon engraved with crest and initials CWM (Sir Charles W. Malet, Baronet); five marks on silver trigger guard are initials MB (Moses Brent) in rectangle, date letter for 1786, lion passant, lion head crowned, and sovereign's head; two ramrod pipes; ramrod with engraved silver finial and, on opposite end, iron spiral worm.

This pistol is from a cased pair. Cases were usual for dueling pistols, but sometimes they were also used for officer's pistols toward the end of the 18th century. William Jover, well known for his Ferguson rifles, appears to have been in partnership with his son from about 1785 to 1795.

Jover & Son, London, 1786
Overall length 16½ in.; barrel 10 in.
Caliber .70 (14 gauge). Weight 2½ lb.

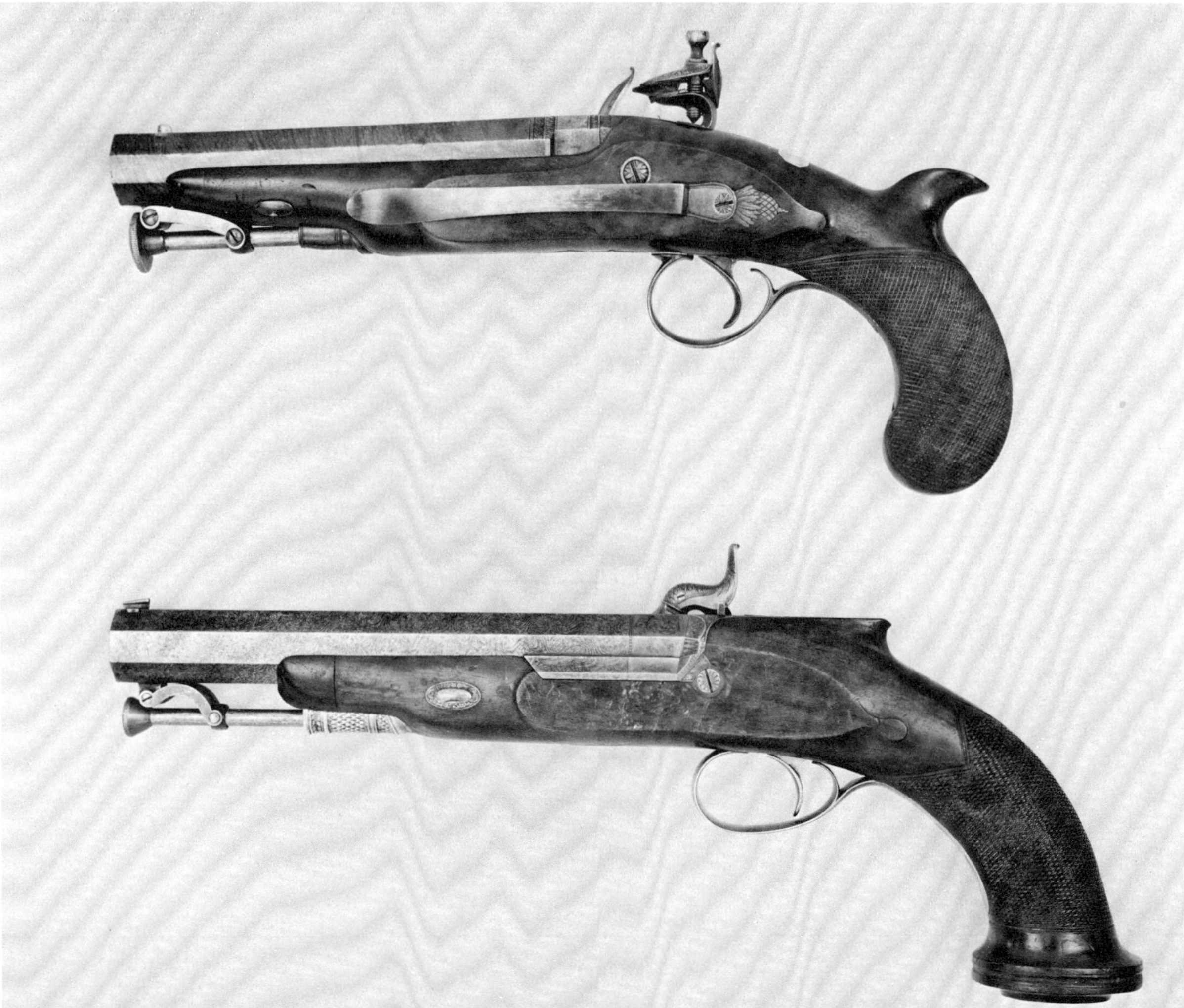

36. Officer's Pistol   (Bedford 410)

Barrel, browned twist, with flattened top, standing rear sight, silver blade front sight, two transverse gold lines inlaid at breech, two barrel slides, gold-lined vent; barrel inscribed in gold inlaid letters DURS EGG LONDON. Lock plate, flat faced, inscribed DURS EGG, filed with beveled edges and engraved with flower sprays; roller bearings on pan cover and feather spring; bolt safety locking cock and pan at half cock. Walnut stock with horn fore-end, checkered butt; engraved steel furniture; trigger guard of French form with floral finial.

For information on Durs Egg, see no. 74.

Durs Egg, London, about 1780

Overall length 15¾ in.; barrel 10 in.

Caliber .69 (14 gauge). Weight 2½ lb.

37. Holster Pistol   (Bedford 865)

One of a pair. Barrel in two stages, separated by molded girdle, breech stage octagonal changing to polygonal, forward stage circular; breech stage finely damascened in silver with floral scrolls enclosing ribbon inscribed WILKINSON LONDON; London proofmarks; false breech damascened in gold; standing rear V-sight, silver bead front sight; two barrel slides. Lock plate, flat faced, blued, inscribed WILKINSON on inlaid gold ribbon and damascened in gold with floral sprays; roller bearings on pan cover and feather spring; platinum-lined vent, gold-lined pan; bolt safety functions at half cock. Walnut stock inlaid over its entire length with scrolling silver wire merging into flowers and leaves of cut and engraved silver sheet; furniture of gilt bronze, cast and chased with trophies of arms in high relief; butt cap, with short spurs, displays trophies on matted

ground and is heavily mercury gilded; side plate, trigger guard, blank escutcheon, and rear ramrod pipe are decorated to correspond with butt cap; single side nail; ramrod has gilded brass tubular finial that is attached by small transverse screw and, at opposite end, elongated brass finial.

This is evidently a presentation pistol, and in view of its gilt-bronze mounts and rather old-fashioned form, it must have been intended for a Near Eastern or Indian recipient. Usually the ornament of such a pistol included some Eastern detail, but none is present here. The pair would originally have been placed in a lavishly fitted case.

James Wilkinson succeeded Henry Nock, his father-in-law (see no. 169), in 1805 at Ludgate Hill. He was himself succeeded by his son, Henry, who traded as James Wilkinson & Son at 27 Pall Mall from 1829 to 1852. Henry Wilkinson was the author of an authoritative volume entitled *Engines of War*, published in London in 1841. The Wilkinson firm is today best known as a producer of razor blades.

Henry Wilkinson, London, about 1805–10

Overall length 19¼ in.; barrel 13⅛ in.

Caliber .61 (20 gauge). Weight 2½ lb.

38. Officer's Pistol   (Bedford 1251)

One of a pair. Barrel, browned twist, octagonal, with patent breech, inscribed PALMER ROCHESTER, platinum-lined vent, brass blade front sight; single barrel slide. Lock plate, flat faced, engraved with leaf border and trophies of arms and inscribed PALMER; roller bearing on both steel and feather spring; Manton-type perforated pan. Walnut stock with saw grip of unusual form, checkered butt; blued and engraved steel furniture; trigger guard with pineapple finial, swivel ramrod; belt hook.

This pistol belonged to Benyon Kent, Esq. (1779–1856) of Tatefield Hall, Yorkshire.

Palmer, Rochester, about 1820
Overall length 13 in.; barrel 6¾ in.
Caliber .67 (16 gauge). Weight 2 lb.

39. Rifled Percussion-cap Holster Pistol
(Bedford 1022)

One of a pair. Barrel, Damascus twist, browned, octagonal, rifled with six grooves, top facet inscribed SAML. & CHAS. SMITH, PRINCES STREET LEICESTER SQUARE LONDON; patent breech stamped SMITHS PATENT within platinum border; standing rear leaf U-sight, iron blade front sight adjustable for windage. Lock plate with percussion lock with dolphin-head hammer, engraved with scrollwork and inscribed SAML. & CHAS. SMITH PRINCES ST. LONDON; case-hardened finish; bolt safety engages at half cock. Walnut three-quarter stock with rudimentary saw handle, checkered butt; engraved, blued steel furniture; silver ramrod pipe; single barrel slide with engraved slots; swivel ramrod.

The hammer of this pistol has an unscrewable nose. The patent, dated 1830, number 5978, refers to "Smith's Patent Imperial Cap." This was wider and flatter than the usual cap, and the priming was placed in a small indentation in the center of the inside surface. The firm of Samuel & Charles Smith was at 64 Princes Street from 1832 to 1870.

Samuel & Charles Smith, London, about 1830–40
Overall length 15 in; barrel 8 in.
Caliber .66 (16 gauge). Weight 2¼ lb.
Literature: Winant, *Early Percussion Firearms*, pp. 110–112.

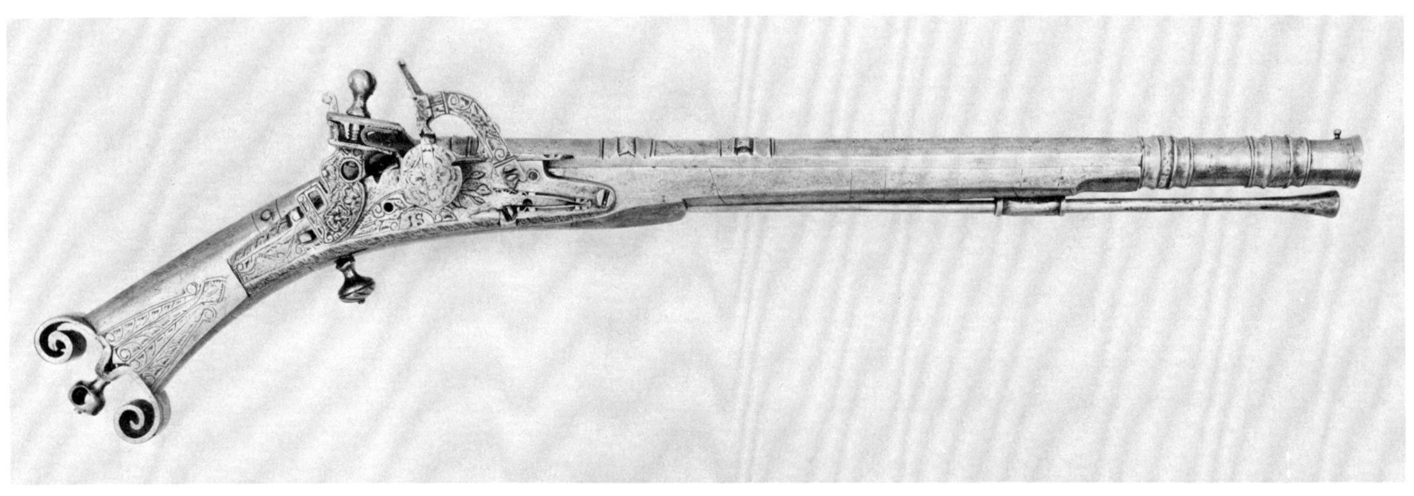

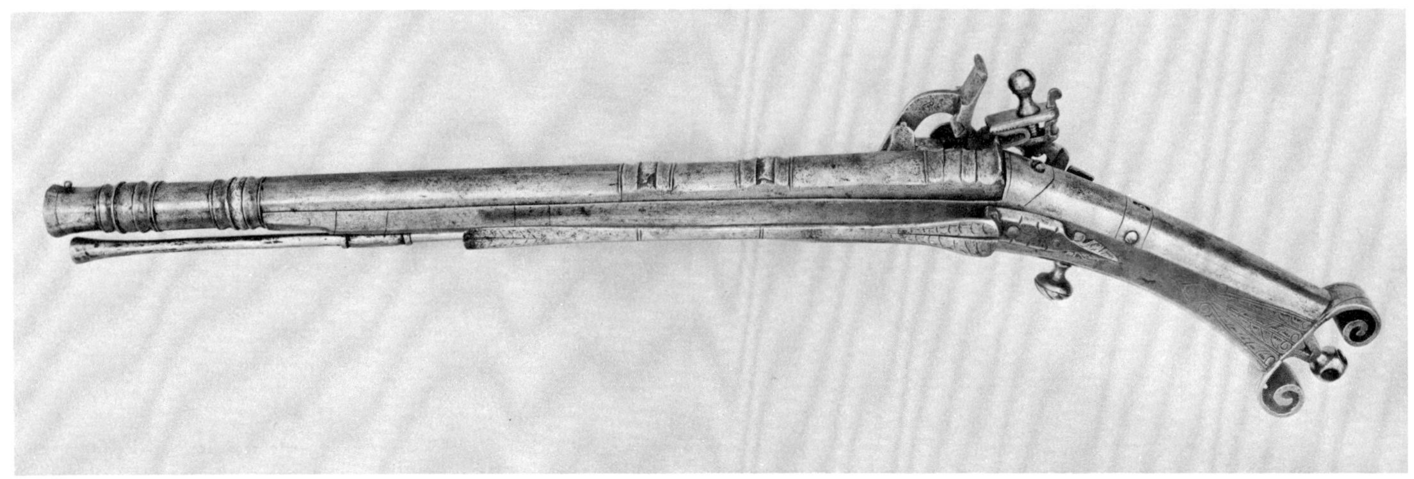

3

SCOTTISH PISTOLS

These signed Scottish pistols, of brass or steel engraved and chased, show the principal mechanisms and types. They date from 1619 to the late 18th century. Among the characteristic features that distinguish Scottish pistols from all others are: steel or brass stocks, the style of butt, the picker (used to clear the lock of powder fouling) that fits into the butt, globular triggers, the lack of a trigger guard, and the profuse ornamentation of scrolls and Celtic strapwork, often inlaid with silver. Furthermore, they were made in pairs, the 17th-century ones with right- and left-hand locks. There are four principal types of Scottish pistol, distinguished by their butts: the fishtail, heart-shaped, lobe-shaped, and scroll or ram's horn. The lock mechanisms used are the snaphance (dated examples range from 1598 to 1686) and the flintlock.

The records of the Incorporation of Hammermen in Scotland include the names of gunmakers at least as early as 1585. By 1646 a minor Scottish industry had been established at Doune in Stirlingshire by Thomas Caddell and others. A long line of pistolmakers followed, and at the beginning of the 18th century the all-metal flintlock pistol, with either a lobe-shaped or a ram's-horn butt, was a part of the ordinary Highland full dress.

40. Boy's Snaphance Belt Pistol
[Not illustrated] (Bedford 1582)

Of brass, except for the action. Barrel engraved with flowers and scrolls, with five raised bands and raised octagonal muzzle; blank shield for owner's crest and date 1619 across extreme rear of breech. Lock plate bears maker's mark I.D.; lock plate and stock engraved with scrolls and panels. Stock terminates in concave-sided octagonal ball butt, engraved overall; long slender belt hook; ramrod and top jaw and screw of cock are replacements.

> 1619
> Overall length 12 in.; barrel 8½ in.
> Caliber .375.

41. Scroll-butt Snaphance Pistol
(Bedford 1532)

Barrel alternately faceted and round; divisions marked by molded rings, three of them overlaid with engraved silver; engraved along top facet, a running leaf design; iron bead front sight; stationary rear sight. Lock plate engraved with thistles and Tudor rose, also gunmaker's initials IS (John Stvart); horizontal sear passes through lock plate and engages rectangular perforation in heel of cock; flat-faced cock with descent arrest; pan with discoid fence engraved with rose and dated 1683; pan is separate piece; steel has long arm engraved with conventional foliage; spirally filed button trigger; trigger tang, pivoted by transverse peg, moves in rectangular slot on top of grip. Stock, of steel, engraved on each side with conventional foliage; picker (blade lacking) has spherical perforated head and is screwed into butt between scrolls; on reverse of stock is steel belt hook; long steel ramrod passes through one pipe.

John Stvart was one of the best of the late 17th-century Scottish gunmakers. His place of residence, not known, is believed to have been one of the smaller towns in northeastern Scotland. His signature in full appears on a very fine pair of Scottish flintlock pistols, similar in proportion to no. 41 though with heart-shaped butts, in the Royal Swedish Armory, Stockholm. A Scottish flintlock pistol with lock inscribed IO STVART is in the George F. Harding Museum, Chicago (inv. no. 1487).

> John Stvart, 1683
> Overall length 19⅝ in.; barrel 14⅛ in.
> Caliber .62 (20 gauge). Weight 2 lb.
> Ex coll.: Major Jakobsson, Stockholm; Marquis de Bute; Roy G. Cole, Hamilton, Ontario.
> Literature: Hoff, "Scottish Pistols in Scandinavian Collections"; Whitelaw, *Treatise on Scottish Hand Firearms*, pl. 2, no. 5.

42. Scroll-butt Flintlock Pistol
(Bedford 1061)

Barrel round, except for middle part of hogsback form and octagonal muzzle; divided into sections by silver bands engraved with conventional floral designs, one enclosing a blank heraldic shield; hogsback section inlaid with silver diamonds and roundels engraved with design simulating foliage. Lock plate, inscribed *T. Caddell* (in script), is rounded and engraved with conventional foliage; cock engraved en suite; faceted steel attached to pan by screw, head of which is inside lock; horizontal sear; half cock set by sear passing through rectangular aperture in lock plate in front of cock; ball trigger. Stock, of steel, engraved with panels of conventional foliage and inlaid with transverse bands

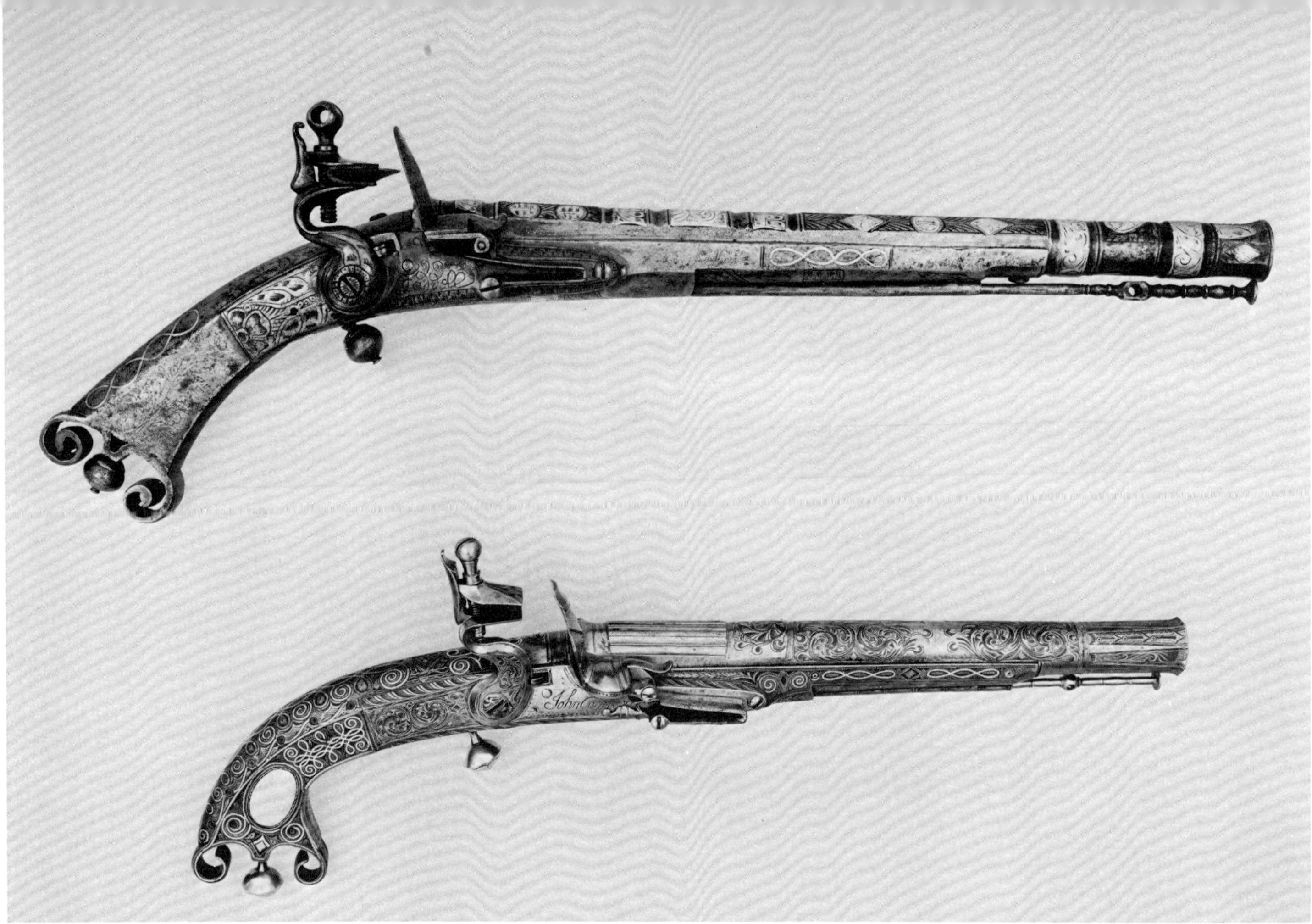

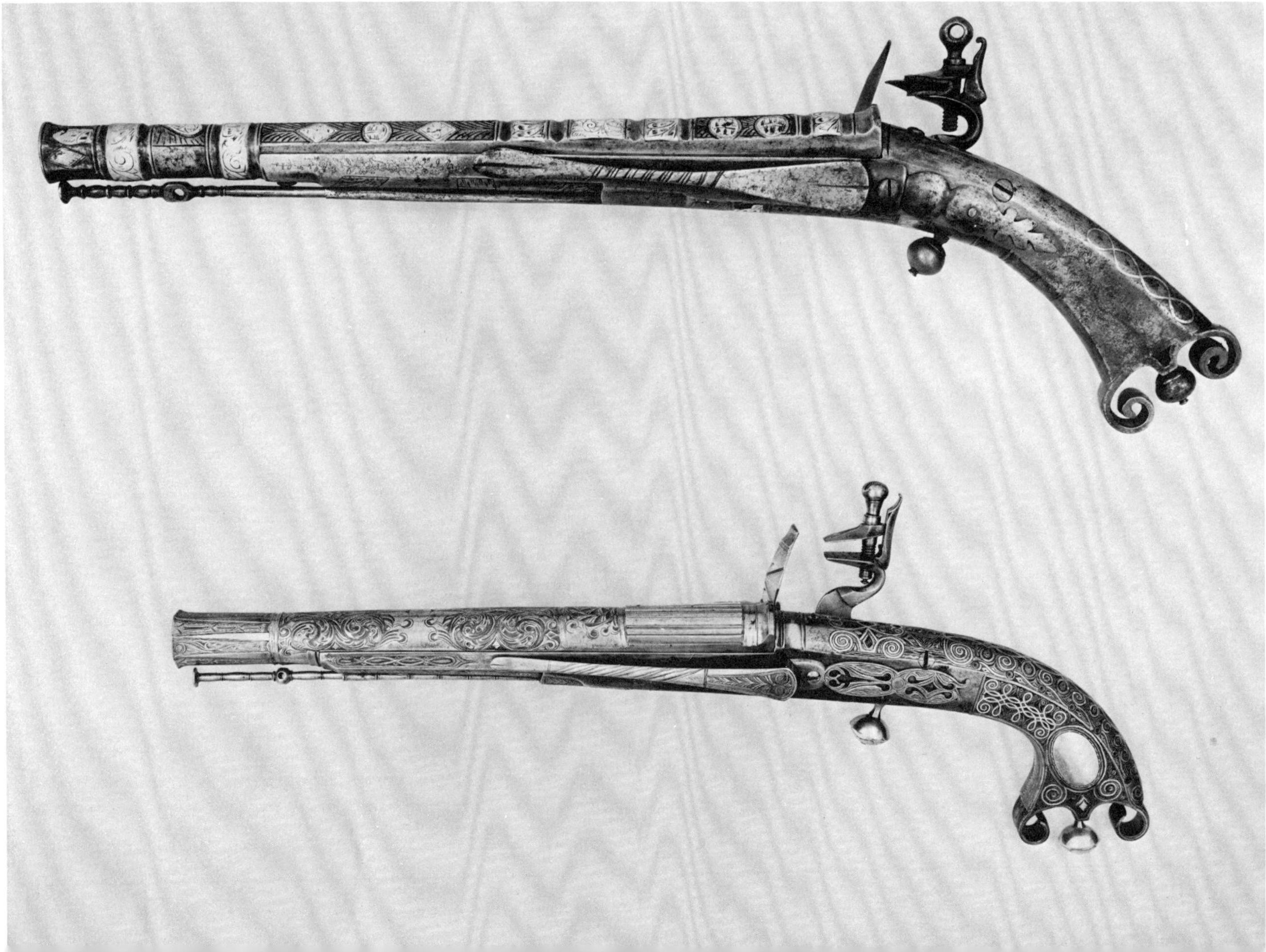

of silver also engraved with foliage; upper surface inlaid with silver scrolls, sides engraved with foliage with traces of gilding and bluing; between scrolls is screwed picker with spherical head; belt hook with lines and foliate finial; under belt hook is original blued and gilded surface of stock; steel ramrod, with spiral worm and baluster head, is perforated for a rod to assist in turning it when a ball is being removed from barrel.

The Caddells of Doune, Sterlingshire, were gunmakers for several generations. The first Caddell is said to have come from Muthill to Doune about 1640; the last was living in the fourth quarter of the 18th century. This pistol probably was made by the second generation. See no. 45 for a later Caddell pistol. A flintlock pistol with lock plate inscribed THOS. CADDELL and silver plaques inscribed CAPT. JAMES LOCKHART OF GENERAL COLYEAR'S REGT. is in the George F. Harding Museum, Chicago (inv. no. 1489); a pair of Thos. Caddell flintlock pistols are in Windsor Castle (Laking, *Catalogue*, nos. 7–8, ill.).

> Thomas Caddell, Doune, about 1695
> Overall length 17½ in.; barrel 12¹⁄₁₆ in.
> Caliber .70 (14 gauge). Weight 2 lb.
> Literature: Blackmore, *Firearms*, pp. 70–71, ill.;
> Blackmore, *The Art of the Armourer*, no. 230, ill.

43. Scroll-butt Flintlock Pistol
(Bedford 1127)

One of a pair, exceptional by reason of profuse gold inlay in the stock, in addition to the more usual silver inlay. Barrel of conventional form, fluted at breech, octagonal at muzzle, intervening section round; rear sight cut in elevated end of breech. Lock plate, flat, engraved with name *John Campbell* (in script); horizontally acting sear passes through square aperture in lock plate to engage front of cock at half cock; bridle between pan and pan-cover screw; front of steel faceted. Stock has on each side of butt a blank gold oval plaque; between scrolls of butt is globular gold-headed picker; gold button trigger; opposite lock plate is belt hook filed with spiraled ornament, its tail pierced and engraved; underneath and around belt hook the original blued surface is preserved; single elongated steel ramrod pipe; steel ramrod with perforated ball to aid in turning ramrod.

There were three generations of pistol makers in the Campbell family. The first was apprenticed to the first Thomas Caddell of Doune; the last retired from business shortly before 1798.

> John Campbell, Doune, about 1760
> Overall length 14½ in.; barrel 8¾ in.
> Caliber .62 (19 gauge). Weight 1¾ lb.
> Literature: Whitelaw, *A Treatise on Scottish Hand Firearms*, pp. 95–96, pl. VII, fig. 25.

44. Scroll-butt Flintlock Pistol
(Bedford 1271)

Although generally of Scottish character and signed by the Scottish maker Christi, this bears the place name London on the lock plate, and also a London private proof. Furthermore, instead of the typical Scottish ornament, the butt and barrel are engraved with much more typically English, or even French, decoration. Barrel of usual Scottish form, but circular section is deeply engraved with rococo scrollwork, flowers and shells enclosing a crest, and demi-eagle with wings displayed holding crown in its beak; between this section of barrel and fluted breech, separated by molded rings, is section engraved with trophy of arms. Lock plate, rounded, engraved with trophy of arms and, in scrolls, name and place CHRISTI LONDON; steel engraved with scrollwork and filed with vertical rib. Stock of silver gilt, engraved with scrolls and flowers; behind raised breech, a crowned thistle is engraved within scrolls; between butt scrolls is silver picker head engraved with a rose; silver-gilt globular trigger is similarly engraved; on reverse side of pistol is belt hook inlaid with gold, its finial finely pierced on gold ground; the original oval plaques on each side of grip have been replaced with gilt-bronze plaques decorated with hatching; trigger tang, pivoted at sides of the grip, does not extend to open slot in grip, unlike the arrangement in the normal Scottish pistols in this exhibition; steel ramrod with disk finial passes through elongated silver pipe.

Another pistol by Christi, in the Royal Collection at Windsor, also has a stock entirely of silver, in which the Celtic ornament is replaced by rococo scrollwork of more European or Continental character (Whitelaw, *A Treatise on Scottish Hand Firearms*, pl. VIII, fig. 30). A John Christie, known to be a maker of Scottish pistols, worked in the Tower of London from 1794 to 1830. Murdoch of Doune produced a series of presentation pistols in which stocks of copper gilt take the place of the usual iron or brass. In the same way, decoration of English or Continental character replaces the usual Celtic interlays. For a pair by J. Murdoch, see Hayward, *The Art of the Gunmaker*, vol. II, pl. 72.

> Christi, London, about 1760
> Overall length 11⅝ in.; barrel 7³⁄₁₆ in.
> Caliber .53 (32 gauge). Weight 1½ lb.

45. Scroll-butt Flintlock Pistol
(Bedford 773)

One of a pair. Barrel of usual Scottish form, fluted at breech, octagonal at muzzle, intervening section round. Lock plate, flat faced, inscribed *Thos Caddell* (in script); perforated disk engraved with rose surmounts comb of cock; horizontal sear passes through lock plate to set at half cock. Stock of steel, bottom inlaid with three transverse bands of silver, top of butt inlaid with interlacing silver scrolls; both sides of butt inset with oval silver plaques, on obverse engraved with crest of owner (armored arm holding a flail), and on the reverse his initials; between butt scrolls is silver picker head engraved with a rose; silver button trigger is engraved to correspond; on reverse of pistol is screwed belt hook with spiraled filing, the finial pierced and engraved; elongated ramrod pipe; steel ramrod with perforated ball to aid in turning ramrod.

This pistol was probably made by the last of the Caddells. For a pistol by a Thomas Caddell of a previous generation, see no. 42.

> Thomas Caddell, Doune, third quarter of the 18th century
> Overall length 12¾ in.; barrel 8¼ in.
> Caliber .57 (25 gauge). Weight 1½ lb.

46. Lobe-shaped-butt Flintlock Pistol
(Bedford 788)

One of a pair. Barrel of usual Scottish form. Lock plate, flat, with engraved tail and cock, is inscribed I. MURDOCH; horizontal sear passes through lock plate and engages at half cock. Stock, of steel, inlaid with transverse bands of engraved silver; remaining surface engraved with conventional foliage; butt inlaid with triangles and bands of silver; button trigger of silver engraved with a rose; on reverse side of pistol is belt hook with pierced finial; elongated ramrod pipe and steel ramrod with discoid finial.

John Murdoch, who was still working in 1798, was the last of the successful Scottish gunmakers. Another of his pistols of this type is in The Metropolitan Museum of Art (acc. no. 19.53.52).

> John Murdoch, Doune, last quarter of the 18th century
> Overall length 12¾ in.; barrel 7¾ in.
> Caliber .58 (24 gauge). Weight 1½ lb.

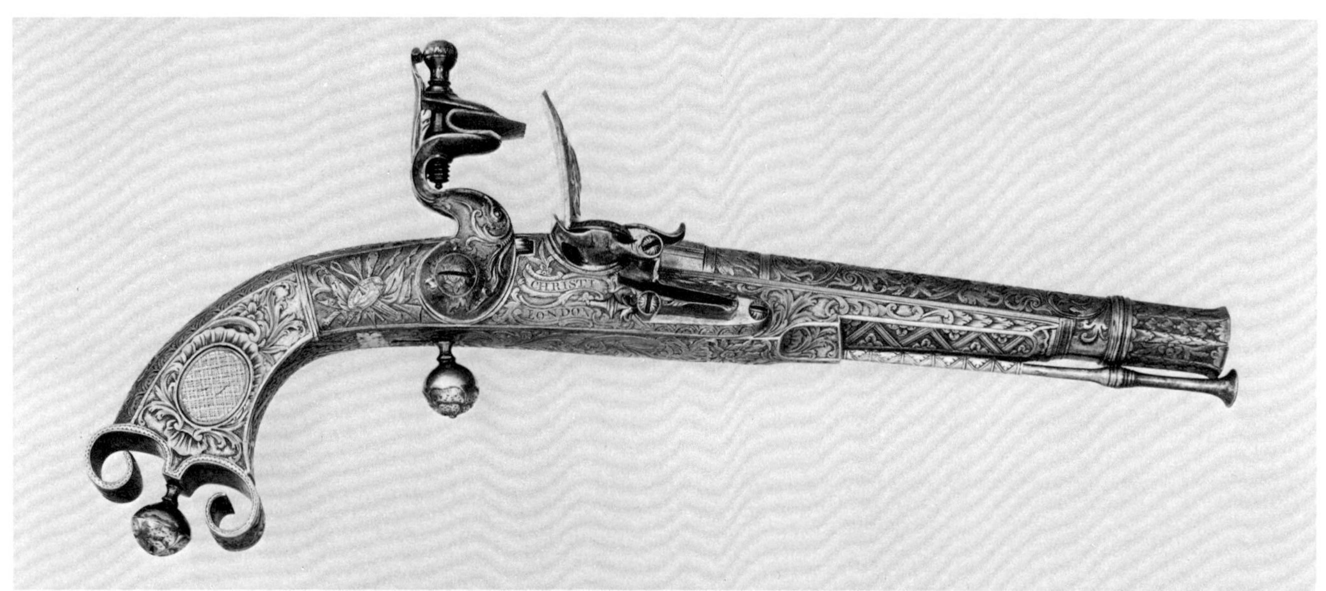

44

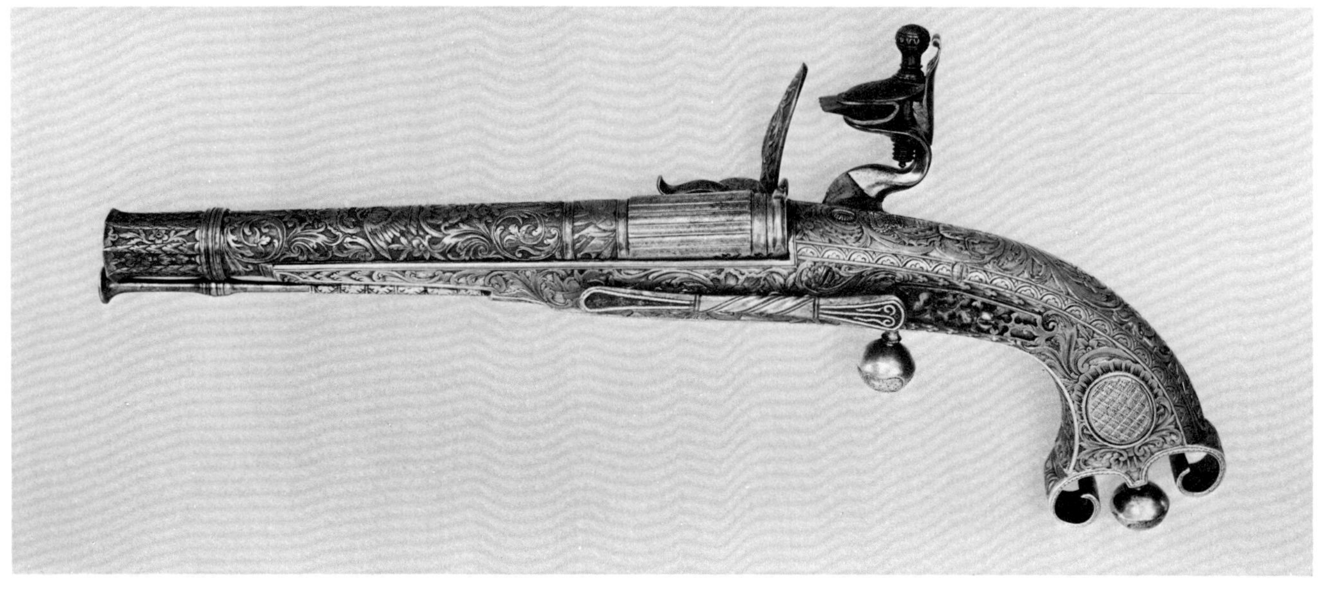
44

45

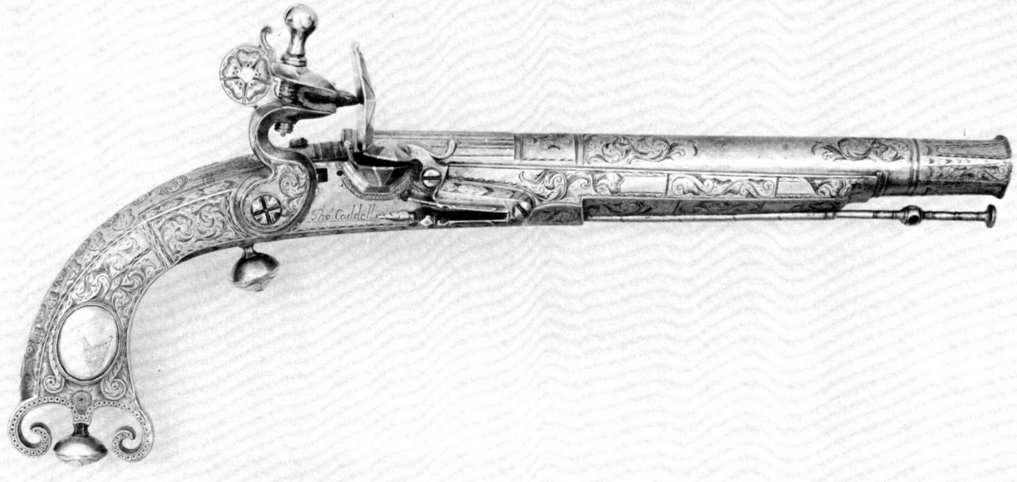

46

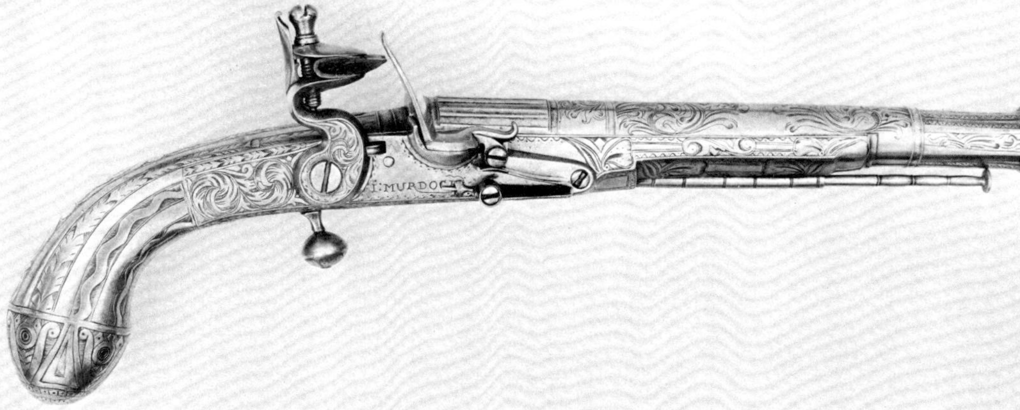

45

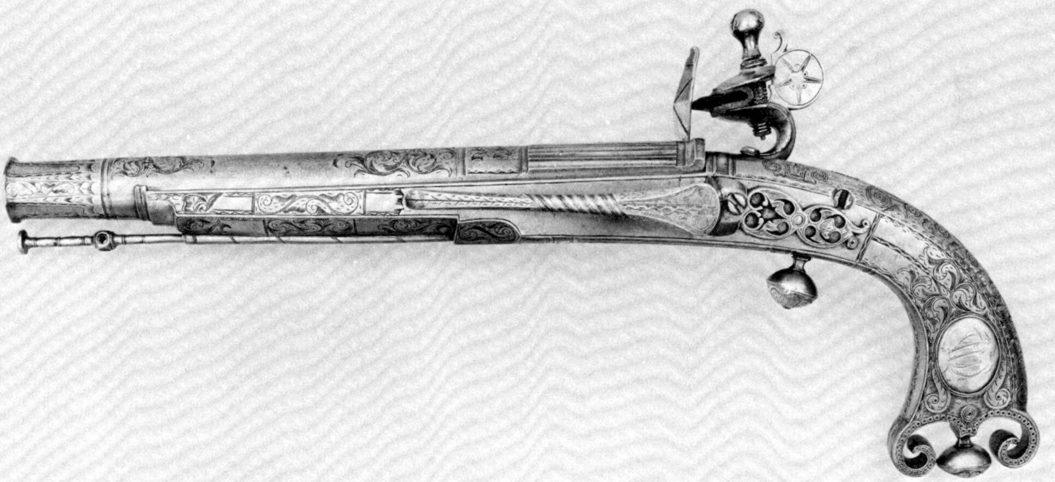

46

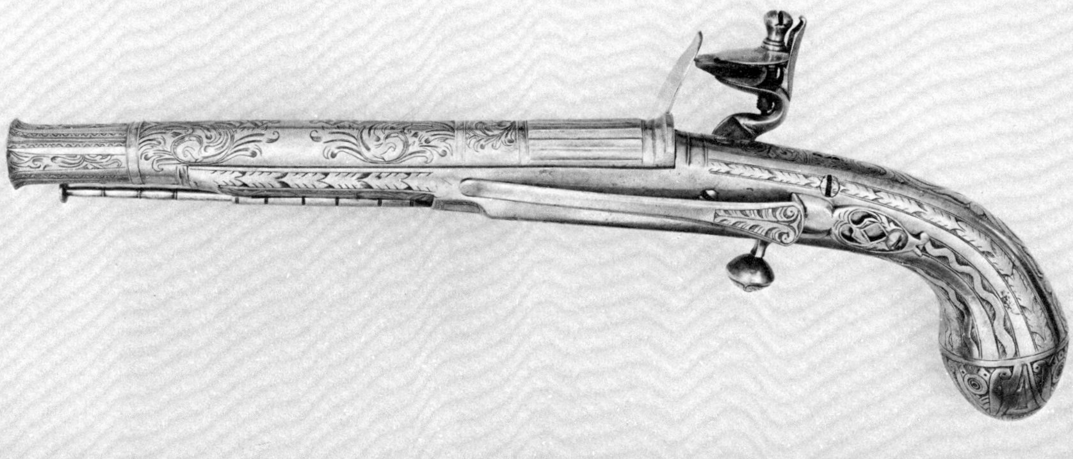

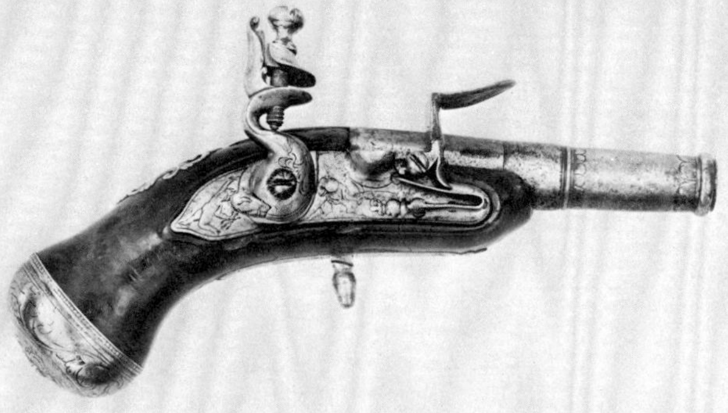

47

48

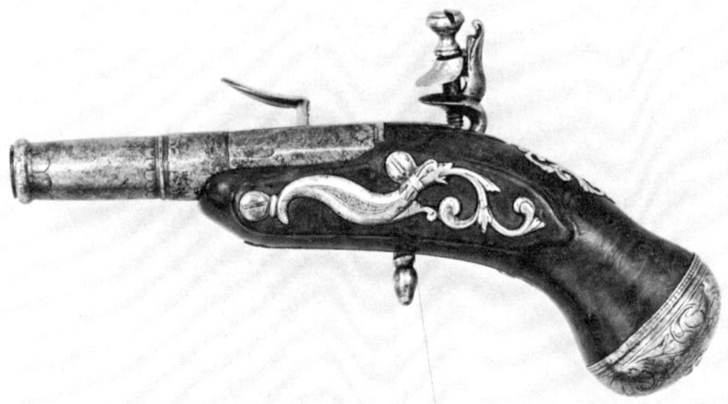

47

48

4

TURNOFF PISTOLS

These twenty examples of turnoff pistols were made over a period of 140 years, the earliest dating from about 1660. They were made in pairs, and all except one are signed. Besides London, the gunmakers represented here worked in Oxford, Warwick, and Whitehaven. The turnoff type of horse pistol is not as graceful in contour as the full-stock holster pistol. However, some of the examples have an attractive burl-walnut stock, in certain instances inlaid with silver scrollwork, and some have silver spurred pommels, though a small mask pommel was more widely used. A silver side plate and silver wire scrolling were also used.

A feature of these horseman's pistols is a construction in which the lock plate and housing were made integrally with the breech, thereby reducing the walnut stock to the grip. The term *turnoff* indicates a barrel that unscrews in front of the chamber so it can be loaded with a ball that fits the bore more tightly than is possible with a muzzle-loader. Many of these turnoff barrels are rifled. The combination of a tight fit and rifling increased both power and accuracy, the result being a firearm capable of piercing the breastplates of cuirassiers. No. 50 has the forward part of the barrel permanently attached to the stock by a ring and link that prevented the barrel from slipping away when being loaded on horseback. A number of the exhibited pistols have an elongated lug on the underside of the barrel that was engaged by a wrench fitted with a slot for screwing the barrel onto the breech.

Of especial interest in this group are two items by James Freeman, both made about 1720. One (no. 57) is a pair of flintlock pistols with left- and right-hand locks, the other (no. 54) a flintlock with fixed cannon barrel. Thus, ordinary muzzle-loading pistols with fixed barrels similar in form to turnoff barrels continued to be used in the period of the turnoff breech-loading type. Here we should also mention the two-shot superimposed-load breech-action flintlock turnoff pistol by Israel Segalas, Jr., made about 1750.

The series ends with two box-lock pistols in which the cock, instead of being placed on the side, occupies a position on top in the center of a boxlike area; the pan and pan cover are likewise at the top of the breech. From the end of the 18th century, turnoff barrels were confined almost exclusively to pocket pistols.

47. Rifled Pocket Flintlock Pistol
(Bedford 1104)

Barrel rifled with eight grooves, in two stages with molded girdle between; breech octagonal changing to polygonal, engraved with flowers and pendant ribbon enclosing name W. UPTON (partly obliterated), forward stage round, ending in muzzle ring. Lock plate with molded face engraved with nude warrior; horizontal sear of original construction; pivoted dog safety catch engaging between half and full cock. Walnut half stock carved with raised borders; steel furniture except for silver escutcheon; oval butt cap engraved with foliage enclosing human half figures and serpents; serpentine side plate; acorn trigger; no trigger guard.

Since the butt is so small, the trigger is pivoted unusually far forward on the rear side nail. A link extending forward over the tumbler was necessary to connect the trigger with the sear. W. Upton was among the highly skilled provincial gunmakers of the second half of the 17th century. He provided pistols (still extant) for the use of the Estates Bursar of Magdalene College, Oxford. He became a freeman of the city of Oxford in 1647 and was elected a constable of the city in 1681. He is recorded working up to 1698.

William Upton, Oxford, about 1660
Overall length 6⅛ in.; barrel 3⅛ in.
Caliber .35. Weight ¼ lb.

48. Rifled Flintlock Pistol   (Bedford 860)

Barrel rifled with eight grooves; forward part secured by ring and link to stock for ease when loading on horseback; barrel in two stages, separated by girdle, breech octagonal stamped with London proofmarks, forward stage round with molded muzzle ring. Rounded lock plate engraved with strawberry leaves and fruit; early type of vertically acting sear without bridle to tumbler. Walnut half stock; iron furniture; spurred pommel fluted and engraved with conventional foliage; serpentine side plate; blank vase-shaped escutcheon; globular trigger.

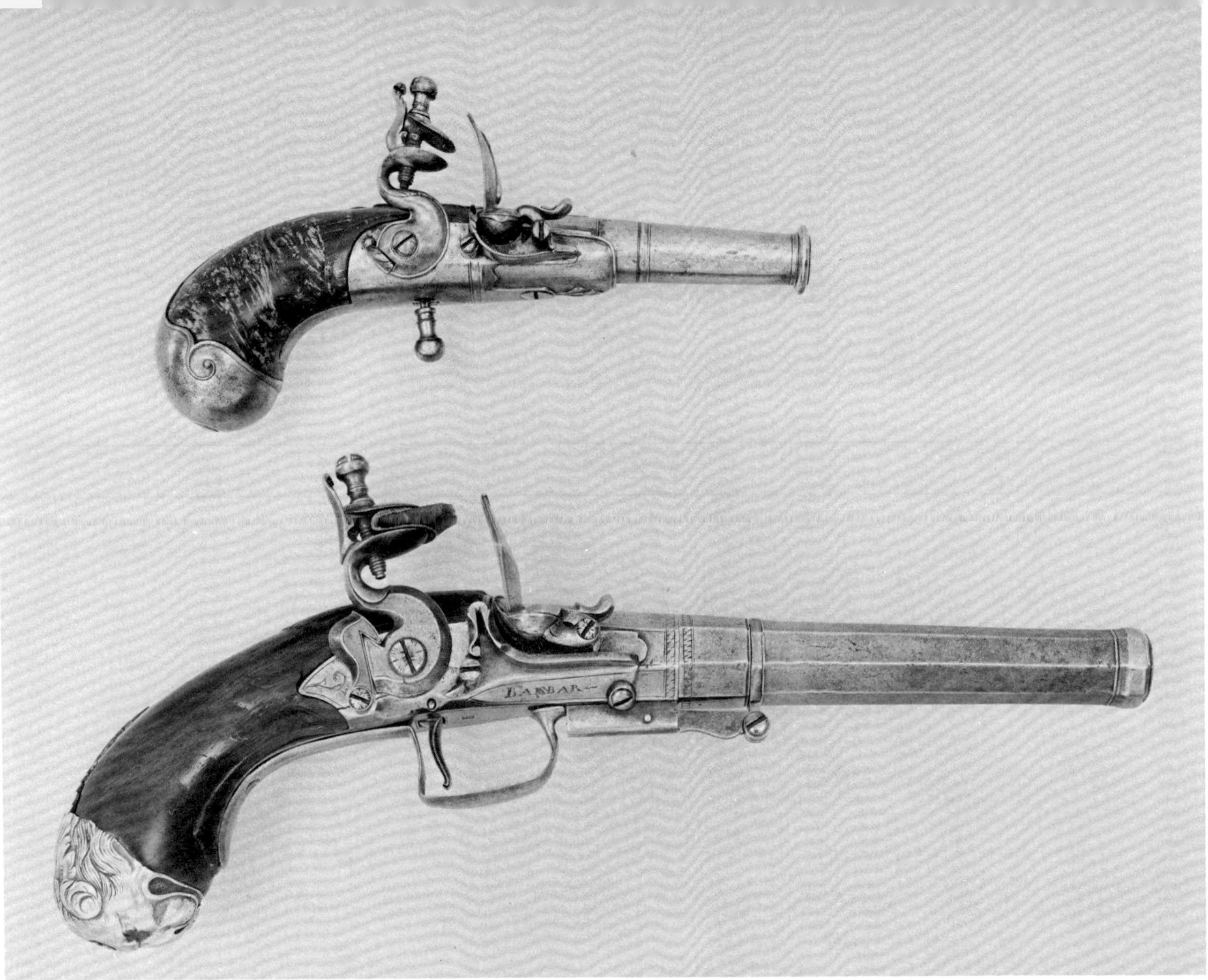

49

50

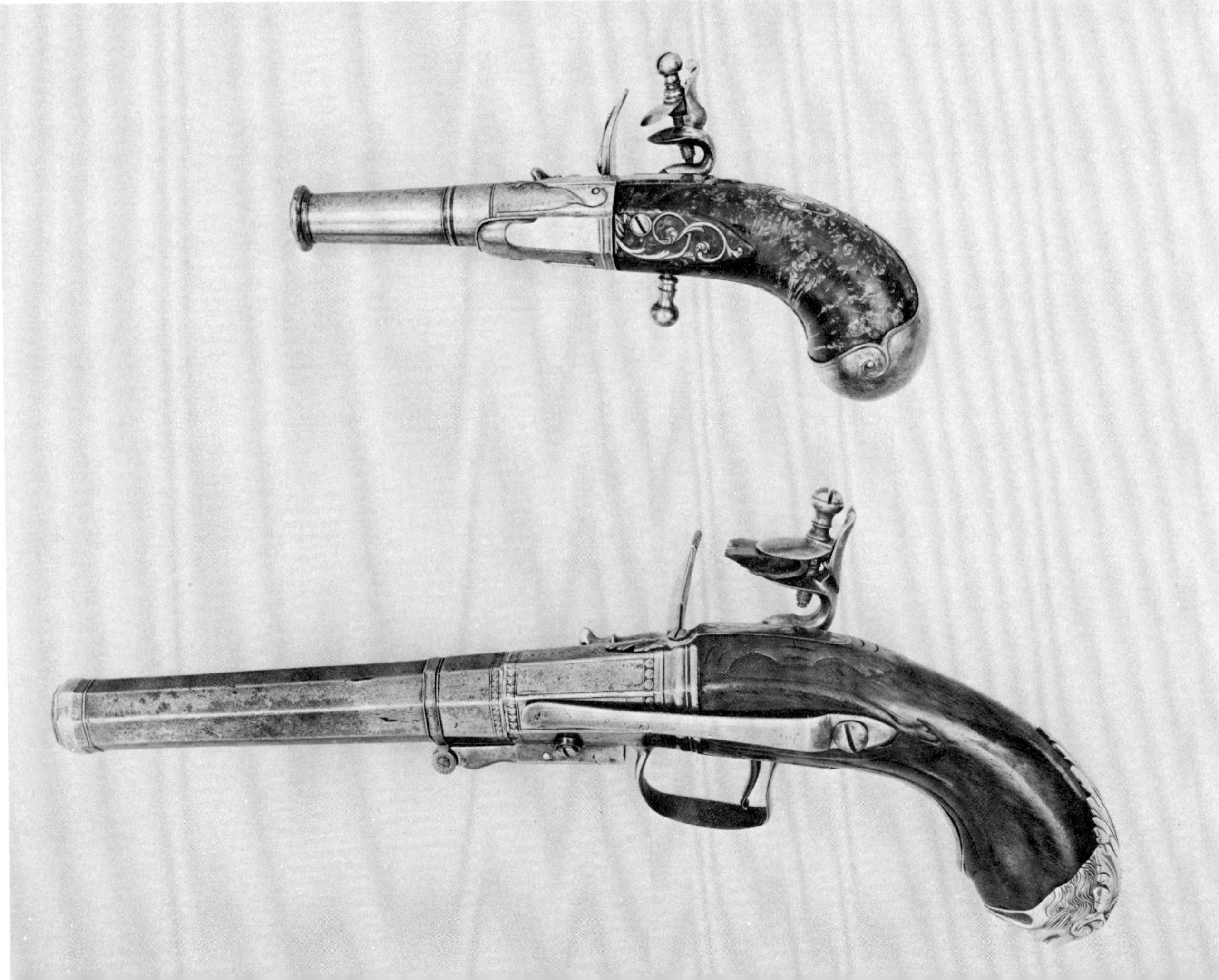

49

50

The attribution to Edward Nicholson is based on the close similarity of this pistol to one by Nicholson in the Mark Dinely collection, Berwick St. John, England (Hayward, *The Art of the Gunmaker*, vol. II, pl. 16 a). Nicholson was master of the Gunmakers' Company in 1697.

Edward Nicholson, London, about 1670
Overall length 11⅜ in.; barrel 6 in.
Caliber .45 (50 gauge). Weight 1 lb.

49. Rifled Pocket Flintlock Pistol
(Bedford 1190)

Cannon barrel rifled with six grooves, in two stages separated by molded girdle, ending in expanded muzzle ring; flattened top at breech terminating in leaf ornament. Dog safety operating between half and full cock; single-leaf upward-curved "steel" spring. Butt of figured burl-walnut; steel furniture; rounded pommel, chased with raised edges and volutes; side plate pierced with floral scrolls; single side nail; blank escutcheon with pierced pendant swags; button trigger; no trigger guard.

Henry Ellis, Doncaster, about 1690
Overall length 6⅞ in.; barrel 3⅝ in.
Caliber .36. Weight ¾ lb.
Literature: Hayward, *The Art of the Gunmaker*, vol.
II, p. 328, pl. 15 b.

50. Flintlock Pistol
(Bedford 1173)

One of a pair. Octagonal cannon barrel in three stages, separated by engraved and then molded girdle, terminating in muzzle ring; barrel hinged to extensible

iron rod sliding in socket under breech for convenience in loading when on horseback; inscribed LONDINI on top facet of barrel and BARBAR on facet below lock. Flat-faced cock with dog catch engaging between half and full cock; faceted steel, its face channeled in Spanish manner; inverted-V "steel" spring. Walnut butt carved with cartouche around barrel tang; silver butt cap, chased as lion's head with acanthus-leaf mane, is

secured by engraved exterior iron screw; steel trigger guard; steel belt hook.

This pistol displays the earliest form of the Queen Anne cannon barrel.

Lewis Barbar, London, about 1710–15
Overall length 11⅛ in.; barrel 4⅞ in.
Caliber .62 (20 gauge). Weight 1½ lb.

51. Pocket Flintlock Pistol
(Bedford 854)

One of a pair. Barrel in three stages, octagonal at breech, forward stages round separated by molded girdle, ending in muzzle ring; projection under breech takes key for unscrewing. Side lock, cock with flattened face engraved with foliage; faceted pan and faceted steel with engraved borders; inscribed below lock D. WYNN LONDINI. Walnut butt, carved behind barrel tang with leaf ornament; silver furniture; border of butt cap engraved with lines merging into leaves, center chased with flower; side plate chased with foliate scrolls and dolphin head; escutcheon surmounted by grotesque mask and engraved with crest (double-headed bird); steel trigger guard with acorn finial, same form on forward finial of barrel tang.

David Wynn was admitted freeman of the Gunmakers' Company in 1715.

David Wynn, London, about 1710–20
Overall length 7¼ in.; barrel 3⅜ in.
Caliber .50 (37 gauge). Weight ¾ lb.

52. Flintlock Pistol
(Bedford 1530)

One of a pair. Cannon barrel in three stages, octagonal changing to polygonal, then circular, then circular again; around breech and muzzle ends are chased girdles of acanthus foliage, and at central point of barrel, molded girdle, all three of silver; WILLMORE LONDON inscribed on top facet of breech; stamped on underside of breech are London proofmarks and crowned F for foreigner; projection under breech takes key for unscrewing. Lock plate, rounded, inscribed WILLMORE; cock engraved with strawberry foliage; vertical ridge carved below center of front of steel. Stock, figured burl-walnut, carved with shell and foliage around barrel tang; silver furniture; pommel, of fine workmanship, cast and chased with floral scrolls developing into dogs' heads and grotesque masks; side plate formed of S-scrolls developing into foliation; escutcheon cast and chased with crest, ducal coronet surmounted by raised goat's head with branch folded in mouth; trigger guard engraved with hunting trophy and leaf finial.

It is exceptional to find Queen Anne pistols with a silver muzzle ring. According to family tradition, this

51

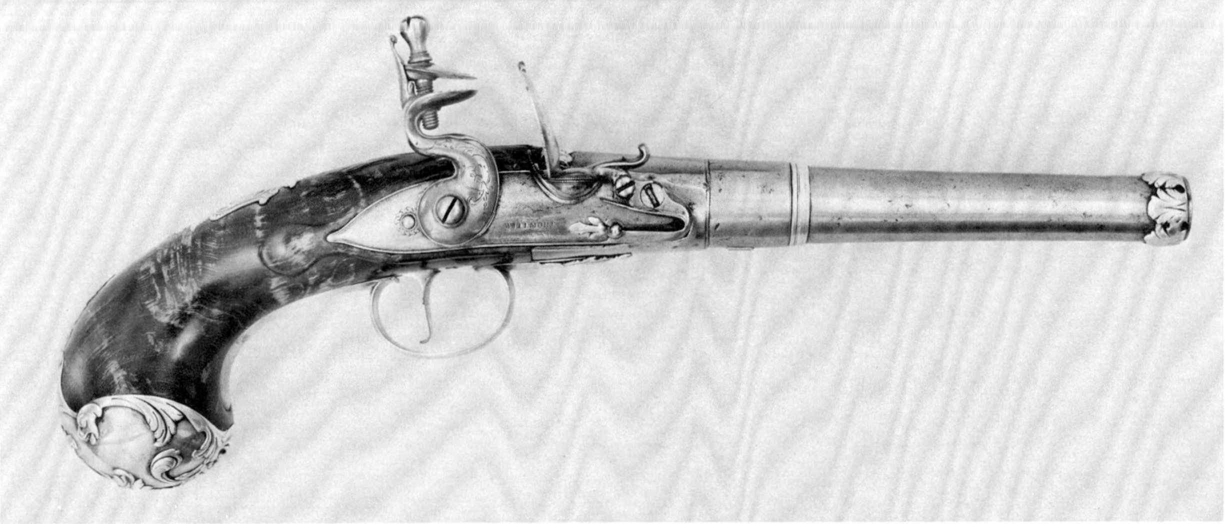

52

51

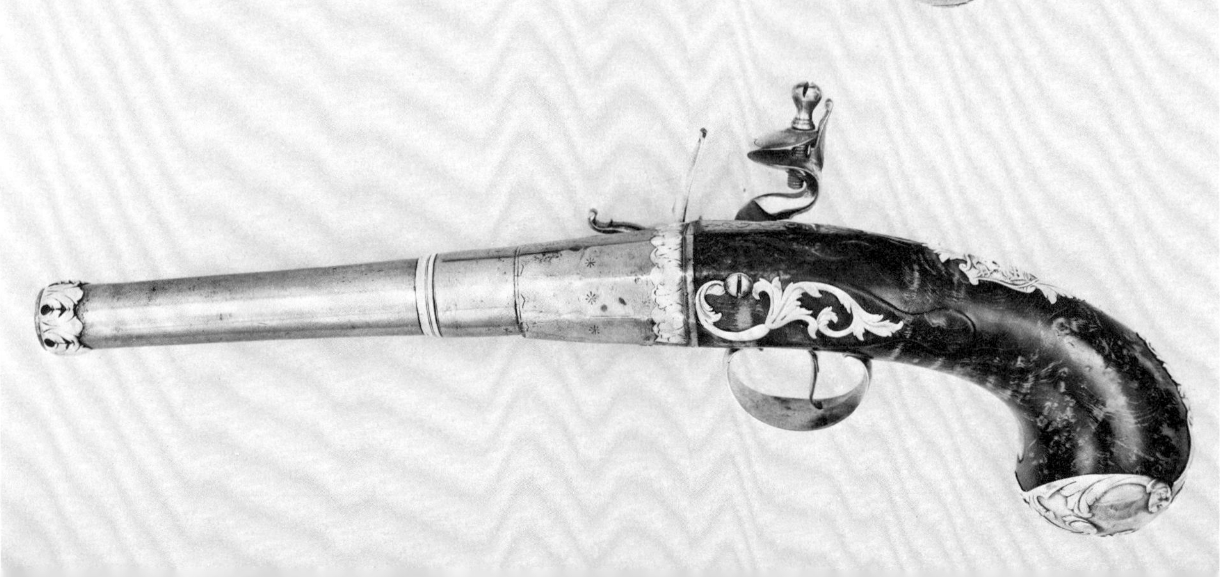

52

pistol and its mate were owned by a relative of the Dumaresq family, who carried them in the 18th century on his daily ride to London along the Edgeware Road as protection against highwaymen. James Willmore was not a freeman of the Gunmakers' Company. His premises in Leicester Fields were sometimes searched for

unproved firearms. In 1740 he was appointed Gunmaker in Ordinary to the king, with a grant of lodgings in Whitehall. He provided the locks for a fine double-barreled flintlock gun in the Royal collection at Windsor Castle that was made for one of the Royal dukes; the barrels for this gun were supplied by James Barbar, son of Lewis Barbar (Blackmore, *Royal Sporting Guns at Windsor*, p. 34, pl. 14).

> James Willmore, London, about 1720
> Overall length 12 in.; barrel 7 in.
> Caliber .65 (17 gauge). Weight 1¼ lb.
> Literature: Sotheby's sale, May 19, 1970, lot 145, ill.

53. Pocket Flintlock Pistol   (Bedford 1286)

Cannon barrel in two stages with molded girdle between, terminating in muzzle ring; engraved acanthus foliage around breech; top of barrel inscribed LONDON; London proofmarks and barrelsmith's mark ET surmounted by fleur-de-lis (Edward Turvey); elongated projection under barrel to aid unscrewing. Side lock with bolt safety engaging at half cock; steel carved with vertical ridge below center; under inverted-V "steel" spring inscribed H. DELANY. Butt, walnut, carved behind barrel tang with leaf and inlaid all over with scrolling silver wire; silver furniture; butt cap chased with leafy borders and grotesque mask and engraved with hunting trophy; leafy S-scroll side plate; blank escutcheon surmounted by grotesque mask; steel trigger guard.

Henry Delany, a Huguenot, was admitted freeman of the Gunmakers' Company in 1715. He worked in Long Acre, Holborn, and was nominated overseer of the Huguenot church there in 1722. Edward Turvey, who made the barrel of this pistol, was the father of gunmaker William Turvey and was master of the Gunmakers' Company in 1713.

> Henry Delany, London, about 1720
> Overall length 6½ in.; barrel 3 in.
> Caliber .50 (37 gauge). Weight ½ lb.
> Literature: Hayward, "The Huguenot Gunmakers of London," pp. 124–125.

54. Flintlock Pistol   (Bedford 1197)

Fixed cannon barrel in three stages, octagonal changing to polygonal at breech, forward stages round, separated by molded girdles, ending in muzzle ring; engraved borders around breech and muzzle; no proofmarks. Lock plate and cock with rounded face and engraved borders, former inscribed FREEMAN LONDINI; inverted-V "steel" spring under pan cover. Butt, walnut, carved to outline mounts and with leaf behind barrel tang; silver furniture; butt cap cast and chased with conventional foliage and finely engraved with chimerical animal head and cherub's head amid strawberry foliage; silver sheet shaped and chased as dragon inlaid on each side of barrel tang; dragon side plate; blank escutcheon; steel trigger guard; iron ramrod, passing through iron ramrod pipe beneath barrel and engaging in tubular socket attached to forward end of trigger guard, is restored.

The cannon barrel turnoff form evidently became so popular that pistols of the normal type loading from the muzzle were made according to the same pattern. James Freeman was master of the Gunmakers' Company in 1732. Characteristic of his firearms is the silver dragon scroll inlaid on each side of the barrel tang. These are found on nearly all of his Queen Anne turnoff pistols and also on some of his holster pistols.

> James Freeman, London, about 1715–20
> Overall length 12 1/16 in.; barrel 7⅝ in.
> Caliber .70 (14 gauge). Weight 1½ lb.

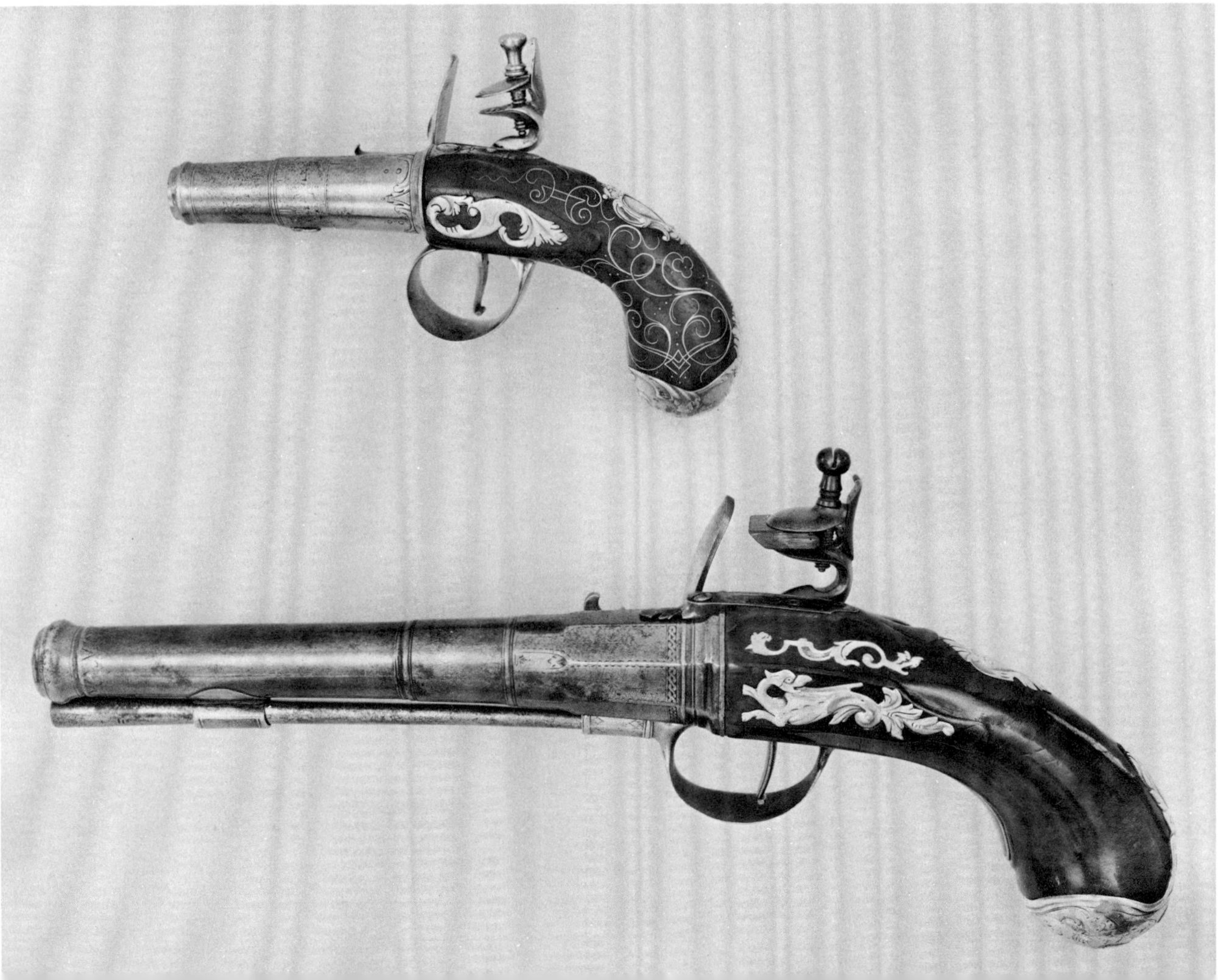

H. DELANY

FREEMAN · LONDON

53
55
54
56

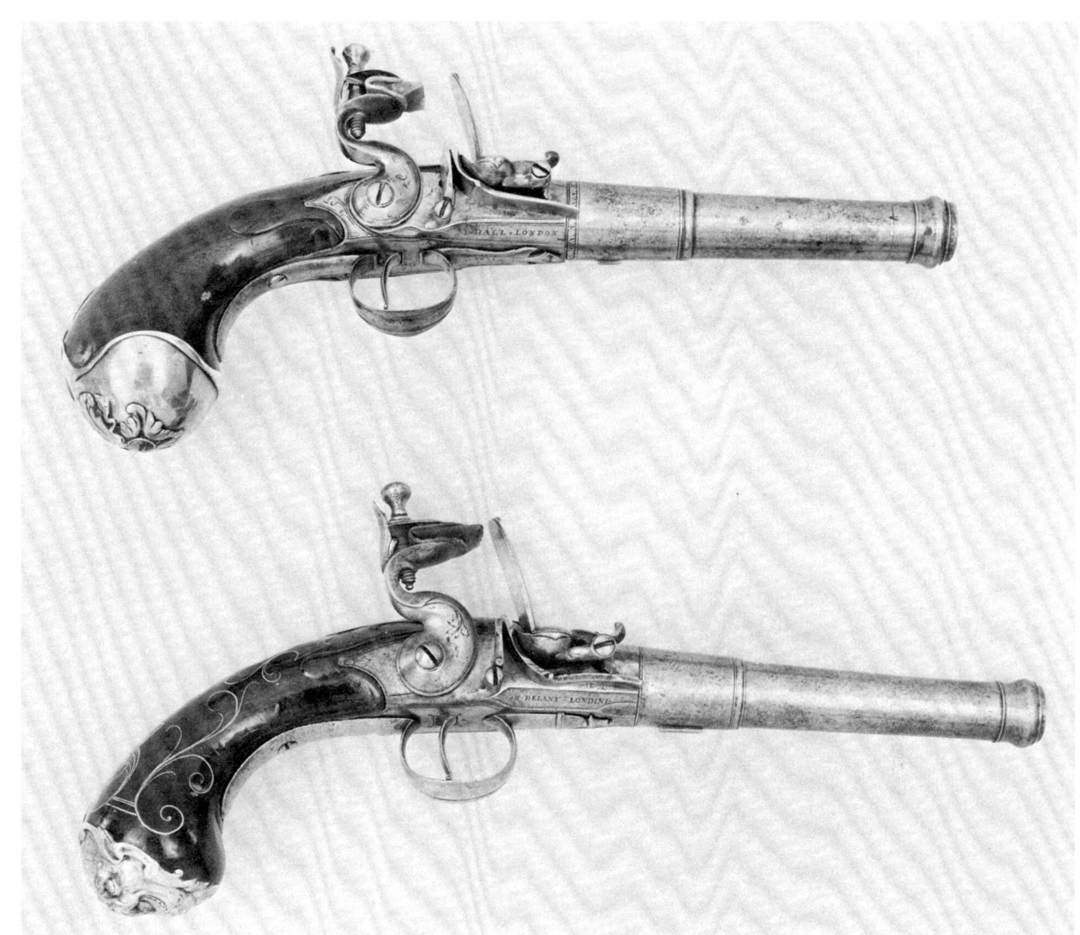

53
55
54
56

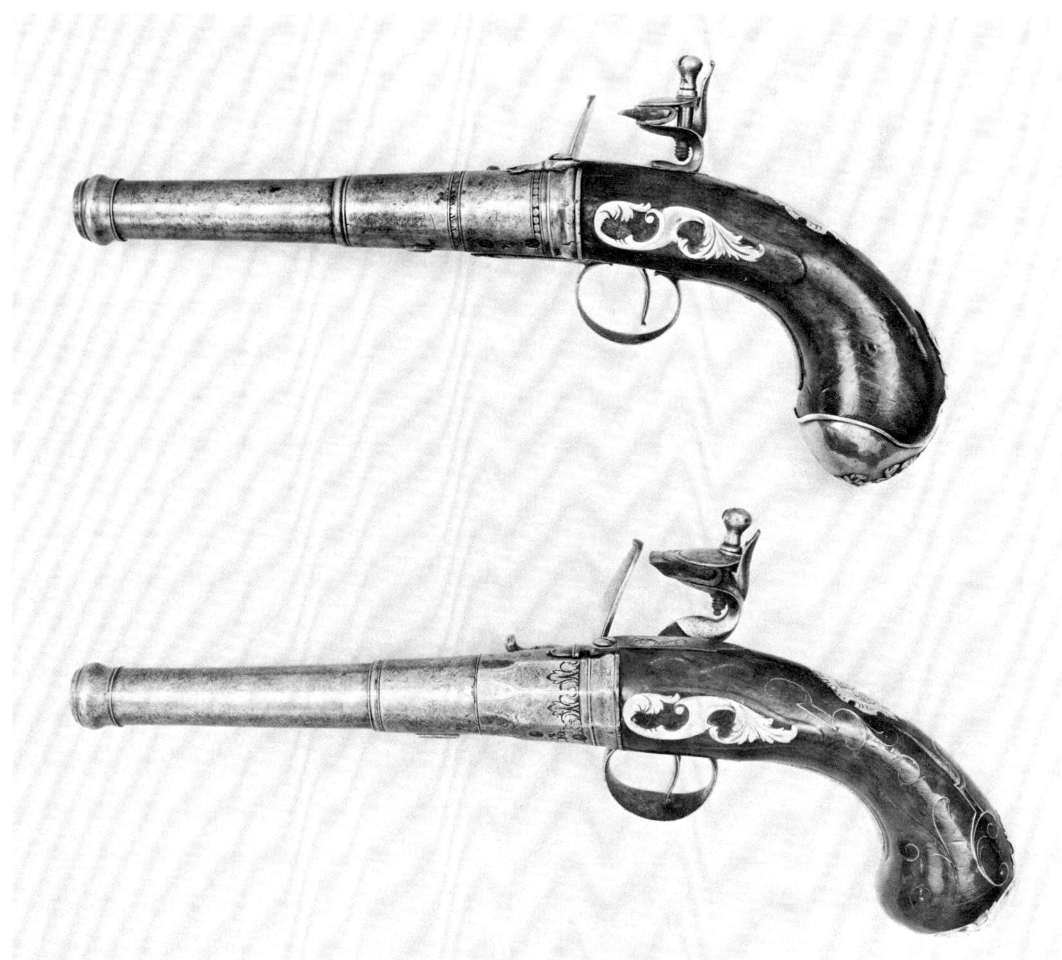

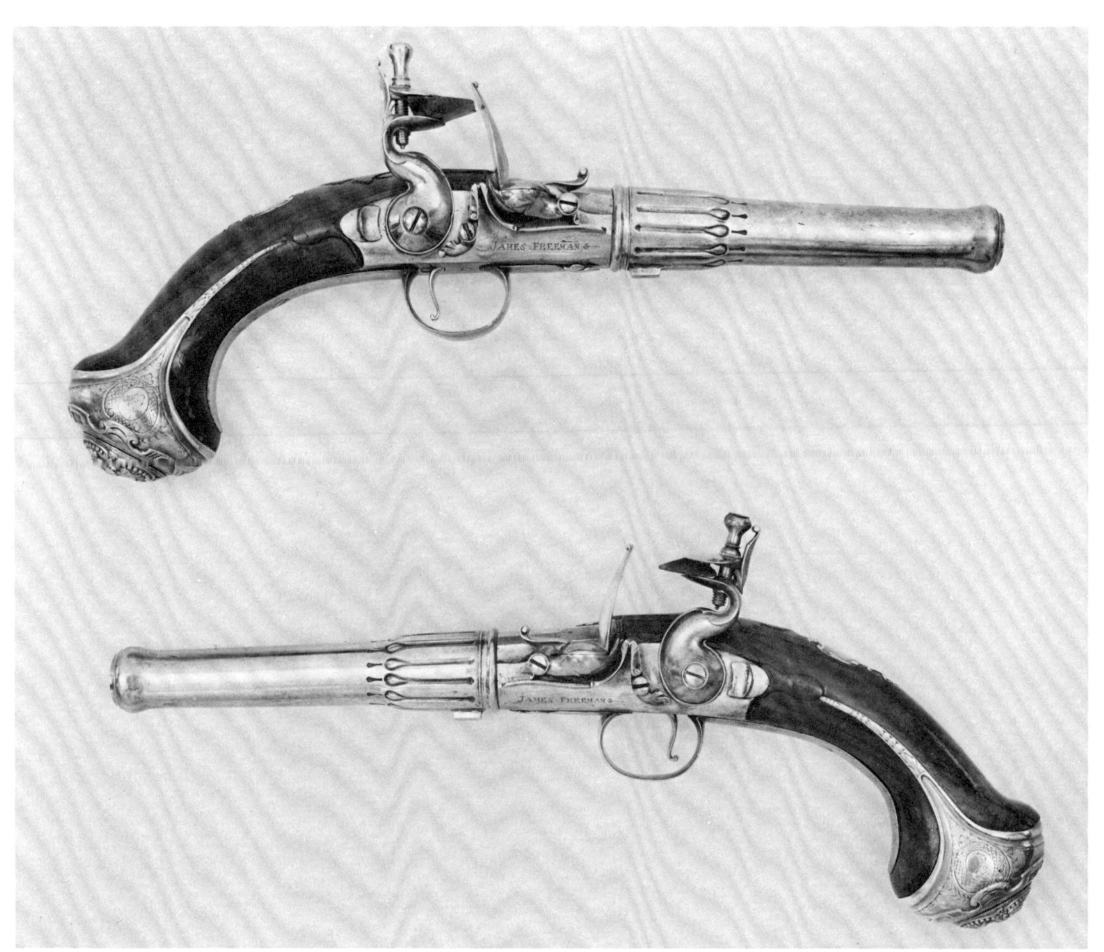

57

57

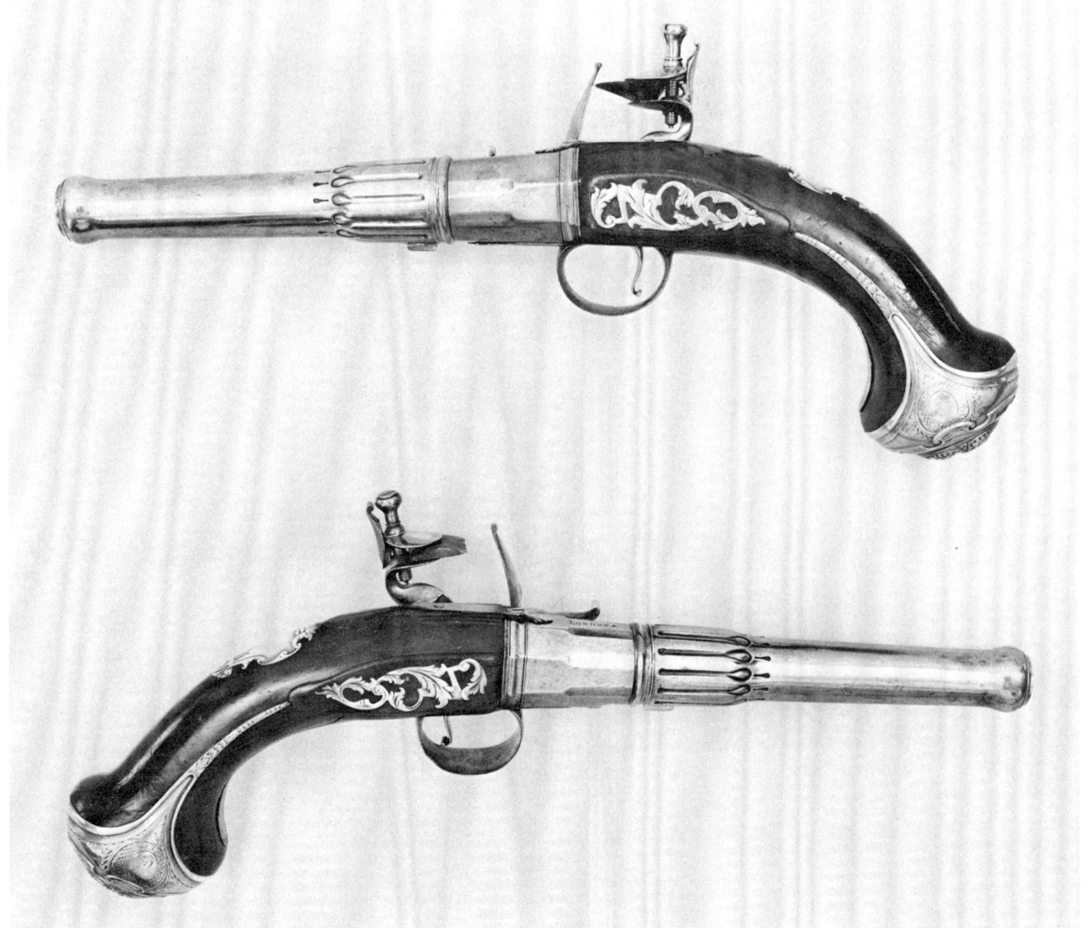

57

57

55. Flintlock Pistol   (Bedford 1126)

One of a pair. Cannon barrel in two stages with molded girdle between, engraved border at breech and muzzle ring; at breech stamped with London proofmarks and barrelsmith's mark HA over diamond (John Hall); bottom of breech inscribed I. HALL LONDON. Lock plate forged integrally with breech, inscribed I. HALL LONDON; cock with rounded surface engraved with scrolls; steel engraved with grenade; barrel tang has cut-leaf finial. Stock, walnut, carved behind tang with leaf; silver furniture; butt cap cast and chased with conventional flowers; side plate of S form developing into leafy scrolls; escutcheon has blank oval in center and is framed with leaves; steel trigger guard has leaf finial.

John Hall was admitted freeman of the Gunmakers' Company in 1702 and was master in 1726.

John Hall, London, about 1720
Overall length 10⅞ in.; barrel 6 in.
Caliber .65 (17 gauge). Weight 1½ lb.

56. Flintlock Pistol   (Bedford 1125)

One of a pair, cannon barrel in three stages with girdles between, octagonal changing to polygonal at breech, forward stages round ending in molded muzzle ring; at breech engraved with conventional leaves; on one of left side facets are stamped London proofmarks between which is mark HD crowned (Henry Delany); projection under breech to aid in unscrewing; breech signed under lock H. DELANY LONDINI. Lock plate forged integrally with barrel; round-faced cock; inverted-V "steel" spring. Butt, walnut, carved with leaf behind barrel tang and inlaid with silver wire scrolls; silver furniture; grotesque-mask butt cap; pierced scrolled side plate; escutcheon engraved with mirror monogram beneath an earl's coronet.

Henry Delany, about 1720.
Overall length 12 in.; barrel 6⅞ in.
Caliber .66 (16 gauge). Weight 1½ lb.
Literature: Hayward, *The Art of the Gunmaker*, vol. II, pl. 22 a.

57. Pair of Flintlock Pistols with Left- and Right-hand Locks   (Bedford 1176)

Barrel in three stages, octagonal changing to polygonal, then circular with ring of deep grooves, then circular terminating in muzzle ring; breech inscribed LONDON; London proofmarks and barrelsmith's mark IF crowned (James Freeman); on underside is elongated projection for barrel wrench. Lock plate inscribed JAMES FREEMAN; cock and steel with rounded face and raised edges; bolt safety engages between half and full cock; inverted-V "steel" spring. Butt, walnut, carved to outline mounts and with leaf behind barrel tang; silver furniture; spurred pommel, spandrels engraved with busts of warriors within foliate cartouches; frame chased in relief-scroll strapwork; butt cap cast and chased with full-face bust of classical warrior

within inner dotted cartouche; pierced foliate side plate; blank escutcheon with mask above and shell below; steel trigger guard with leaf finial.

This pair of Queen Anne turnoff pistols is one of the finest of its type extant.

James Freeman, about 1720
Overall length 12¾ in.; barrel 7 in.
Caliber .65 (17 gauge). Weight 2 lb.

58. Flintlock Pistol   (Bedford 1086)

Cannon barrel in three stages, separated by girdles, ending in muzzle ring; at breech engraved with acanthus foliage and inscribed N. PARIS WARWICK; underside of breech has Birmingham private proofmarks. Lock plate forged integrally with breech; round-faced cock engraved with foliage; steel trigger guard; sliding trigger-guard tongue fits into notch in top of trigger to act as safety; pan has flash fence; inverted-V "steel" spring.

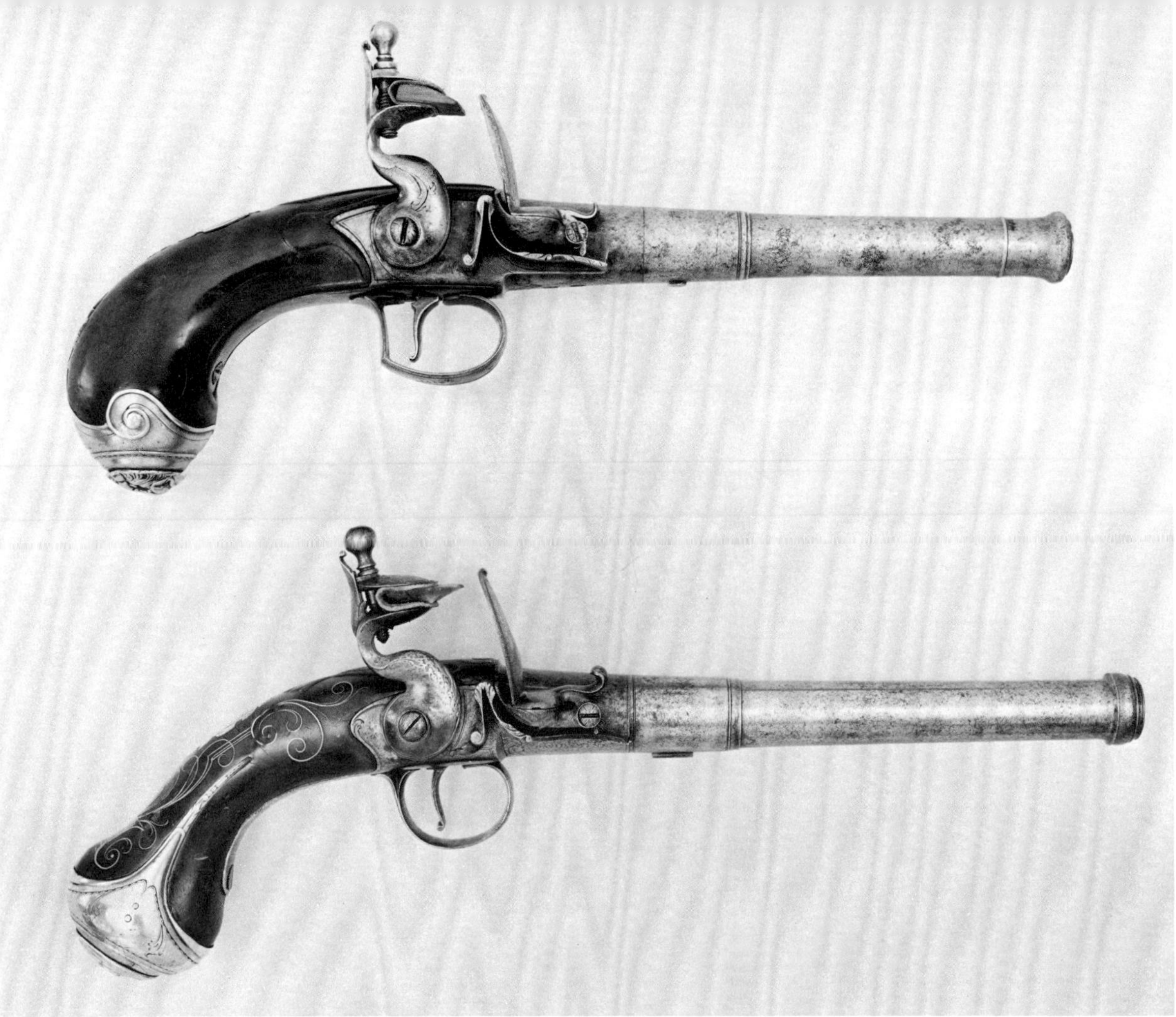

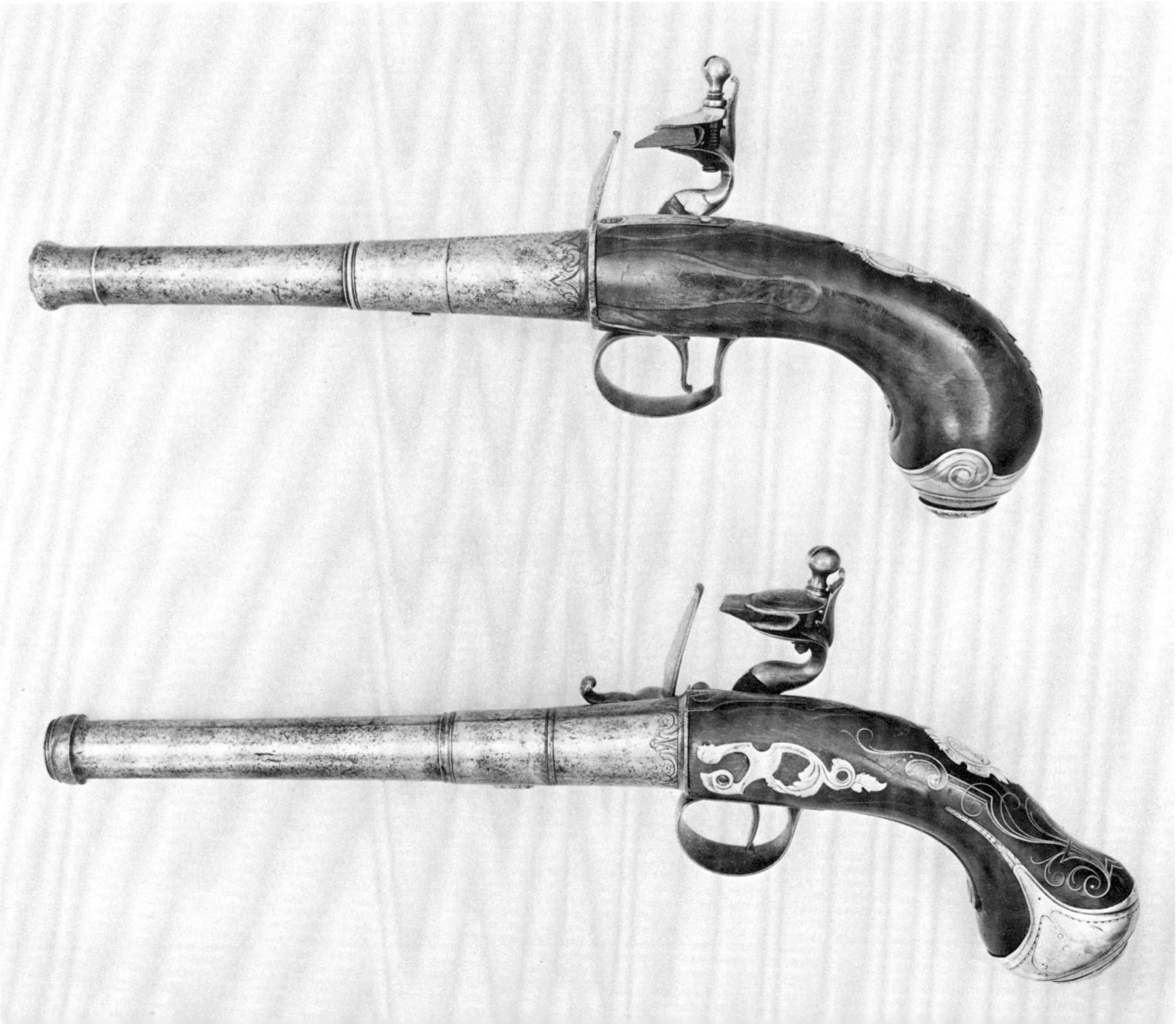

Butt, walnut, carved with shell behind barrel tang and with raised edges; pommel engraved with eagle and formalized leaf, cap itself chased with lion's mask; no side plate; silver escutcheon surmounted by grotesque mask and engraved with owner's crest, stag's head erased.

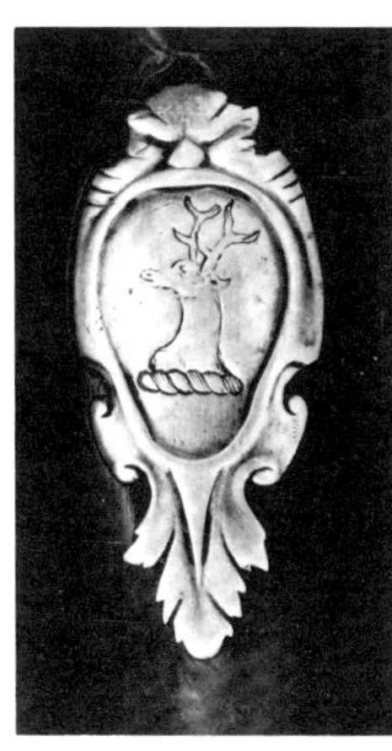

There were two gunmakers named Nicholas Paris working in Warwick in the first half of the 18th century. The elder arrived in Warwick in 1680 and died there in 1716. This pistol is the work of his son, who sometimes signed his work: Nicholas Paris, Junior, Warwick. An ingenious gunmaker, he produced six-barreled revolving guns with automatic primer and a breech-loading shotgun that bears the arms of the Duke of Buford, the latter in the Tower of London Armouries. He was employed by Lord Leigh of Stoneleigh, whose descendants preserved several of his firearms until recently.

Nicholas Paris, Jr., Warwick, about 1725–40
Overall length 12⅜ in.; barrel 7⅛ in.
Caliber .63 (17 gauge). Weight 1¾ lb.
Literature: Hayward, *The Art of the Gunmaker*, vol. II, pp. 71–72.

59. Flintlock Pistol   (Bedford 761)

One of a pair. Barrel of circular section in three stages, molded girdles between, ending in muzzle ring;

at breech engraved with acanthus foliage and inscribed LONDON; lower part of barrel at breech stamped with London proofmarks between which is mark DW surmounted by fleur-de-lis (David Wynn). Lock plate inscribed DAVID WYNN; lock forged integrally with breech; cock and action with engraved borders, rounded face; inverted-V "steel" spring. Stock, walnut, carved with leaf behind barrel tang and inlaid with scrolling silver wire; silver furniture; spurred pommel with engraved borders, cap cast and chased with grotesque mask with tongue sticking out; pierced foliate side plate; oval escutcheon engraved with crest, turreted tower within baroque cartouche.

David Wynn, London, about 1725–30
Overall length 13⁵⁄₁₆ in.; barrel 8 in.
Caliber .65 (17 gauge). Weight 1¾ lb.

60. Flintlock Pistol   (Bedford 1229)

One of a pair. Barrel in three stages with molded girdles between, terminating in muzzle ring; acanthus foliage engraved around breech; underside of breech stamped with London proofmarks between which is barrelsmith's mark LB (Lewis Barbar); two vents and left- and right-hand locks, both firing same charge. Locks forged integrally with breech; on underside of breech inscribed BARBAR LONDON; round-faced cocks with engraved borders; inverted-V "steel" spring. Butt, walnut, carved with shell behind barrel tang; silver furniture; spurred pommel with engraved borders, butt cap cast with old man's mask showing his tongue within cartouche of shells and scrolls; escutcheon with shell above and leaf below engraved with owner's initials JS.

This pistol and its mate (not in the Bedford collection) are the only recorded English pistols in which a single trigger releases both cocks simultaneously. This double ignition is more valuable than a reserve lock, as there might not have been time to fire the second lock in an emergency. No. 60 has evidently seen

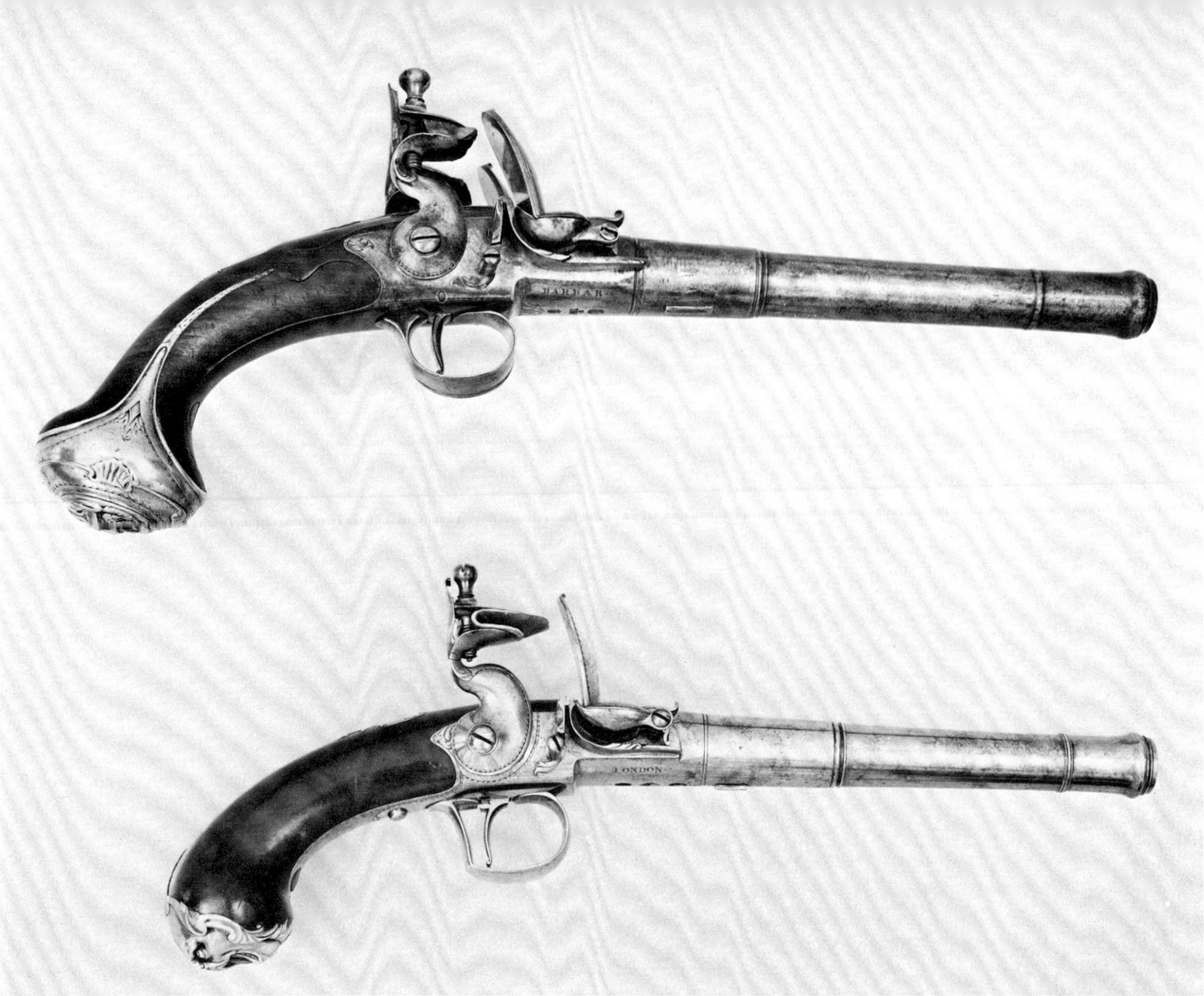

BARBAR

LONDON

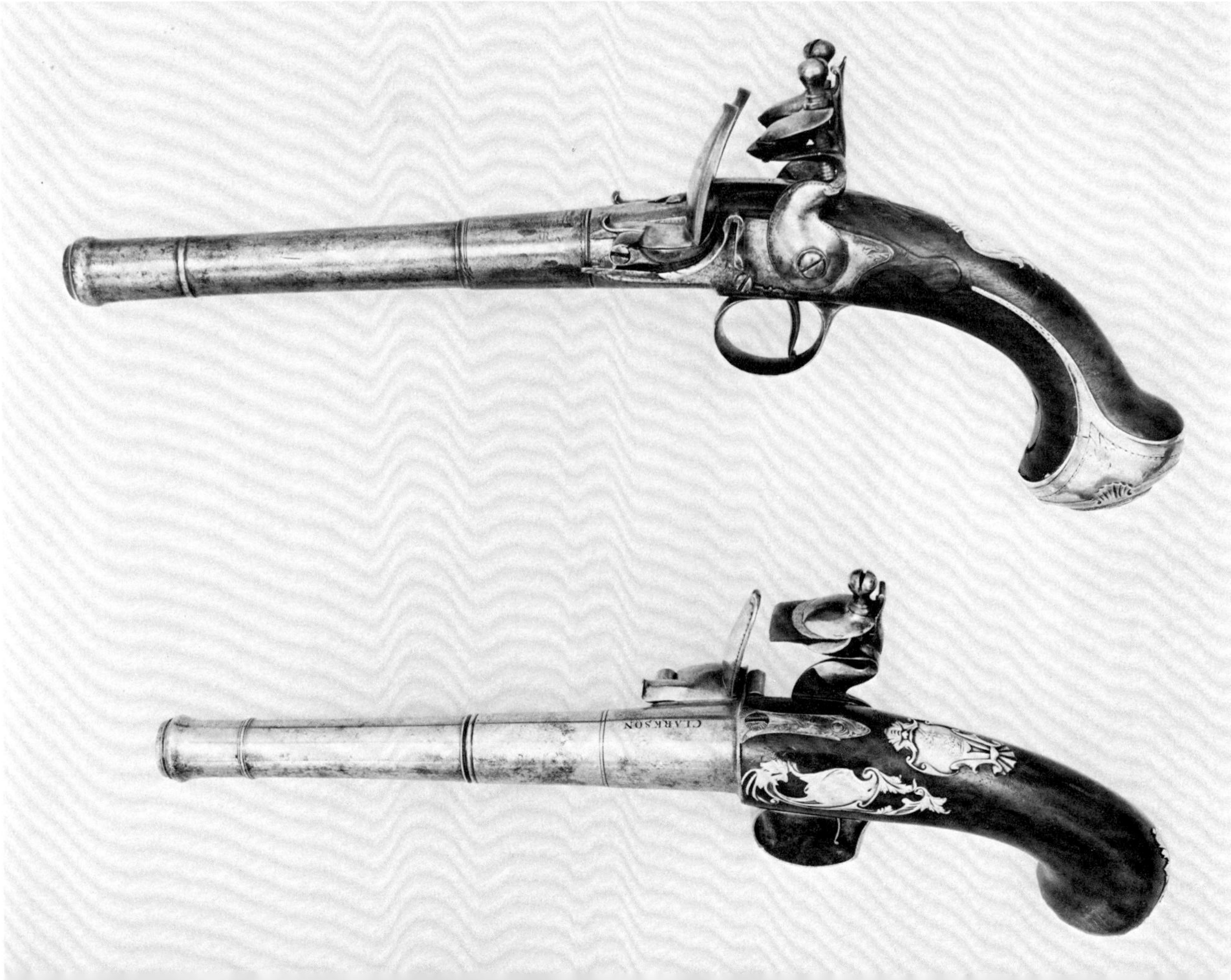

CLARKSON

much use, as both steels have had a second inner face attached to them.

Lewis Barbar, London, about 1730–40
Overall length 13¾16 in.; barrel 7¹⁵⁄₁₆ in.
Caliber .63 (17 gauge). Weight 2 lb.
Literature: Winant, *Firearms Curiosa*, p. 229, fig. 256.

61. Flintlock Pistol (Bedford 1201)

One of a pair. Barrel in three stages with molded girdles between, ending in muzzle ring; name CLARKSON inscribed on breech; on underside of breech, London proofmarks between which is barrel-smith's mark IC (J. Clarkson); barrel stamped with numeral 2 adjacent to projection that fits barrel wrench; breech end of barrel has corresponding numeral; below lock, barrel inscribed LONDON. Lock forged integrally with breech; rounded lock plate, cock, action, and steel have engraved borders; steel trigger guard; when stud behind trigger guard is depressed, trigger guard can be pushed forward to lock trigger; this safety can be oper-ated at half cock or when cock is down; lock cannot be moved from safety without button release first being pressed; inverted-V "steel" spring. Butt of walnut; silver furniture; grotesque-mask butt cap; side plate of scroll-ing foliage incorporating mask and asymmetrical cartouche; escutcheon with mask above and shell below engraved with owner's crest, antelope's head erased rising from ducal coronet.

Joseph Clarkson was admitted freeman of the Gunmakers' Company in 1715.

Joseph Clarkson, London, about 1730–40
Overall length 11¹⁵⁄₁₆ in.; barrel 7¼ in.
Caliber .61 (21 gauge). Weight 1½ lb.

62. Two-shot Superimposed-load Breech-action Flintlock Pistol
(Bedford 1053)

Cannon barrel in three stages with girdles between, muzzle ring; at breech inscribed LONDON; breech, under trigger guard, stamped with London proofmarks between which are initials IS surmounted by fleur-de-lis (Israel Segalas). Lock plate forged integrally with barrel and inscribed SEGALAS; revolving (tap-action) turnover priming pan cutting off rear vent when communicating with forward vent; upper area of revolving priming pan connects with forward vent through channel to fire forward charge; when pan is revolved priming powder connects with rear vent; ball for rear chamber and forward charge are loaded from muzzle end, in order that rear ball can be firmly seated before rear chamber is loaded with powder, thus eliminating risk of powder adhering to walls of chamber and causing flashback when forward load is discharged; rear powder charge loaded through screw hole in bottom of barrel, opened by unscrewing trigger guard; inverted-V "steel" spring. Butt of walnut; silver furniture; butt cap chased with mask.

Israel Segalas, Jr., was born in 1714 and appren-ticed to his father, a Huguenot immigrant. He was admitted freeman of the Gunmakers' Company in 1745 and was proofmaster from 1763 to 1772. The Minutes of the London Gunmakers' Company list "IS with a Flower de Lis over it" as also the mark of Jonathan Stanton, whose proof piece and mark were approved in 1754. The mark is no. 69 on the mark plate of the Lon-don Gunmakers' Company (Blackmore, "The Mark Plate of the Gunmakers' Company," p. 128, pl. XIV, no. 69).

Israel Segalas, Jr., London, about 1750
Overall length 13 in.; barrel 6⁵⁄₁₆ in. (8 in.)
Caliber .63 (18 gauge). Weight 1½ lb.
Literature: Baxter, *Superimposed Load Firearms, 1360–1860*, pp. 167–168, pl. 94; Hayward, "The Huguenot Gunmakers of London," pp. 124, 126, pl. XVII; C. R. Suydam, "Two-Shot Superimposed Queen Anne Flintlock Pistol by Israel Segalas," pp. 58-59, 4 ills. and cover color ill.

63. Flintlock Pistol (Bedford 1234)

One of a pair. Cannon barrel of circular section with two molded girdles and muzzle ring, engraved with foliage and inscribed GRIFFIN LONDON at breech; underside of barrel at breech stamped with London proofmarks between which is barrelsmith's mark IH surmounted by leaf. Cock with rounded face and line border; inverted-V "steel" spring below priming pan. Butt of walnut carved with shell behind barrel tang; silver furniture of rococo design; grotesque-mask butt

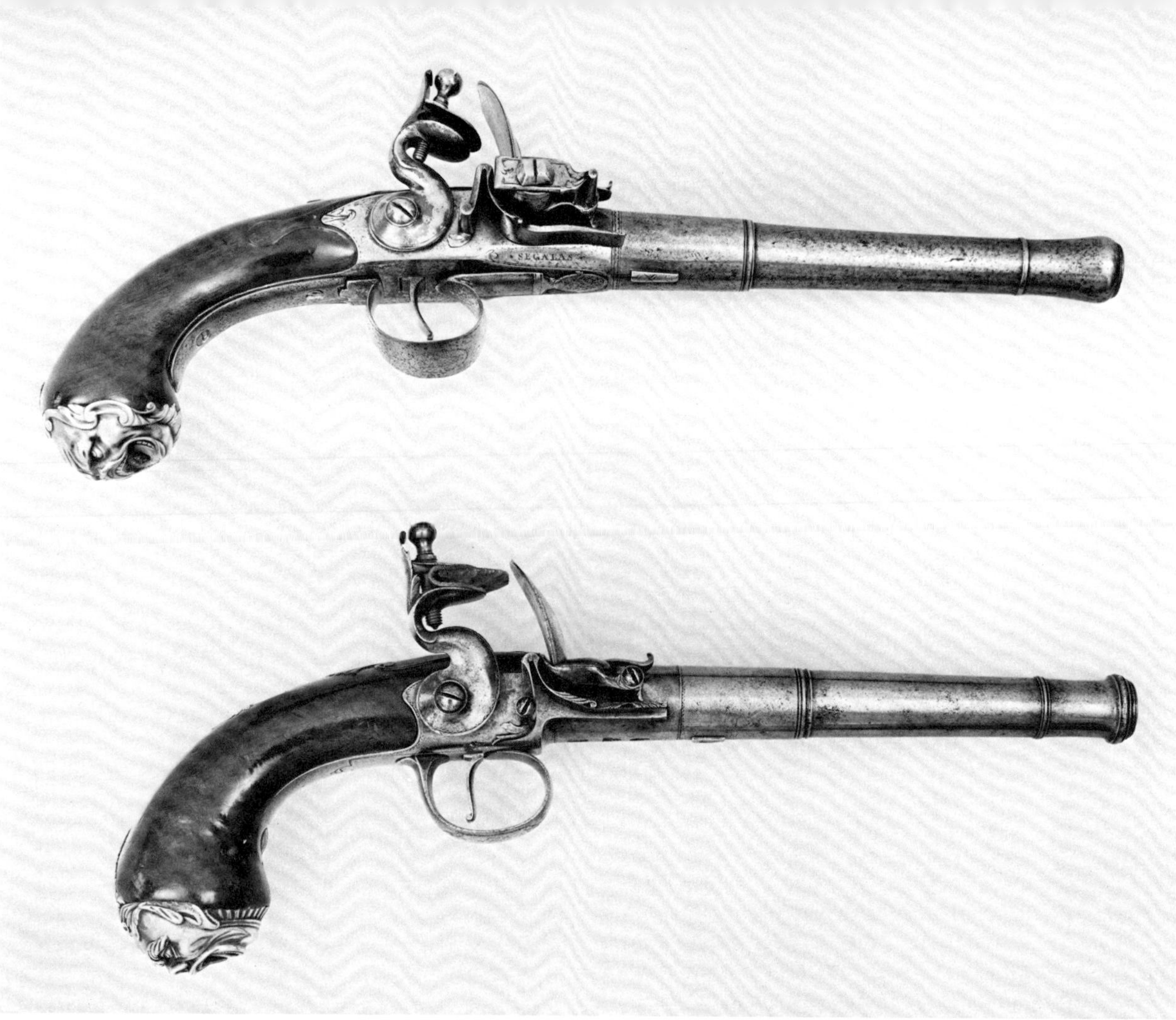

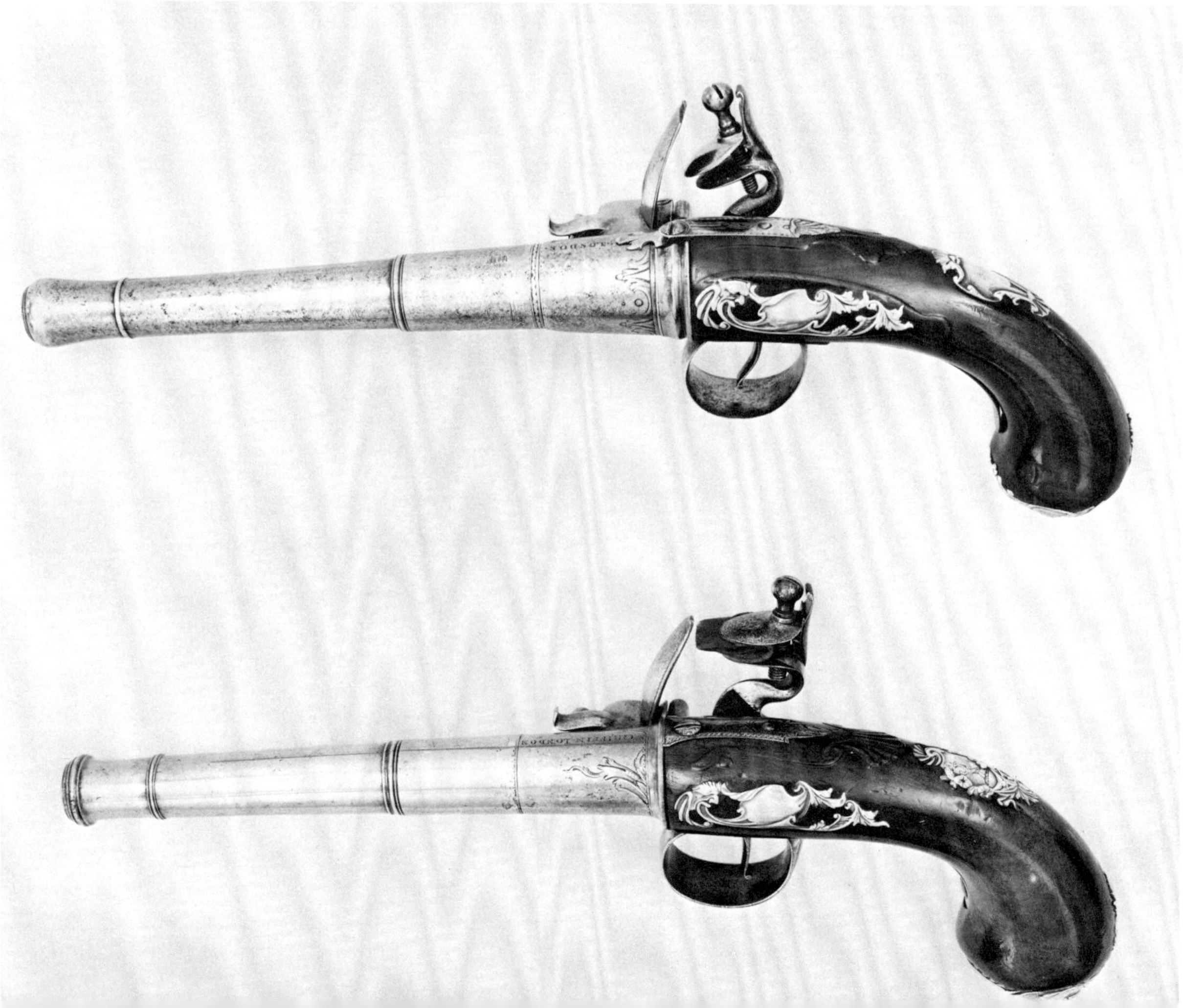

cap; escutcheon engraved with owner's crest, dove with wings displayed holding branch in beak.

Joseph Griffin was, after Lewis Barbar, the leading London maker of flintlock horse and cannon-barrel pistols during the middle decades of the 18th century. He was admitted freeman of the Gunmakers' Company in 1750 and was master in 1763–64. He worked in Bond Street from about 1763 until about 1770, when he went into partnership with John Tow.

Joseph Griffin, London, about 1756–66
Overall length 12⅜ in.; barrel 5⅝ in. (7⁵⁄₁₆ in.)
Caliber .65 (17 gauge). Weight 1½ lb.

64. Flintlock Pistol (Bedford 883)

One of a pair. Cannon barrel in three stages with molded girdles between, molding at breech, and muzzle ring; near breech engraved WT HAVEN (Whitehaven); Birmingham private proofmarks between which is the barrelsmith's stamp TP (T. Peele). Separate side lock, with rounded face and cut, raised borders, inscribed PEELE; inverted-V "steel" spring under pan. Walnut half stock, with steel fore-end, is carved with shell

and foliage around barrel tang and profusely inlaid with scrolling silver wire ending in flower heads; silver furniture; grotesque-mask butt cap with silversmith's mark JK (John King), lion passant, and sterling mark; side plate chased with trophies; blank escutcheon surmounted by helmet, trophies of arms below.

T. Peele, Whitehaven, about 1760
Overall length 13⁹⁄₁₆ in.; barrel 8⁵⁄₁₆ in.
Caliber .63 (17 gauge). Weight 1½ lb.
Literature: Pollard, *A History of Firearms*, pl. opp. p. 48, fig. 4.

65. Flintlock Pistol (Bedford 886)

One of a pair. Cannon barrel rifled with eight grooves, in three stages with molded girdles between, ending in muzzle ring; Birmingham private proofmarks and stamp TR (Thomas Richards). Box lock forged integrally with breech, name T. RICHARDS engraved on ribbon within rococo scrolls. But, walnut, inlaid

with silver wire scrolls; silver furniture; grotesque-mask butt cap with Birmingham hallmark and mark TR; steel trigger guard.

The pistol is unusual in that the gunmaker also provided the silver mounts. In London the Worshipful Company of Goldsmiths would not have permitted a gunmaker to cast and finish his own mounts. Evidently in Birmingham there was more freedom.

Thomas Richards, Birmingham, about 1780
Overall length 12½ in.; barrel 6¾ in.
Caliber .60 (21 gauge). Weight 1¼ lb.

66. Flintlock Pocket Pistol (Bedford 1067)

Short circular barrel with girdle of foliage engraved around muzzle; London proofmarks. Box lock forged integrally with breech; on reverse of lock inscribed S. BRUNN and on obverse No. 55 CHARING CROSS, LONDON; concealed trigger opening automatically

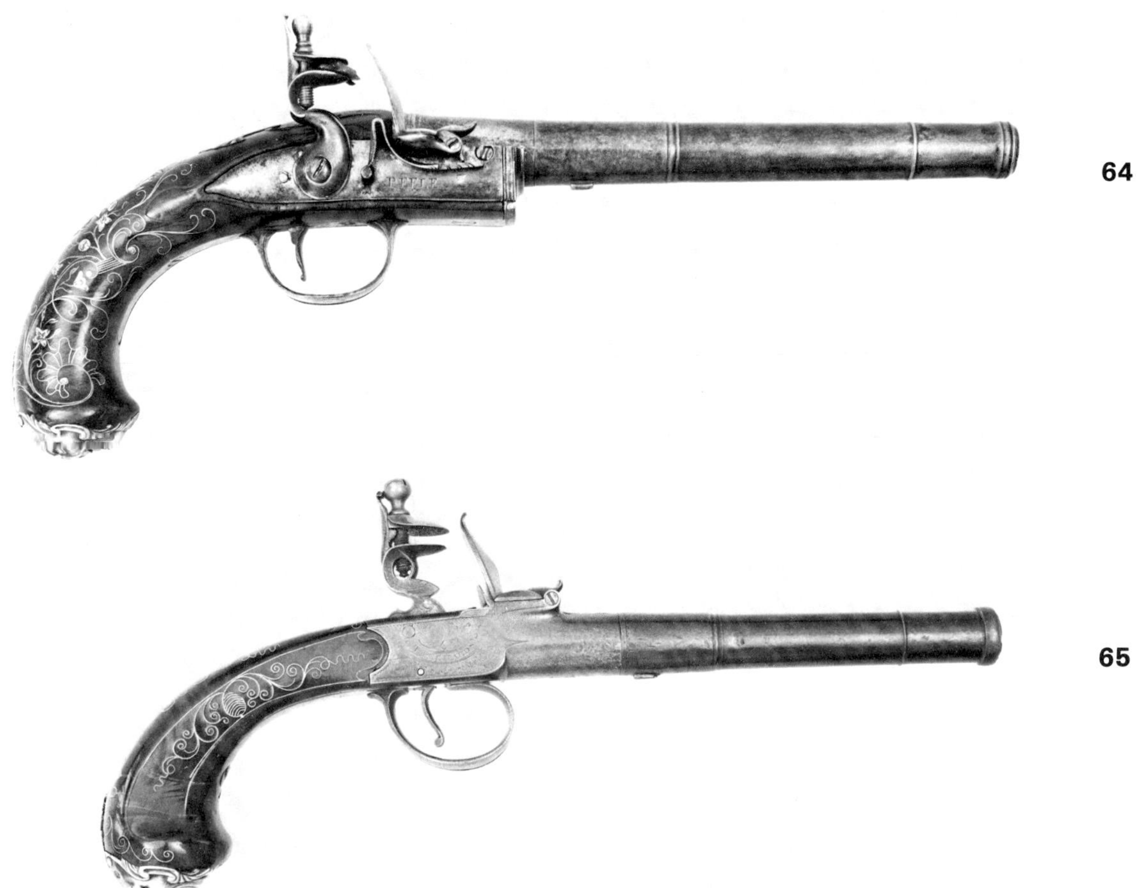

64

65

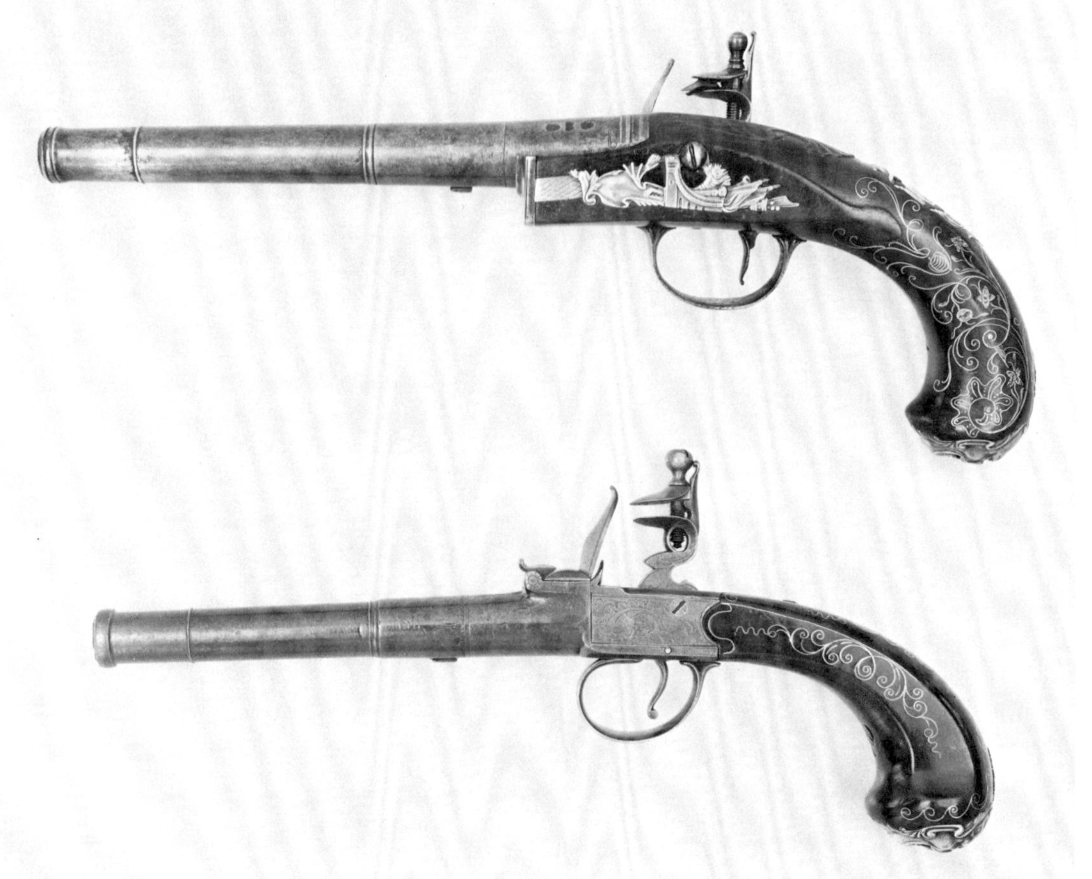

64

65

when pistol is cocked; bolt safety locking cock and steel at half cock. Butt, walnut, flat side, inlaid on three sides with cut silver sheet of floral design.

Samuel Brunn was also a sword cutler. He took over the premises of John Knubley at 55 Charing Cross in 1795 after the latter's death. Brunn supplied a number of expensive guns to the Prince of Wales, including a steel pistol with a magazine that loaded twelve times in a minute.

Samuel Brunn, London, about 1800
Overall length 6¾ in.; barrel 3 in.
Caliber .60 (21 gauge). Weight ¾ lb.

66

66

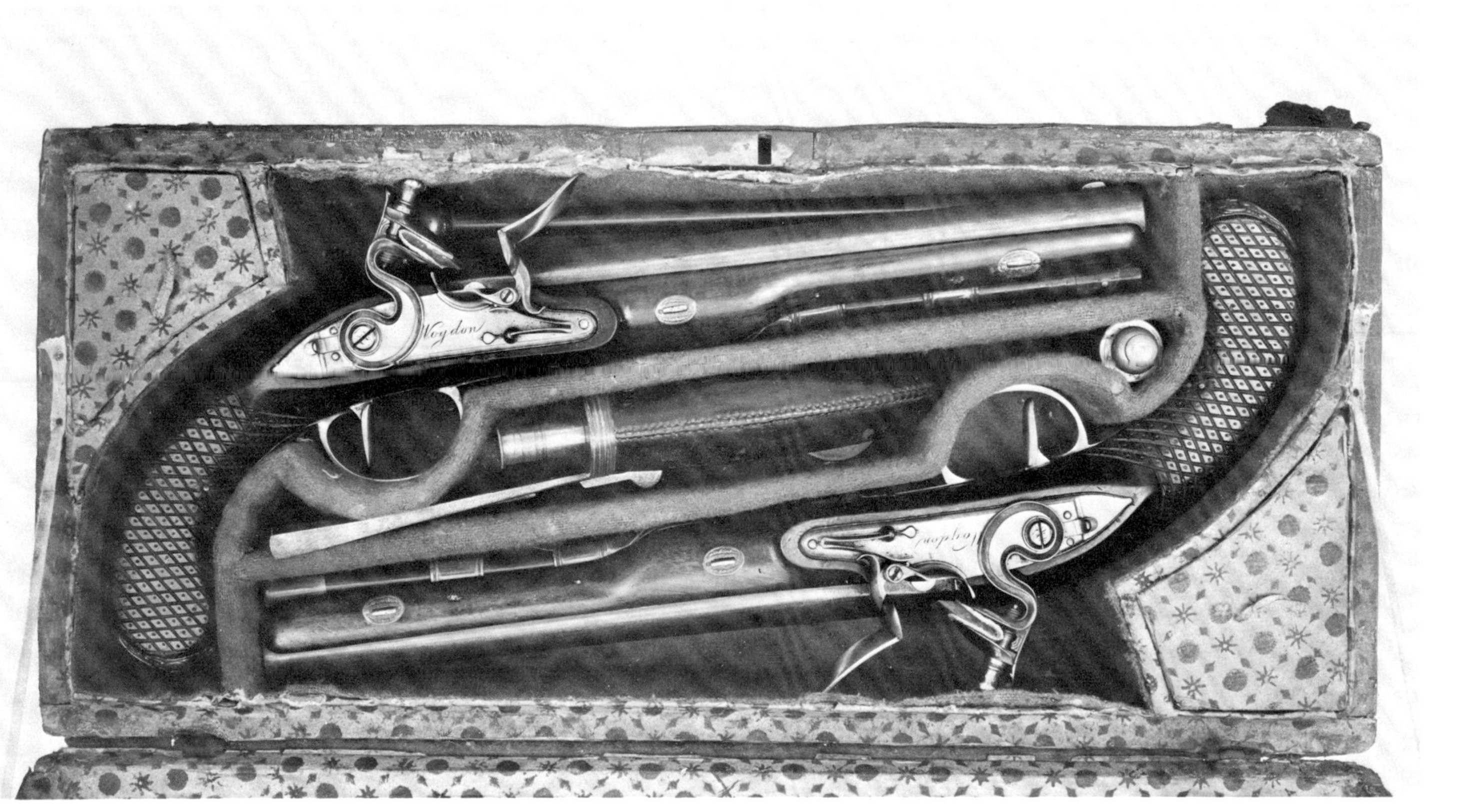

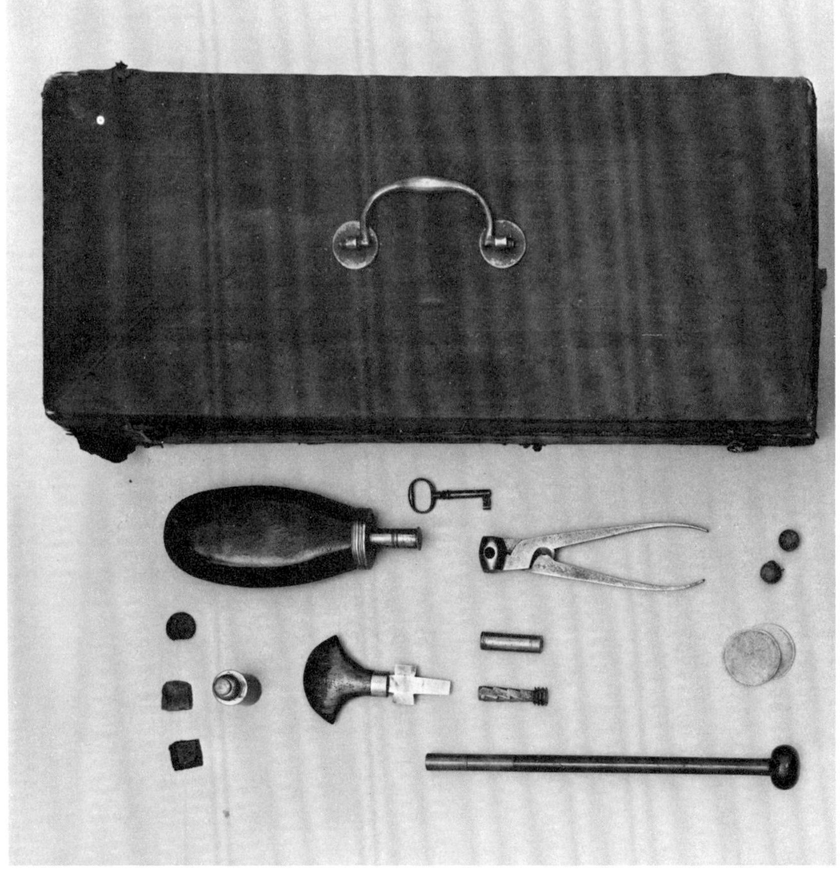

5

DUELING AND TARGET PISTOLS

After 1770, dueling with swords went out of favor, and affairs of honor were settled with the pistol. Every gentleman required a pair of dueling pistols, and these were produced by most of the better British gunmakers. They came in a handsome hardwood case that was divided into compartments for the pistols, the loading and cleaning accessories, and tools. These normally included powder-and-bullet flask, ramrod, wooden mallet, bullet mold, patch box, wad cutter, oilcan, cleaning rod, bullet extractor, screwdriver, and spare flints.

This group of nineteen dueling pistols covers a period of some sixty years, beginning in 1776. Cased pairs are well represented in the Bedford collection, but only three cased pairs of flintlock pistols and one of patch-lock pistols, all with accessories, are included in the exhibition. In the other instances, only a single pistol from the case is shown. The majority of the 18th-century examples have full stocks; the later pistols have three-quarter stocks, except for no. 83, with a half stock. The furniture is usually of blued steel, which resisted rust and prevented reflection, an important consideration in a duel. Judging from the decorative motifs on the steel furniture, skilled engravers worked for any gunmaker who required their services. The pineapple trigger-guard finial appears on nine items, each by a different gunmaker, the acorn on three. The spur trigger guard appears on seven items; it was apparently a common feature, intended to give a steady grip.

Noteworthy is the cased pair by Robert Wogdon (no. 67). The leather-covered wood case with a lining of green baize and printed paper is the earliest known example of its type. The locks include a hair trigger. Another noteworthy pistol is the left-hand flintlock made by John Twigg (no. 72). It was Twigg who, soon after 1770, introduced the fully octagonal barrel bored smooth for dueling. Of the cased pair of percussion-cap pistols, made by Joseph Egg (no. 83), one is smooth bore, the other rifled. Rifling was not usual in dueling pistols. Also in the exhibition is a rifled percussion-cap target pistol made by Westley Richards of Birmingham (no. 84).

Most of our dueling pistols have barrels of laminated or twisted iron and steel. These were called "Damascus" because a pattern like that of damask silk appeared during the etching process and, furthermore, because the fame of Damascus steel provided a good trade name. The bore of our pistols varies from .50 caliber to .62 caliber, the barrel lengths from approximately 9 to 10¼ in., the weights from 1½ to 2½ lb.

In the history of gunmaking, the period 1805–35 was a critical one, for then all gunmakers (and there were a great many) were experimenting to do away with the flintlock. The chief disadvantage of the flintlock was the delay between the fall of the cock and the ignition of the charge. The detonating system, which substituted a fulminate for flint as a means of igniting the charge of powder, was patented by the Reverend Alexander Forsyth in 1807. Forsyth's invention gave instantaneous discharge and greatly improved the certainty of fire. Following Forsyth, the percussion system went through the various undeveloped stages of loose detonating powder, pellets, patch lock, and tube primers, and emerged as the perfected percussion cap.

67. Cased Pair of Flintlock Dueling Pistols   (Bedford 1167)

Barrel, browned, of circular section except for top facet inscribed WOGDON LONDON, engraved border at breech, hooked breech, gold-lined vent; stationary rear sight on barrel tang; silver blade front sight; Tower private proofmarks (crown and crossed scepters) between which is barrelsmith's mark RW (Robert Wogdon); two barrel slides with oval slots. Lock plate, flat faced, inscribed WOGDON, has beveled edge; bolt safety engaging at half cock, hair trigger, and detent. Walnut full stock; early form of wide-cut checkering on grip; silver furniture; butt cap chased with seated figure of Britannia within rococo scrollwork; opposite lock plate is oval plaque engraved with owner's initials RCB; trigger guard, with acorn finial, stamped with initials IK (John King), date letter for 1776, crowned lion head, and leopard passant; two ramrod pipes, ramrods have horn finials.

The butt cap of silver cast and chased with a figure of Britannia seems to have been used only by Wogdon. The crown and crossed scepters was the private proofmark of the British Board of Ordnance. From the mid-18th century it was struck twice on the work of all private gunmakers proved at the official government proofhouse at the Tower, and from 1797 in Birmingham as well.

The leather-covered wood case, with brass loop handle and a lining of green baize and printed paper, is the earliest known example of its type. Interior of case, fitted for the pistols, has additional partitions for the leather-covered powder flask, bullet mold, cleaning

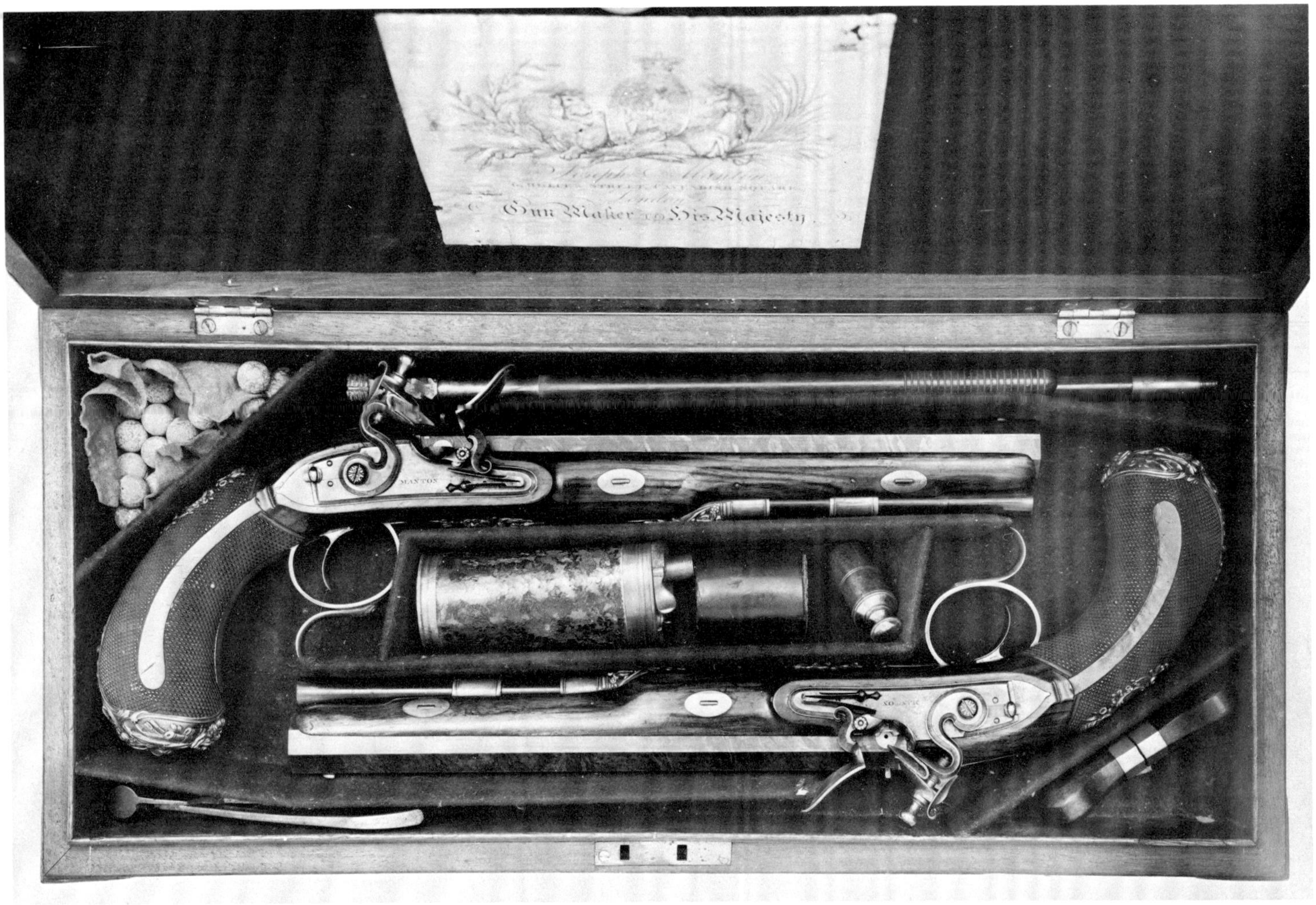

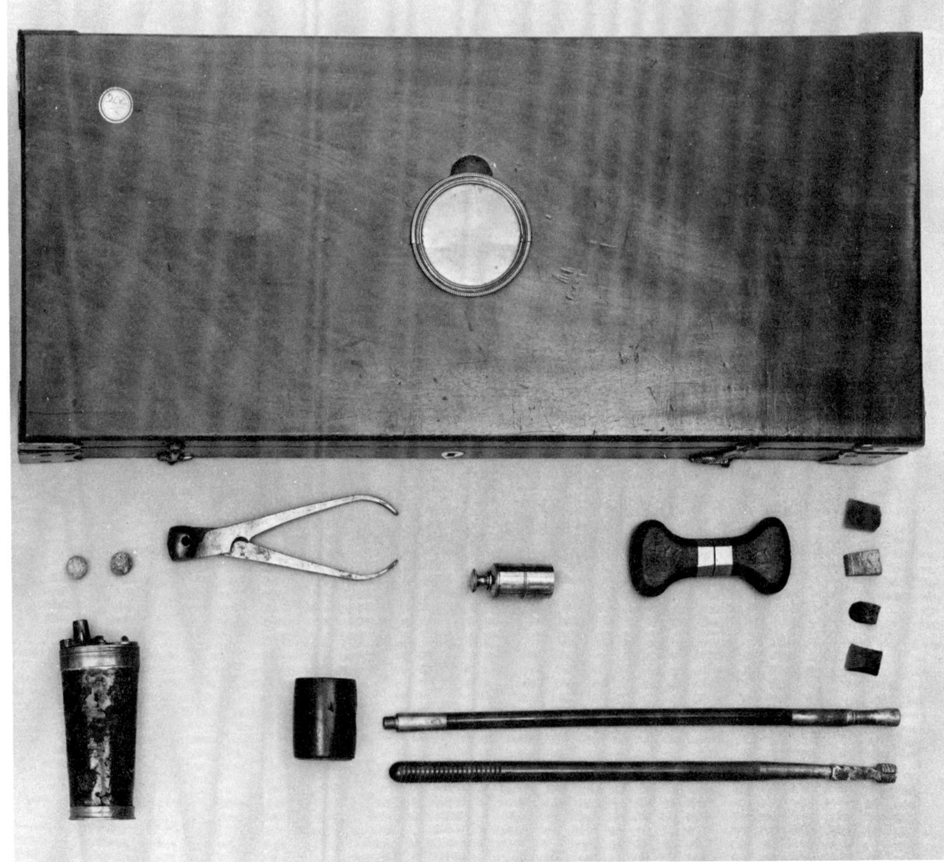

implements and screwdriver, and, in the two corners, balls and patches. Under one pistol is a cleaning rod with ebony handle.

Robert Wogdon worked at the Haymarket from about 1772 to 1800.

Robert Wogdon, London, 1776
Overall length 13½ in.; barrel 8⅞ in.
Caliber .52 (33 gauge). Weight 1½ lb.
Case 16¾ in. x 7¼ in. x 3⅛ in.
Literature: W. Keith Neal, "Pistols for Two," pp. 157–170, 16 ills.

68

68. Cased Pair of Flintlock Dueling Pistols (Bedford 1161)

Barrel, browned twist, octagonal, with single gold transverse line at breech, gold-lined vent, inscribed in gold MANTON LONDON; stationary rear sight and gold front sight; hooked breech; two barrel slides with oval silver slots. Lock plate, flat faced, with beveled edge, inscribed MANTON; semiwaterproof gold-lined pan, pan cover with roller bearing riding on elliptical ridge on feather spring; bolt safety, operating at half cock, locks both cock and pan. Walnut full stock with checkered grip; silver furniture; butt cap chiseled in relief with trophies and faun's head and stamped with initials MB (Moses Brent) and date mark for

1797; side plate chiseled in high relief with trophies of arms; escutcheon asymmetrical surrounded by trophies of arms; trigger guard engraved with trophies of arms has applied spur for third finger; Manton serial number 2837.

The original brass-bound, baize-lined mahogany case has compartments fitted for the pistols and accessories, including powder-and-ball flask, bullet mold, screwdrivers, mallet, and balls. Inside cover is a trade label: Joseph Manton, 6 Holles Street, Cavendish Square, London, Gunmaker to his Majesty. The presence of John Manton pistols in a Joseph Manton case can presumably be explained by the pistols' having

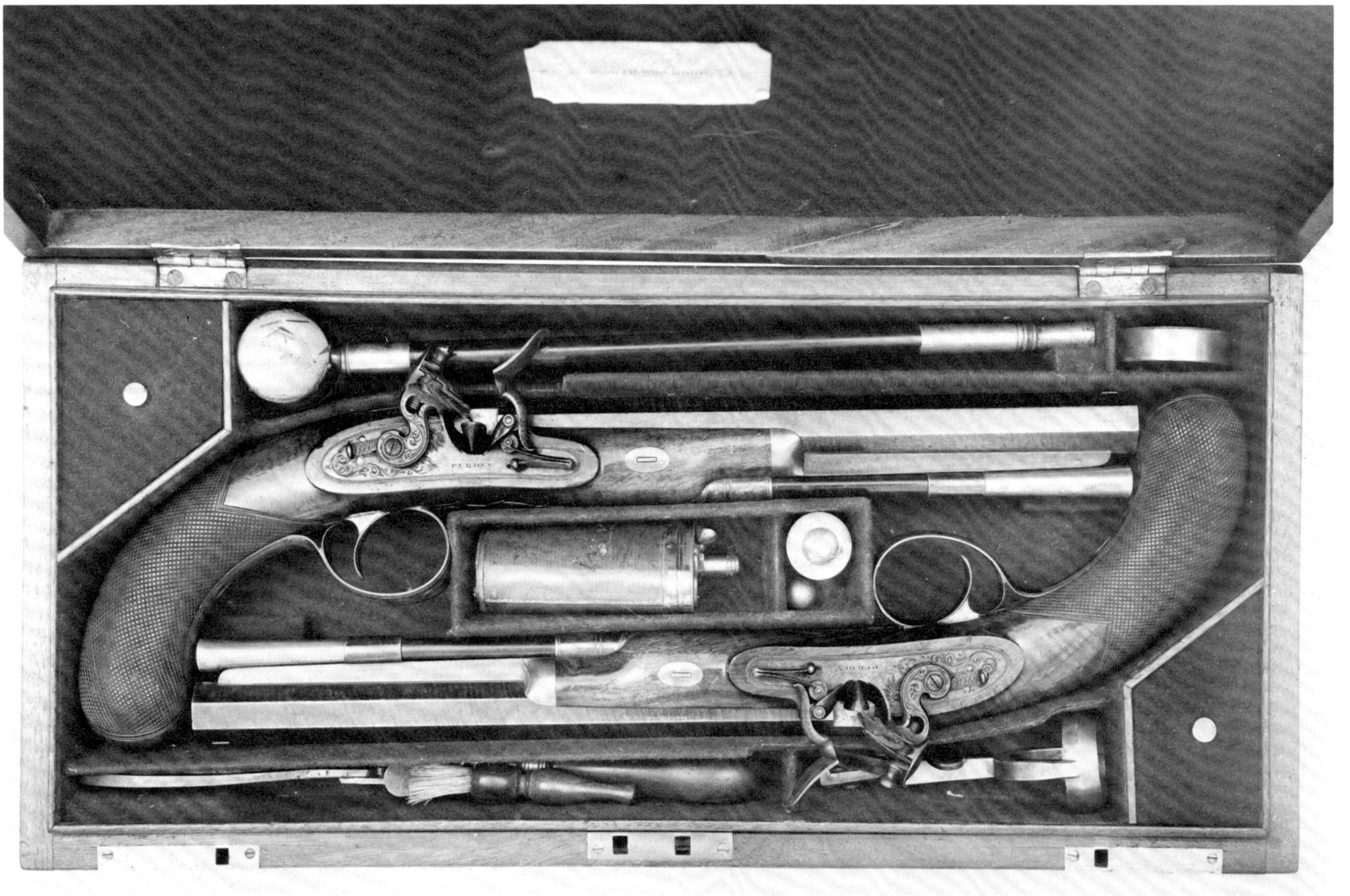

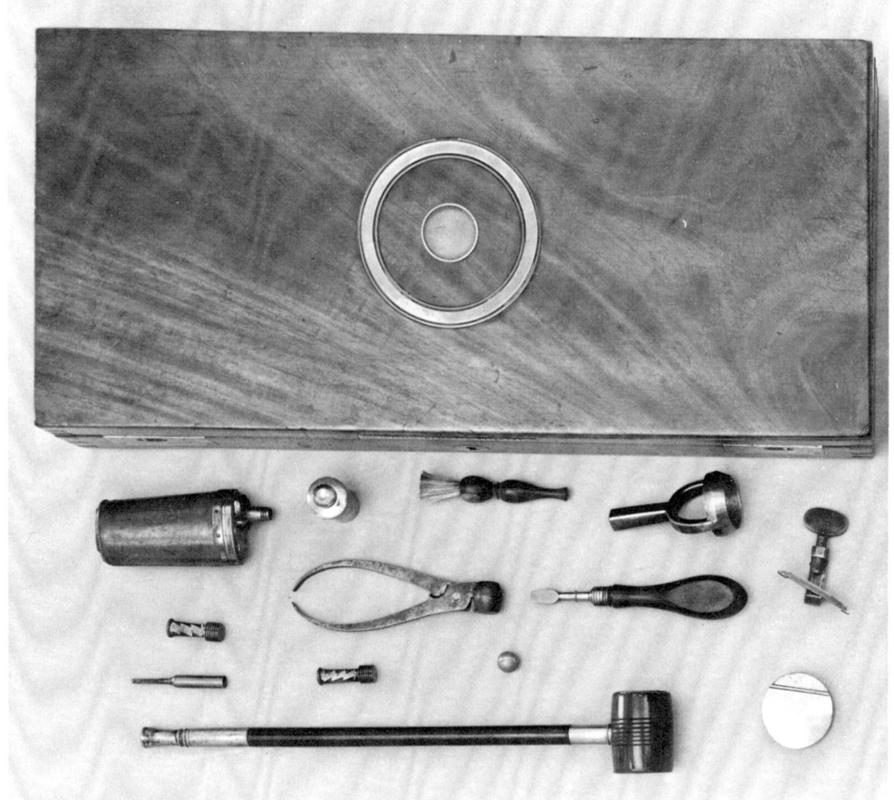

been sent to Joseph Manton for cleaning or repair and his having put his own label in the case. Of exceptionally fine quality, these pistols were apparently presentation pieces.

John Manton, London, 1797
Overall length 50⅛ in.; barrel 10 in.
Caliber .53 (28 gauge). Weight 2¾ lb.
Literature: Neal and Back, *The Mantons: Gunmakers*, p. 73; Christie's sale, November 22, 1965, lot 202, pl. XVI.

69. Cased Pair of Flintlock Dueling Pistols
(Bedford 1245)

Barrel, browned twist, octagonal, with patent breech, single platinum transverse line; top facet inscribed I. PURDEY PRINCES STREET LEICESTER SQUARE LONDON; recessed in top of patent breech is platinum-lined mark inscribed PURDEY LONDON; stationary leaf sight on false breech; steel blade front sight; London proofmarks; under-barrel rib; single barrel slide with oval slots. Lock plate, flat faced, with engraved borders and scrollwork and inscription PURDEY; platinum-lined vent, waterproof pan, patent pan cover with roller bearing on toe and on steel spring; small loop-necked cock; bolt safety operating at half cock; flash fence acts as descent arrest. Walnut three-quarter stock has silver fore-end and checkered grip; blued steel furniture; blank octagonal escutcheon; trigger guard engraved with trophies of arms, pineapple finial; two ramrod pipes; ramrods have brass finial and, on opposite end, brass powder measure. Purdey serial numbers 764 and 765.

The original green-baize-lined mahogany traveling case bears the maker's original trade label: J. Purdey, Gun Manufacturer, 4 Princes Street, Leicester Square. Case is fitted with compartments for the pistols and for the accessories, including leather flask, oil bottle, wad cutter, screwdrivers, and mallet.

James Purdey, Sr., was born in 1784, the son of another James Purdey, who was a gunmaker in the Minories. After serving a six-year apprenticeship with Thomas Hutchinson, beginning in 1797, he worked for Joseph Manton as a stocker and finisher from 1803 to 1806, and later for Forsyth on early percussion guns. He set up business in Princes Street in 1814 and thereupon began to number his guns. In 1826 he took over Joseph Manton's premises at 314½ Oxford Street after Manton had gone bankrupt. At first he changed the number to 315 Oxford Street, but shortly afterward he changed it back to 314½, which remained the address until 1882. James Purdey, Sr., died in 1863.

James Purdey, Sr., London, about 1820
Overall length 15½ in.; barrel 9¼ in.
Caliber .53 (31 gauge). Weight 2½ lb.
Literature: Akehurst, *Game Guns and Rifles*, pp. 150–154.

70. Cased Pair of Patch-lock Dueling Pistols
(Bedford 1280)

Barrel, browned twist, octagonal, with patent breech that has recessed gold-lined mark inscribed S. NOCK LONDON; single gold transverse line; case-hardened finish to patent breech and false breech; stationary leaf V-sight on false breech; iron bead front sight; single barrel slide with silver slots; under-barrel rib. Patch lock with flat-faced lock plate inscribed SAMUEL NOCK REGENT CIRCUS and having engraved borders and scrolls; hammer has removable striker; neck of striker has groove on each side; spring on exterior has tip that fits into groove to lock striker; when striker is revolved a quarter turn, it can be withdrawn to be replaced by another striker fitted with patch; lock has hammer buffer plate adjacent to water drain; platinum-lined safety vent. Walnut three-quarter stock with horn fore-end, checkered grip; blued steel furniture; blank rectangular silver escutcheon; trigger guard has spur for third finger, is engraved with trophies, and has pineapple finial; two ramrod pipes; ramrods have horn finials, with brass powder measure on opposite end of one and iron worm on opposite end of other. Nock's serial number 6705.

The green-baize-lined mahogany case with a sunken brass carrying ring in the top bears the maker's trade label showing the Royal Arms of George IV or William IV and reading: Patent Breeching; Nock, Gunmaker to his Majesty, Regent Circus, Piccadilly, London. At bottom of label is the warning: A number of guns and pistols having been made of a very inferior description

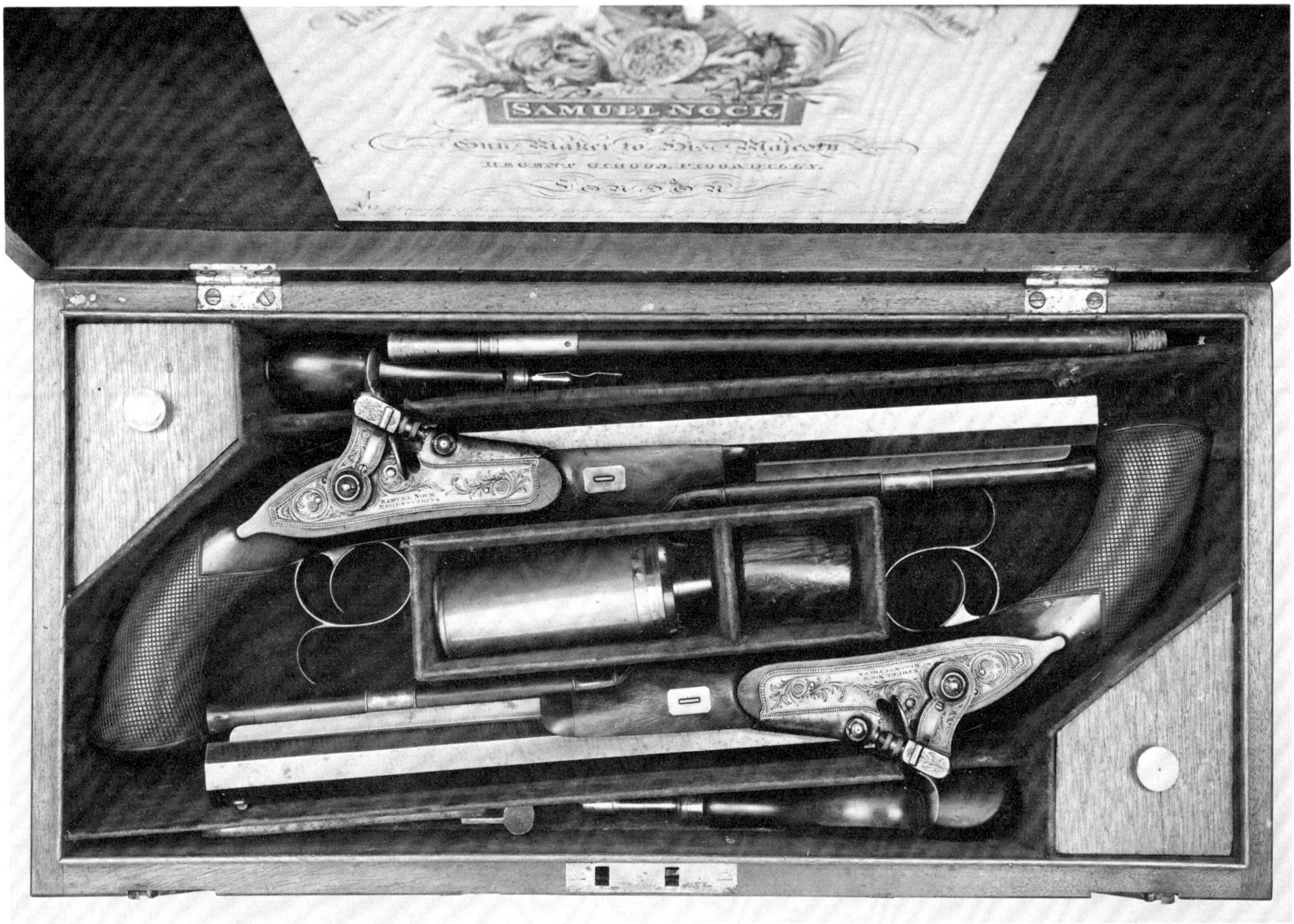

marked S. Nock, or H. Nock. None are genuine but
what have Samuel Nock engraved thereon. Case has
partitions for leather flask, mallet, bullet mold, and
nipple key.

Samuel Nock was apprenticed to his uncle Henry
in 1800. In 1806 he set up business at 180 Fleet Street,
moving in 1826 to 43 Regent Circus. He was made
freeman of the Gunmakers' Company in 1800 and was
master in 1836.

Samuel Nock, London, about 1830
Overall length 15¾ in.; barrel 10³⁄₁₆ in.
Caliber .53 (31 gauge). Weight 2½ lb.

71. Flintlock Dueling Pistol (Bedford 1115)

One of a pair. Barrel, browned twist, polygonal,
inscribed WOGDON; stationary rear sight, silver blade
front sight; gold-lined vent. Lock plate, flat faced with
faceted edges, inscribed WOGDON on oval gold plaque
surmounted by engraved drapery swags; cock engraved
with foliage; bolt safety; hair trigger. Walnut full stock
with later checkering on butt and added silver strength-
ening plaque on obverse; silver furniture; butt cap

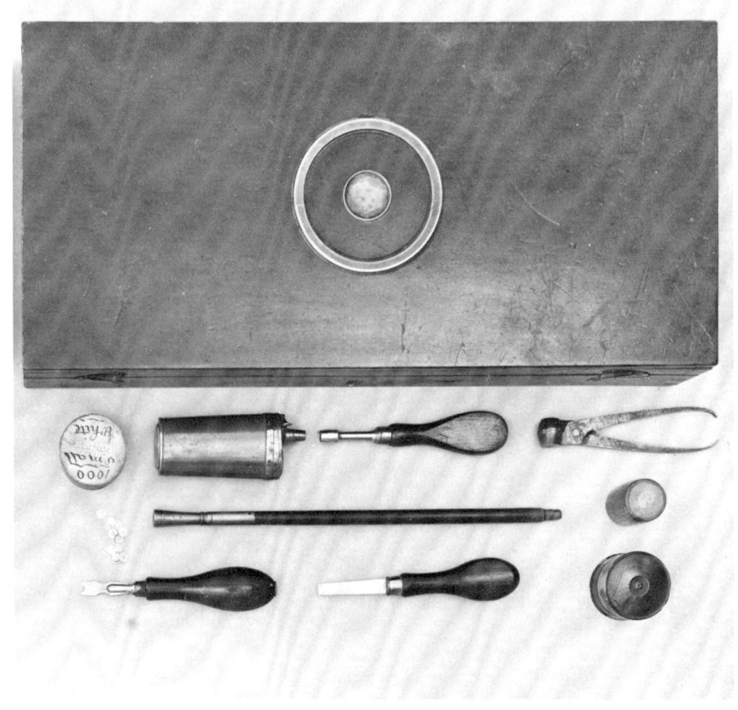

chased with seated Britannia within rococo scrolls; pierced side plate with Roman helmet and sword; trigger guard with acorn finial.

This is the earliest fully evolved dueling pistol

in the exhibition. Robert Wogdon's firm was established about 1772 in the Haymarket.

Robert Wogdon, London, about 1772–75
Overall length 16¼ in.; barrel 10 in.
Caliber .59 (24 gauge). Weight 2 lb.

72. Left-hand Flintlock Dueling Pistol (Bedford 1526)

Barrel, browned twist, octagonal, false breech, gold-lined vent; stationary rear sight, blade front sight; barrel and lock inscribed TWIGG; London proofmarks and mark IT (John Twigg). Lock set in left-hand side for left-handed man. Lock plate, flat faced with faceted edges; bolt safety engaging at half cock and locking pan cover; hair trigger; roller bearing in toe of pan cover moving on projection on top of feather spring. Walnut full stock with checkered grip, carved with rococo shell behind barrel tang; engraved, blued steel furniture.

This is one of the earliest dueling pistols made by Twigg, who shared with Wogdon first place among the earlier makers of the dueling pistol. Between them, they perfected a form that was emulated throughout Europe. Twigg, whose weapons are invariably plain, was one of the first gunmakers to introduce checkering of the stock.

John Twigg, Piccadilly, London, about 1775
Overall length 15¼ in.; barrel 9⅞ in.
Caliber .56 (28 gauge). Weight 1¾ lb.

73. Flintlock Dueling Pistol (Bedford 1206)

One of a pair. Barrel, browned, octagonal, inscribed WOGDON; London proofmarks; stationary rear sight and silver blade front sight; gold-lined vent; two barrel slides with oval slots. Lock plate, flat faced, inscribed WOGDON in oval cartouche surmounted by swags; cock engraved with foliage; case-hardened finish. Walnut full stock with rounded butt; engraved, blued steel furniture; acorn trigger-guard finial; ram-

rod with reversible head for loading charge directly into chamber.

Robert Wogdon, London, about 1780
Overall length 15⅛ in.; barrel 10 in.
Caliber .56 (28 gauge). Weight 1¾ lb.

74. Flintlock Dueling Pistol (Bedford 1228)

One of a cased pair. Barrel, browned twist, octagonal, struck over breech with gold-lined stamp consisting of inscription D. EGG LONDON and crown, surrounded by three gold-lined, stamped fleurs-de-lis; two transverse gold lines at breech; stationary rear leaf sight, silver blade front sight; gold-lined vent and pan; two barrel slides. Lock plate, flat faced with beveled edges, engraved with flower sprays; roller bearing on pan-cover toe; bolt safety operating at half cock on both cock and pan cover; hair trigger and detent. Walnut full stock carved with floral spray behind barrel tang, checkered butt, horn fore-end; blued steel furniture engraved with trophies of arms; butt cap engraved with floral motif in center; trigger guard of French form with flower finial; two ramrod pipes; ramrod has horn finial and, on opposite end, elongated iron tube.

Durs Egg was one of the most successful London gunmakers of the late 18th and early 19th centuries. One of his principal patrons was the Prince of Wales. Born in the village of Oberbuchsiten near Solothurn in Switzerland in 1745, Egg presumably emigrated first to

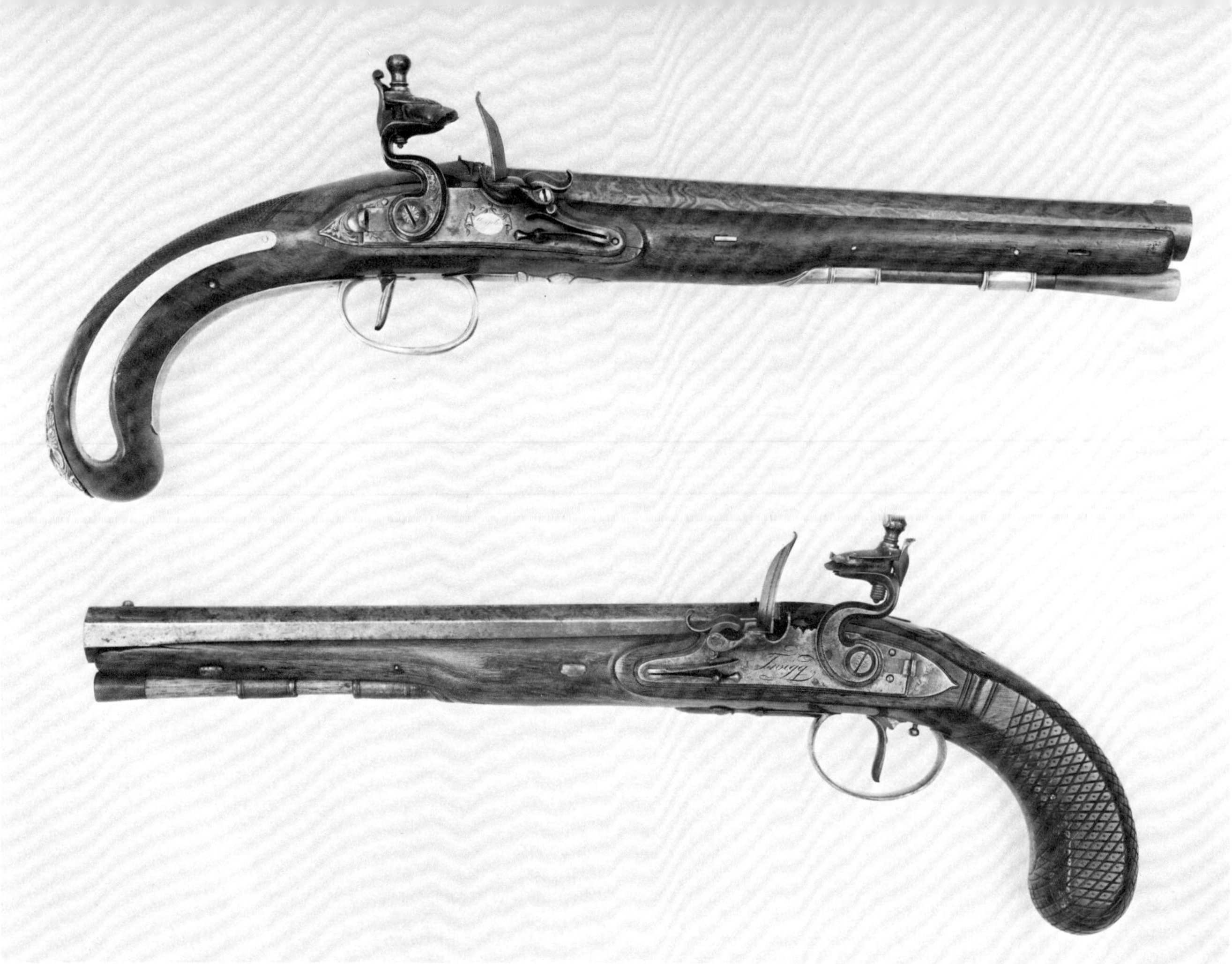

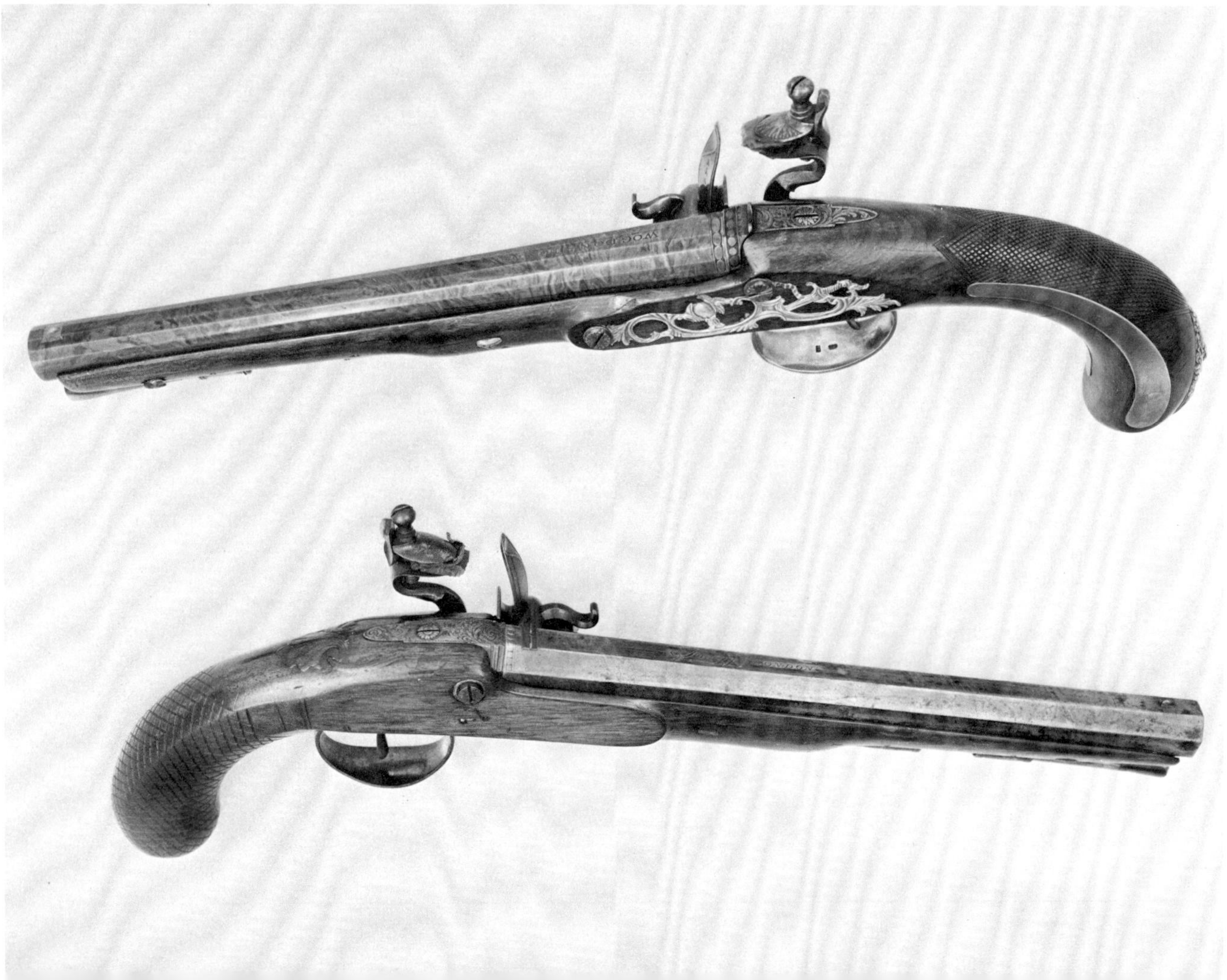

71 73

72 74

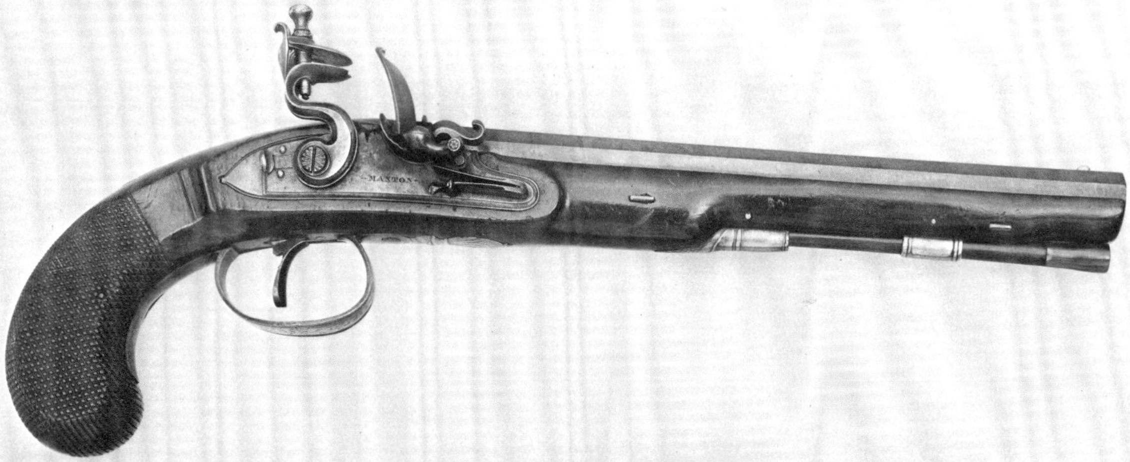

71 75

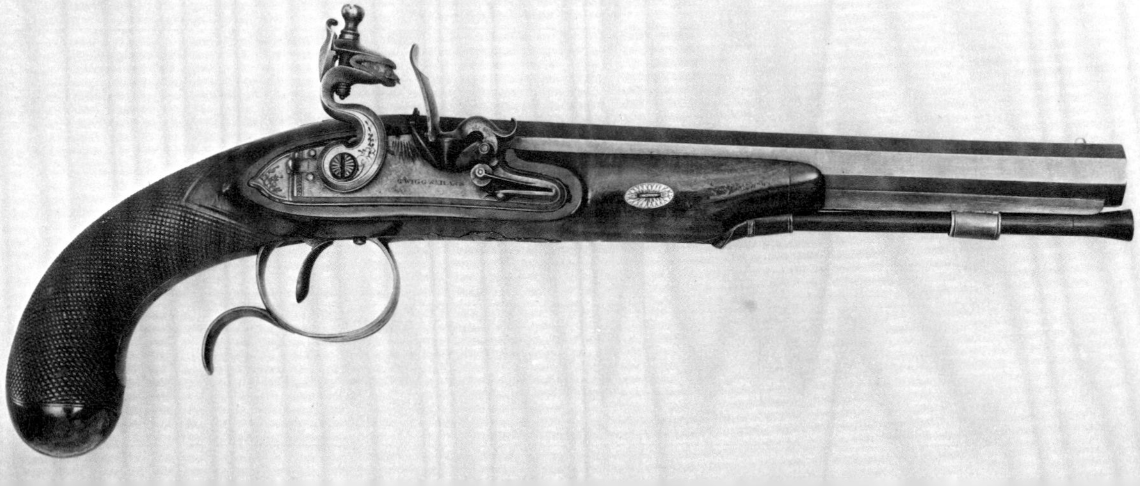

72 76

France and then came in 1772 to London, where he remained until his death in 1831. He is best known for his double-barreled shotguns and his superb pairs of dueling pistols. His earliest pieces, such as no. 74, show strong French influence, here noticeable in the flower spray carved behind the barrel tang and in the form of the trigger guard. His most strongly French-influenced piece was a Ferguson rifle made about 1782 for the Prince of Wales and now in the Windsor Castle Armoury (Blackmore, *Royal Sporting Guns at Windsor*, see "Egg" in Index, frontispiece, pl. 16).

> Durs Egg, London, about 1775–80
> Overall length 14⅞ in.; barrel 10 in.
> Caliber .50 (37 gauge). Weight 1½ lb.
> Literature: Blair, "The Eggs and their Origins."

75. Flintlock Dueling Pistol (Bedford 1266)

Barrel, browned twist, octagonal, inscribed in gold letters MANTON LONDON, hooking into false breech; two barrel slides, stationary rear sight, silver blade front sight; London proofmarks; gold-lined vent and pan. Lock plate, flat faced, filed with beveled edges and signed MANTON; roller bearing on pan cover, riding on elliptical ridge on feather spring; bolt safety operative at half cock. Walnut full stock with checkered grip; engraved steel furniture originally blued; pineapple trigger-guard finial.

John Manton was one of the best-known London gunmakers of the late 18th and early 19th centuries. He

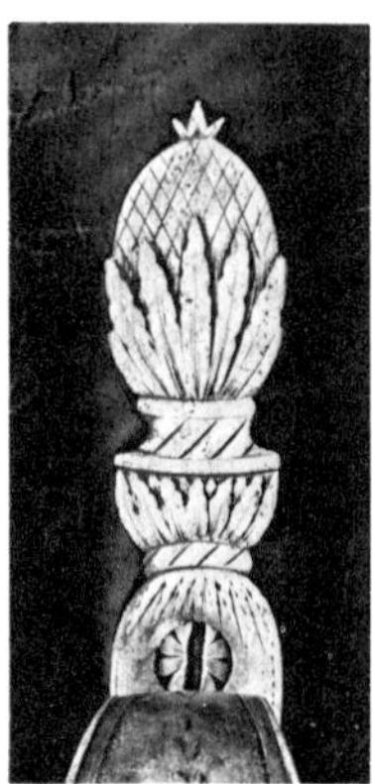

was born in 1752 in Grantham, where he was apprenticed to a gunmaker in 1768, but by 1770 he had moved to London and was employed by the famous maker of dueling pistols Twigg of Piccadilly. He rose to be foreman of that firm. In 1781 he started his own business at 6 Dover Street, remaining there until his death in 1834. He patented many improvements on flintlock firearms and in 1788 began to give serial numbers to all those he made. This pistol antedates the numbered series.

> John Manton, London, about 1785
> Overall length 15½ in.; barrel 10 in,
> Caliber .62 (20 gauge). Weight 1½ lb.

76. Flintlock Dueling Pistol (Bedford 1543)

Barrel, browned twist, octagonal, patent breech with one gold transverse line; on patent breech, gold-lined stamp inscribed TWIGG & BASS LONDON; single barrel slide with oval gold slots, stationary rear sight on false breech, gold blade front sight; under-barrel rib; London proofmarks; gold-lined vent. Lock plate, flat faced, inscribed TWIGG & BASS has engraved flower sprays and filed, beveled edges; waterproof pan; roller bearings on pan cover and feather spring; bolt safety engaging at half cock; hair trigger and detent. Walnut three-quarter stock with horn fore-end, checkered butt; engraved and blued steel furniture; trigger-guard finial has pineaple rising from vase.

This is an early example of the evolved form of dueling pistol with three-quarter stock and under-barrel rib, which was first introduced at the end of the 18th century. A spur was added to the trigger guard to make the pistol easier to steady. John Twigg went into partnership with John Bass in 1787 and produced this up-to-date type. Twigg died in 1790.

> Twigg & Bass, London, about 1790
> Overall length 15½ in.; barrel 10⅛ in.
> Caliber .58 (24 gauge). Weight 1¾ lb.

77. Flintlock Dueling Pistol (Bedford 1507)

One of a pair. Barrel, browned twist, octagonal; patent breech, with single gold transverse line, has sunken rectangular gold inlaid mark inscribed JOSEPH MANTON PATENT, surmounted by crown; two barrel slides with silver oval slots, stationary rear sight, silver blade front sight; London proofmarks; recessed gold-lined vent and gold-lined pan of patent form. Lock plate, flat faced, inscribed JOSEPH MANTON LONDON, border engraved with an overlapping leaf design; pan cover with roller bearing riding on elliptical ridge on feather spring; bolt safety operating at half cock; semi-waterproof pan. Walnut full stock, checkered butt; engraved steel furniture with traces of bluing; small iron butt cap with engraved central flower and screw head; silver escutcheon engraved with crest of Hamilton: tree with label inscribed THROUGH surmounted by a baron's coronet; pineapple trigger-guard finial. Manton's serial number 305.

Joseph Manton was even more famous than his older brother John as a maker of dueling pistols and double-barreled shotguns. He was born in Grantham in 1766 and died in London in 1835. Apprenticed first to a Grantham gunmaker, he subsequently worked with his brother. He ended his apprenticeship before 1789 and began to work on his own. Like his brother, he patented numerous improvements for the flint and percussion-cap action. He produced over 10,000 firearms numbered in sequence. From April 1792 until 1825, he worked at 25 Davis Street, Berkley Square, and he subsequently went to 11 Hanover Square. In 1826 he was bankrupt. Later he went to debtor's prison.

Joseph Manton, London, about 1792–93
Overall length 14½ in.; barrel 10⅛ in.
Caliber .58 (24 gauge). Weight 2½ lb.
Literature: Neal and Back, *The Mantons: Gunmakers;* Christie's sale, December 8, 1969, lot 80, ill.

78. Flintlock Dueling Pistol (Bedford 1538)

One of a cased pair. Barrel, browned twist, octagonal, inscribed in gold inlay D. EGG LONDON, patent breech with transverse gold lines, under-barrel rib; single barrel slide with silver oval slots, rear stationary leaf sight, gold blade front sight; London proofmarks; vent and waterproof pan are gold lined. Lock plate, flat faced, inscribed D. EGG and engraved with flower sprays; roller bearings on feather spring; separate flash fence; bolt safety engages at half cock and also locks pan cover; small movable section of rear of lock plate is variation of normal sliding bolt safety; hair trigger and detent. Walnut three-quarter stock with checkered grip and steel fore-end; blued, engraved steel furniture; butt cap engraved with central flower; oval gold escutcheon with owner's initials; trigger guard of French type with pineapple final and additional spur for third finger; ramrod with horn tip has steel worm on opposite end.

The pistol was modernized, some years after it was made, by the addition of a spur to the trigger guard. The French shape of the trigger guard suggests a date before 1800.

Durs Egg, London, about 1790–1800
Overall length 16 in.; barrel 10⅜ in.
Caliber .56 (27 gauge). Weight 2½ lb.

79. Flintlock Dueling Pistol (Bedford 1576)

Barrel, browned twist, octagonal, patent breech has inlaid gold ribbon with maker's signature together with spray of roses, shamrocks, and thistles in gold; barrel inscribed GUNMAKER TO HIS MAJESTY; under-barrel rib; London proofmarks; single barrel slide with silver oval slots; gold sight, surrounded by gold sunburst; gold lines inlaid around breech and muzzle. Lock plate, flat faced, inscribed H. W. MORTIMER & CO., filed with beveled edges; vent and pan are gold lined; roller bearing on pan cover and on feather spring; bolt safety locking both cock at half cock and pan; hair trigger and detent. Walnut three-quarter stock with silver fore-end; checkered butt; blued steel furniture engraved with trophies of arms; shield-shaped escutcheon; spurred trigger guard with pineapple finial.

H. W. Mortimer worked at 89 Fleet Street from 1782. Holding the appointment of Gunmaker to the

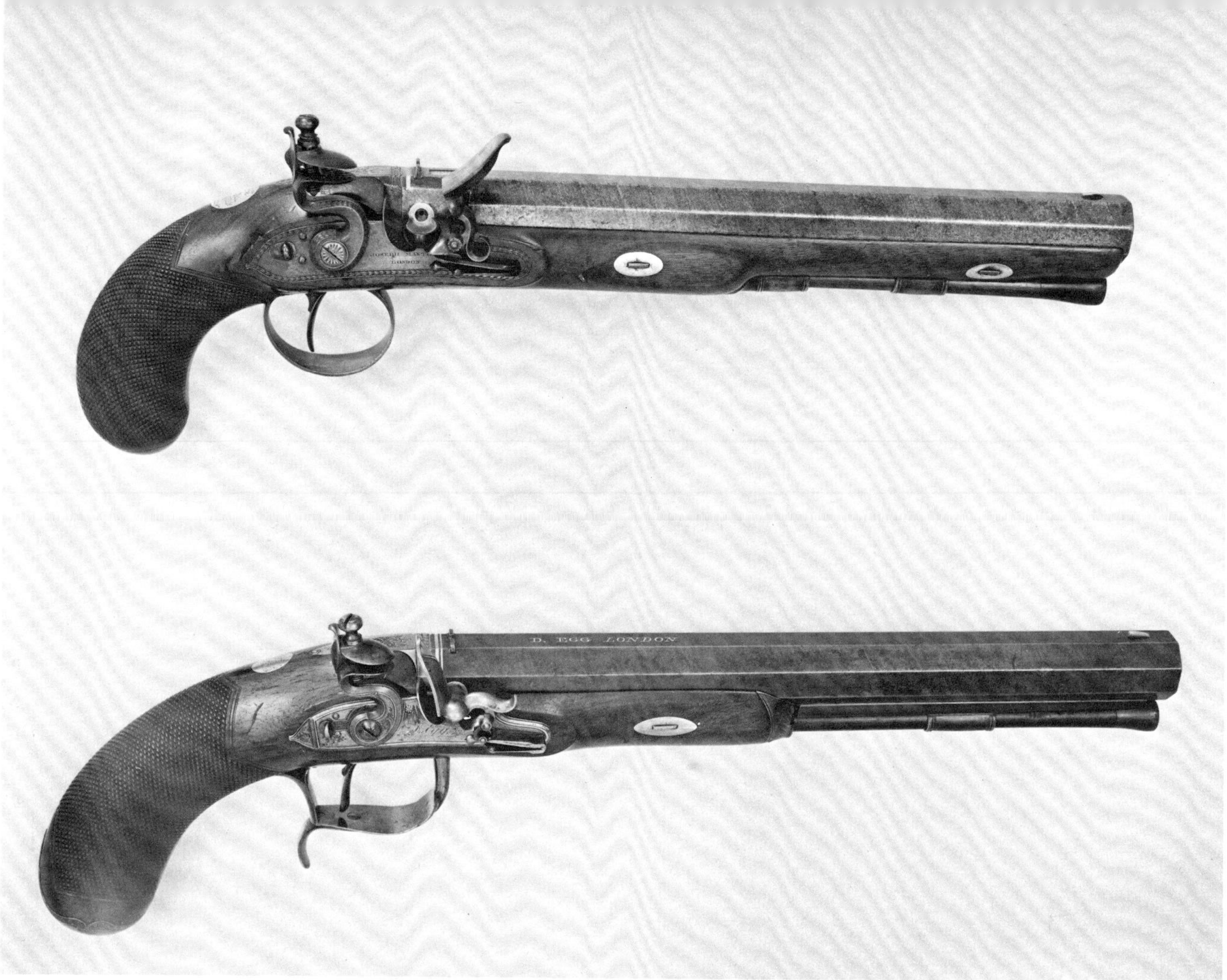

D. EGG LONDON
J.W. Mortimer & Co

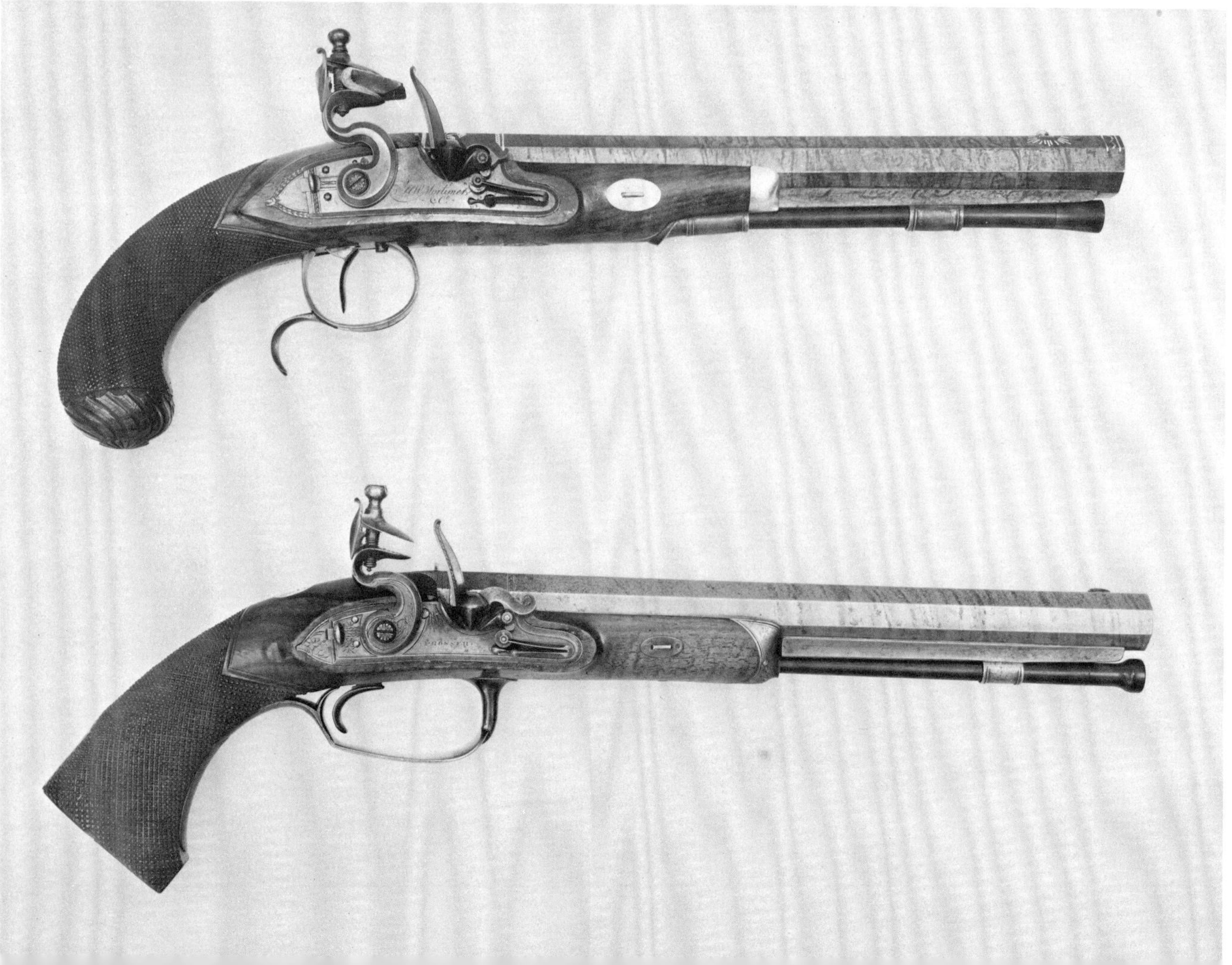

King, he produced firearms on a large scale. This dueling pistol with its fine gold damascening is one of his best productions.

> H. W. Mortimer & Co., London, about 1795–1800
> Overall length 15½ in.; barrel 9⅞ in.
> Caliber .60 (21 gauge). Weight 2 lb.

80. Flintlock Dueling Pistol (Bedford 1240)

One of a cased pair. Barrel, octagonal, with patent breech, single gold transverse line, top facet inscribed PROSSER CHARING CROSS LONDON; under-barrel rib, London proofmarks, single barrel slide; stationary rear sight on false breech, silver blade front sight; gold-lined vent. Lock plate, flat faced, inscribed PROSSER, with beveled edges and engraved sprays of flowers, numbered 64 on inside; waterproof pan; flash fence; roller bearing on pan cover and on feather spring; cock has descent arrest; bolt safety engaging at half cock. Walnut three-quarter stock with engraved steel fore-end; checkered butt of unusual form, cut at angle; engraved, blued steel furniture; butt with angle mount of silver signed PROSSER and dated 1803; silver escutcheon with owner's crest (lion passant) and initials; trigger guard of French type has bud finial.

John Prosser was a retail supplier of arms, swords, and uniforms as well as a working gunmaker from 1796 to 1854. The curious form of butt is said to have become popular with English officers who had served in the Iberian Peninsula and become familiar with the Catalan shape of stock, but this pistol antedates the Peninsular War.

> John Prosser, London, 1803
> Overall length 16 in.; barrel 10 in.
> Caliber .57 (27 gauge). Weight 2 lb.

81. Flintlock Dueling Pistol (Bedford 478)

One of a cased pair. Barrel, browned twist, with case-hardened patent breech engraved with trails of foliage and inset with platinum plaque inscribed MORTIMER & SON, LONDON; barrel inscribed LUDGATE HILL GUNMAKERS TO HIS MAJESTY; serial number 2519 on breech tang; single transverse gold line; sta-

tionary rear sight on false breech, brass front sight; under-barrel rib, single barrel slide. Lock plate, flat faced, inscribed T. MORTIMER & SON, with engraved overlapping-leaf border and flower sprays; platinum-lined vent, waterproof pan, roller bearing on feather spring; bolt safety engaging cock at half cock and pan cover; loop-necked cock. Figured walnut three-quarter stock with saw handle and silver fore-end; engraved, blue steel furniture; silver escutcheon engraved with crest of Hawkins, boar's head, and motto LIBERTATE ET NATALE SOLUM.

This pistol and its mate were made for the first Baron Hawkins of Killincarrick, County Wicklow, Ireland; his coat of arms is engraved on the lid of the case. No. 81 represents the highest development of the flintlock dueling pistol before it gave way to the percussion-cap pistol. The firm of Thomas Mortimer & Son was at Ludgate Hill from 1809 to 1824.

> Thomas Mortimer & Son, about 1820
> Overall length 15¾ in.; barrel 10¼ in.
> Caliber .52 (33 gauge). Weight 2½ lb.

82. Percussion-lock Dueling Pistol
(Bedford 428)

One of a pair; converted from flintlock to percussion-cap action about 1830. Barrel, browned twist, octagonal, with patent breeching added at time of conversion; single gold transverse line; two barrel slides with silver slots; stationary rear sight on false breech, gold front sight. Oval gold plaque inscribed RIGBY inset in barrel and in lock plate. Lock plate, flat faced, engraved with floral sprays, filed with beveled edges, vertical inlaid gold line; dolphin hammer, nipple with platinum safety vent; hair trigger and detent. Walnut full stock, checkered butt; blued steel furniture engraved with trophies of arms; owner's crest, demi-lion rampant and initial, engraved on gold plaque and set in barrel tang; trigger guard with pineapple finial; ramrod with special loading device.

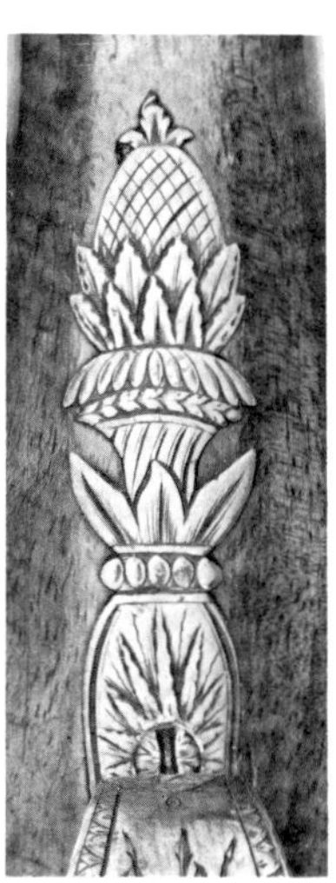

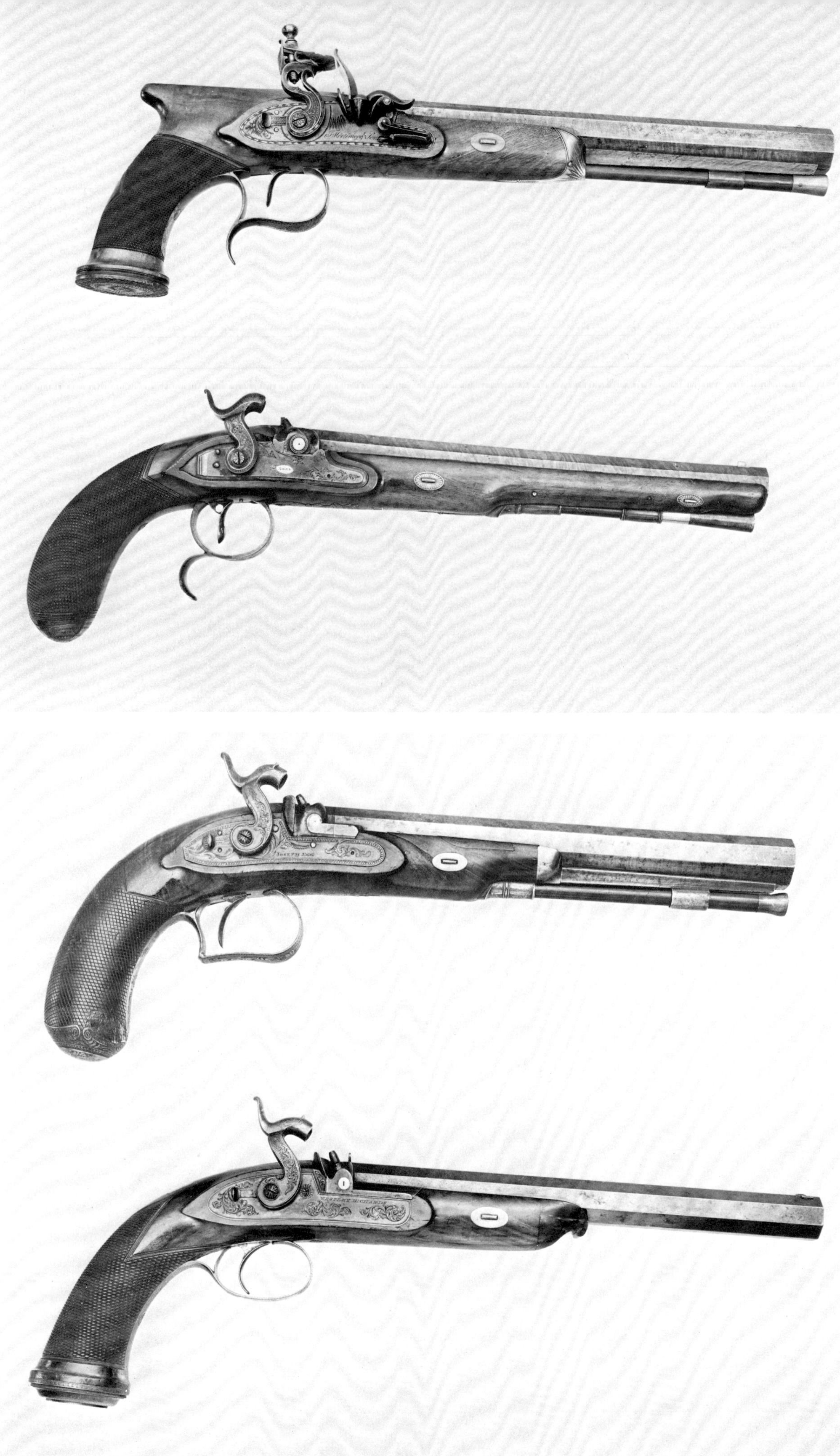

John Rigby of Dublin, established in 1735, belonged to a family of gunmakers whose firm continues today. The conversion from flint to percussion is exceptional in that the full stock has been left intact instead of being cut back with a rib added to the barrel.

John Rigby, Dublin, about 1790
Overall length 15¾ in.; barrel 10¼ in.
Caliber .52 (33 gauge). Weight 2 lb.
Literature: Akehurst, *Game Guns and Rifles*, pp. 154–155.

83. Rifled Percussion-cap Dueling Pistol
(Bedford 1072)

One of a cased pair, one pistol with smooth bore, the other rifled. Barrel, browned twist, octagonal, with patent breech, under-barrel rib, stationary rear sight on false breech, blade front sight; top facet inscribed JOSEPH EGG, PICCADILLY, LONDON; barrelsmith's mark WF (William Fullerd); platinum-lined safety vent. Lock plate with engraved edges and foliate scrolls inscribed JOSEPH EGG; dolphin hammer, bolt safety, hair trigger, detent. Walnut half stock with silver fore-end checkered grip; engraved, blued steel furniture; gold escutcheon.

Joseph Egg, a nephew of Durs Egg, was born in 1774 in Huningue, Alsace. Presumably he came to England to join his uncle, but the earliest reference to him, which dates from 1800, shows him to have been working in Great Windmill Street. In 1801 he went into partnership with Henry Tatham, gunmaker and sword cutler, of 37 Charing Cross. In 1814 or 1815 Joseph Egg set up his own business at 1 Piccadilly, where he remained until his death in 1837. His business was carried on by his sons. Besides specializing in small-scale double-barreled pistols (see no. 211), he patented in 1813 an inverted flintlock (Blair, "Joseph Egg's Inverted Flintlock," p. 174).

Joseph Egg, London, about 1830
Overall length 15½ in.; barrel 10 in.
Caliber .52 (30 gauge). Weight 2½ lb.
Literature: Blair, "The Eggs and their Origins," p. 355.

84. Rifled Percussion-cap Target Pistol
(Bedford 1142)

One of a pair. Barrel, browned twist, octagonal, with polygroove rifling; top facet inscribed WESTLEY RICHARDS 170 NEW BOND ST., LONDON; patent breech with case-hardened finish inlaid with transverse platinum lines; stationary rear sight, silver blade front sight. Lock plate, flat faced, inscribed WESTLEY RICHARDS, engraved with floral sprays; platinum-lined safety vent, dolphin hammer, bolt safety operating at half cock. Walnut three-quarter stock with horn fore-end, checkered grip; engraved, blued steel furniture; flattened butt with engraved oval butt cap; blank silver escutcheon; trigger guard with pineapple finial engraved with figure of man in contemporary costume holding pistol, ready for duel.

In view of the rifled barrel, this was probably a target pistol rather than a dueling pistol. The firm of Westley Richards was established in Birmingham in 1812 by William Westley Richards. The factory was in High Street. Many of their firearms were sold through their agency at 170 Bond Street, London. The firm still continues in business in Birmingham.

Westley Richards, Birmingham, about 1830
Overall length 15¹¹⁄₁₆ in.; barrel 9½ in.
Caliber .56 (26 gauge). Weight 2 lb.
Literature: Taylor, *A Brief History of the Westley Richards Firm, 1812–1913*.

85. Tube-lock Dueling Pistol (Bedford 493)

One of a cased pair. Barrel, browned twist, octagonal, with case-hardened patent breech, signed on recessed stamp JOSEPH MANTON PATENT, surmounted by crown; London proofmarks; serial number 10080; single transverse line of platinum; stationary rear sight on false breech, silver bead front sight. Lock plate, flat faced, engraved with floral sprays and inscribed JOSEPH MANTON; bolt safety. Walnut three-quarter stock with horn fore-end, checkered butt; engraved, blued steel furniture; trigger guard has engraved shell finial.

The tube lock was patented by Joseph Manton on August 3, 1818, patent number 4285. A slender copper tube, filled with a detonating compound containing fulminate of mercury, fits directly into the touchhole where it is held by a spring. The hammer strikes the tube, exploding the contents and igniting the powder charge. It is somewhat surprising to find a tube lock being made as late as 1837, when the percussion-cap action was already well established.

Joseph Manton, London, about 1837
Overall length 14$^{15}/_{16}$ in.; barrel 10 in.
Caliber .50 (37 gauge). Weight 2½ lb.
Literature: Neal and Back, *The Mantons: Gunmakers*, pp. 176, 282.

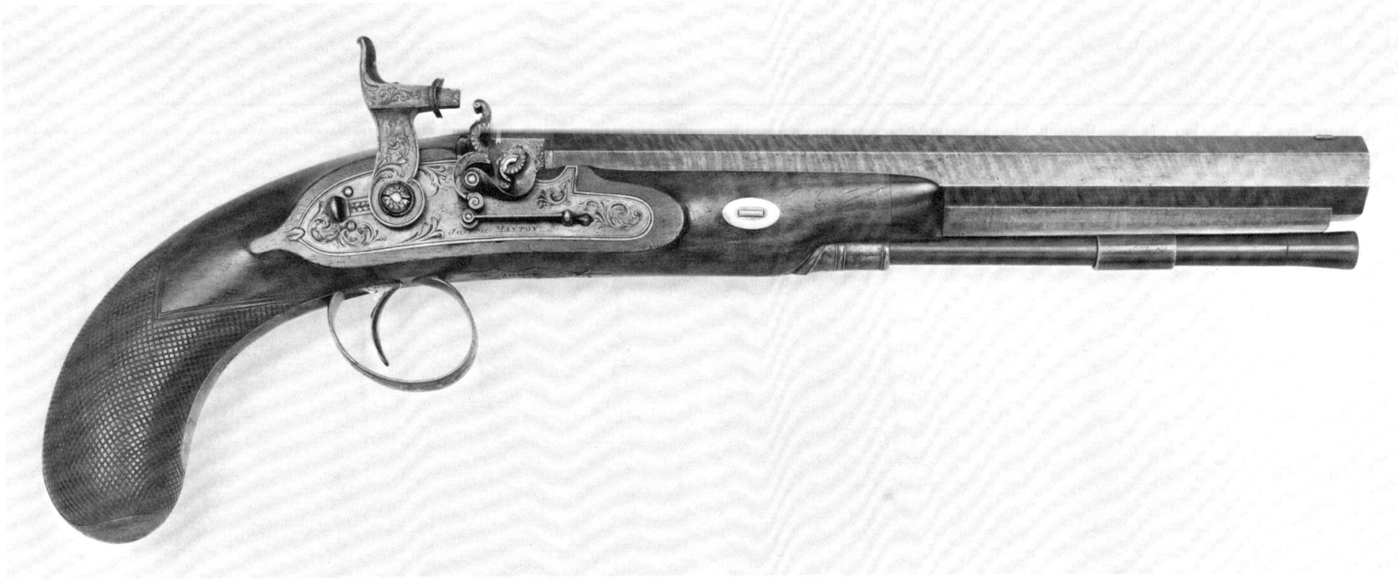

6

SPORTING GUNS AND OFFICER'S FUSILS

Guns designed specifically for hunting were being made on the Continent in the 16th century. In England, however, firearms were not used for sport until much later, perhaps because there was little large game and the weapons of the time were unsuited to shooting birds. In due course, the deficiency of the weapons was remedied with the development of superior precision locks by British gunsmiths.

The restoration of the monarchy in 1660 saw the beginnings of shooting as a sport. During their exile in France, Charles II and his courtiers had acquired a taste for shooting birds in flight. Pepys in his Diary of the year 1665 relates that "Sir Robert Long [Charles II's secretary during his exile] told us of the plenty of partridges in France, where he says the King of France and his company killed with their guns, in the plain de Versailles, 300 and odd partridges at one bout." *Pteryplegia: Or, The Art of Shooting Flying*, a poem written by George Markland and published in 1727, is in the Clay Bedford library. It contains much practical information on the sport.

The overall shape and mechanical details of shotguns changed little during the first half of the 18th century. During this time, English gunmakers were at the stage where they were able to build first-rate firearms. The stocks were only slightly carved, and the barrels and locks had a minimum of engraving and chasing. During the second half of the century it became possible to shorten the barrel because of the better quality of the powder and also because of the invention by Henry Nock in 1787 of patent breeching, which caused the powder to be ignited in its center, thus improving the strength and regularity of the shooting. In the last twenty years of the century, the best type of sporting gun was a half-stocked shotgun with a pair of barrels 30 or 32 in. in length; the bend of the stock was less pronounced than in the earlier guns, and the stock had a checkered grip. The double-barreled sporting gun, well developed by the end of the 18th century, was further improved and refined in the first thirty years of the 19th. Altogether these guns were functional and plain, but with graceful lines.

Of the eight sporting guns in the exhibited group, the first six are flintlocks; they date from about 1730 to 1797, the latest being a double-barreled shotgun by John Manton (no. 91). The last two items in the group are cased double-barreled percussion-cap shotguns, one made by William Mills in 1828 (no. 93), the other by James Purdey in 1837 (no. 92). Four of the guns have steel furniture, and four have silver furniture, in three instances by the silversmith John King. Two of the pieces are considered to be officer's fusils because of the presence of military features, one having a socket bayonet (no. 88), the other provision for a sling (no. 91). The guns range in caliber from .65 to .78; barrel lengths vary from 29½ to 38 in.

86. Flintlock Sporting Gun (Bedford 1375)

Barrel, circular, in two stages separated by molded girdle, facet over breech inscribed CLARKSON LONDON; stamped near breech with London proofmarks between which is barrelsmith's mark IC within diamond (Joseph Clarkson); sighting V cut in false breech; silver blade front sight; three barrel slides; gold-lined vent. Lock plate with rounded face, inscribed CLARKSON;

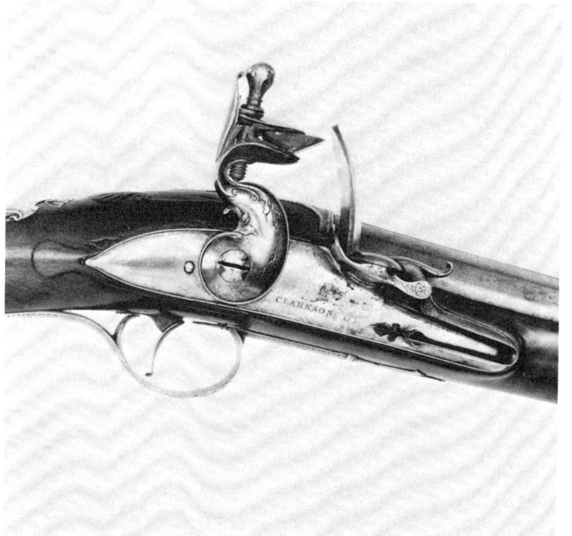

bridle between pan and pan-cover screw; cock finely chiseled with leafage. Walnut full stock carved with shells behind barrel tang and rear ramrod pipe; steel furniture; butt plate with tang and engraved borders; side plate pierced and chiseled with trophy of arms and secured by screws indented for rectangular keys; blank polished escutcheon; three engraved ramrod pipes; ramrod with horn finial.

Joseph Clarkson, London, about 1730
Overall length 51⅕ in.; barrel 36 in.
Caliber .78 (10 gauge). Weight 6 lb.

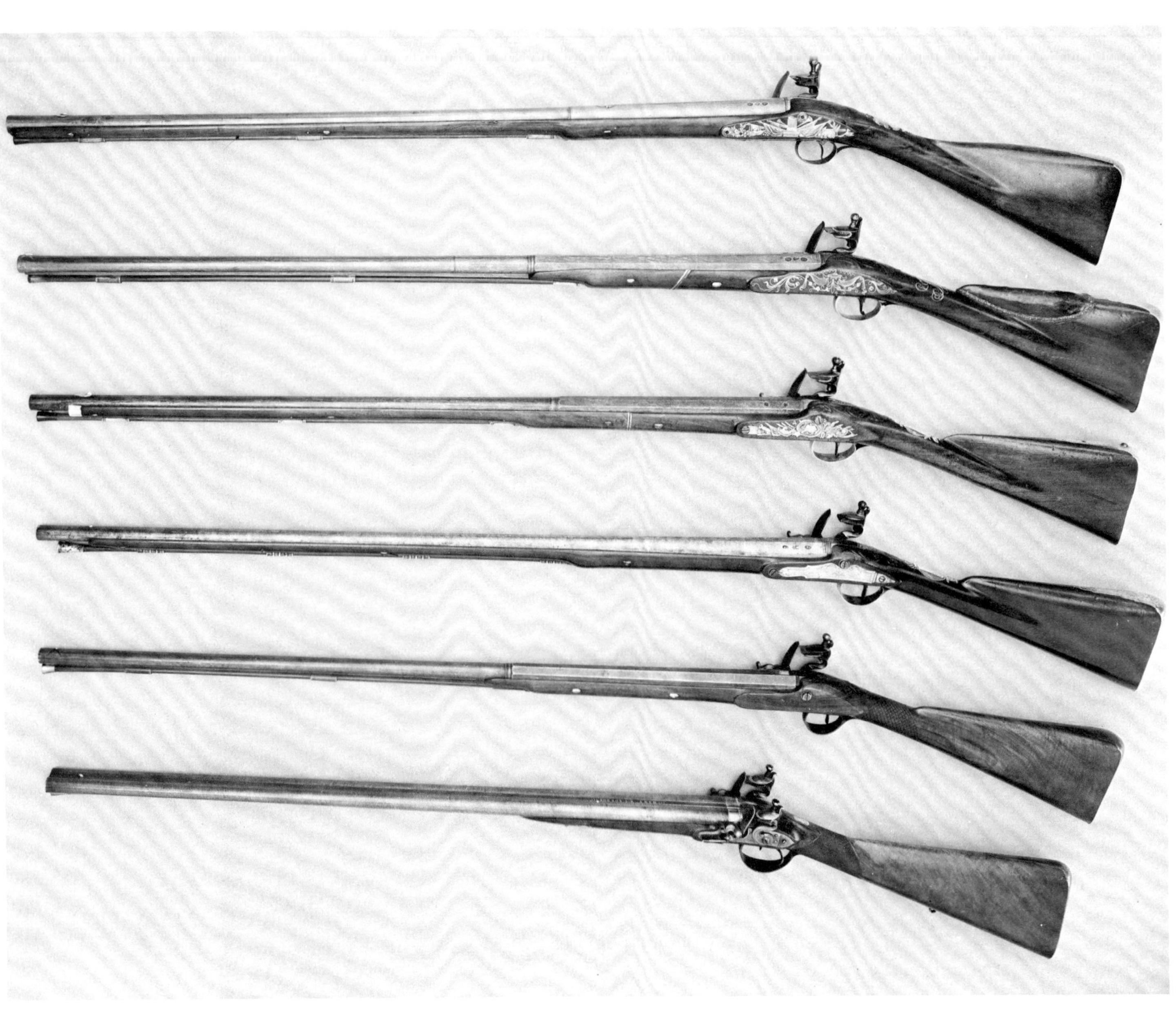

87. Flintlock Sporting Gun (Bedford 1350)

Barrel in three stages, separated by girdles, octagonal breech, two forward stages of circular section; barrel inscribed W. BAILES, RUSSELL STREET, LONDON; barrel struck on top facet in Spanish fashion with lion rampant and name LONDON surmounted by a crown; London proofmarks and barrelsmith's mark F for foreigner, that is, one not a member of Gunmakers' Company; two barrel slides. Lock plate inscribed W.

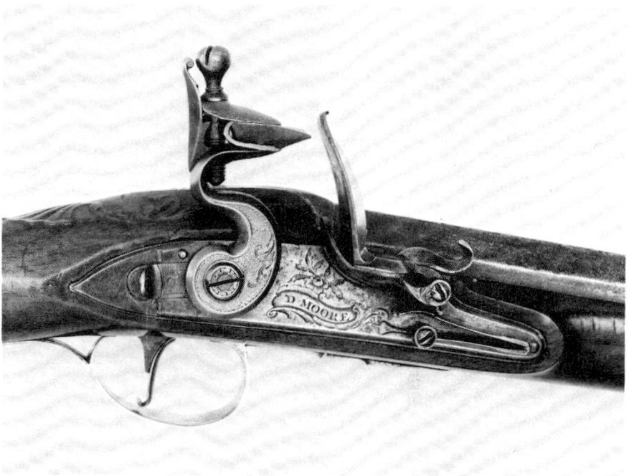

BAILES. Walnut three-quarter stock, forward section detachable, carved with shell behind barrel tang; leather pad on comb; silver furniture engraved with floral designs and with dotted borders, bearing London hallmark and silversmith's mark JK (John King); owner's initials JH inlaid in silver wire on small; leaf trigger-guard finial.

William Bailes, London, 1759
Overall length 53 in.; barrel 37½ in.
Caliber .75 (11 gauge). Weight 6¾ lb.

88. Flintlock Sporting Gun (Bedford 1376)

Barrel with hooked breech, in two stages with molded girdle between, octagonal at breech, remainder of circular section; inscribed COOK BATH, possibly name of provincial gunmaker or owner's name; two Birmingham proofmarks near breech; false breech grooved for rear sight, silver bead front sight; four barrel slides. Lock plate, flat, inscribed D. MOORE in ribbon, engraved with floral sprays, and filed with beveled edge; cock has descent arrest; bolt safety engaging at half cock; flash fence. Walnut full stock divides into two parts six inches in front of lock, carved behind barrel tang with shell and foliage; forestock has silver finial; silver furniture; butt plate with tang engraved with trophies; trap in butt cap opens to disclose small socket bayonet that fits over stud on underside of muzzle; butt plate has mark JK (John King) and date letter for 1770; side plate pierced and chased with trophies of arms; escutcheon surmounted by helmet, cannon be-

low, engraved with armored arm holding spear; trigger guard, with acorn finial, has four marks: JK (John King), lion passant, leopard's head, and date letter for 1770; three ramrod pipes; ramrod has horn finial.

Although this gun corresponds to the usual fowling piece in design, the presence of a socket bayonet suggests that it must, in fact, have been intended for use as an officer's fusil. Daniel Moore submitted his proof piece and was admitted to the Gunmakers' Company in 1758. At the same time his mark, the letters DM sur-

mounted by a coronet in a square shield, was approved.

Daniel Moore, London, 1770
Overall length 52 in.; barrel 36½ in.
Caliber .65 (16 gauge). Weight 6¼ lb.

89. Flintlock Sporting Gun (Bedford 1349)

Barrel of round section except for top facet over breech, engraved transverse border at breech, top facet terminating in loop; barrel inscribed JOHN TWIGG LONDON; London proofmarks and Twigg's mark, IT surmounted by crown; hooked breech; three barrel slides; iron bead front sight. Lock plate, rounded, with engraved borders, inscribed TWIGG. Walnut full stock

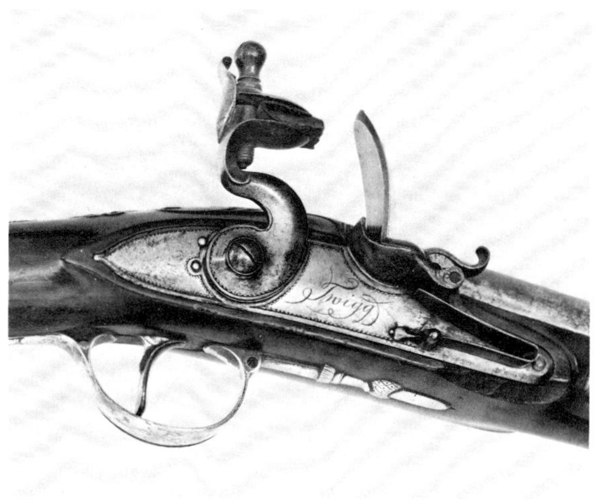

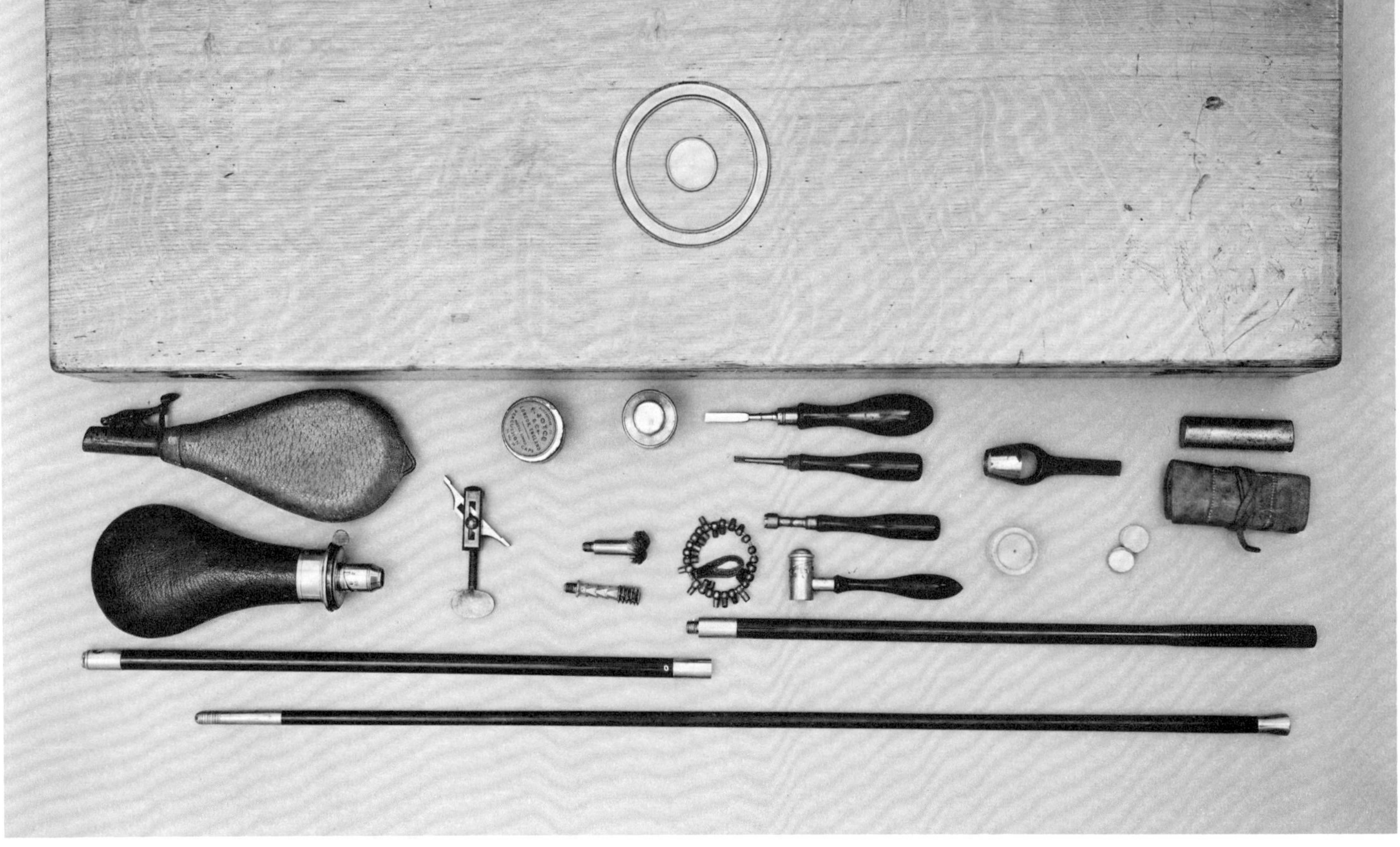

carved with shell and foliage behind barrel tang; stock stops short of muzzle to allow place for socket bayonet; silver furniture bearing London hallmark and silversmith's mark JK (John King); butt plate with engraved borders and rococo foliage; flat side plate engraved with bow, arrow, and quiver within rococo scrollwork; oval escutcheon with shield above and pedestal below engraved with owner's coat of arms and motto PRO ARIS ET FOCIS; trigger guard with acorn finial.

This gun was originally an officer's fusil, as is demonstrated by the hole for sling swivel through the forward part of the trigger guard.

John Twigg, London, 1777
Overall length 53½ in.; barrel 38 in.
Caliber .65 (17 gauge). Weight 6¼ lb.

90. Flintlock Sporting Gun (Bedford 1336)

One of a pair. Barrel, browned twist, in two stages separated by molded girdle, octagonal at breech, forward stage of circular section; at breech, gold recessed mark inscribed TWIGG, with star below, then LONDON, the whole surmounted by crown; two barrel slides; silver bead front sight; hooked breech; under-barrel rib. Lock plate with flat face inscribed TWIGG, filed with beveled edges; flash fence integral with pan;

pan cover with roller bearing riding on elliptical ridge on feather spring; bolt safety engaging at half cock; gold-lined vent. Walnut three-quarter stock with horn fore-end, checkered small, carved with rococo shell behind barrel tang; engraved, blued steel furniture; butt plate has tang engraved with foliate scrolls; single side nail with engraved head; trigger guard with acorn finial; ramrod with brass finial, tube at opposite end is half brass and half iron.

John Twigg, London, about 1780
Overall length 52¼ in.; barrel 36¾ in.
Caliber .65 (17 gauge). Weight 5¼ lb.

91. Double-barreled Flintlock Gun
(Bedford 1327)

Barrels, browned twist, with rib between, patent breech with engraved gold transverse lines; on rib near breech inscribed in gold MANTON LONDON; gold bead front sight; barrel hooked into false breech; single barrel slide. Flat-faced left- and right-hand locks inscribed MANTON with semiwaterproof pans; cocks have descent arrest; flash fence integral with pan; roller bearings on pan cover and feather spring; gold-

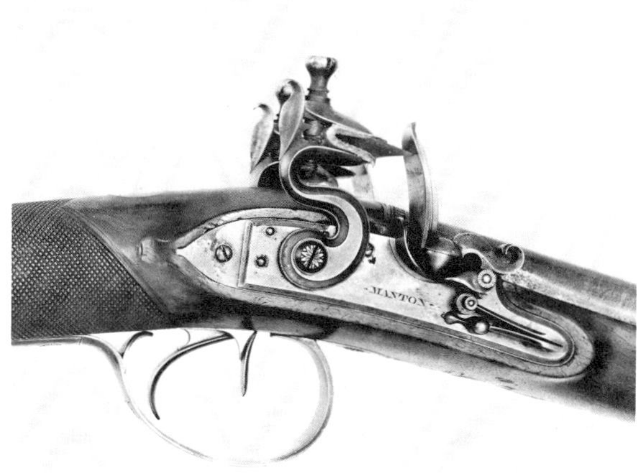

lined pan and vents; long, curved rear trigger is for left lock. Walnut half stock with checkered grip; engraved, blued steel furniture; butt plate with tang engraved with trophy; escutcheon engraved with crest of dukes of Bedford; pineapple trigger-guard finial; iron loops for shoulder sling; ramrod with brass finial, at opposite end is threaded brass tube for attaching worm.

This gun is typical of the fine-quality sporting arms that the Manton brothers supplied to the nobility of England at the end of the 18th century and early in the 19th.

John Manton, London, 1797
Overall length 49⅝ in.; barrel 34 in.
Caliber .66 (16 gauge). Weight 7½ lb.
Literature: Neal and Back, *The Mantons: Gunmakers*, p. 71.

92. Cased Double-barreled Percussion Sporting Gun (Bedford 1369)

Barrels, browned twist, with raised concave rib inscribed J. PURDEY 314½ OXFORD STREET LONDON; breech blocks have view marks on underside; on underside of each barrel, mark JP (James Purdey), London proofmarks, and serial number 2966; on underside at muzzle, raised area prevents ramrod from ac-

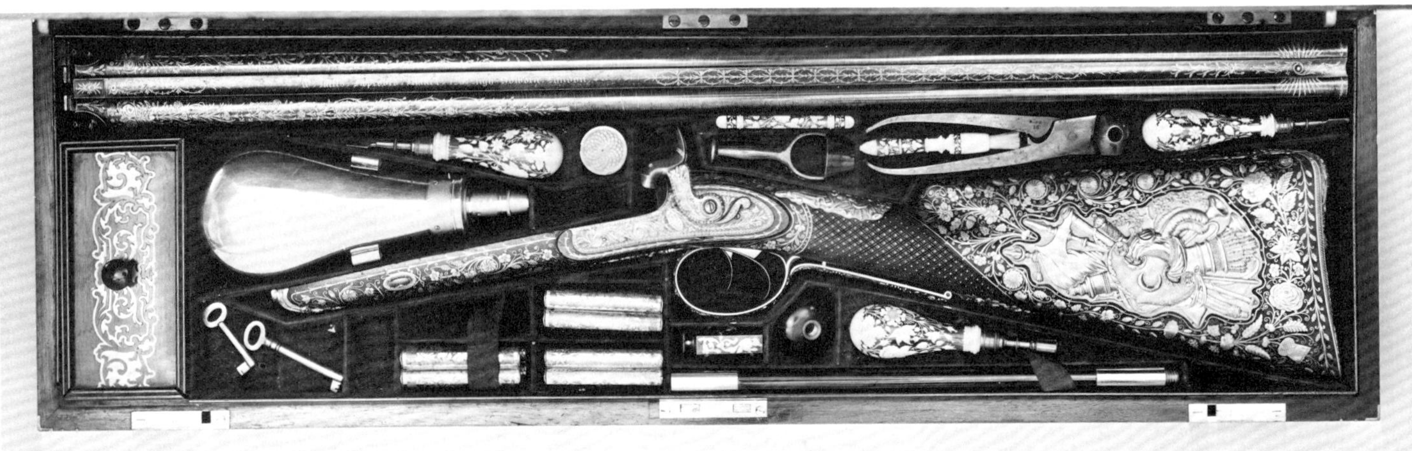

cidentally falling out; patent breech with platinum line, case-hardened finish; silver bead front sight. Lock plates, flat faced, inscribed PURDEY, with engraved borders and scrollwork; dolphin hammers; platinum-lined vents. Figured walnut three-quarter stock with checkered small and forestock; engraved, blued steel furniture; butt plate with tang engraved with foliation; blank oval silver escutcheon; trigger guard engraved with foliation and serial number 2966; ramrod attached to barrel has finial with serial number 2966 and, on opposite end, brass tube with iron worm, tube threaded for cap.

Complete in original red-baize-lined oak case with brass carrying handle. Case contains shot-and-powder flask, cleaning rod, wad cutter, oil bottle, and all other fittings. Maker's trade label headed by Royal Arms reads: J. Purdey, 314½ Oxford Street (near Hanover Square) London, Gun Manufacturer. Added in ink: Charge for this gun 2½ dms, No. 2 powder, to 1 oz. shot, No. 6 or 5.

> James Purdey, London, 1837
> Overall length 47 in.; barrel 29½ in.
> Caliber .70 (14 gauge). Weight of barrels including ramrod 4 lb.; stock 2½ lb.
> Case 33 x 10 x 3¼ in.
> Literature: Akehurst, *Sporting Guns*, p. 53, ill. at top.

93. Cased Double-barreled Percussion-cap Shotgun   (Bedford 1303)

Barrels, browned twist, with raised concave rib between; inscribed in gold W. MILLS IMPROVED MAKER 120 HIGH HOLBORN LONDON; London proof-marks; patent breech with case-hardened finish; breech extending to nearly half of barrel length, finely damascened in gold with scrollwork bearing roses, acorns, and other flowers and terminating in sprays of grasses; entire length of central rib similarly damascened in gold; muzzles have damascened girdles; gold front sight within gold sunburst; single barrel slide; false breech

also damascened in gold with floral scrolls and roses. Lock plates, flat, richly damascened with gold scrolls on blued ground, in gold oval engraved W. MILLS IM-PROVED; dolphin-head hammers damascened all over in gold with scrolls bearing leaves and roses; hall-mark of 1828; goldsmith's mark SW; dog safety catch engaging at half cock. Walnut three-quarter stock with checkered small, studded with silver nailheads; entire length of stock profusely inlaid with silver wire scroll-work bearing roses, thistles, daisies, acorns, and various other flowers; silver furniture cast in high relief and finely chased with floral motifs; butt-plate tang cast and chased with shell surmounted by trophy of arms and, above, classical urn from which rises bunch of flowers; escutcheon chased with trophy of arms; on each side of butt in high relief is irregular plaque with trophies of arms, each with shield bearing one or three crescents; trigger guard has pivoted silver safety and is inscribed SAFETY.

Original blue-velvet-lined rosewood case; exterior and top of one compartment of interior profusely inlaid with brass ornament in Buhl technique. Four compartments contain six shot-measures, each of steel etched with scrollwork against gray ground. All tools, including screwdriver, nipple wrench, and brush, have ivory handles etched against dark ground with flowers corresponding to those on stock; silver powder flask with silver-gilt spout bears London hallmark for 1830. On lid, gunmaker's trade label, missing, is replaced by colored print entitled Partridge Shooting From an Original Painting by C. H. Weigall London Henry Lee 22 Warwick Lane.

This must be one of the most elaborately decorated firearms ever produced in England. The presence of crescents in the silver plaque on the butt implies that it was a presentation piece, probably intended for an Indian ruler or Near Eastern official. William Mills worked in High Holborn from 1822 to 1838.

> William Mills, London, 1828
> Overall length 47 in.; barrel 30 in.
> Caliber .70 (14 gauge). Weight of barrels including ramrod 4 lb.; stock 4½ lb.
> Case 32³⁄₁₆ x 9¾ x 3 in.

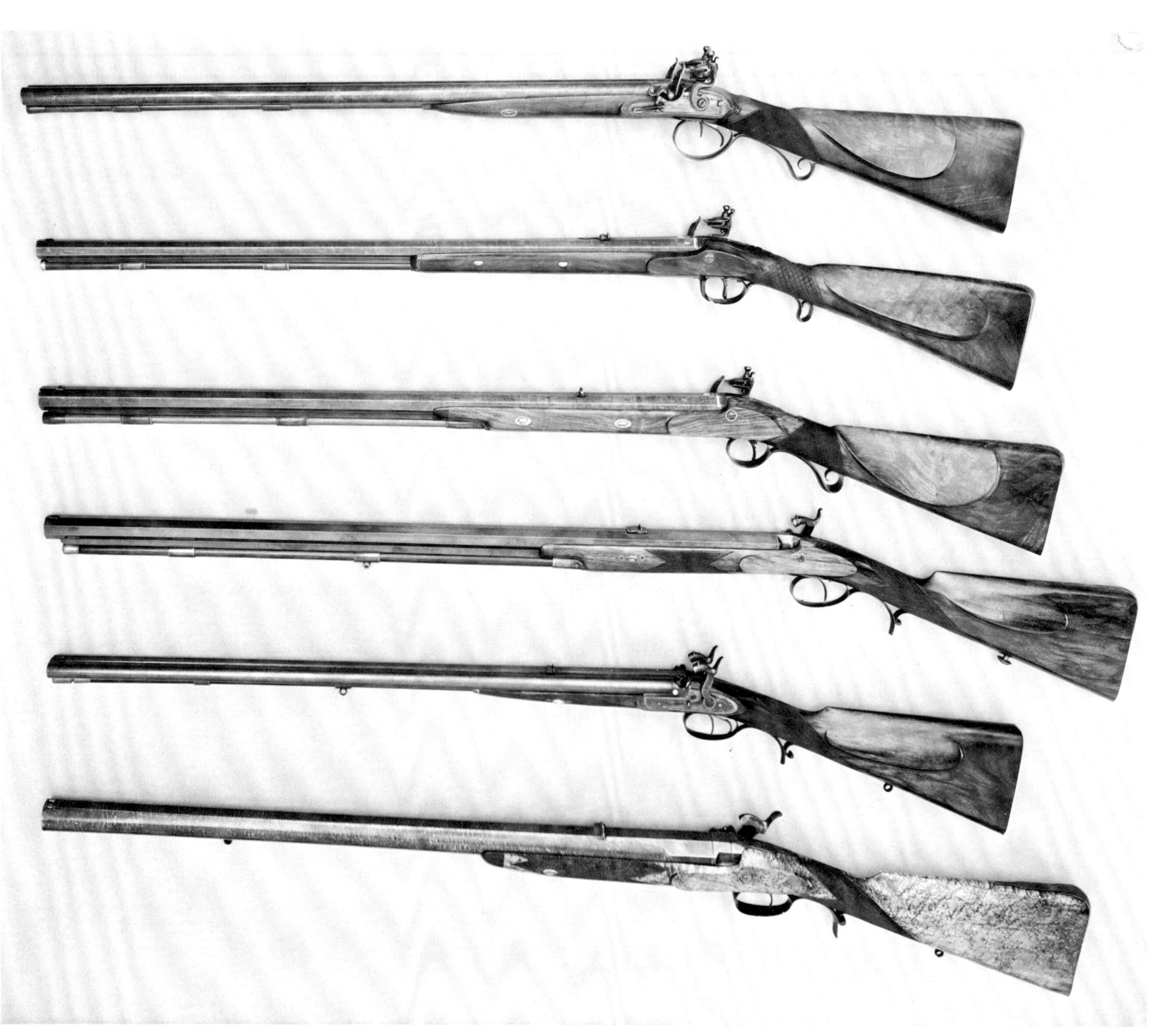

7

SPORTING RIFLES

The rifle was first developed as a sporting piece, since improvements were generally applied to weapons made for noble huntsmen before they were extended to military weapons. The rifle was already highly developed in the 16th century, when a German writer stated that "just as it was considered no art to live well with wine, so too it was no art to shoot well with rifled guns." Both on the Continent and in England, only the privileged hunted, hence there were comparatively few marksmen. A patent for rifled barrels granted in London in 1635 to Arnold Rotsipen has already been mentioned (page 11), but apparently rifling was not widely practiced in England until the 18th century. Benjamin Robins, a mathematician, gave the first known scientific explanation of the superiority of rifled barrels over smooth bores in his *New Principles of Gunnery*, published in London in 1742.

The rifles in the exhibited group date from about 1790 to 1875, before gunmaking became industrialized. During this period, the English makers occupied a position of supremacy, and their skill stimulated a demand for fine sporting rifles. The names John and Joseph Manton, Durs Egg, and James Purdey were internationally known and respected, and their rifles are still esteemed by collectors and sportsmen. Among the exhibited pieces are three specialized rifles; a boar rifle (no. 96), a rifle for shooting American buffalo (no. 97), and an elephant rifle (no. 99). The two Manton rifles (nos. 94 and 96) bear the crest of the dukes of Bedford.

94. Double-barreled Flintlock Rifle
(Bedford 1331)

Barrels, browned twist, with central rib, each rifled with nine grooves; patent breech with transverse gold lines; inscribed in inset gold-lined stamp JOSEPH MANTON PATENT, surmounted by a crown; stationary rear sight on false breech, silver blade front sight. Lock plates flat faced, inscribed JOSEPH MANTON LON-DON and filed with beveled edges; roller bearing on

pan cover riding on elliptical ridge on feather spring; bolt safety engaging at half cock; semiwaterproof gold-lined pan; flash fence integral with pan; cocks have descent arrests. Walnut half stock, with pineapple fore-end; blued steel furniture engraved with flower sprays; butt plate has tang engraved with hunting dog; butt with cheekpiece, checkered at small; oval escutcheon engraved with crest of dukes of Bedford, goat surmounted by coronet; trigger guard of Continental type with pineapple finial; two ramrod pipes; ramrod has

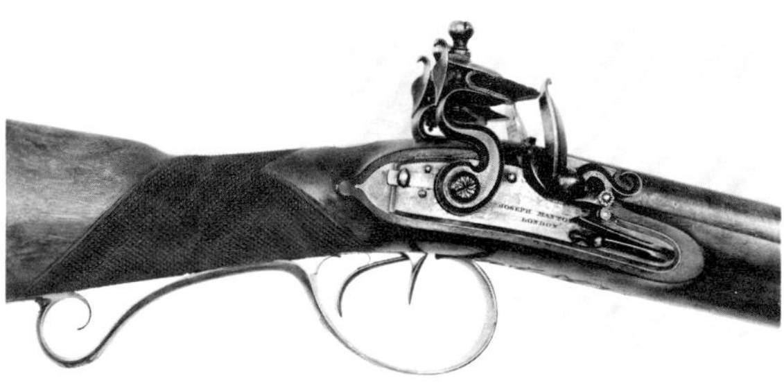

horn finial with concave tip for seating bullet; on opposite end, iron cylindrical powder charger $3\frac{13}{16}$ in. long. Serial number 112.

This number is the earliest known on a firearm by Joseph Manton. The rifle is in mint condition.

Joseph Manton, London, about 1790
Overall length $45\frac{3}{4}$ in.; barrel 30 in.
Caliber .64 (18 gauge). Weight $9\frac{1}{4}$ lb.
Literature: Neal and Back, *The Mantons: Gunmakers*, p. 225, figs. 70–73.

95. Flintlock Rifle
(Bedford 1332)

Barrel, browned twist, octagonal, rifled with nine grooves, top facet over breech with recessed gold-lined mark inscribed D. EGG LONDON, surmounted by crown and flanked on each side by fleur-de-lis; gold transverse band; false breech, with case-hardened finish, engraved with hound; London proofmarks; rear three-leaf sight, silver blade front sight; two barrel slides with silver slots; under-barrel rib. Lock plate, flat faced, inscribed D. EGG, engraved with flower sprays and hound, and filed with beveled edges; vent and pan both gold lined; roller bearing on pan cover riding on elliptical ridge on feather spring; movable tail of lock plate acts as bolt safety locking cock and pan at half cock; hair trigger and detent. Walnut half stock, with carved cheekpiece and spray of flowers behind barrel tang, is checkered at small and has engraved iron fore-end; engraved, blued steel furniture; oval escutcheon engraved with crest of dukes of Bedford, goat surmounted by coronet; single side nail with engraved head secures lock plate; trigger guard has engraved covered-vase

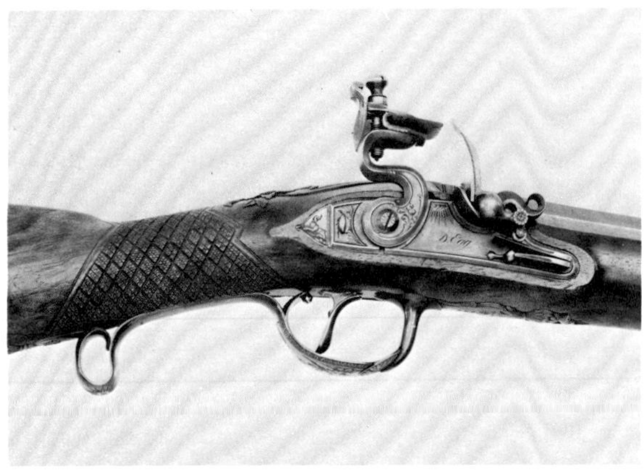

finial; two ramrod pipes; ramrod has brass bullet-seater finial. This rifle is in mint condition.

> Durs Egg, London, about 1785–90
> Overall length 46½ in.; barrel 31 in.
> Caliber .60 (22 gauge). Weight 6½ lb.
> Ex coll. Duke of Bedford

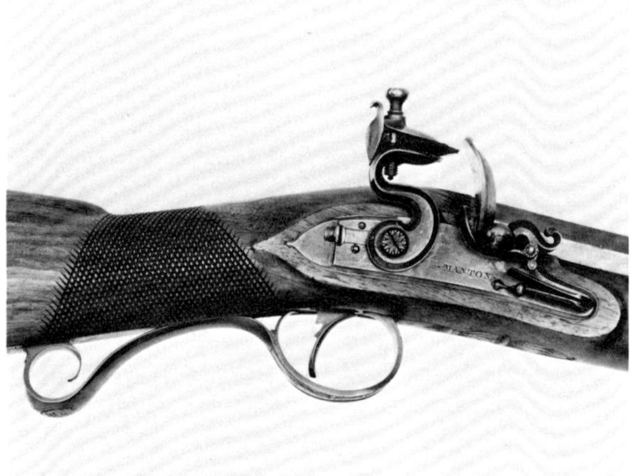

96. Flintlock Boar Rifle (Bedford 1325)

Barrel, browned twist, octagonal, with multi-grooved rifling; top facet at breech has sunken gold oval mark stamped MANTON LONDON with beaded border; London proofmarks on underside of barrel; two barrel slides with silver slots; barrel tang engraved with wounded stag; transverse gold band at breech; brass blade front sight, stationary rear single-leaf iron V-sight; under-barrel rib; gold-lined vent. Lock plate, flat faced, inscribed MANTON, filed with beveled edges; cock has descent arrest; pan cover with roller bearing riding on elliptical ridge on feather spring; flash fence integral with pan; bolt safety engaging at half cock. Three-quarter stock of figured walnut with checkered small, cheekpiece, horn fore-end; blued steel furniture; butt plate engraved with boar; single engraved side nail secures lock plate; gold escutcheon engraved with initial B for duke of Bedford surmounted by coronet; three ramrod pipes; ramrod terminates in

bullet seater. Serial number 1231.

> John Manton, London, 1790
> Overall length 48 in.; barrel 32½ in.
> Caliber .68 (15 gauge). Weight 8¾ lb.
> Ex coll. Duke of Bedford
> Literature: Neal and Back, *The Mantons: Gunmakers*, pp. 66–67, fig. 51.

97. Percussion-cap Rifle (Bedford 1301)

Barrel, Damascus twist, octagonal, rifled with ten grooves, top strap inscribed J. PURDEY 314½ OXFORD STREET LONDON; patent breech with single platinum transverse line, case-hardened finish; under-barrel rib; iron blade front sight, rear three-hinged leaf sight. Lock plate, flat faced, inscribed with name PURDEY, borders engraved with leaf pattern, remainder with scrollwork; dolphin hammer, bolt safety engaging at half cock; flash fence; hair trigger and detent; platinum-lined vent. Figured walnut full stock carved with cheekpiece, and with checkered small and forestock; blued steel furniture engraved with scrollwork; butt plate, checkered, tang engraved with scrolls; obverse of butt has engraved butt trap, interior of cover stamped POWDER 1⅝; single side nail secures lock plate; single barrel slide with engraved iron slots; Continental-type trigger guard, engraved with serial number 4536, has long spur for three fingers, is checkered, and has engraved floral finial; stud and loop for attachment of sling; three ramrod pipes; ramrod with brass rammer and, at opposite end, threaded brass tube with transverse perforation for attaching barrel-cleaning swab.

This rifle, in mint condition, is said to have been made for shooting buffalo on the American plains. It is probably by James Purdey, Jr. (1828–1909), who was apprenticed to his father in 1843 and who took over the business in 1863 when his father died. The firm is still the leading manufacturer of sporting guns in London.

> James Purdey, Jr., London, 1850
> Overall length 52 in.; barrel 36 in.
> Caliber .675 (16 gauge). Weight 10 lb.

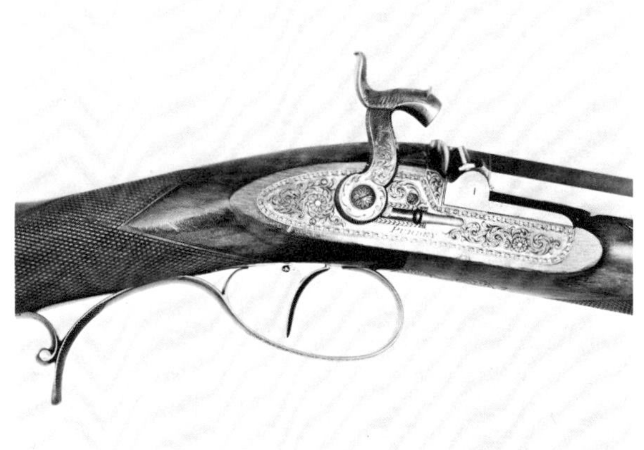

98. Double-barreled Percussion-cap Rifle (Bedford 937)

Barrels, Damascus twist, browned, round in section, each rifled with two wide grooves for belted ball; raised central rib inscribed J. PURDEY 314½ OXFORD STREET LONDON; patent breech with single platinum line, engraved with scrollwork, as is barrel tang; single barrel slide with engraved iron slots; stationary rear sight with two hinged leaves, silver blade front sight. Lock plates, flat faced, inscribed PURDEY and engraved with scrollwork; dolphin hammers; bolt safeties

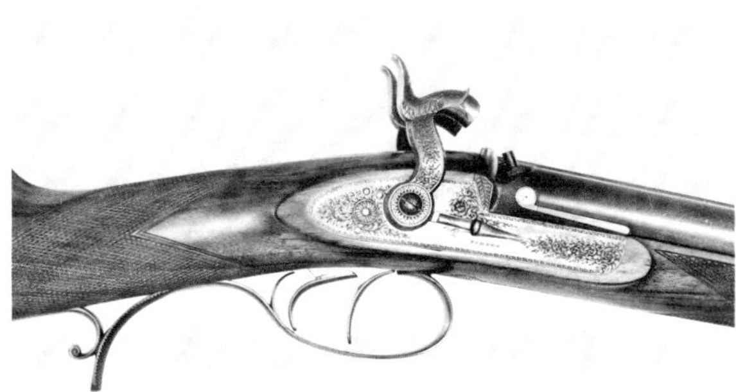

engaging at half cock; platinum-lined safety vents. Figured walnut three-quarter stock with carved cheekpiece, checkered small and forestock; blue steel furniture engraved with scrollwork; butt plate checkered and inscribed CHARGE 3½ DMS NO. 6 POWDER; butt trap on obverse, hinged cover engraved with scrollwork; serial number 6636 engraved on trigger guard; trigger-guard spur is for resting three fingers; two triggers, front one for right lock; ring loops under barrel and butt for sling; two ramrod pipes; ramrod has tubular brass finial (bullet seater) and, on opposite end, elongated brass finial stamped with serial number 6636.

This rifle, in mint condition, was acquired from Messrs. J. Purdey & Sons.

James Purdey, London, 1863
Overall length 47¼ in.; barrel 31 in.
Caliber .50 (37 gauge). Weight 9 lb.

99. Percussion-cap Elephant Rifle (Bedford 1321)

Barrel, browned twist, octagonal at breech, remainder of circular section, but with top facet inscribed CHAS OSBORNE LONDON; rifled with five grooves; patent breech, barrel tang engraved with scrollwork; rear sight with two leaves, one hinged; steel blade front sight; single barrel slide with engraved slots. Lock plate, flat faced, engraved with scrollwork and overlapping-leaf borders and inscribed with name

CHAS OSBORNE; dolphin hammer; platinum-lined safety vent. Three-quarter stock of figured bird's-eye maple, checkered small and forestock, horn fore-end; number 76 stamped near butt on obverse of stock; engraved, blued steel furniture; single side nail secures lock plate; silver escutcheon on underside of butt; ring loops under barrel and butt for sling.

Charles Osborne set up business in 1858 and appears to have worked until about 1865.

Charles Osborne, London, about 1865
Overall length 51 in.; barrel 34 in.
Caliber ¹⁵⁄₁₆ in. (4 gauge). Weight 13¼ lb.

100. Cased Double-barreled Percussion-cap Rifle (Bedford 966)

Barrels, browned twist, rifled with two grooves for belted ball, with raised central rib inscribed J. PURDEY 314½ OXFORD STREET LONDON; underside of each breech stamped with London view mark; underside of each barrel stamped with numeral 17, London proofmarks, and serial number 4474; patent breech with case-hardened finish and platinum safety plugs; stationary rear leaf sight with three hinged leaves, rear one stamped 100; blade front sight; two barrel slides with oval slots. Lock plate, flat faced, inscribed with name PURDEY and engraved with scrollwork; dolphin hammers; bolt safeties engaging at half cock; two triggers, front one releasing right-hand lock. Walnut three-quarter stock, carved with cheek rest, has checkered forestock and small; blued, engraved steel furniture; butt plate is checkered and has engraved tang; trigger guard engraved with serial number 4474, has checkered extension that serves as rest for three fingers; iron ring on stock and on center ramrod pipe for attaching sling.

Complete with original baize-lined oak case with compartments for rifle powder, powder flask, bullet bag, bullet molds, and other accessories. Fittings are engraved with name MAJOR MACNAGHTON. Trade label of James Purdey surmounted by the Royal Arms of William IV and manuscript label giving instructions

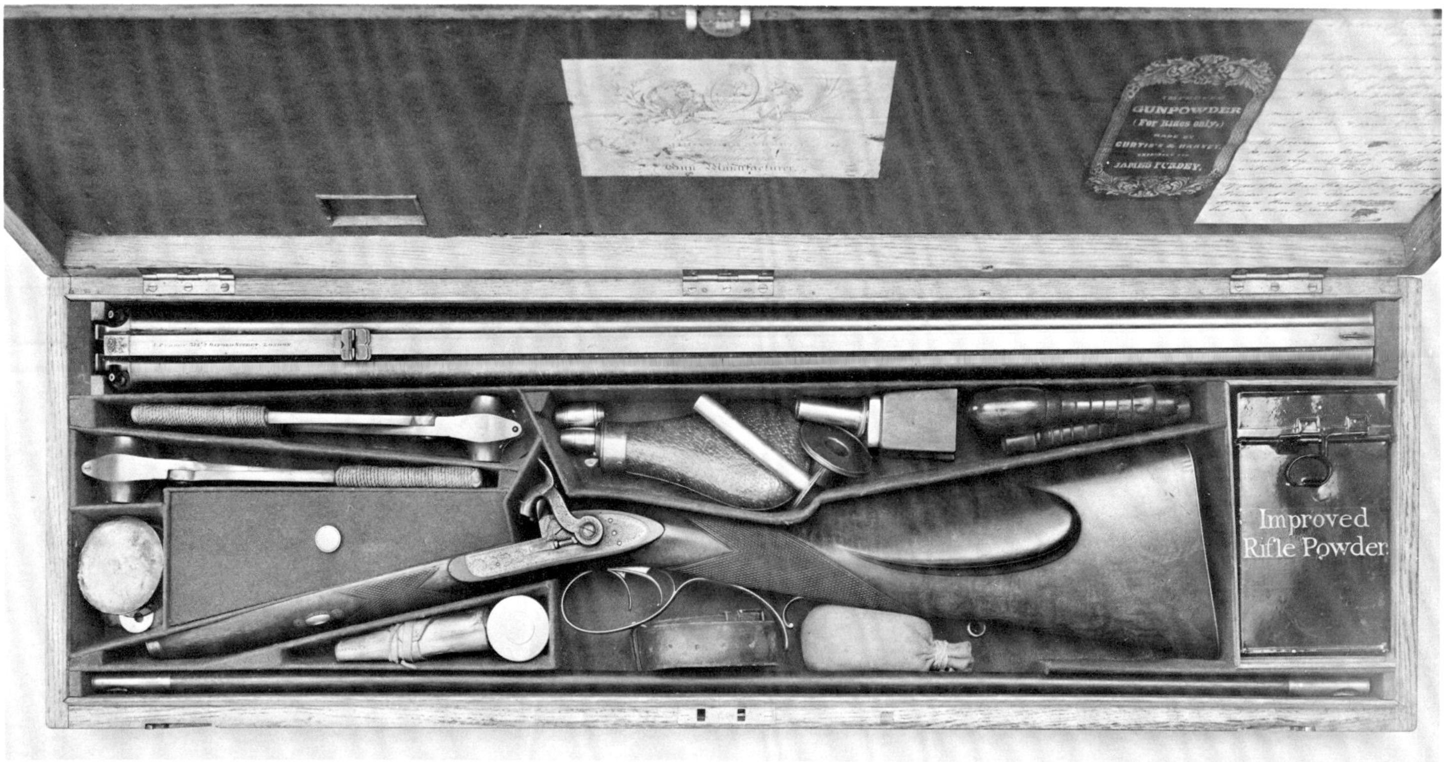

GUNPOWDER
(For Rifles only,)
MADE BY
CURTIS & HARVEY,
SHIPPED TO
JAMES PURDEY.
Improved
Rifle Powder.

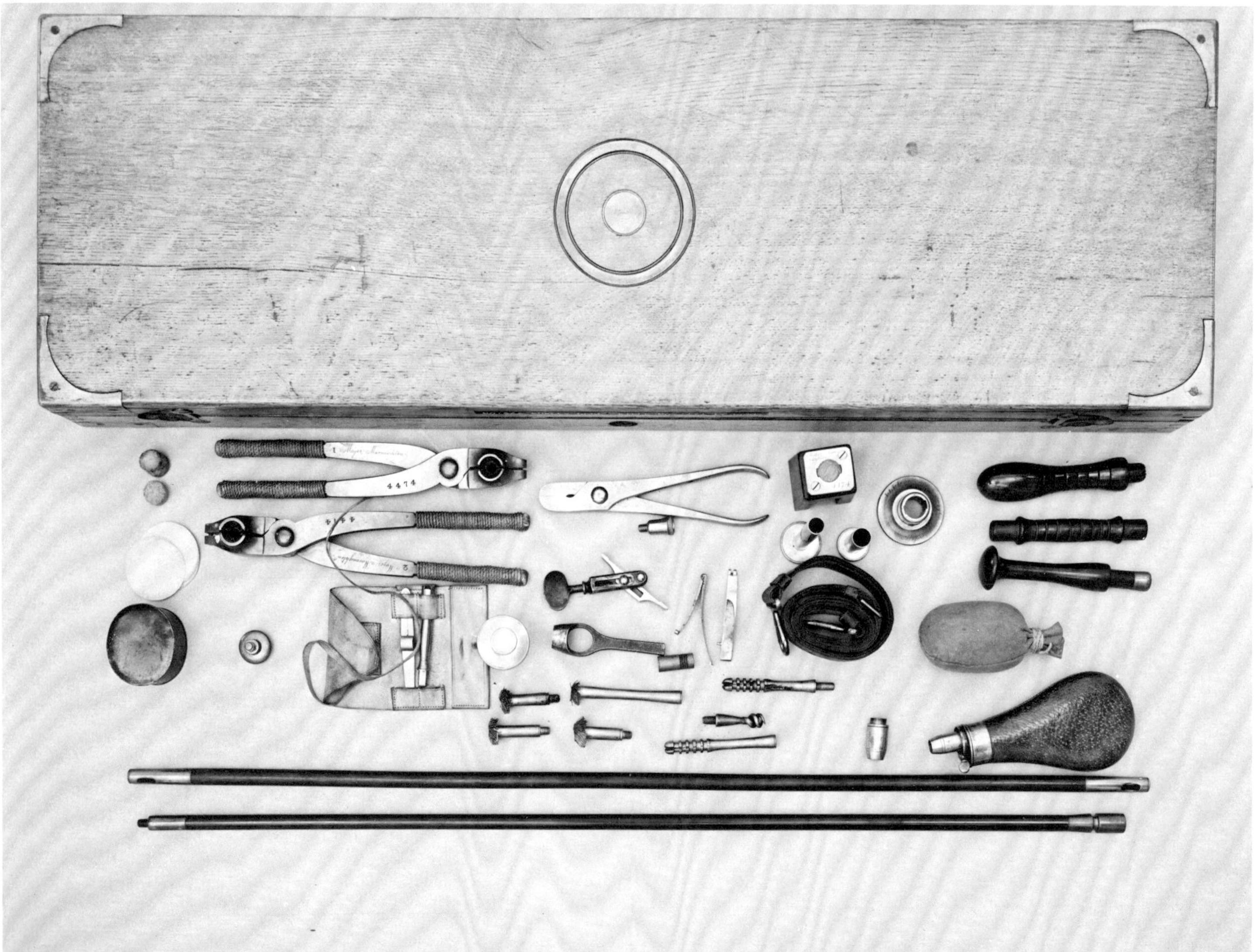

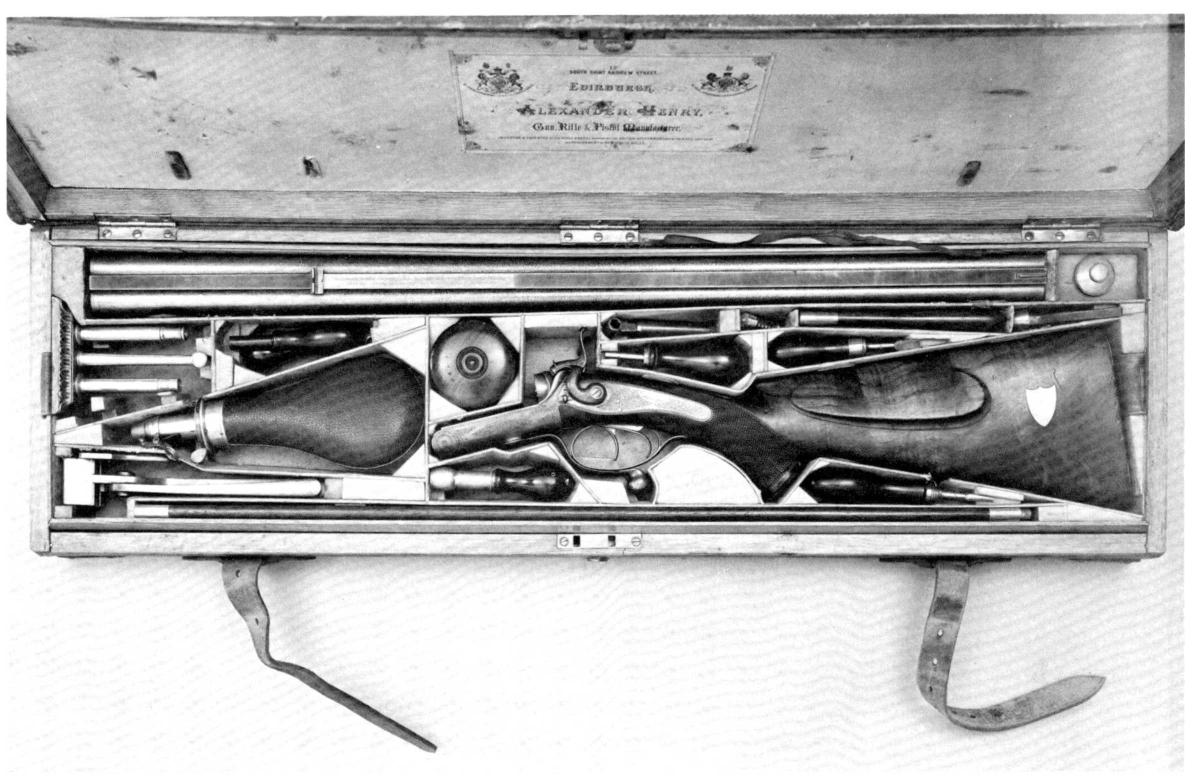

for loading. Also a printed label reading: Improved Gun Powder for Rifles only made by Curtiss & Harvey, expressly for James Purdey. In compartment below the box for black powder is original letter reading: My dear Sir: Please you shoot without the pig and deer, you kill another animal. I will come tomara morning. Signed: Bey Nee Sing Mhorf. The letter is addressed: To the Major, Sir Macnaughton, 8th Hoosier.

James Purdey, London, about 1850

Overall length 31 in.

Caliber .69 (17 gauge). Weight of barrels including ramrod 7 lb.; stock 3¼ lb.

Case 34⅛ x 10⅞ x 3¼ in.

101. Cased Double-barreled Center-fire Cartridge Rifle (Bedford 909)

Barrels, Damascus twist, with polygroove rifling and with raised central rib; barrelsmith's mark AH (Alexander Henry); serial number 3210; in front of rear sight, barrel rib inscribed ALEXR HENRY, 12 SOUTH ST. ANDREW STREET, EDINBURGH. PATENT NO. 2377. MAKER TO THEIR ROYAL HIGHNESSES, THE PRINCE OF WALES AND DUKE OF EDINBURGH; stationary rear sight, and one hinged leaf; blade front sight. Action and back-action locks engraved with scrollwork. Separate half stock and forestock. Figured walnut butt inlaid on obverse with gold shield inscribed FROM VR [Victoria Regina] TO J. BROWN, ESQR CHRISTMAS 1875.

Complete in original leather-covered, pigskin-lined oak case with powder flask and all fittings. Maker's trade label with arms of the Prince of Wales and the Duke of Edinburgh reading: Alexander Henry, Gun, Rifle and Pistol Manufacturer, Inventor & Patentee of the rifle barrel adopted by the British Government and of the rifle adopted by the government of New South Wales. Stamped in gold letters on exterior of case: J. Brown, Esquire, HMP Attendant, Balmoral.

John Brown, Queen Victoria's favorite gillie, eventually became her personal attendant.

Alexander Henry, Edinburgh, about 1875

Overall length 45½ in.; barrel 28 in.

Caliber .45. Weight of barrel 5 lb.; stock 3¼ lb.

Case 34 x 10 x 4½ in.

8

MILITARY GUNS

M ilitary firearms were plain weapons. Edward Davies, in his book *The Art of War* . . . , published in London in 1618–19, gives the soldier this advice: "Hee that lovyth the saftie of his owne person and delights in the goodness and bewtie of a peece, let him always make choice of one that is double breeched, and if it be possible, a myllan [Milan] peece, for they be of tough and perfecte temper, light, square and big of breech, and very strong where the powder doth lie, and where the violent force of the fire does consist, and, notwithstanding, trimme at the ends. Our English peeces approache very nigh unto to them in goodnesse and bewty (theyr heavinesse onlie excepted) so that they be made on purpose, and not one of those common sale peeces with round barrels, whereunto a beaton [experienced] souldier will have a great respect, and rather choose to pay double money for a good peece than to spare his purse and endanger himselfe."

The exhibited group includes pieces dating from about 1580 to about 1775; service firearms for all the rulers from Queen Elizabeth I to George III are included. Two Elizabethan guns, a matchlock musket that was carried in the Trained Bands (no. 102) and a snaphance carbine (no. 103), are extraordinarily rare. Another rarity is the James II grenade flintlock rifle made about 1687 by James Peddell (no. 105). The name *Brown Bess* is now used to describe all types of British military flintlock muskets made from 1720 to 1840. Three examples (nos. 108–110), two of which are signed by gunmakers and dated, are included. The Ferguson breech-loading rifle made by the distinguished gunmaker Durs Egg is of historical interest (no. 111). It was developed and patented in 1776 by Captain Patrick Ferguson of the 71st Highlanders to counteract the American riflemen, who were an effective arm of the American forces. One hundred of these rifles were made for the British army in 1776. Despite its origin, Ferguson's breechloader is regarded as American because its first appearance as a weapon of war was on the battlefields of America.

102. Matchlock Musket (Bedford 1312)

Barrel, octagonal, stationary rear sight, bead front sight. Matchlock action, match holder of steel, shaped in form of eagle's head and pierced with aperture to represent eye; pan forged separately from lock plate and attached by screw; pivoted pan cover with pear-shaped grip; large flash fence, end of which keys into right-hand side of rear sight. Walnut full stock profusely inlaid throughout entire length with engraved staghorn and mother-of-pearl; shoulder stock with iron heel plate cut with deep depression for thumb; butt inlaid with birds and monsters and mother-of-pearl roundels within staghorn scrolls; on obverse of butt, mother-of-pearl shield engraved with arms of Worshipful Company of Haberdashers, London; on cheek side, similar shield engraved with initials OC (original owner); iron trigger guard with extension for third and fourth fingers; horn ramrod pipes engraved with warrior's head and similar horn plaque inlaid in front of trigger guard.

102

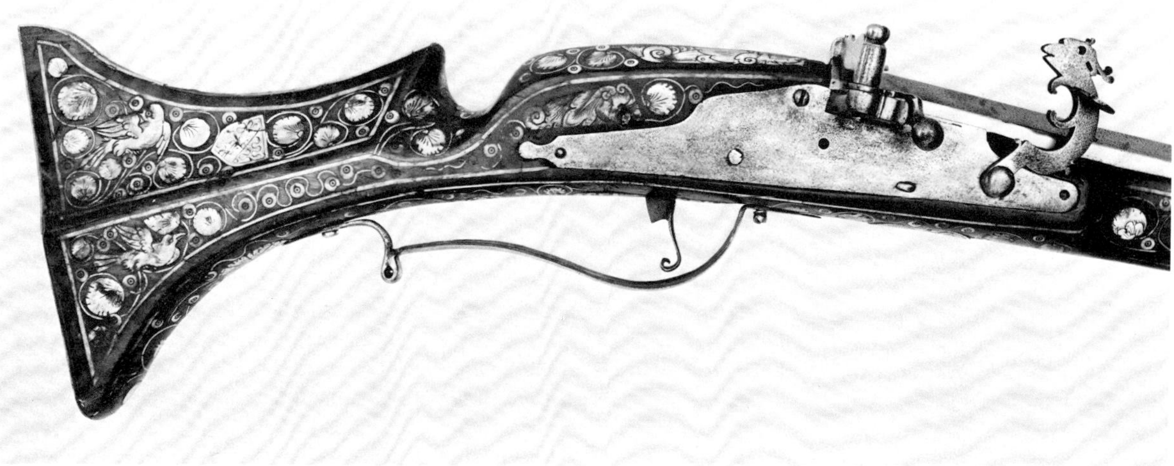

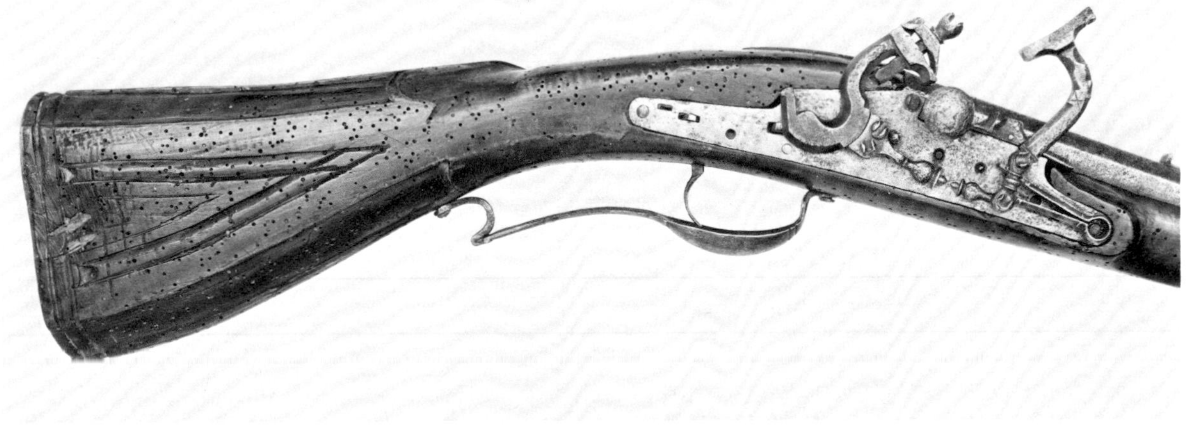

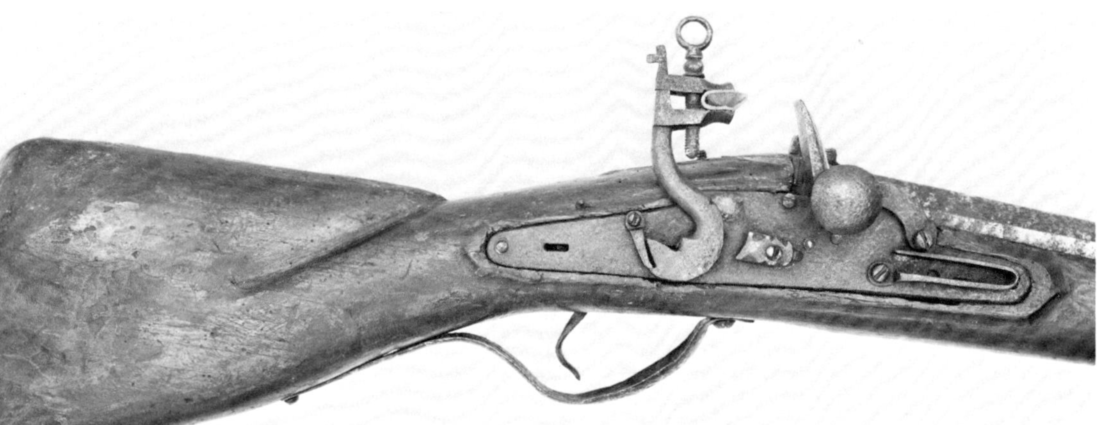

This musket seems to be the only surviving example of a weapon carried by the London Trained Bands in the reign of Elizabeth I. The owner was evidently in the Haberdashers' Company, members of which were responsible for paying for their own firearms.

About 1580

Overall length 62½ in.; barrel 48 in.

Caliber .78 (10 gauge). Weight 11½ lb.

Literature: Hayward, "English Firearms of the 16th Century."

secured by two side nails; trough-shaped trigger guard, with extension for third and fourth fingers, secured by two screws, front screw continuing vertically through stock to secure barrel tang.

This is the only known surviving example of an Elizabethan snaphance carbine.

About 1600

Overall length 42 in.; barrel 27⅞ in.

Caliber .68 (16 gauge). Weight 5½ lb.

103. Elizabeth I Snaphance Carbine
(Bedford 1341)

Barrel, octagonal, with large circular vent, rear stationary leaf sight, iron bead front sight. Lock plate, flat faced, half cock set by pivoted dog catch (lacking) engaging toe of cock, full cock by sear passing through lock plate and resting on heel of cock; buffer with vase finial for arresting fall of cock; pan forged separately, screwed to lock plate; steel and feather spring with vase finial, secured by bridle screws. Walnut full stock, forestock restored, butt and stock in front of lock carved with ridged and paneled ornament; iron furniture; lock

104. James I Dog-lock Musket
(Bedford 1316)

Barrel in two stages with molded girdle between, octagonal at breech, forward stage round; stationary rear sight, bead front sight. Lock plate, flat faced, with horizontal sear; half cock set by dog catch engaging heel of cock, full cock by sear passing through aperture in lock plate and engaging top of heel of cock; cock buffer and pan cover screwed to lock plate; ring-headed cock-jaw screw. Club-butt full stock; wrought-iron furniture; two sheet-iron barrel bands, no butt plate, lock secured by three side nails; flat strip trigger guard,

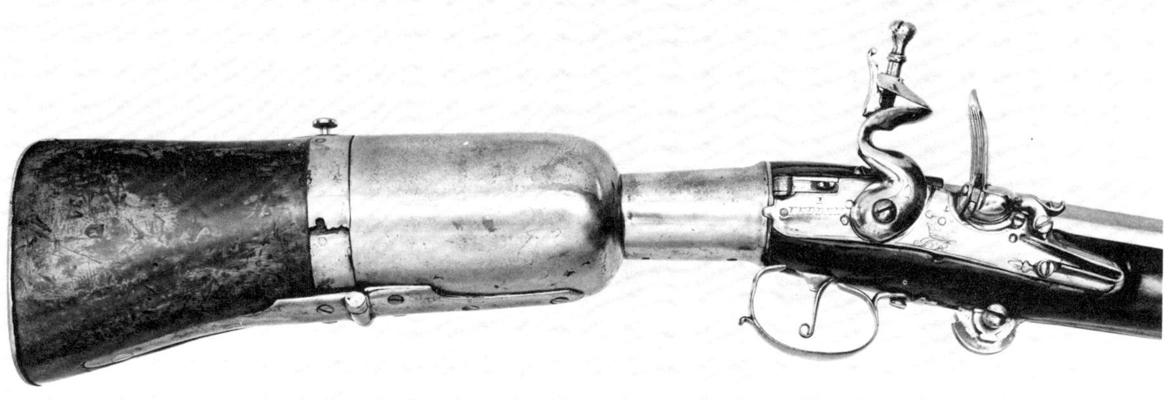

105

forward screw that secures trigger guard continues through stock to barrel tang.

    About 1610

    Overall length 70 in.; barrel 54¼ in.

    Caliber 13⁄16 in. (9 gauge). Weight 19 lb.

    Literature: Blackmore, *British Military Firearms*, pp. 33, 51.

105. James II Grenade Flintlock Rifle
(Bedford 923)

Barrel in three stages separated by molded girdles, octagonal changing to polygonal at breech, forward stages of circular section ending in muzzle ring; Ordnance proofmarks; blade front sight; single barrel band; barrel tang is extended backward to reach circular brass plate forming base of mortar-grenade barrel; latter is deep cup-shaped receptacle of steel hinged to rear part of butt and stamped on base with crowned cipher JR (James Rex). Lock plate with rounded face inscribed I. PEDDELL and engraved with crowned cipher J2R (James II); steel has vertically serrated inner face. Flintlock adapted to fire either charge in barrel or charge in chamber of grenade barrel; tube runs along inside of lock plate connecting priming pan to grenade cup; this can be filled with priming powder through rectangular receptacle with hinged door behind cock; receptacle is controlled by shutter in rear of pan, which can be raised when grenade is to be fired. Walnut stock, stamped 234 near butt end, in two parts, butt hinged by iron strap to underside of grenade cup; brass butt plate; forestock with brass serpentine side plate in front of which is recess with ramrod; three brass ramrod pipes; folding iron supporting rest is hinged to forestock in front of trigger guard; rest is locked in place by hinged stirrup near muzzle.

John Tinker, an Ordnance fireworker, invented this combined musket and grenade thrower in 1681 and was awarded a pension of five pounds per quarter for it. A minute in the Ordnance Records refers to three gunmakers, among them James Peddell, stocking and locking brass hand mortar pieces made by the Ordnance

brass founder William Wightman at Moorfields. Three only of these combined weapons are known to have survived; the other two are in the Tower of London. James Peddell was master of the Gunmakers' Company from 1703 to 1705.

    James Peddell, London, about 1687

    Overall length 53¾ in.; barrel 38½ in.

    Caliber .69 (14 gauge). Weight 12 lb.

    Literature: Grose, *Military Antiquities*, vol. II, p. 363, pl. 49; Blackmore, *British Military Firearms*, p. 35, pl. 9; Sherlock, "Early British Grenade Launchers."

106. William III Service Flintlock Musket
(Bedford 904)

Barrel in two stages, octagonal changing to polygonal at breech, remainder round, with molded girdle between; blade front sight; Ordnance proof and barrelsmith's initials RC. Lock plate with rounded face engraved with crowned cipher WR (William III); lock, with vertically acting sear, secured by three side nails. Walnut full stock with iron strap trigger guard; butt plate and ramrod pipes of brass.

    1695–1700

    Overall length 61 in.; barrel 45¾ in.

    Caliber .77 (10 gauge). Weight 11 lb.

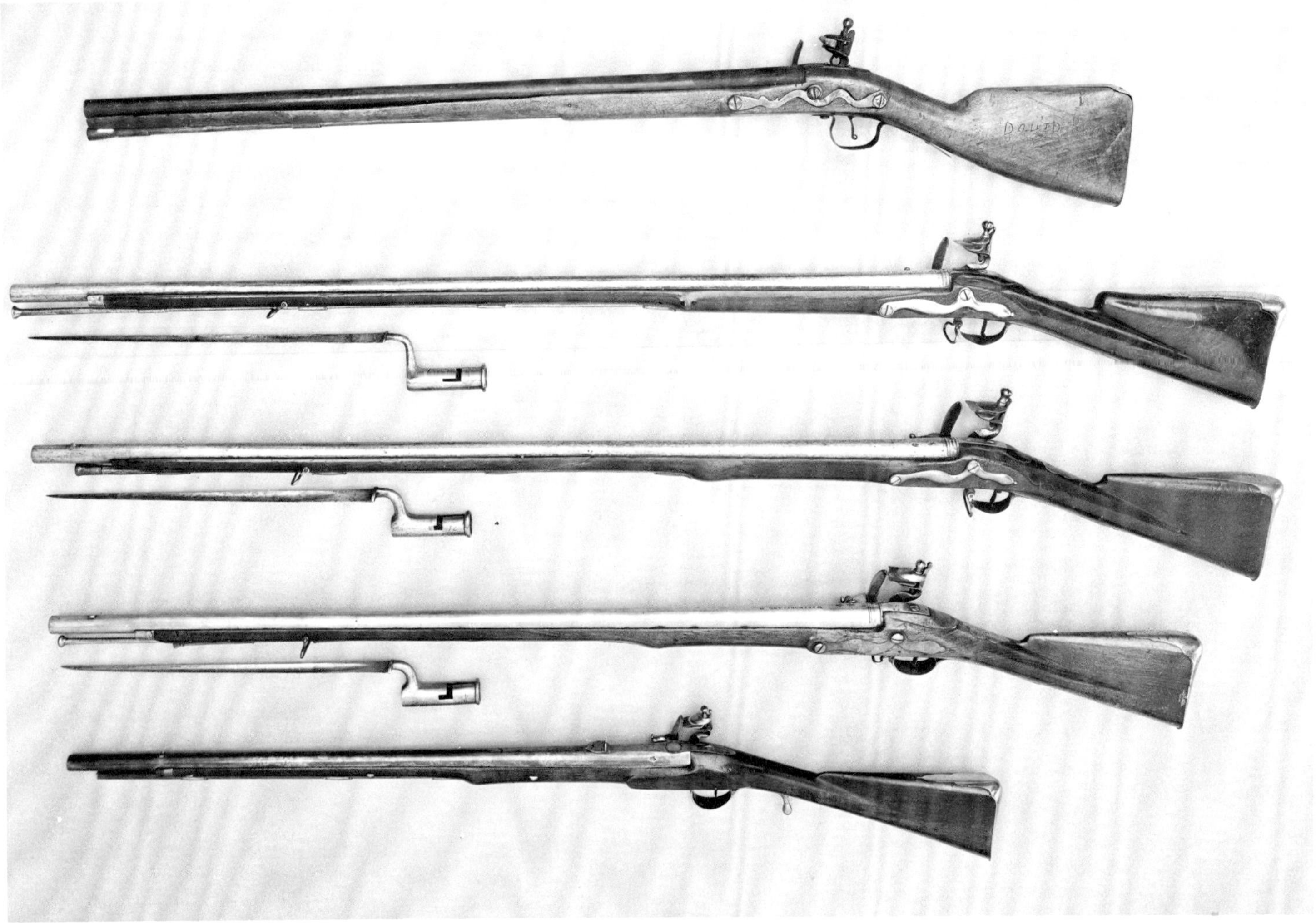

107. Queen Anne Service Dog-lock Musket
(Bedford 1314)

Barrel of circular section cut down from 45 in.; Ordnance proofmarks; three barrel pins. Lock plate, flat faced, with dog catch engaging between half and full cock; engraved with crowned cipher AR (Anne Regina) and broad-arrow mark, on tail are name I. BENNETT and numeral 7, apparently meaning 1707;

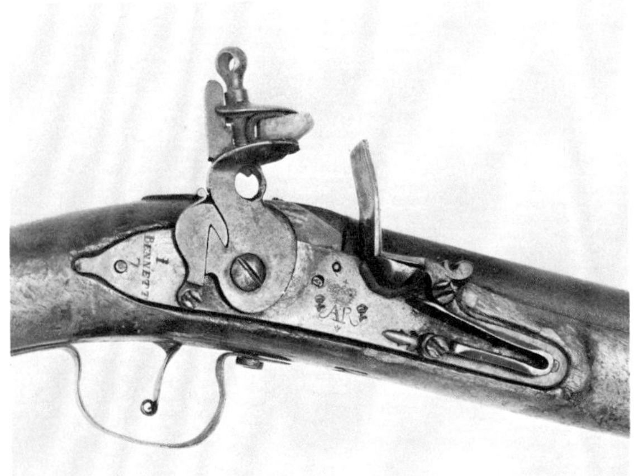

loop-neck cock. Walnut full stock, cut down at same time as barrel, carved with initials WT in front of trigger guard; brass furniture; butt inscribed at later date with name DAVID BALCH; flat strip butt plate; serpentine side plate with three side nails; iron trigger guard; two brass ramrod pipes; ramrod with bone finial.

John Bennett was admitted freeman of the Gunmakers' Company in 1686 and was master in 1721.

John Bennett, 1707

Overall length 50½ in.; barrel 35¼ in.

Caliber .80 (9 gauge). Weight 9 lb.

Literature: Blackmore, *British Military Firearms*, p. 42, pl. 5, ill. at bottom; p. 282, no. 86.

108. George I Brown Bess Flintlock Musket with Bayonet
(Bedford 964)

Barrel of circular section, engraved over breech L D J O N KERR (Lord John Kerr); Ordnance proofmark; on front of barrel is stud for securing socket bayonet and serving as front sight. Lock plate, rounded with engraved borders, crowned cipher GR (George Rex), signature and date CLINTON 1726 on tail, and number 1; flash fence. Walnut full stock, cut back slightly for socket bayonet, has steel strap fore-end; iron furniture; butt with shaped comb; serpentine side plate with two side nails; butt plate with tang; escutcheon; trigger guard with vase finial; sling swivel attached to front of trigger guard and in front of second ramrod pipe.

Lord John Kerr, a younger son of the Earl of Crawford, presumably used this musket when a volunteer.

    Clinton, 1726
    Overall length 62¼ in.; barrel 46 in.
    Caliber. 78 (12 gauge). Weight 10 lb.; bayonet 1 lb.
    Literature: Blackmore, *British Military Firearms*, pl. 12, p. 283, fig. 88.

109. George II Brown Bess Flintlock Musket with Bayonet   (Bedford 355)

Barrel of rounded section, inscribed over breech ROYAL WELSH FUZILIERS; four barrel pins. Lock plate, rounded, with engraved borders, stamped with broad arrow and crown, and crowned cipher GR (George Rex), on tail signed ES COLE (Elias Cole) and dated 1730. Walnut full stock set back slightly for socket bayonet; brass furniture; tang of butt plate engraved with name CAPT. BERNARD and NO. 39; serpentine side plate with two side nails; escutcheon engraved with letter H (H Company) and NO. 39; trigger guard with bottle-shaped finial, two sling swivels; four ramrod pipes; wood ramrod with brass rammer finial. Socket bayonet marked $\frac{5}{11}$; tapering triangular blade with mid-ridge on one side extending entire length; numeral 6 stamped on flat face, at junction of blade and socket is inspector's mark.

This type of firearm was known as the long land musket. In view of the musket's great weight, it seems unlikely that it was carried by an officer. Perhaps H Company was commanded by Captain Bernard.

    Elias Cole, 1730
    Overall length 62 in.; barrel 46 in.
    Caliber .78 (10 gauge). Weight 10½ lb.; bayonet 1 lb.
    Literature: Blackmore, *British Military Firearms*, pl. 15, no. 1.

110. George III Brown Bess Flintlock Musket with Socket Bayonet   (Bedford 365)

Barrel of circular section, engraved over breech WESTMORELAND M (Militia); Ordnance proofmark. Lock plate, rounded, with engraved borders, stamped with broad arrow crowned and crowned cipher GR (George Rex), on tail inscribed TOWER. Walnut full stock, set back for socket bayonet, has brass fore-end; brass furniture; butt plate with tang has pedestal-and-vase finial; flat serpentine side plate has two side nails; vase-shaped escutcheon inscribed with numbers 8 and 39; these numbers are also inscribed on iron ramrod, which has expanded finial for ramming ball; steel ramrod pipe; two steel sling swivels; socket bayonet stamped with maker's name GILL.

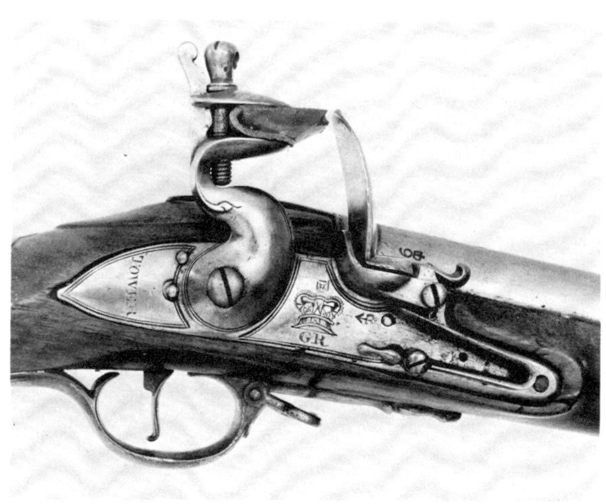

This type of musket was known as the short land patent, or militia new patent.

About 1765

Overall length 57½ in.; barrel 42 in.

Caliber .80 (8 gauge). Weight 10 lb.; bayonet 1 lb.

Literature: Blackmore, *British Military Firearms*, pl. 15, no. 3.

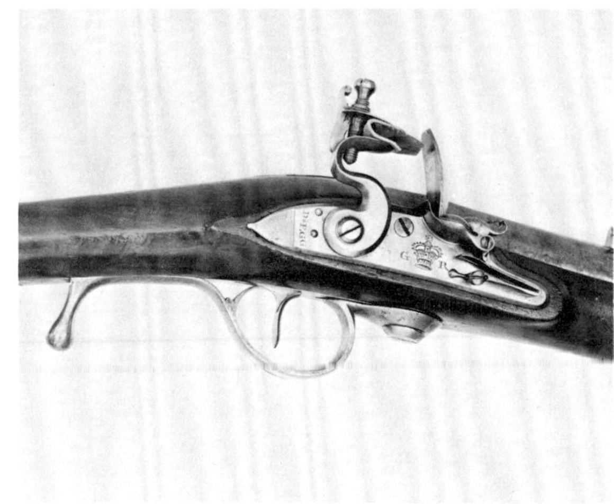

111. George III Ferguson Breech-loading Rifle   (Bedford 337)

Barrel of circular section, except for top facet over breech, inscribed D. EGG LONDON; rifled with seven grooves; rear two-leaf sight; blade front sight; three barrel slides; under-barrel stud for socket bayonet. Lock plate, flat faced, with beveled edges, signed D. EGG on tail, engraved with crowned cipher GR (George Rex); lock screwed on from lock side; breech screw attached to trigger guard opens breech by single turn of ten-threaded screw-bolt handle; trigger guard locked by peg on trigger plate that fits into slot in trigger guard. Walnut full stock, set back at muzzle for socket bayonet, has brass band at fore-end; brass furniture; butt plate with tang; three ramrod pipes; wood ramrod with brass finial and, on opposite end, threaded brass tube for attaching interchangeably worm and jag.

Durs Egg, London, about 1776

Overall length 47½ in.; barrel 32¼ in.

Caliber .64 (18 gauge). Weight 8 lb.

Literature: Blackmore, *British Military Firearms*, pp. 71–72, 82–86, pl. 24, fig. 12.

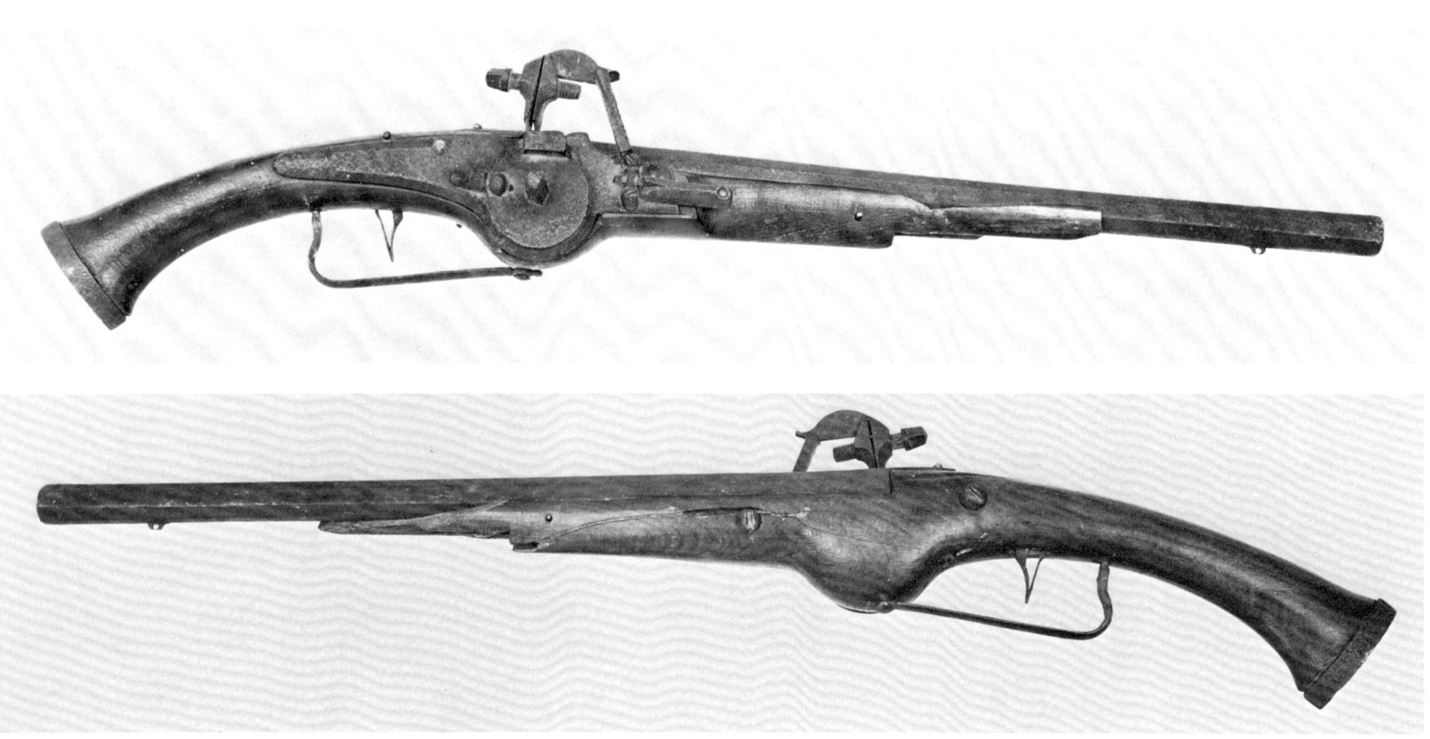

9

MILITARY PISTOLS

The thirteen service cavalry pistols catalogued here were used during the reigns of James I to George III. They date from 1610 to 1796. The inclusion of the royal cipher on several of the pistols is helpful in identifying the reign to which each belongs. The first successful pistols used the wheel-lock mechanism, a single wheel-lock pistol dating about 1610 being represented here. The particular merit of the wheel-lock pistol is that it could be fired with one hand and thus could be used by a horseman. However, it was so costly to produce that it was not used on a large scale. Following the wheel-lock chronologically are two pistols with English locks and a sequence of flintlocks. Five of the lock plates are dated and bear the word Tower (Small Gun Office in the Tower of London), or the name of the contractor who made the arm.

These service pistols were carried by enlisted men. Officers carried pistols that generally resembled the issued pistols but were custom-made and frequently shorter and lighter (nos. 6–39). Nevertheless, the military pistols were made under the direction of the best contemporary gunmakers. Two of the pistols (nos. 115 and 118) are signed, one by Robert Brooke, the other by John Sibley, both of whom were masters of the Gunmakers' Company. During the short reign of James II (1685–88), the contract for supplying the new weapons, the first English "Government Arm" of a distinctive type, made exactly to pattern and intended for the use of the regular troops, was given to Robert Brooke.

Early militia arms had been subject only to regulations fixing their caliber and barrel length. The service pistols described here vary in caliber from .55 to .78 and in barrel length from 9 to 15 inches, the earliest pistol, the wheel-lock, having the longest barrel, and the flintlock pistol made about 1796 having the largest caliber, .78 (10 gauge). Since no standard bore was observed for these early pistols, each pair was provided with a bullet mold, in which the trooper cast his own "shott."

112. James I Wheel-lock
Holster Pistol (Bedford 1535)

Barrel, octagonal, shows traces of mark near end

of breech, is fixed by pins and single screw passing from underside of stock into barrel tang. Flat-faced wheel lock with wheel guide; bridle connects cock and cock spring. Beech stock, forward part lacking; fishtail butt encircled by iron band; three side nails secure lock plate; iron trigger guard, spring behind trigger; trigger tang secured by pin above lock plate.

This pistol is known to have hung on the wall of Petworth House from the period of the English Civil War (1640–49) until recently. Although most of its features are international, the form of the butt makes an English provenance likely.

About 1610
Overall length 23¼ in.; barrel 15 in.
Caliber .55 (28 gauge). Weight 2¼ lb.
Literature: Christie's sale, July 8, 1970, lot 25.

113. Charles I English-lock
Holster Pistol (Bedford 894)

Barrel in two stages, breech octagonal changing to polygonal, remainder round, with molded girdle between; London proofmarks near breech. Lock plate, flat faced, through which passes horizontally operating sear to engage tail of cock at half cock; dog safety catch operating between half and full cock; buffer screwed to front of lock to arrest cock; head of cock screw is perforated and does not have groove for screwdriver; perforation was aid when replacing used flints; bridle between steel and feather-spring screws; exterior iron screw secures separate pan cover; lock secured by three side nails. Varnished walnut full stock with fishtail butt; iron collar around butt, that around fore-end missing; embryonic leaf carved behind barrel tang; flat strip trigger guard; single ramrod pipe; ramrod passes through pipe and into stock socket.

A number of English-lock pistols have survived, some in homes with Civil War associations, wherefore there is no reason to doubt that they represent the type of the period. This pistol differs from no. 114 in the following respects: the horizontal sear passes through the lock plate; there is an applied buffer; a bridle joins the steel and feather spring. Both pistols have a priming pan, secured by a screw, that is not integral with the lock plate.

About 1640
Overall length 21½ in.; barrel 13½ in.
Caliber .60 (22 gauge). Weight 2 lb.

114. English-lock Pistol (Bedford 812)

Barrel in two stages, breech octagonal changing to polygonal, forward stage round, separated by molded girdle; London proofmarks and indistinct barrelsmith's mark, letter P surmounted by leaf. Lock plate, flat faced, with horizontally acting sear that, unlike the one on

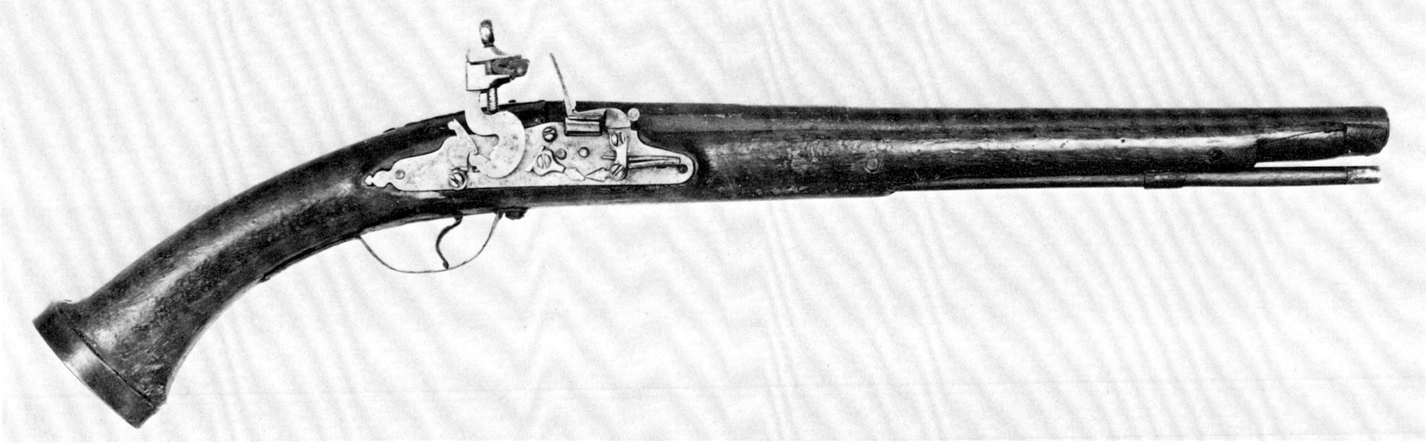

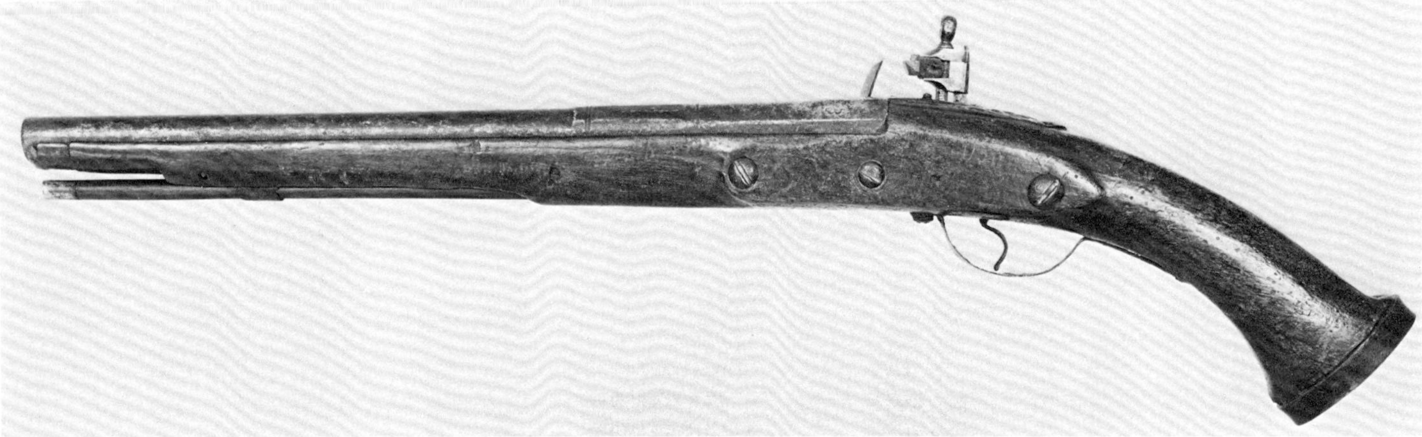

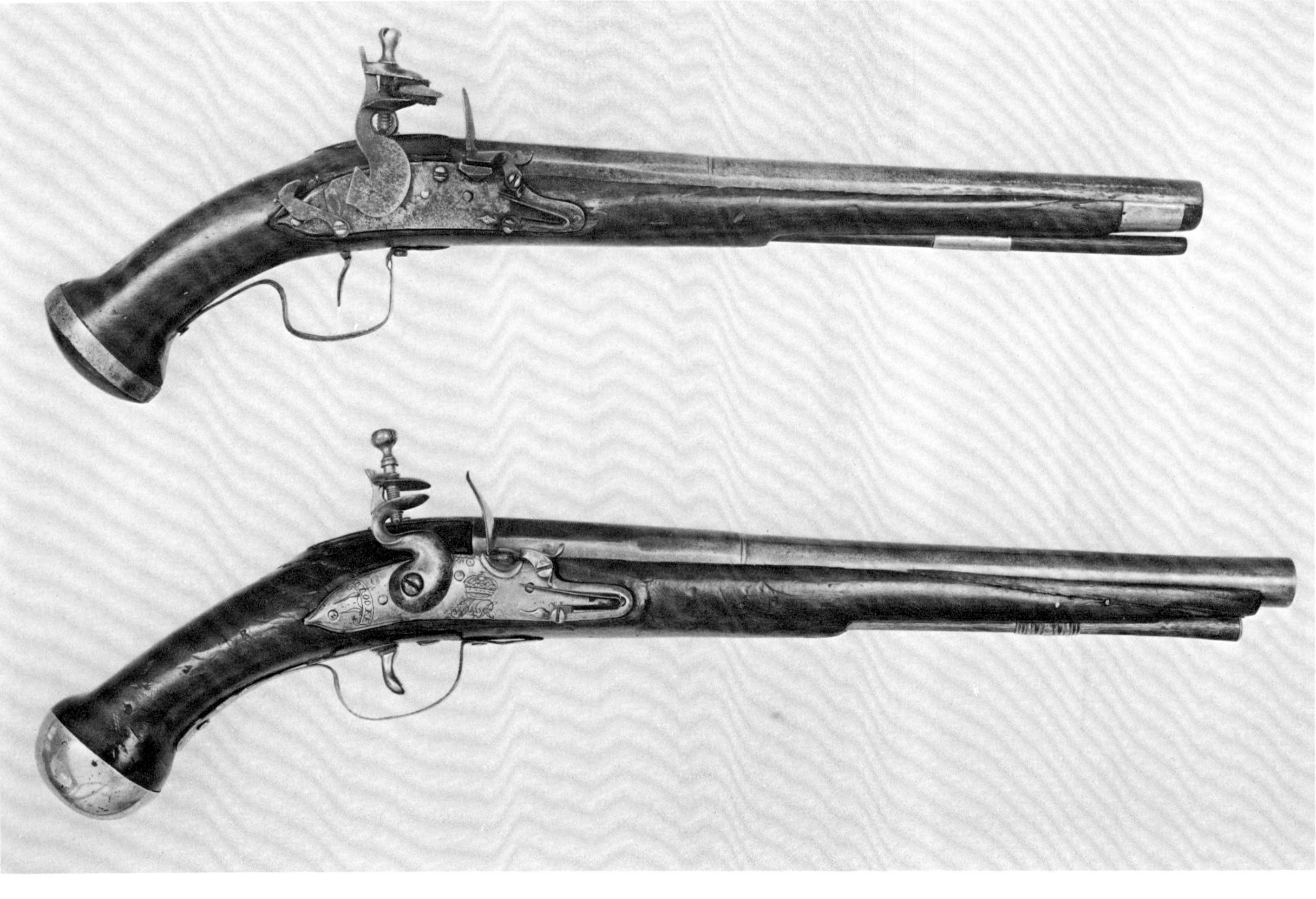

no. 113, does not penetrate lock plate; dog safety; three side nails; steel of rectangular outline; flat-faced cock has shoulder on inner face that acts on descent arrest; priming pan is separate element. Walnut full stock with fishtail butt reinforced by iron band; brass band around fore-end; iron strip trigger guard; screw securing front end of trigger guard passes vertically through stock and secures barrel tang; brass ramrod pipe.

> About 1645–50
> Overall length 19¼ in.; barrel 12⅝ in.
> Caliber .59 (23 gauge). Weight 2 lb.

115. James II Service-pattern Horse Pistol   (Bedford 1196)

Barrel in two stages, octagonal at breech changing to polygonal, remainder round, girdle between; on top of barrel, Ordnance proofmark and barrelsmith's mark RB crowned (Robert Brooke); tang wrought with barrel and secured by vertical screw inserted from underside of stock. Lock plate, round faced, with vertically acting sear, engraved with name BROOKE in ribbon and crowned cipher JR (James Rex). Walnut stock roughly carved behind barrel tang; three side nails; brass pommel cap; baluster ramrod pipe, trigger plate, and ramrod disk finial; iron trigger guard restored; thick trigger shaped for finger.

Robert Brooke was master of the Gunmakers' Company in 1679–80. He died in 1689. The earliest and latest dates of references to Brooke and his widow Mary in the ledgers of the Board of Ordnance are 1678 and 1694.

> Robert Brooke, London, about 1685–89
> Overall length 20¾ in.; barrel 13⅞ in.
> Caliber .59 (23 gauge). Weight 3½ lb.
> Literature: Blackmore, *British Military Firearms*, p. 55, ill. at top; p. 281, mark 42; May, "Some Board of Ordnance Gunmakers," p. 202; Hewitt, "Notice of the Combined Use of the Match-lock and the Flint-lock, in the Progressive Improvements of Firearms" (lock plate engraved with the name Brooke and the crowned cipher JR).

116. James II Service-pattern Horse Pistol   (Bedford 1177)

Barrel has unidentifiable barrelsmith's mark. Lock engraved with cipher J2R (James II) surmounted by crown. Iron trigger guard and barrel tang secured by iron nail that extends vertically through stock.

> About 1687
> Overall length 21¼ in.; barrel 13¹¹⁄₁₆ in.
> Caliber .61 (21 gauge). Weight 2½ lb.
> Literature: Blackmore, *British Military Firearms*, p. 283, ills. 82–83.

117. William III Service-pattern Horse Pistol   (Bedford 1032)

Barrel in two stages, octagonal changing to polygonal at breech, forward stage round, girdle between; on top facet are Ordnance proofmark and barrelsmith's mark R in oval; barrel secured by two transverse pins, and barrel-tang screw inserted from bottom of stock. Lock plate, rounded, inscribed with cipher WR surmounted by crown, as used by William III after death of Queen Mary in 1694; lock secured by two side nails. Maple full stock with brass butt cap and brass baluster ramrod pipe; plain ramrod fits through pipe and into stock socket; iron trigger guard has vase finial.

This pistol was restocked in America between 1700 and 1725. The rear end of the lock plate, broken before then, is now secured by two instead of three side nails.

> About 1696
> Overall length 21 in.; barrel 14 in.
> Caliber .63 (17 gauge). Weight 2½ lb.
> Literature: Blackmore, *British Military Firearms*, p. 281, fig. 40; Mayer, *Flintlocks of the Iroquois, 1620–1687*, p. 35, fig. 17.

118. Queen Anne Service-pattern Horse Pistol   (Bedford 1541)

Barrel in two stages, octagonal changing to polygonal at breech, forward stage of round section, girdle between; barrel stamped with Ordnance proofmark and barrelsmith's mark IS (John Sibley); barrel tang secured by vertical screw inserted from bottom of stock. Lock plate, rounded, engraved with cipher AR (Anne Regina) surmounted by crown, broad arrow crowned, name I SIBLEY, and numeral 6 for 1706; cock with descent arrest; flash fence integral with pan cover. Walnut full stock carved with ridge around barrel tang; brass furniture; grip stamped H6C; butt cap engraved on each side with monogram AR; flat strip side plate.

John Sibley is recorded between 1687 and 1715 in the Board of Ordnance Ledger in the Admiralty Library, London. He was admitted freeman of the Gunmakers' Company in 1685 and was master in 1705.

> John Sibley, London, 1706
> Overall length 20¾ in.; barrel 13⅞ in.
> Caliber .63 (17 gauge). Weight 3 lb.
> Literature: Blackmore, *British Military Firearms*, p. 55, ill. at bottom; May, "Some Board of Ordnance Gunmakers," p. 203.

119. George I Service-pattern Horse Pistol   (Bedford 723)

Barrel round, stamped near breech with cipher GR crowned (George Rex), broad arrow, and crossed scep-

113
113
114
115

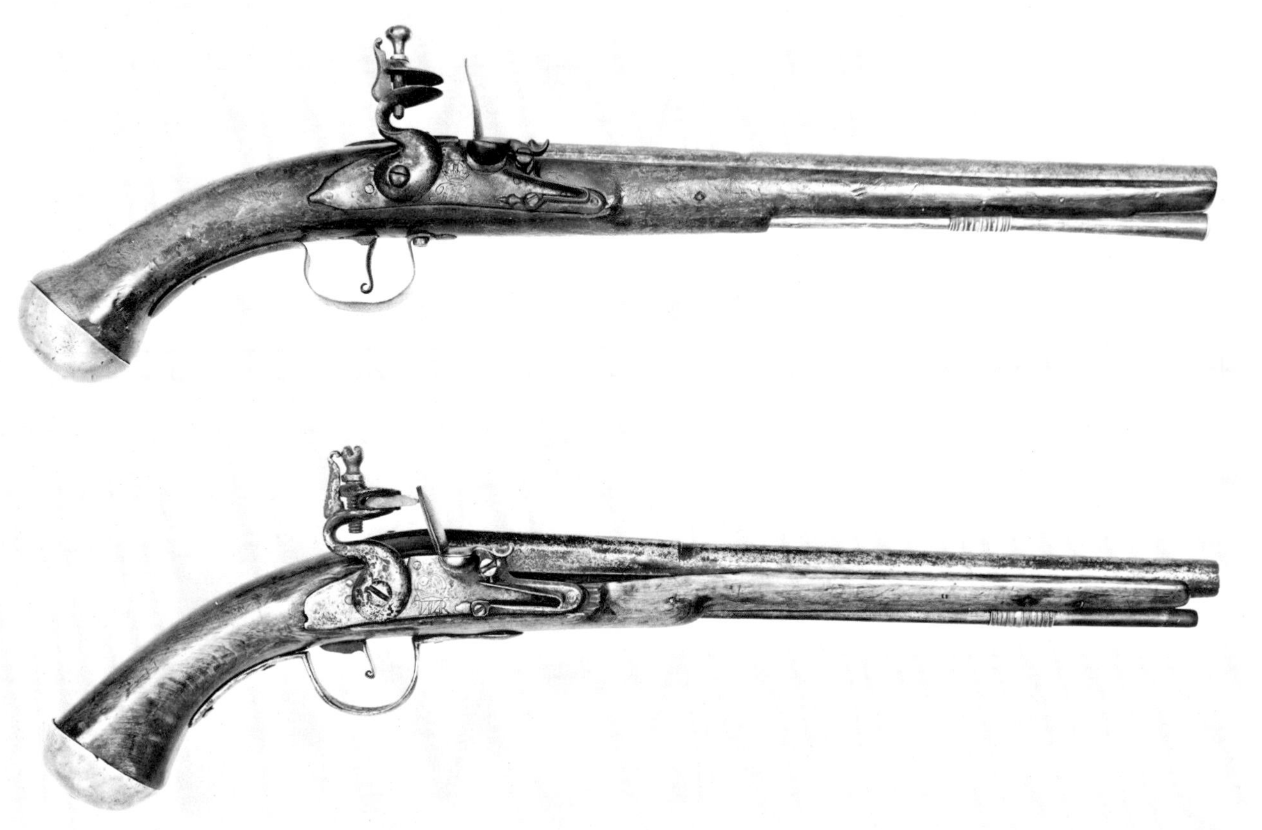

116

117

ters crowned, last mark also on barrel tang. Lock plate flat faced, engraved with double-line borders and strawberry foliage; on lock tail name I. WHIT, numeral 19 for 1719, and broad-arrow stamp; flash fence integral with priming pan; flat loop-neck cock has descent arrest; cock-screw head is both grooved for screwdriver and perforated. Walnut full stock, fore-end restored (old restoration); brass furniture with engraved borders; pommel has spurs engraved with foliage; reverse-curved side plate with leaf engraved on tail and two nails; two ramrod pipes; ramrod with brass tube finial.

This pistol has the high finish characteristic of military pistols in the reign of George I. John White was admitted freeman of the Gunmakers' Company in 1705.

John White, 1719
Overall length 19 in.; barrel 12⁹/₁₆ in.
Caliber .67 (16 gauge). Weight 2½ lb.

120. George II Service-pattern Horse Pistol
(Bedford 876)

Barrel, round, stamped at breech with cipher GR crowned, broad arrow crowned, Ordnance proof, numeral 8 surmounted by star, and barrelsmith's stamp IR.

Lock plate, rounded, engraved with line borders, cipher GR crowned, and broad arrow, and on tail, TOWER and date 1742; cock has descent arrest; flash fence integral with priming pan, which has bridle through which "steel" screw passes. Walnut full stock carved to outline mounts; brass furniture; spurred pommel; S-form side plate with tail; two ramrod pipes, rear pipe with tang extending beyond stock socket; plain ramrod with brass tube finial.

1742
Overall length 18¾ in.; barrel 12 in.
Caliber .60 (22 gauge). Weight 2¾ lb.
Literature: Blackmore, *British Military Firearms*, p. 97, ill. at top.

121. George III Light-dragoon Horse Pistol
(Bedford 1081)

Barrel, round, stamped near breech with Ordnance proofmark, cipher GR, and broad arrow; numeral 4 stamped near breech on right side of barrel. Lock plate, flat faced, engraved with line borders and cipher GR crowned, tail engraved with TOWER, date 1761, and

118

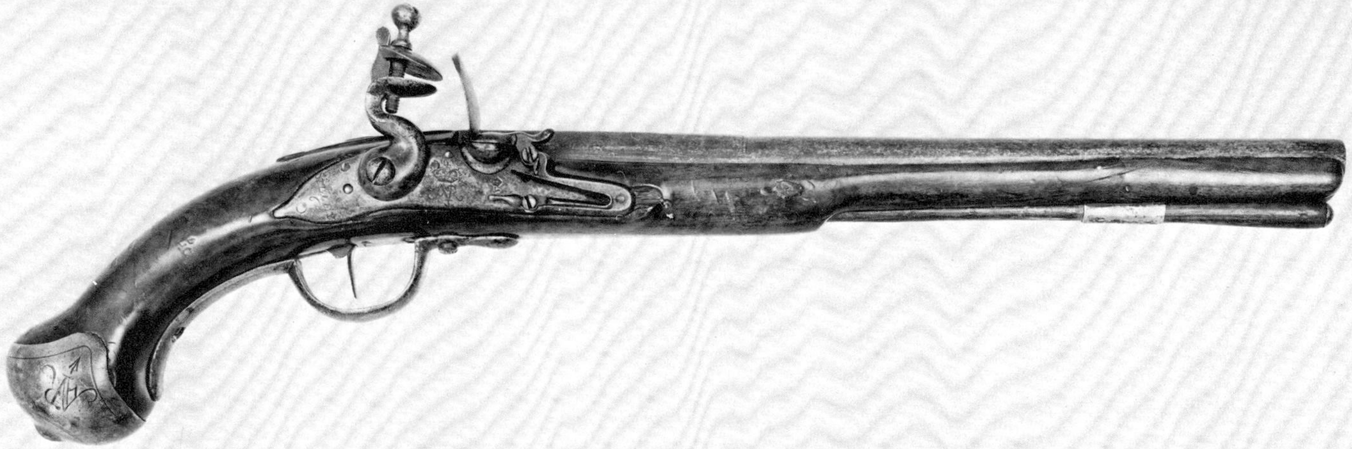

119

118

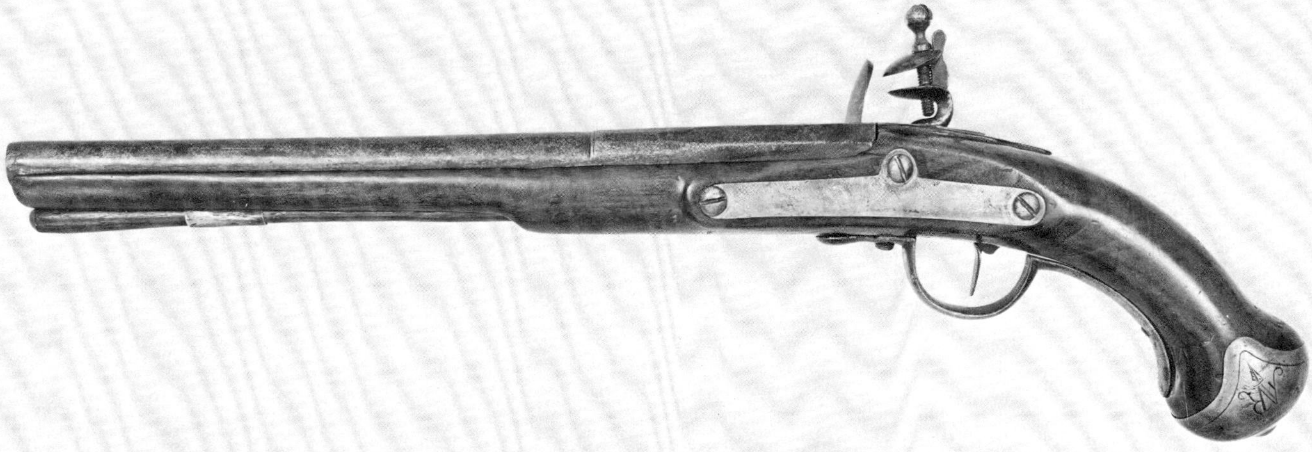

119

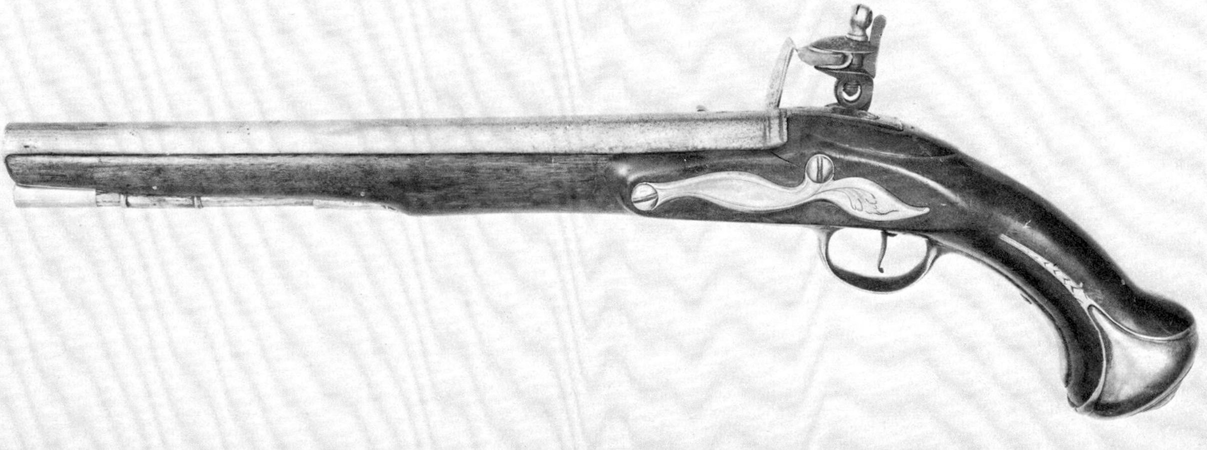

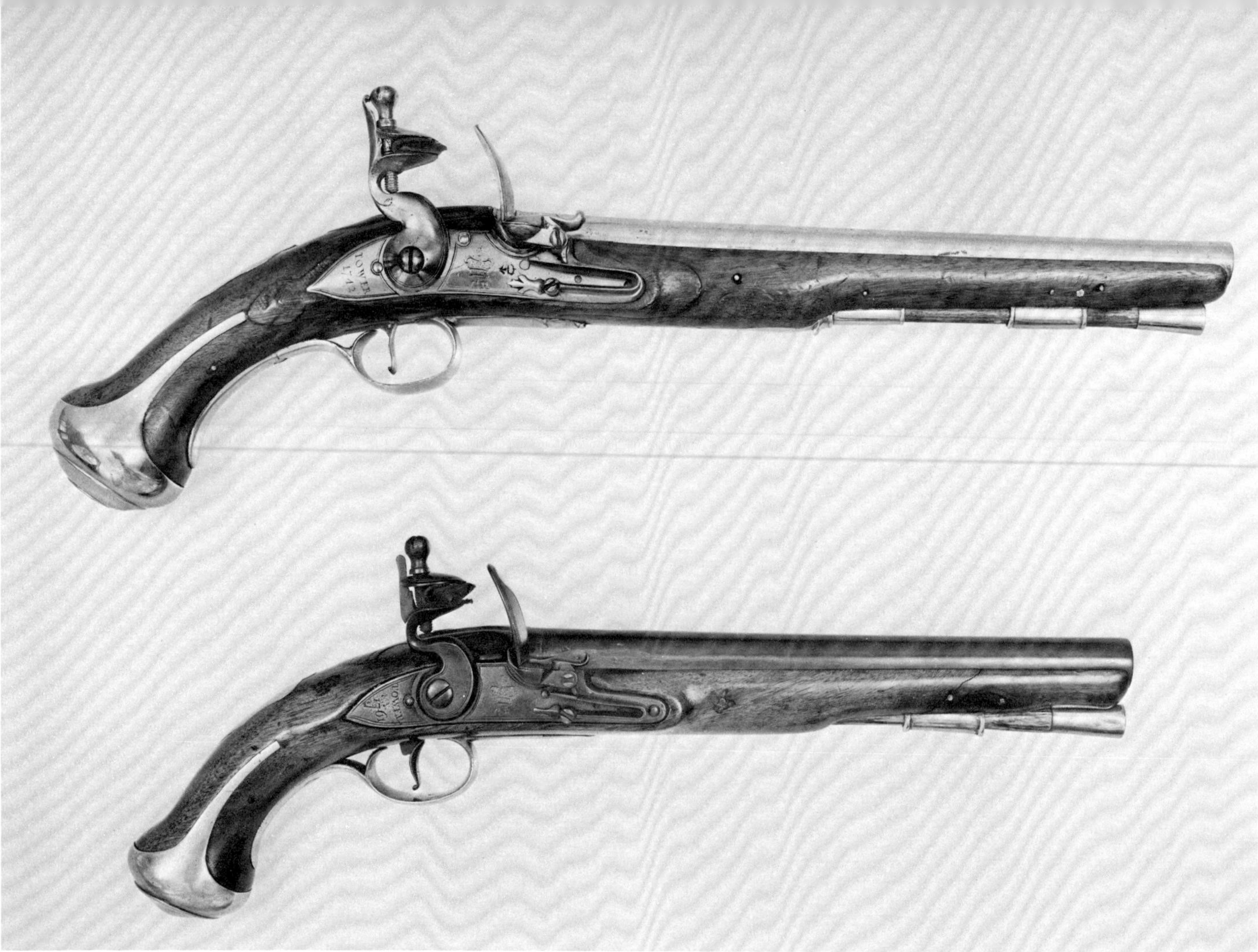

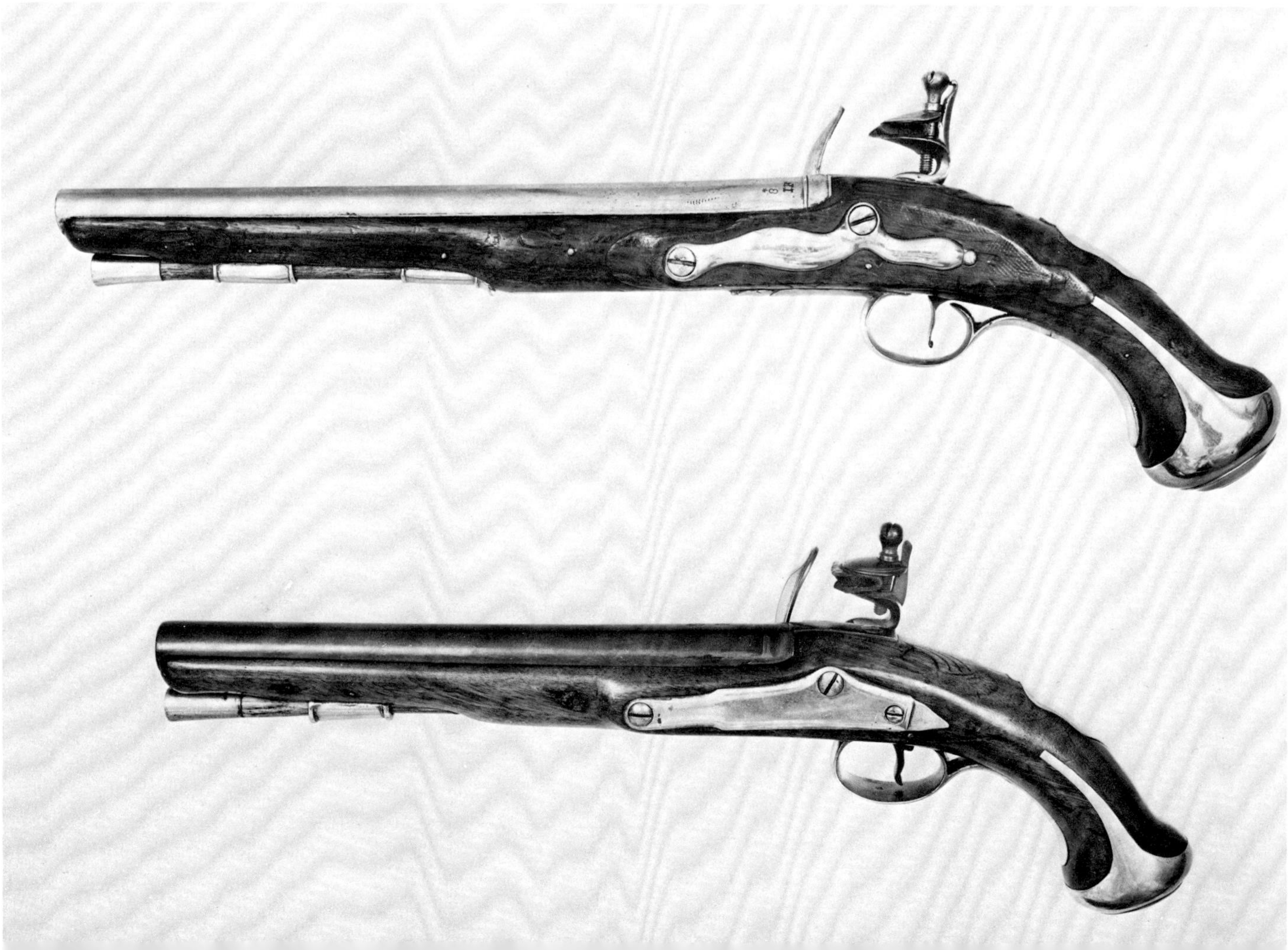

TOWER
1742

1745
VERNON

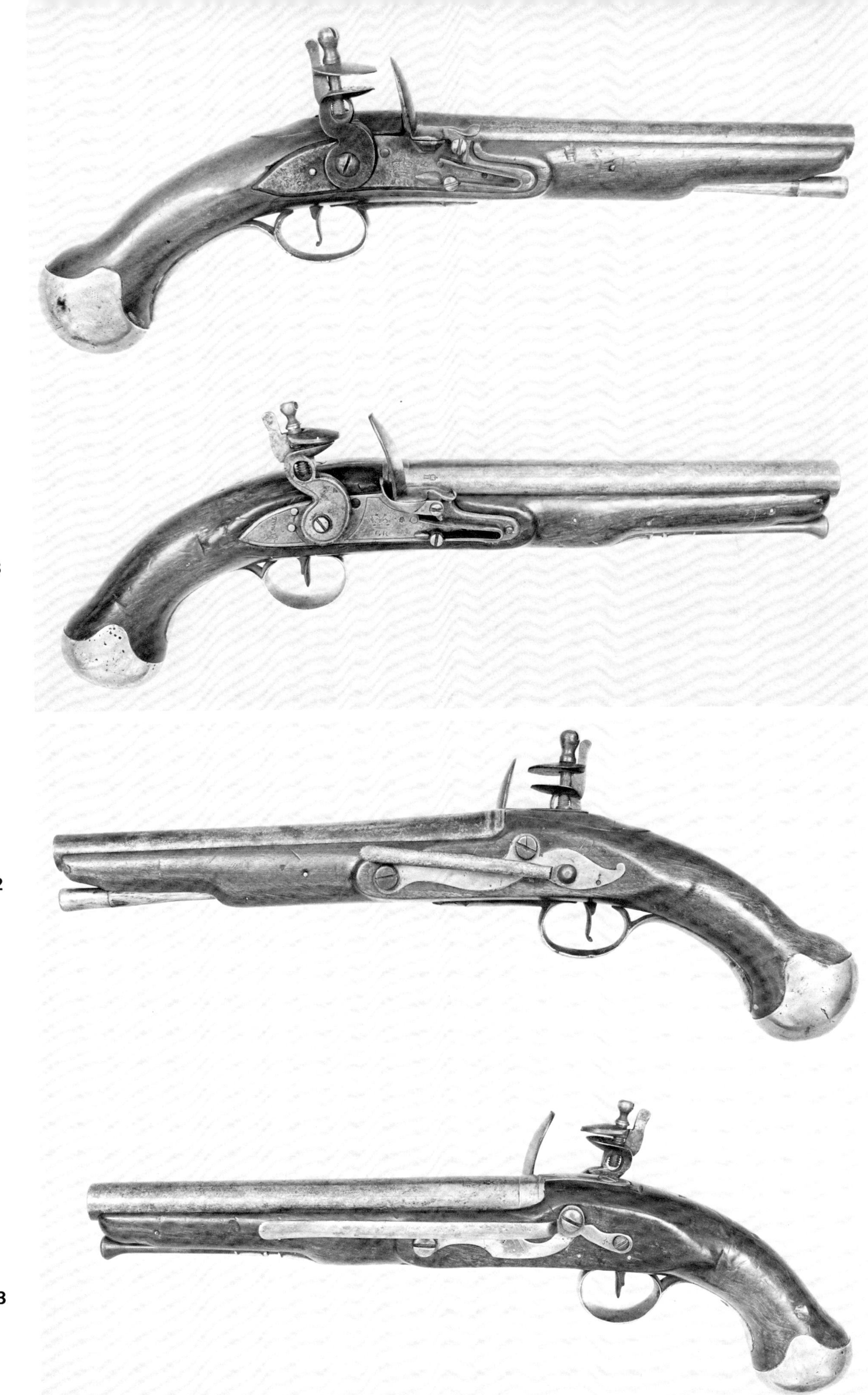

120 122

121 123

120 122

121 123

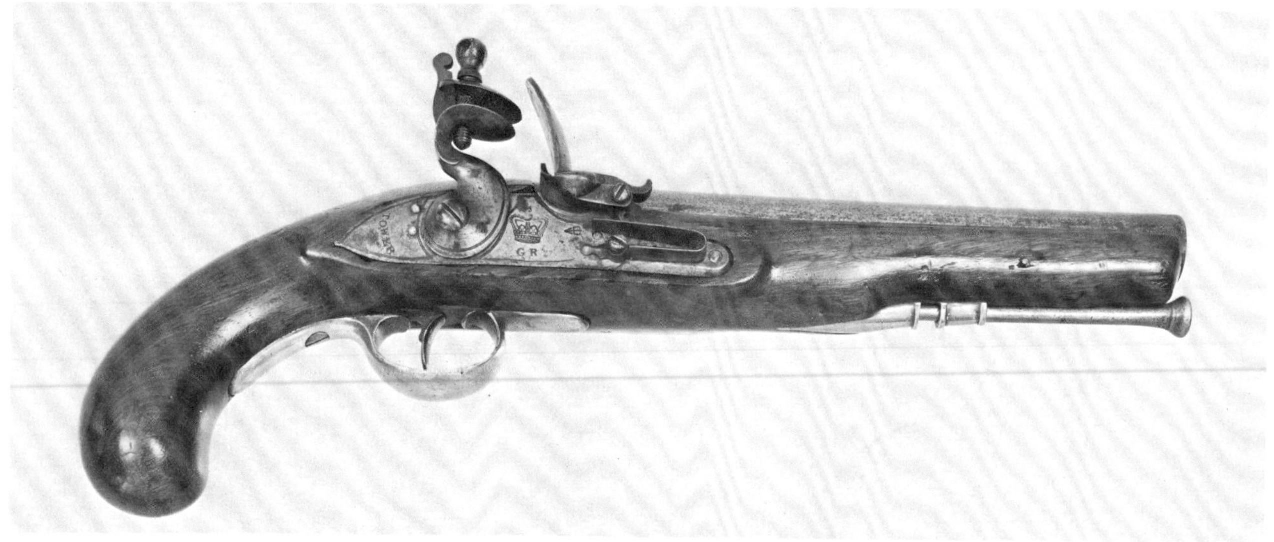

broad-arrow mark; cock has descent arrest; flash fence integral with priming pan; bridle between pan and pan-cover screw. Walnut full stock with shell roughly carved behind barrel tang; brass furniture; spurred pommel; flat side plate with three side nails; blank vase-shaped escutcheon; single ramrod pipe; plain ramrod with brass tube finial.

    1761

    Overall length 16¼ in.; barrel 10 in.

    Caliber .68 (15 gauge). Weight 2½ lb.

    Literature: Blackmore, *British Military Firearms*, p.
       97, ill. in center.

122. George III Sea-service Pistol   (Bedford 1094)

Barrel, round, stamped near breech with Ordnance proof, cipher GR, and broad arrow. Lock plate, flat faced, engraved with cipher GR crowned, broad arrow, and name VERNON, date 1762 on tail; loop-neck cock

has descent arrest. Walnut full stock; brass furniture; flat side plate; steel belt hook; ramrod with brass tube finial fits into stock socket.

    Vernon, 1762

    Overall length 16¼ in.; barrel 9 in.

    Caliber .59 (23 gauge). Weight 2½ lb.

123. George III Service-pattern Navy Pistol   (Bedford 1063)

Barrel, round, stamped with Ordnance proof, broad arrow with cipher GR, and numeral 1 crowned. Lock plate engraved with line border and marks TOWER, GR crowned, and broad arrow; top cock jaw is replacement; jaw screw has transverse perforation; loop-neck cock has descent arrest; flash fence integral with pan; bridle between pan and pan cover. Walnut full stock has broad-arrow mark and initials BO near barrel tang; butt cap, trigger guard, side plate, and two ramrod pipes of brass; brass pins secure barrel and ramrod pipes; rear pipe with tang extending beyond stock socket; one-piece iron ramrod with bullet seater.

About 1775

Overall length 15 in.; barrel 9 in.

Caliber .60 (22 gauge). Weight 2¾ lb.

Literature: Blackmore, *British Military Firearms*, p. 97, ill. at bottom.

124. Flintlock Service Pistol (Bedford 1216)

Barrel, round, stamped near breech with Ordnance proof, cipher GR, and broad arrow. Lock plate marked with TOWER, cipher GR, and broad arrow, and signed WILKES on inside; cock has descent arrest; cock-screw head is both grooved for screwdriver and perforated; flash fence integral with priming pan; bridle between pan and pan-cover screw. Walnut full stock stamped with date 1826 on small and with initials VL and six-pointed star behind side plate; brass furniture; reverse-curved side plate; trigger guard; one-piece iron ramrod with slot for attaching cleaning cloth; two ramrod pipes, rear pipe with tang extending beyond stock socket.

This pistol was made according to a modified patent of 1796. James Wilkes was a sword cutler and gunmaker of Covent Garden, 1795–1810.

James Wilkes, London, about 1796

Overall length 15 in.; barrel 9 in.

Caliber .78 (10 gauge). Weight 2¾ lb.

Literature: Blackmore, *British Military Firearms*, p. 150, ill. at top.

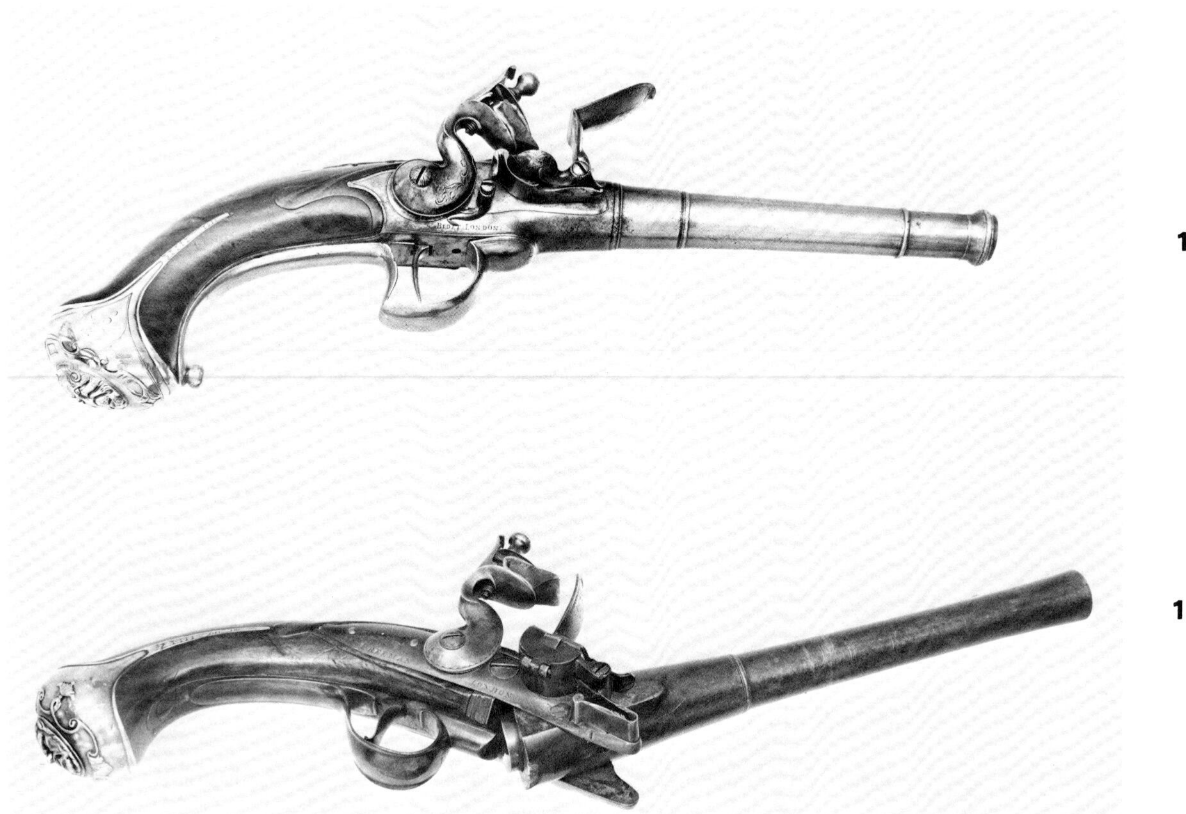

125

126

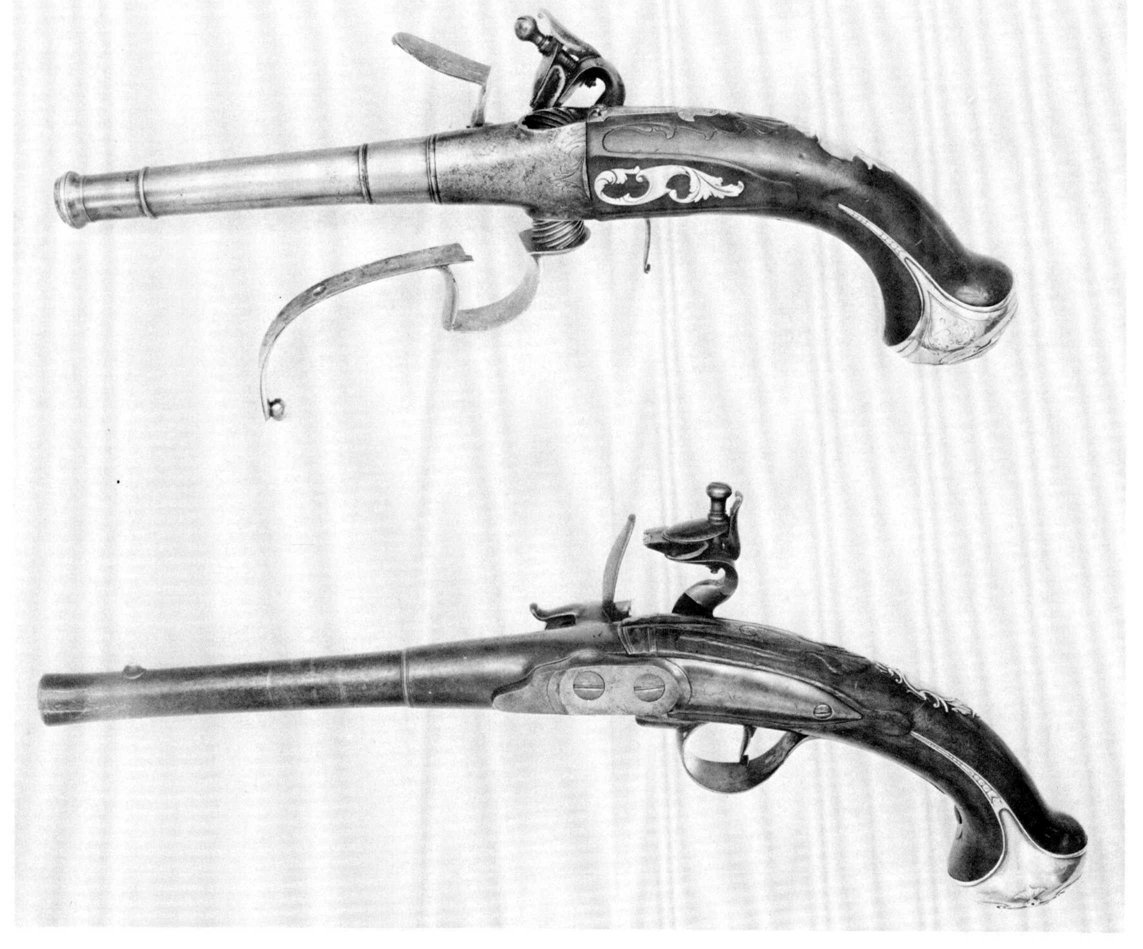

125

126

10

BREECH-LOADING PISTOLS AND GUNS

The convenience of inserting the charge at the breech instead of at the muzzle was very early recognized. Among the surviving early breech-loading firearms are two matchlock guns, originally wheel-locks, that were made for Henry VIII and are preserved in the Tower of London. One is dated 1537, the earliest definitely datable breech-loading small arm extant. Also associated with Henry VIII is the series of breech-loading matchlock gun shields in the Tower, considered to have been made from 1544 to 1547 by Giovanni Battista of Ravenna for the royal bodyguard. The mechanisms of all the foregoing had a removable metallic cartridge. In the present exhibition are two break-action metallic cartridge firearms with barrels that lift, one a gun by Robert Rowland (no. 135), about 1735–40, the other a pistol by James Freeman (no. 126), about 1750, both with steel cartridges. Of greatest rarity is a compressed-air-system rifled pistol (no. 131) made by Samuel Pauly about 1820. The barrel moves downward to give access to a reloadable cartridge. In a percussion cap blunderbuss pistol with Wilkinson action (no. 132) the breech is separate from the barrel and hinged at the rear so that it can be lifted for loading its special cartridge.

In contrast to the break-action breechloaders is a revolving gun with two chambers discharging through a single barrel (no. 134), made about 1700 by Jacques Gorgo.

The magazine breech-loading system of repeating flintlock firearms is widely known as the Lorenzoni system, named after Michele Lorenzoni, a leading Florentine maker who was active in the last quarter of the seventeenth century. The system was adopted by many makers, especially in England. John Cookson, presumably English, used this system on a gun in the Victoria and Albert Museum (no. 77–1893), and Cookson, or possibly his son, published the following advertisement in the Boston (Massachusetts) *Gazette*, April 12, 1756: "BREECH-LOADING GUN. Made by John Cookson, and to be Sold by him at his House in Boston; a handy Gun of 9 Pound and a half Weight; having a Place convenient to hold 9 Bullets, and Powder for 9 Charges and 9 Primings; the said Gun will fire 9 Times distinctly, as quick, or slow as you please, with one turn with the Handle of the said Gun, it doth charge the Gun with Powder and Bullet, and doth prime and shut the pan, and cock the Gun. All these Motions are performed immediately at once, by one turn with the said Handle. Note, there is Nothing put into the Muzzle of the Gun as we charge other Guns." The Lorenzoni system is usually known in America as the Cookson system. Four Cookson or Lorenzoni type firearms, dating in the last quarter of the eighteenth century, are in the exhibition, nos. 127, 129, 130, and 137. One of these (no. 130) was made by H. W. Mortimer, Gunmaker to his Majesty, about 1800; Mortimer made a similar pistol that belonged to Horatio Nelson and is now in The Metropolitan Museum of Art.

Another type popular in England was a breech-loading flintlock employing a breech plug that entered under the barrel and screwed upward to close the breech, which, when the plug was lowered, was open at the top for loading. The best known variant of the system was invented by the Frenchman Isaac de la Chaumette about 1704. An example (no. 125) made in London about 1730 by his compatriot S. Bidet is in the exhibition. A breech-loading rifle (no. 136) made by John Lambe of Salisbury, about 1730, has a screw plug in the top of the breech for loading. Another example of a screw plug rifle (no. 133) but with plug below the breech was made in London about 1700 by the Huguenot immigrant gunmaker Isaac de Seret. In 1776 Patrick Ferguson perfected the breech plug system and was granted a patent in London. In the exhibition are a Ferguson type pistol (no. 128) and a Ferguson type rifle (no. 139), both by William Jover of London and both dating about 1780. Another London gunmaker, Robert Wilson, made the Ferguson type rifled carbine (no. 140).

---

125. Pistol Employing La Chaumette System (Bedford 1555)

Cannon barrel, round, has four girdles and muzzle ring; private proofmarks SB within diamond (S. Bidet) and CM crowned (Isaac de la Chaumette) stamped on underside of barrel at breech; vertical breech screw is operated by turning trigger guard clockwise; screw has no stop. Lock plate, inscribed BIDET LONDON, is forged integrally with barrel of Queen Anne turnoff form. Walnut half stock carved with shell; silver furniture; spurred pommel chased with scrolled cartouche that frames grotesque-mask cap; side plate formed of reverse-curved foliate scrolls.

Isaac de la Chaumette came to England in 1721 and in the same year obtained a patent for pistols charged by the breech through the barrel. He did not make guns himself, but entrusted his compatriot S. Bidet with the manufacture of firearms according to his patent. Bidet made a gun for George I using La

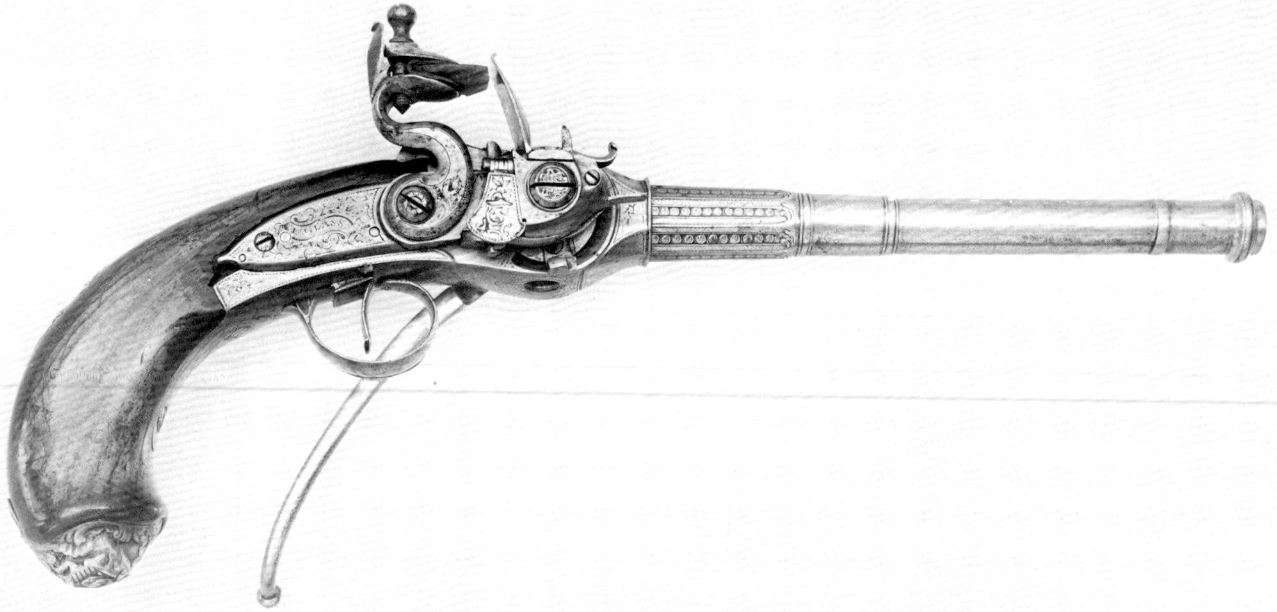

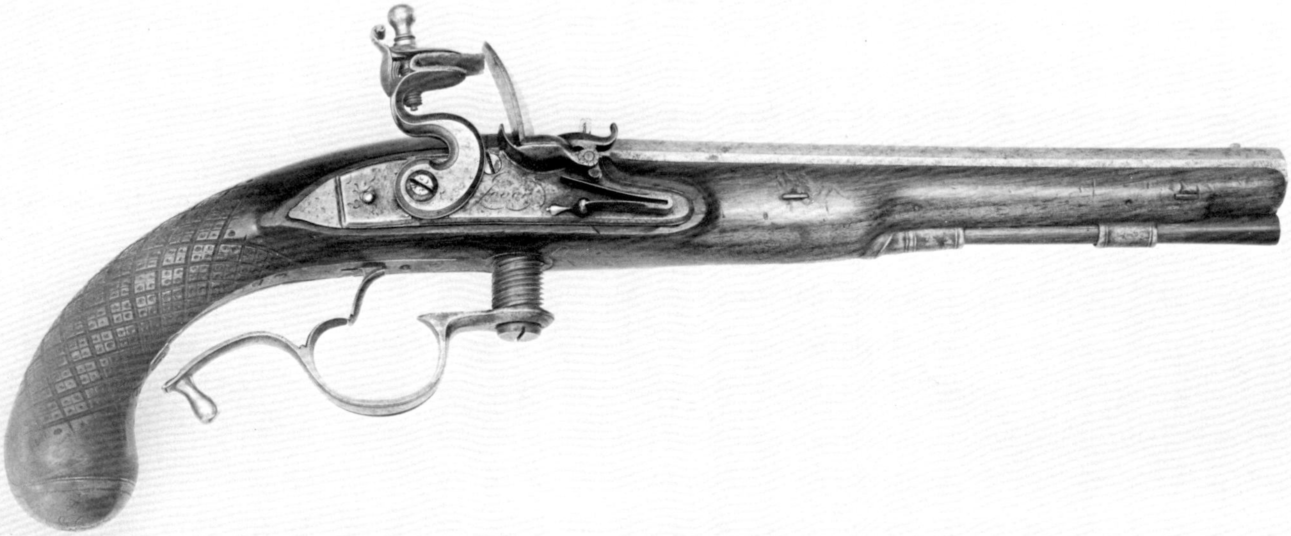

Chaumette's principle; this is now in the collection of H.R.H. The Duke of Brunswick. There are references to Bidet in the Gunmakers' Company Proof Ledger between 1721 and 1731. See no. 111 for the Ferguson version of La Chaumette's system. The Gunmakers' Company tried to contest the La Chaumette patent in 1723 and subsequently refused to prove guns made

after it, hence the absence of the Gunmakers' proof on this pistol.

S. Bidet, London, about 1730
Overall length 14½ in.; barrel 8 in.
Caliber .62 (19 gauge). Weight 2¼ lb.
Literature: Blackmore, *British Military Firearms*, p. 81; Hayward, "The Huguenot Gunmakers of London," pp. 124–125; Mann, *Exhibition of Arms, Armour and Militaria lent by H.R.H. The Duke of Brunswick and Lüneburg*, no. 138, ill.

126. Break-action Metallic-cartridge Pistol (Bedford 717)

Barrel in two stages, both circular, with girdle between; barrel inscribed FREEMAN LONDON at breech, in front of which is engraved Dublin registration number DC 3896; on underside of barrel are stamped London proofmarks, between which is barrel-smith's mark: W over U; when trigger guard is drawn back, break action enables lifting of barrel, causing reloadable steel cylindrical cartridge to fall out; rear sight in false breech; blade front sight. Lock plate, rounded, with back action, inscribed FREEMAN LON-DON; automatic magazine primer with hinged door is adjacent to pan; pan is concave and pivoted to barrel; when barrel is raised, pan scoops up powder from magazine, and pan is revolved to normal position by bringing barrel down to normal position. Walnut half stock; spurred silver pommel, with chased scrolled

cartouche that frames faun-mask cap; silver escutcheon; steel trigger guard.

Nos. 126 and 135 are the only known pistols with break action for metallic cartridge. James Freeman was admitted freeman in 1738 and was master in 1754 of the London Gunmakers' Company. He died in 1756. The Dublin Castle mark was applied by Irish government officials in Dublin. Under an Act of 1843 all owners of firearms were compelled to take out licenses and submit the arms to the police for marking.

James Freeman, London, about 1750
Overall length 16 in.; barrel 9 in.
Caliber .69 (14 gauge). Weight 2½ lb.

127. Rifled Pistol with Automatic Priming Magazine (Bedford 1139)

Barrel in three stages, octagonal at breech, forward stages round, molded rings between, ending in molded muzzle ring. Lock plate, flat faced, inscribed I GLASS on ribbon within engraved scrollwork. Walnut stock; on left side of stock are two compartments, upper one round for balls, lower one rectangular for powder; compartments closed by single hinged door; inside of cylinder hollowed to receive ball and powder; powder compartment separated from ball compartment by blade so that ball cannot accidentally fall in; priming-powder magazine has concave pan pivoted on long cylindrical lever on reverse side that revolves chamber, simultaneously loading it, cocking piece, and causing pan to be automatically loaded and closed. Silver pommel chased with lion rampant holding cannon within rococo scrolls and stamped with anchor of Birmingham, lion passant, and silversmith's initials CF (Charles Freeth).

I. Glass was probably a retailer, either in London or Birmingham.

I. Glass, about 1775
Overall length 15½ in.; barrel 8 in.
Caliber .50 (36 gauge). Weight 2½ lb.

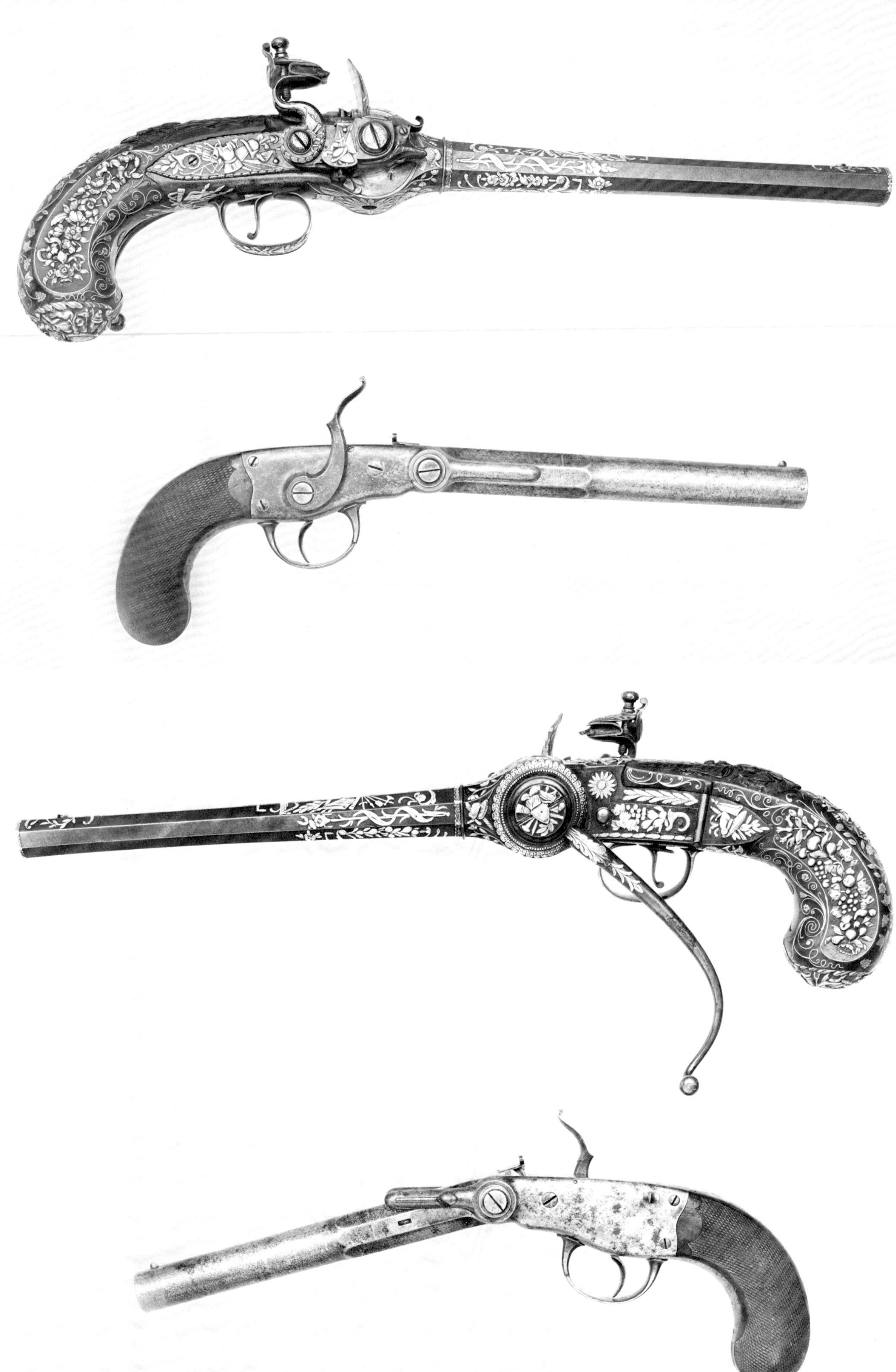

128. Ferguson-type Rifled Pistol (Bedford 1023)

Barrel, octagonal, rifled with eight grooves; top facet of barrel inscribed *Jover* (in script) and LONDON (Roman letters); stationary leaf rear V-sight; blade front sight; two barrel slides; London proofmark at breech end of barrel. Lock plate, flat faced with beveled edges, inscribed *Jover* (script); lock secured by single screw in lock plate and hook; lock plate divided behind cock, and small section of lock plate with raised peg serves as sliding safety; roller bearing between steel and feather spring; hair trigger; pivoted trigger guard with capstan grip is of iron; brass screw plug with flower engraved on top is secured to trigger guard. Walnut full stock with checkered grip; engraved steel furniture.

William Jover, London, about 1780
Overall length 15½ in.; barrel 9¾ in.
Caliber .46 (48 gauge). Weight 2 lb.

129. Lorenzoni-system Magazine Pistol (Bedford 1015)

Turnoff barrel rifled with eight grooves, in four stages with molded rings between, rear two stages octagonal, forward stages round ending in muzzle ring; top facet at breech inscribed *London* (in script); breech engraved with flowers; barrel unscrews to facilitate cleaning of action. Lock plate, flat faced, engraved with rococo cartouche; top strap engraved with trophy of arms; on reverse of stock are chamber with hinged cover for powder and balls, and lever that turns cylinder, automatically cocking piece, covering pan, and filling it with priming powder. Walnut butt profusely inlaid with silver-wire scrolls; silver butt cap, chased with lion rampant and cannon within foliate rococo scrolls, and stamped with anchor of Birmingham, sovereign's head (duty mark), date letter for 1785, and silversmith's mark of Charles Freeth.

This pistol was probably made by a Birmingham gunmaker for sale to a retailer whose name was not engraved on the lock. It was a common practice of Birmingham makers to inscribe the place name London on their guns. In 1813 a bill was laid before Parliament to prevent Birmingham gunmakers from doing so.

Probably Birmingham, 1785
Overall length 11 in.; barrel 5 in.
Caliber .41 (66 gauge). Weight 1½ lb.
Literature: Hayward, *The Art of the Gunmaker*, vol. II, pp. 227–228.

130. Lorenzoni-system Magazine Pistol with Automatic Priming (Bedford 737)

Barrel, octagonal, blued, breech half and muzzle area heavily encrusted with silver chased with trophies of arms, foliation, flower trails, and, in center, shield engraved with decorative coat of arms; on barrel in silver inlaid ribbons are inscribed H. W. MORTIMER LONDON and GUNMAKER TO HIS MAJESTY; silver blade front sight. Back-action lock with flat face, encrusted with trophy of classical arms, cornucopia, and foliage; on reverse side behind cylinder is loading chamber with hinged door for powder and ball. Walnut butt carved in relief behind barrel tang with trophy of arms and armor and laurel leaves, and inlaid with grape foliage and fruit in silver wire and cut sheet; above trigger guard on obverse is inscribed H. W. MORTIMER LONDON; on reverse is inscribed GUN MAKER TO HIS MAJESTY; butt cap gilded and chased with trophy of arms enclosing shield charged with three crescents and stars; silver-gilt escutcheon pierced and chased in high relief with trophy of arms and armor.

This is one of the most richly decorated English pistols extant. The silver work on it, though unsigned and unmarked, is of exceptional quality. It was presumably made for presentation to a Near Eastern or Indian potentate. The coat of arms seems to be decora-

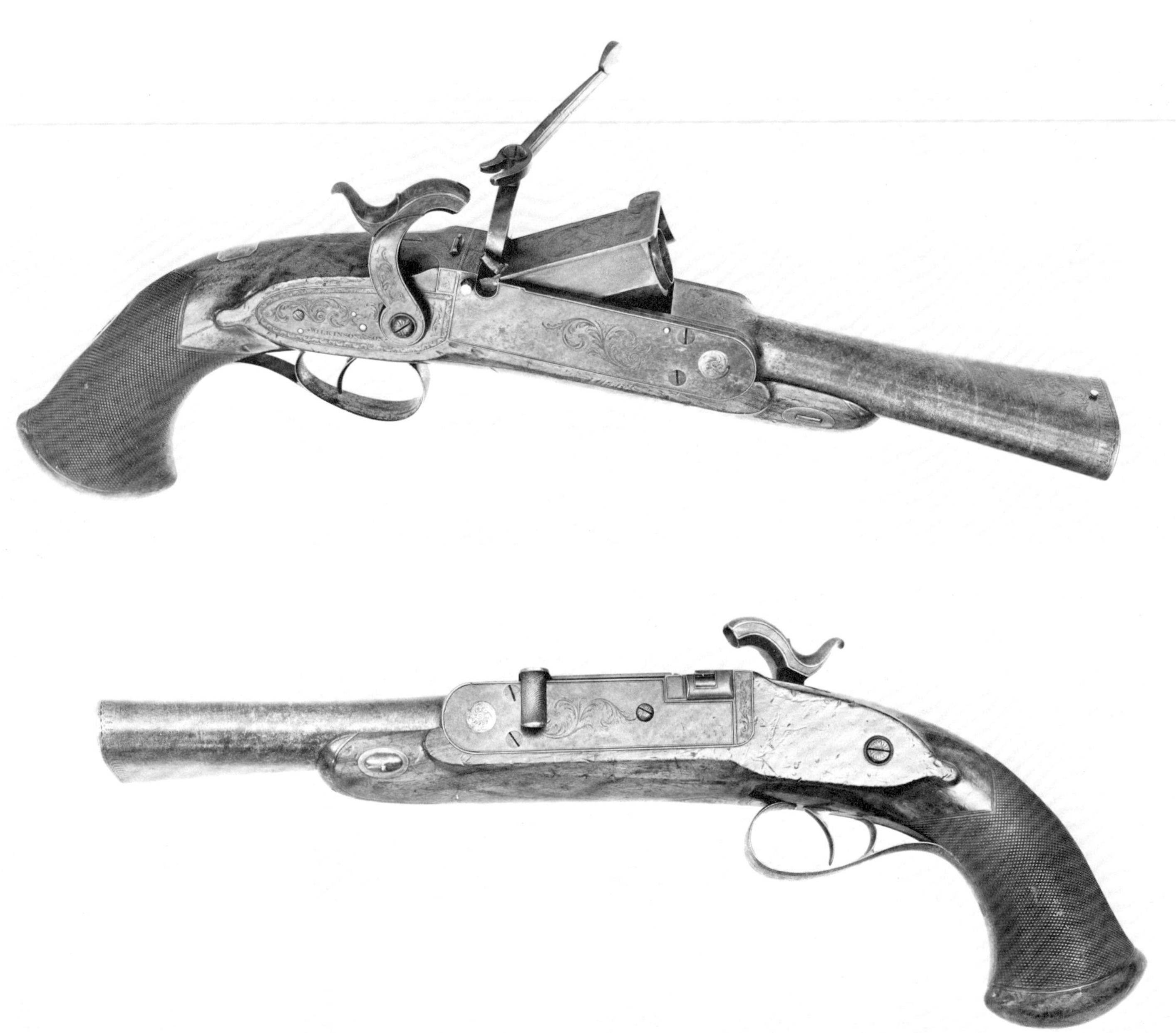

tive rather than heraldically significant. H. W. Mortimer worked at 89 Fleet Street from 1782. His firm became H. W. Mortimer & Son in 1800.

H. W. Mortimer, London, about 1800
Overall length 19¾ in.; barrel 10 in.
Caliber .63 (18 gauge). Weight 4½ lb.
Literature: Grancsay, *The Metropolitan Museum of Art, Loan Exhibition of European Arms and Armor*, 1931, no. 294; Parke-Bernet sale (Edward Hubbard Litchfield collection), December 6, 1951, lot 212, ill.

131. Compressed-air System Rifled Pistol (Bedford 1283)

Twist barrel in two stages, octagonal and round, rifled with eight grooves; rectangular compartment behind barrel encloses compressed-air mechanism that is closed by hinged steel door on top and locked by spring catch; bottom facet of barrel has London proofmarks between which are barrelsmith's initials WF (William Fullerd); iron blade front sight; leaf rear V-sight.

When a stud at the side is pressed, the barrel moves downward, giving access to the breech. The pistol used a brass reloadable cartridge (lacking) with a charge of fulminate at the rear end. When the lock was cocked, a plunger working in a cylinder was drawn back; when the mechanism was released, a blast of hot compressed air was driven forward through a tiny hole in the end of the cylinder, igniting the fulminate in the base of the cartridge and discharging the piece. Examples of this highly ingenious action are rare. It was invented too early for proper exploitation.

Samuel Pauly, about 1820
Overall length 15½ in.; barrel 9⅛ in.
Caliber .66 (16 gauge). Weight 3 lb.
Literature: Reid, "Pauly, Gun-Designer," pp. 181–210, pls. LIII-LXI, pp. 254–258, pl. LXX; Fox, "The Fire Piston and its Origins in Europe," pp. 355–370.

132. Percussion-cap Blunderbuss Pistol with Wilkinson Action (Bedford 1544)

Barrel, browned twist, engraved with scrollwork, muzzle of flattened oval section; silver bead front sight; stationary leaf rear V-sight. Rising breech pivoted at rear, operated by lever at top of lock plate that not only tilts chamber but moves it backward and forward to give obturating effect; lock and action engraved with scrollwork; signed on chamber WILKINSON & SON PALL MALL LONDON and on barrel PATENT; lock plate inscribed WILKINSON & SON. Walnut three-quarter stock with checkered butt; blued and engraved steel

furniture; blank octagonal silver escutcheon; upper part of grip is hollowed and has steel keyhole plate for attachment of shoulder stock (lacking).

Chief of this gun's unusual features is its special cartridge, designed for the elliptical barrel. The paper cartridge contains twelve quarter-circle lead projectiles as well as a charge of powder and a thinly covered detonating cap. The inventor (the system was patented by J. de Burgh, marquis of Clanricarde, on July 15, 1831, British patent number 6139) explained that these projectiles "will be so scattered laterally by the flattened bell shaped end of the barrel as to constitute a most formidable weapon of defence."

James Wilkinson & Son, London, about 1840
Overall length 16 in.; barrel 8⅝ in.
Blunderbuss opening ⅞ x 2 in. Weight 3 lb.
Literature: Winant, *Firearms Curiosa*, p. 256, figs. 301–302.

133. Rifled Carbine (Bedford 1319)

Barrel rifled with eight grooves has ring-handled five-threaded screw plug for insertion of ball below breech; barrel in two stages, octagonal changing to polygonal at breech, remainder round, with faceted and expanded muzzle extension; signed on prolongation of barrel tang I DE SERET A LONDRES. Lock plate forged integrally with barrel, rear end chased with leafy mask; cock and steel with raised borders. Burl-wood

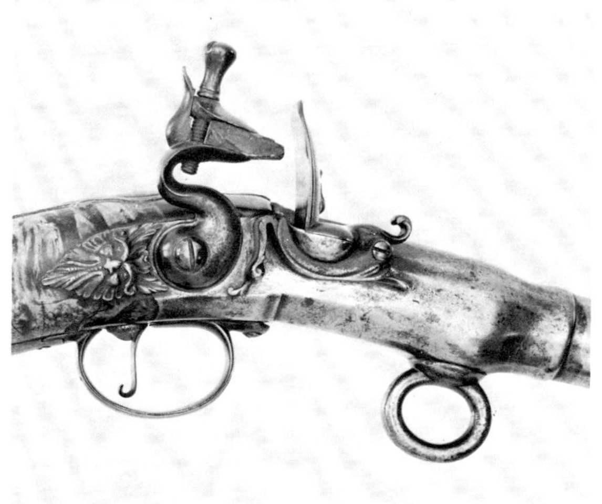

figured butt; steel furniture; pierced sepentine side plate; escutcheon forged integrally into barrel tang.

Isaac de Seret was a Huguenot immigrant from Crespy en Lanois, Aisne. A patron of his was the first duke of Devonshire, the builder of Chatsworth, where two fowling pieces by De Seret are still preserved. He was the father of Samuel de Seret, also a gunmaker, who is mentioned in documents dating from 1690 to 1703. A rifle almost identical to no. 133, apparently

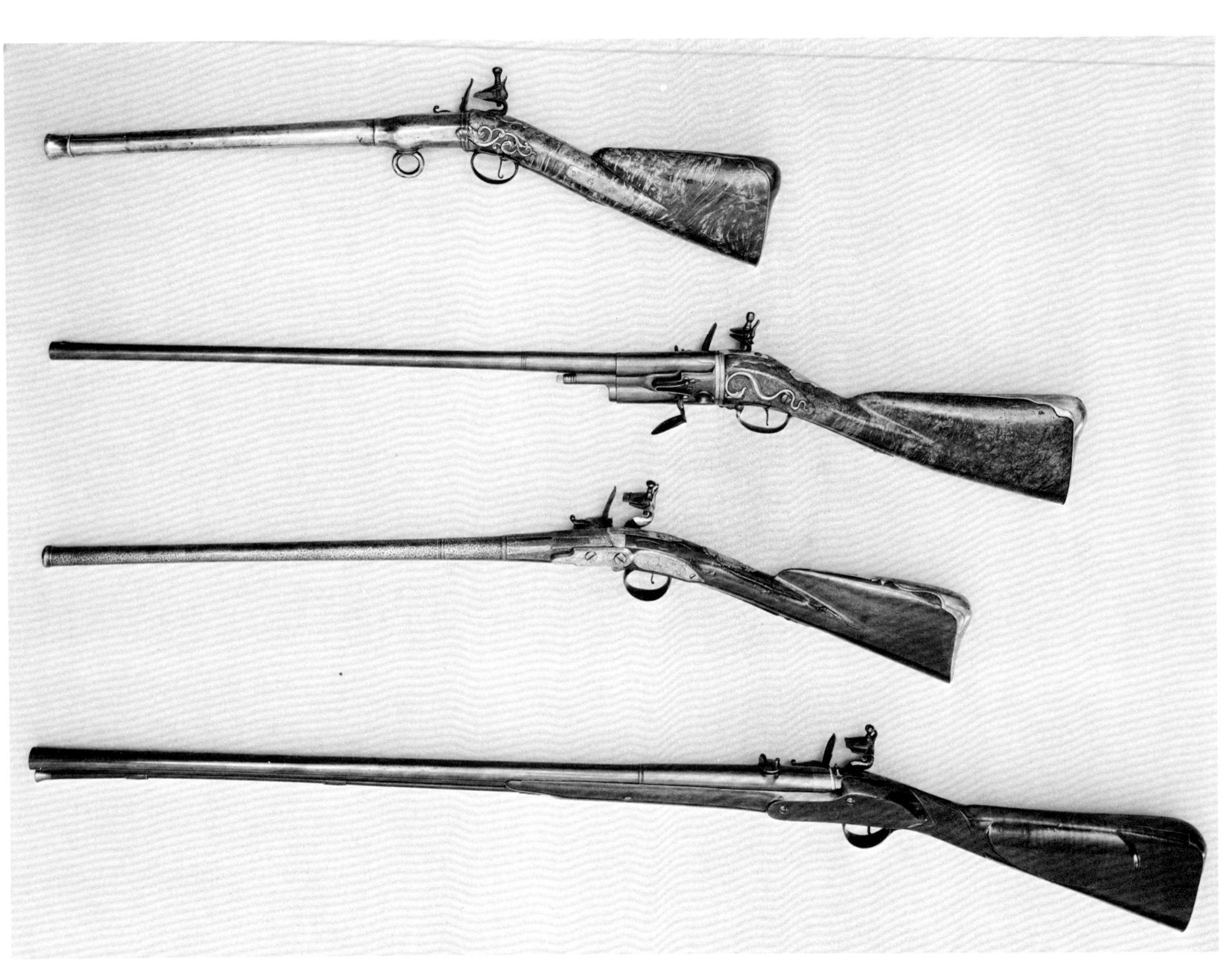

unsigned, is in the Medici Collection in the Museo Nazionale, Palazzo del Bargello, Florence.

Isaac de Seret, London, about 1700
Overall length 32 in.; barrel 19 in.
Caliber .64 (18 gauge). Weight 7¼ lb.
Literature: Hayward, ''The Huguenot Gunmakers of London,'' pp. 117–143, pls. XIII–XXVII; Thomas and Boccia, *Oesterreichische Florenzhilfe, Historische Prunkwaffen*, M50, p. 68.

134. Two-chambered Revolving Gun (Bedford 908)

Two turnover chambers discharging through single barrel, each chamber with separate pan and steel, released by pressing up trigger guard; axle on which chambers turn is extended, and barrel is welded to axle extension; barrel in two stages with molded girdle between; silver blade front sight. Lock plate and cock with raised borders; back-action lock. Burl-wood figured half stock with silver-wire scroll inlay; steel

furniture with raised borders; butt plate, with tang secured by two screws, has hinged door, opened by spring button, leading to compartment; serpentine side plate; chased blank escutcheon.

Jacques Gorgo was a Swiss Protestant immigrant who worked in Grafton Street, Soho. He is recorded in London between 1689 and 1727, in which time he produced a number of breech-loading and repeating arms.

Jacques Gorgo, London, about 1700
Overall length 45½ in.; barrel 30 in.
Caliber .64 (18 gauge). Weight 7½ lb.
Literature: Hayward, ''The Huguenot Gunmakers of London,'' p. 123 and pl. XXI.

135. Gun with Steel Cartridge (Bedford 361)

Barrel in three stages with molded girdles be-

tween, octagonal changing to polygonal at breech, forward stages circular; expanded muzzle end; no proof-marks; barrel inscribed R. ROWLAND LONDON; break action with barrel that lifts and separate reloadable steel cylindrical cartridge; when trigger guard is drawn back, barrel pivots upward, allowing cartridge to fall downward; pan is simultaneously reprimed from magazine primer by means of revolving pan. Lock plate and cock with engraved borders and inscription R. ROWLAND; lock with back action, pan and steel extending

forward along side of breech; dog safety catch; faceted steel. Walnut half stock; engraved steel furniture; butt plate with elongated tang; engraved side plate corresponds in form to lock plate; silver escutcheon chased with two grotesque human masks.

Robert Rowland was admitted freeman of the Gunmakers' Company in 1713. It is surprising that so well known a London gunmaker as Rowland should have sold an unproved gun.

Robert Rowland, London, about 1735–40
Overall length 41½ in.; barrel 26½ in.
Caliber .73 (12 gauge). Weight 7 lb.

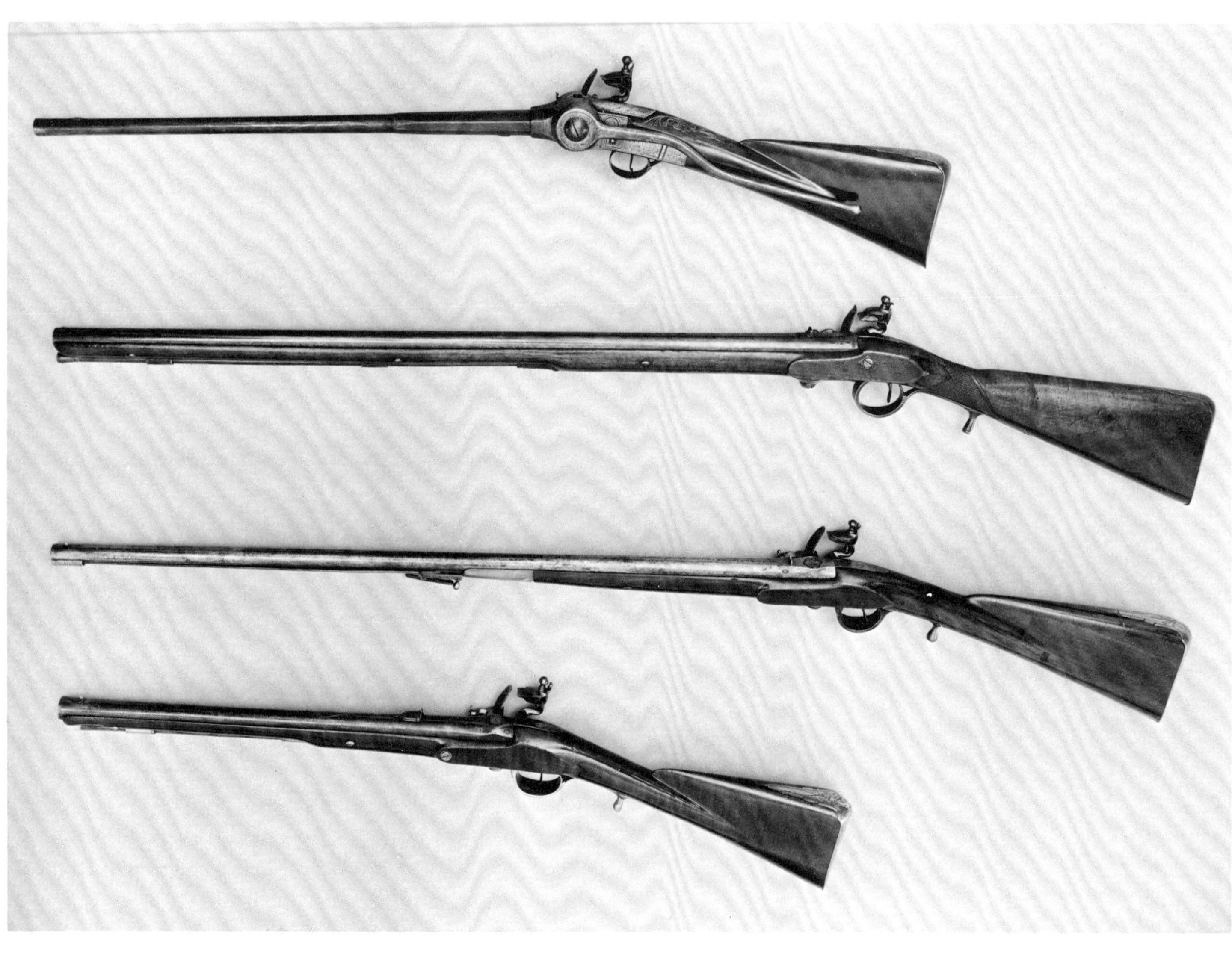

136. Breech-loading Rifle   (Bedford 362)

Barrel, blued, original rifling now bored smooth or much worn, in two stages with molded girdle between; barrel inscribed JOHN (partly obliterated) LAMBE SARUM (*Sarum* is another name for Salisbury); screw plug in top of breech for loading ball; patent breech with platinum-lined touchhole and gold line added after 1790; rear V-sight; bead front sight. Lock plate, flat faced, with line borders, inscribed I. LAMBE.

Walnut half stock with checkered grip of later remodeling and horn finial at fore-end; steel butt plate with tang; trigger guard with elongated tang and early conventional acorn finial.

Joseph Manton is credited with the use of the first platinum-lined touchhole in 1805; thus, the rifle must have been altered more than once.

John Lambe, Sarum, about 1730; modernized about 1790 and later

Overall length 52½ in.; barrel 36½ in.

Caliber .71 (13 gauge). Weight 8 lb.

Literature: George, *English Guns and Rifles*, pl. IX, 2.

137. Lorenzoni-system Magazine Rifle with Automatic Priming   (Bedford 911)

Barrel, rifled with twelve grooves, in two stages, octagonal changing to round at breech, forward stage round; on bottom facet of breech is an elongated projection that fits wrench for screwing barrel; silver bead front sight. Back-action flat-faced lock engraved with foliate scrolls and in ribbons inscribed HEATH & HURDD; action engraved with trophies of arms; brass chambered cylinder. Walnut half stock inlaid with silver wire with shell motif and trophy of arms behind barrel tang; engraved steel furniture.

Guns with this complex breech-loading mechanism were probably produced by one Birmingham specialist, who then sold them to other gunmakers for finishing and retail sale.

Heath & Hurdd, probably Birmingham, about 1770–80

Overall length 40¾ in.; barrel 23¾ in.

Caliber .59 (22 gauge). Weight 8 lb.

Literature: George, *English Guns and Rifles*, p. 139, no. 2, frontispiece.

138. Flintlock Rifle   (Bedford 979)

Barrel, browned twist, rifled with eight grooves; barrel stamped at breech with London proofmarks between which are gunmaker's initials RW; ball is charged through aperture under breech opened by nine turns of screw and removal of trigger guard; stationary rear U-sight; inset silver blade front sight; three barrel slides. Lock plate, flat faced, with roller bearing between steel and feather spring, inscribed with name *Wheeler* (in script). Walnut full stock with checkered wrist; engraved, blued steel furniture; iron butt plate with tang.

Robert Wheeler was a warden of the Birmingham Proof House when it was founded in 1813. He had a warehouse in Cheapside, London, from 1805 to 1808.

Robert Wheeler, London, about 1775–85

Overall length 51¼ in.; barrel 36 in.

Caliber .69 (14 gauge); Weight 8¼ lb.

139. Ferguson-type Rifle   (Bedford 338)

Barrel rifled with six grooves; rear end of trigger guard has bolt handle with slot at base that locks over edge of iron plate; one turn of trigger guard opens breech for loading; top of breech plug engraved with flower; London view mark and proofmark on opposite sides of barrel; top facet of breech inscribed JOVER LONDON; sliding bayonet under barrel; single barrel slide; stationary leaf U-shaped rear sight; iron blade front sight. Lock plate, flat faced, inscribed JOVER, secured by single screw on lock face and hook. Walnut

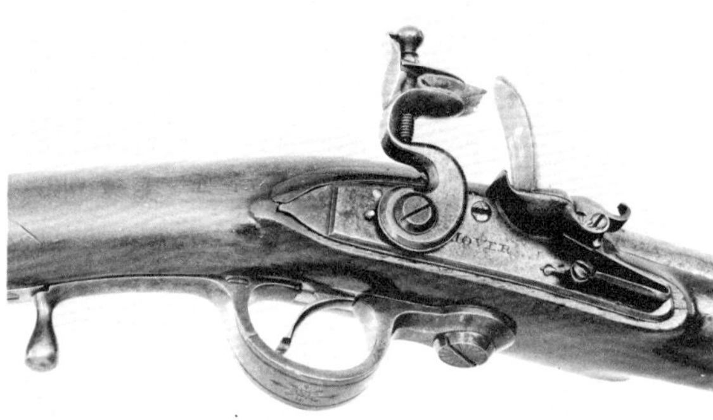

half stock with cow-horn fore-end; brass butt plate with tang engraved with bow, quiver, and arrows.

William Jover seems to have been the first of the London gunmakers to manufacture both rifles and rifled pistols with the Ferguson action (see also no. 128).

William Jover, London, about 1780
Overall length 50¾ in.; barrel 35¾ in.
Caliber .63 (18 gauge). Weight 7 lb.

140. Ferguson-type Rifled Carbine   (Bedford 358)

This carbine is an officer's semiregulation arm. Barrel, browned, rifled with ten grooves, stamped with London proofmarks and inscribed *Minories London* (in script); trigger guard of steel threaded to fit breech end of barrel; one turn of trigger guard opens breech end of barrel for loading; automatic stop on breech plug to prevent removal; rear end of trigger guard has bolt handle; below bolt on underside of trigger guard

is small hollow that fits over raised ball on trigger plate, thus locking trigger guard; stationary leaf rear V-sight in front of which is tall hinged V-sight; silver blade front sight. Lock plate, flat faced with engraved border, inscribed *Wilson* (in script); roller bearing be-

tween steel and feather spring. Walnut full stock with engraved brass furniture; butt plate with tang engraved with trophies; ramrod has cylindrical horn finial and, on opposite end, long iron cylinder with transverse rectangular perforation for attaching swabbing cloth.

Patrick Ferguson, born in 1744, was the second son of a Scottish laird. He first served as a Cornet of Horse in the Scots Greys at the age of fourteen. While Captain in the 70th Regiment, he devised an improved version of La Chaumette's breech-loading action, which he submitted for trial at Woolwich in 1775. In the same year he demonstrated his rifle before the king and royal family at Woolwich, and he was granted a patent shortly after. Ferguson was sent to America in 1777 in command of a detachment armed with his rifle. They suffered heavy casualties in the attack on Brandywine Hill, September 11, 1777. Ferguson lost his life in the battle of King's Mountain, October 7, 1780. Robert Wilson was master of the Gunmakers' Company in 1764 and 1771.

Robert Wilson, London, about 1780
Overall length 36½ in.; barrel 21⅛ in.
Caliber .71 (13 gauge). Weight 5½ lb.
Literature: Blackmore, *British Military Firearms*, pp. 71–80; Ferguson, *Two Scottish Soldiers*, pp. 55–123; Neal, "The Ferguson Rifle."

11

DOUBLE-BARRELED AND OVER-AND-UNDER PISTOLS

The double-barreled pistol was valuable for giving two chances instead of one. A man armed with a single-barreled pistol was weaponless after firing, so single-barreled pistols were usually made in pairs. Multishot mechanisms were devised so that the piece could be loaded with two or more charges and discharged in more or less rapid succession. As a broken spring would render the whole mechanism suddenly useless, the advantage of having a reserve lock and barrel is obvious. Even double-barreled firearms often proved unsatisfactory, hence several improved types were developed. The mechanisms exhibited here show constructions that may be classified as: turnover barrels; fixed over-and-under barrels; box-lock pistols with turnoff barrels; fixed side-by-side barrels. Except for three percussion items, all are flintlocks. Two of our examples, dating from about 1730 and 1760, have turnover barrels (nos. 141 and 143), each barrel with its individual pan and pan cover. A different construction is the fixed over-and-under barrel that appears on two pistols. In one (no. 144), dating about 1740, the right-hand lock serves the upper barrel, the left-hand lock the lower; in the other (no. 151), dating about 1790, the single trigger discharges the right-hand lock first.

A third construction may be seen in four turnoff box-lock pistols. A change in the construction of turnoff pistols (see group 4) took place before the middle of the eighteenth century. The cock was removed from the side and placed centrally behind the barrel. The lock mechanism is held in a box-like enclosure, hence the modern designation box-lock. This change of the position of the action was an important feature, since the new construction presented a smooth surface that was less likely to tear the pocket. The box-lock turnoff-barrel construction continued in pocket pistols (see group 15) until the second half of the nineteenth century. In the present group are three turnoff box-lock flintlock pistols (nos. 145, 147, 148) with side-by-side barrels and a box-lock flintlock converted to percussion cap, with side-by-side fixed barrels (no. 146). They date from 1750 to 1776, and all of them have left- and right-hand locks.

The remaining eight pistols have side-by-side fixed barrels. The five flintlocks date from 1784 to 1818. One of the flintlock pistols (no. 150), made by Francis Innes of Edinburgh about 1790, has a steel-lined socket in the butt for inserting a shoulder stock, enabling one to convert the pistol into a carbine. The three percussion-cap pistols date from 1831 to 1852. The latest percussion pistol (no. 156) is known as a howdah pistol. Such heavy arms, intended to save a big game hunter when attacked by a wounded animal, were carried in the howdah when hunting tigers from the back of an elephant.

For other multishot firearms in the exhibition, see groups 10, 13, 14, and 15.

---

141. Cased Pair of Double-barreled Turnover Flintlock Pistols   (Bedford 497)

Barrels, round, faceted at breech, engraved with shell and rococo scrolls; top facet of each barrel inscribed LONDON, and London proofmark and Tower private proofmarks struck on each barrel; each barrel has individual pan and pan cover and feather spring; barrel released by pulling back steel trigger guard. Lock plate, flat faced, has engraved borders and name I. RICHARDS on ribbon within rococo scrollwork; back-action lock. Walnut full stock in two parts: forestock, and butt carved with shell behind barrel tang; brass furniture; spurred pommel engraved with flower sprays, its cap cast and chased in relief with faun's mask; two ramrod pipes with ramrod.

The original green-baize-lined mahogany case is provided with compartments for the pistols and for the bullet mold and other fittings. Cases of early type, like this one, have a projecting brass swing handle and brass hooks. On the inside the original maker's label reads: New Patent Water-proof Guns and Pistols, By which invention the Touch-holes of the Guns are

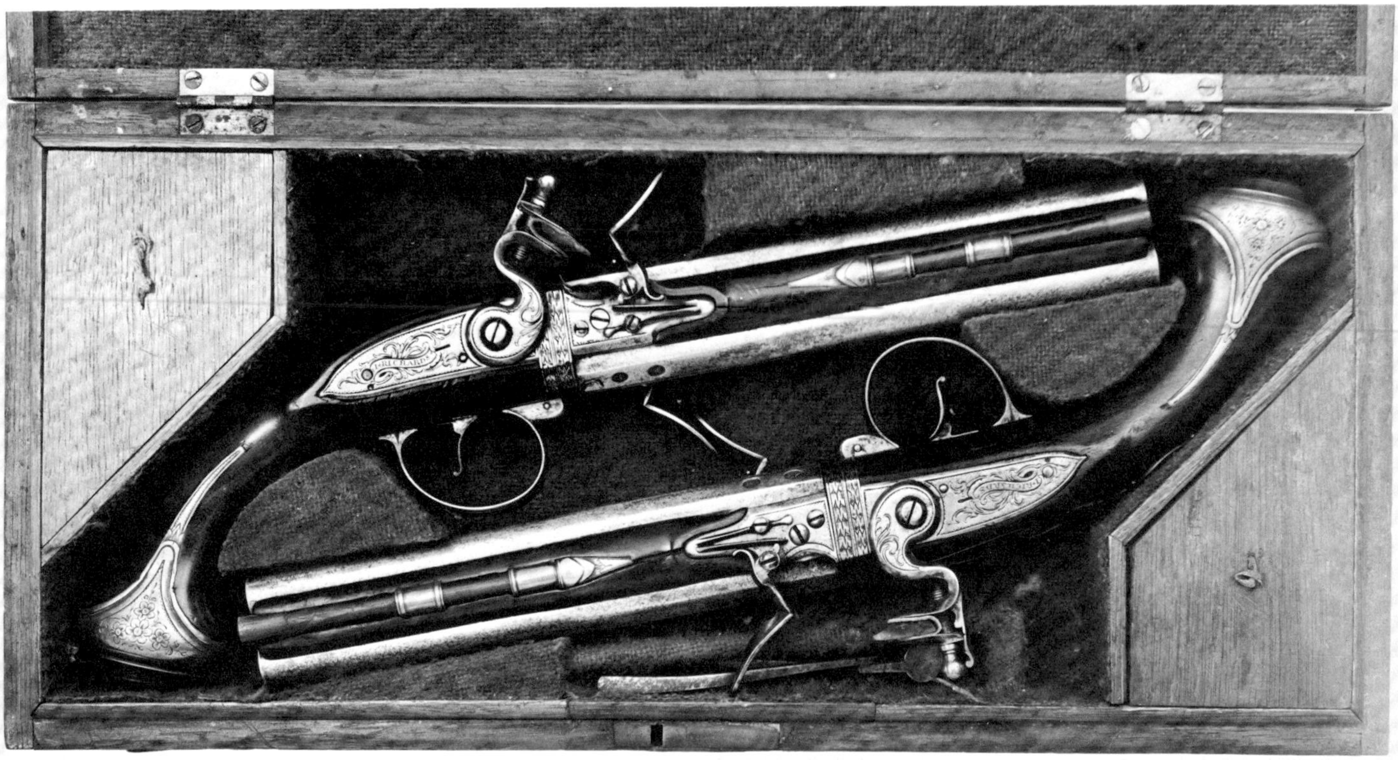

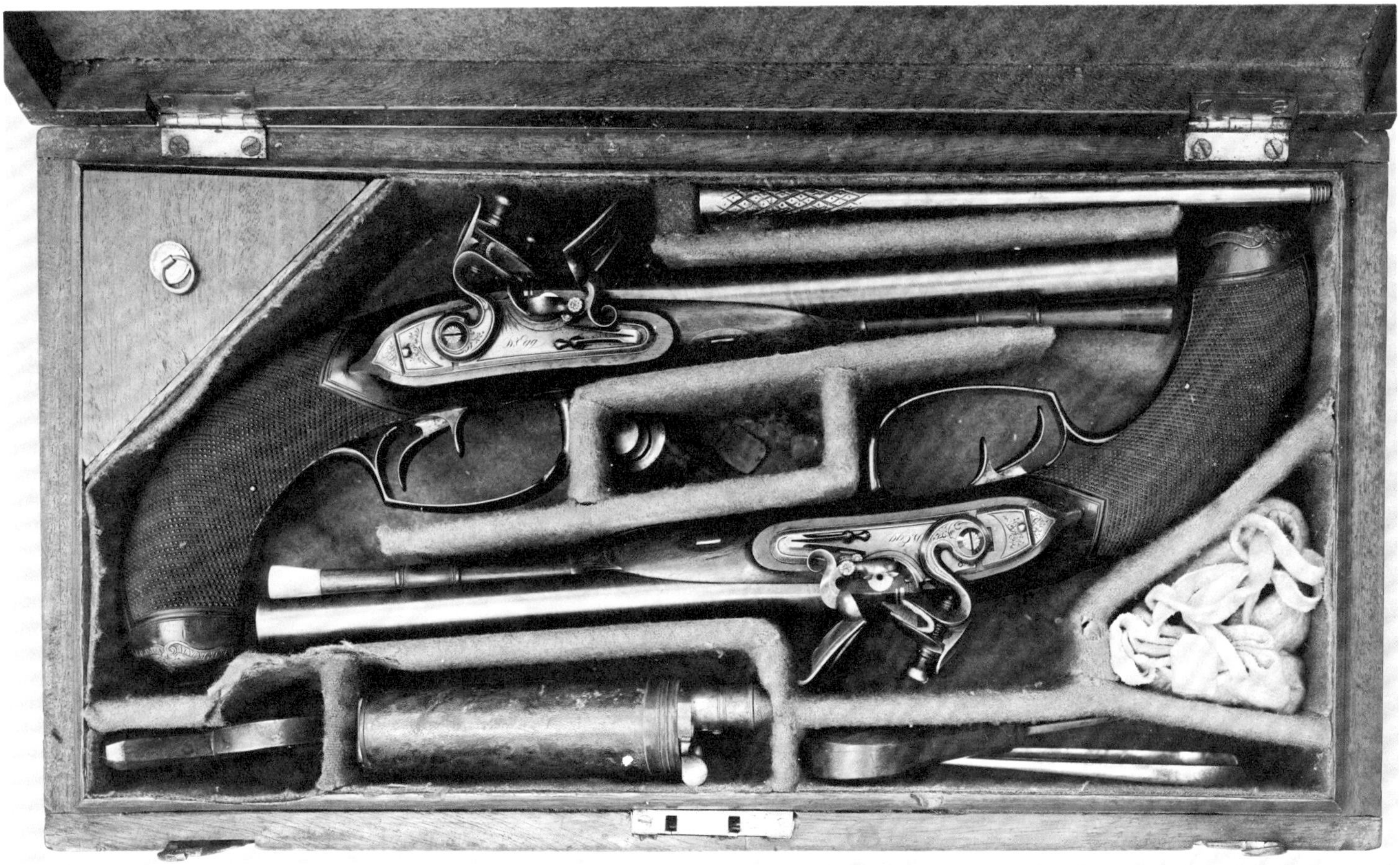

secured from Wet, that no Water can get to by any means (a Contrivance long wanted) for which reason the Guns hang Fire, and often causes Gentlemen to loose their Game. Only to be had of John Richards, Gun-Maker, No. 54, Strand, near the Adelphi, who is the sole Patentee. This invention will be particularly useful in Cock Shooting as the water that drops from the Trees in the Woods communicates with the Prime by which accident their Sport is often spoiled. N.B. The original Shop for the Clean, Strong Gun-Powder.

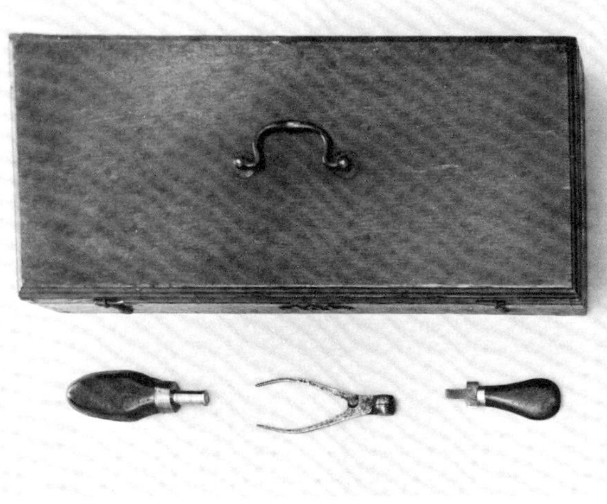

John Richards worked at 54 Strand from 1782 to 1808.

John Richards, London, about 1760
Overall length 16 in.; barrel 8 in.
Caliber .55 (28 gauge). Weight 2½ lb.

142. Cased Pair of Officer's Double-barreled Flintlock Pistols   (Bedford 496)

Barrels, browned twist, side by side with central concave rib, gold transverse lines at breech and London proofmarks; rib inscribed in gold D. EGG, LONDON; false breech; sighting along central rib, gold blade front sight. Lock plate, flat faced, cut with beveled edges engraved with flower sprays and name *D. Egg* (in script); lock plate divided under cock, rear section being movable and acting as safety, locking both cock and pan at half cock; steels with roller bearing riding on raised ridge on feather spring; gold-lined vents; semiwaterproof gold-lined pans with flash fences. Walnut three-quarter stock with checkered butt and engraved steel finial; blued steel furniture with engraved borders and trophies of arms; gold escutcheons engraved with royal ducal crest and initials CHC (or CJC); two triggers, forward one discharging right-hand lock; French-style trigger guard with floral finial; walnut ramrod with horn finial and, at opposite end, steel spiral worm.

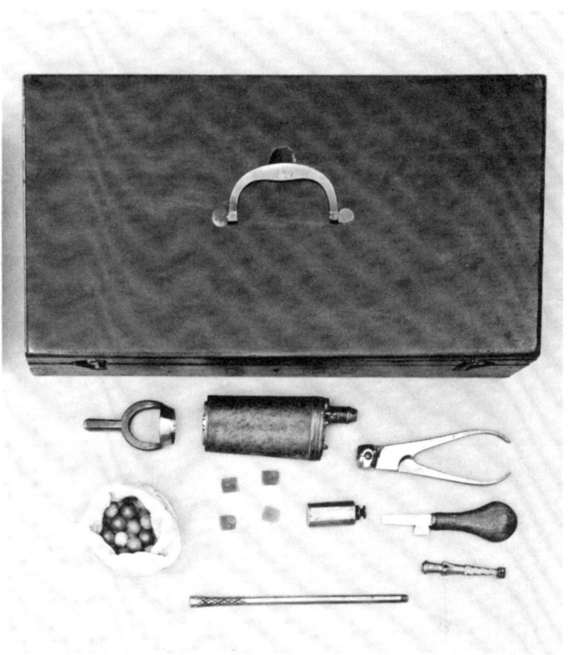

The original green-baize-lined mahogany case is provided with compartments for the pistols, powder flask, wad cutter, bullet mold, and other fittings and maker's label showing the arms of the Prince of Wales and the identification: Egg, Gunmaker to their Royal Highnesses, the Prince of Wales, Duke of York, &c &c Corner of Coventry Street, Hay Market. The case has a pivoted sunken brass handle inscribed with the same initials that are on the pistol's crest.

Durs Egg, London, about 1790
Overall length 13¾ in.; barrel 8 in.
Caliber .51 (36 gauge). Weight 2¼ lb.

143. Double-barreled Turnover Flintlock Pistol   (Bedford 416)

One of a pair. Barrels of brass, inscribed BARBAR, each in three stages, octagonal changing to polygonal at breech, forward two stages circular, molded girdles between; silver blade front sight; top facet of each barrel stamped with London proofmarks and mark LB (Lewis Barbar); each barrel has its own brass pan, ribbed striking surface on steel, and feather spring. Lock plate of brass with back-action lock, engraved borders, name BARBAR engraved on ribbon. Walnut butt and forestock; silver furniture, spurred, polished silver pommel (replacement for original pommel) inscribed *Given by John, Duke of Montague to Henry, Earl of Pembroke Jan. 1733* (in script); side plate of pierced scrollwork; escutcheon chased with arms of John, duke of Montague, surmounted by ducal coronet and enclosed within the garter; steel trigger guard, when pressed up, unlocks barrels so that they can be turned; silver balus-

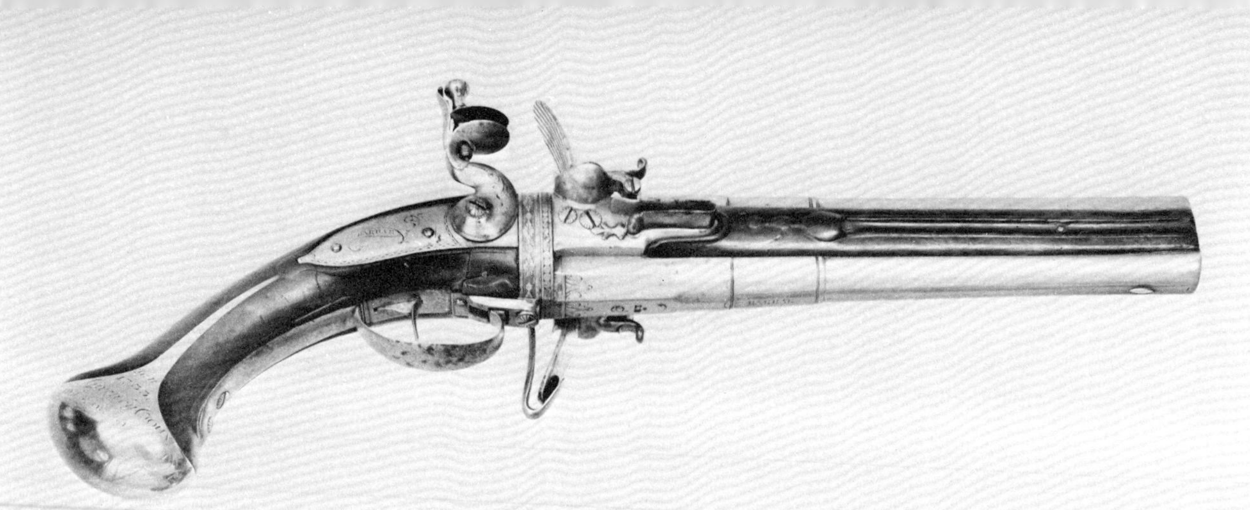

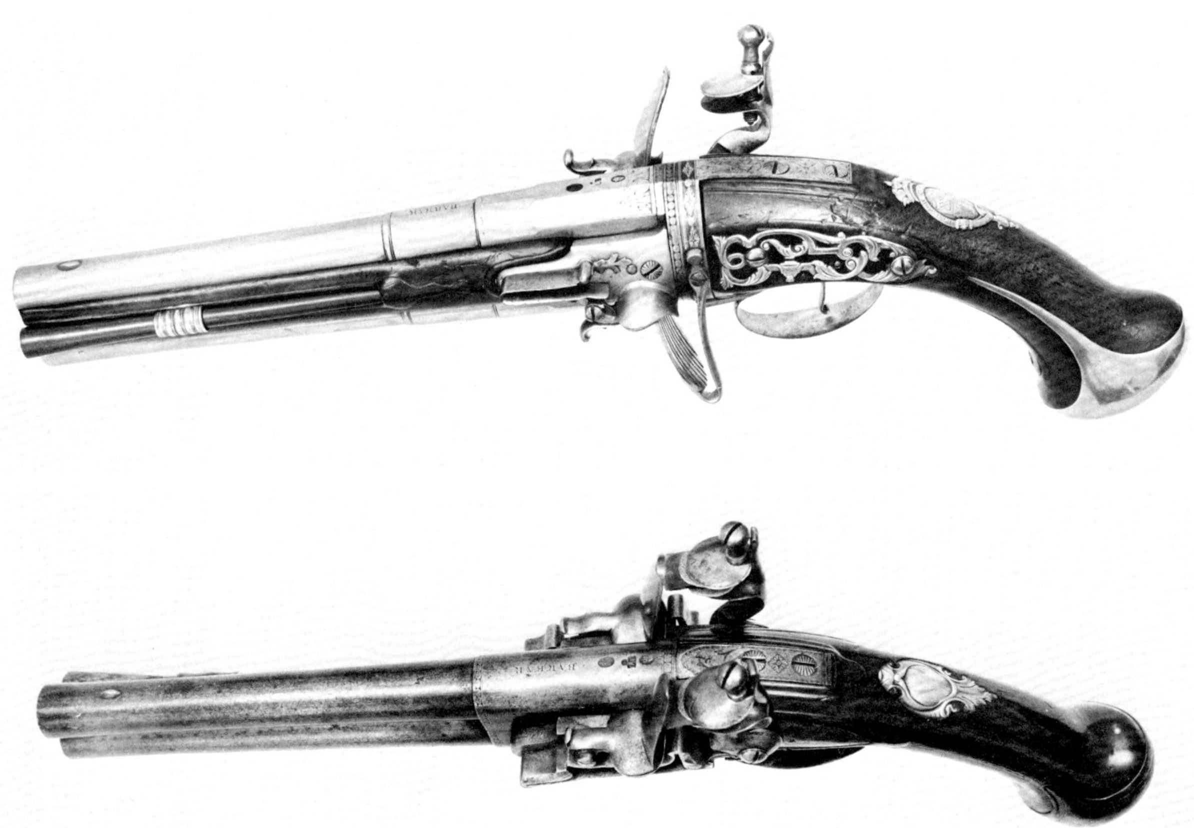

ter ramrod pipe; ramrod of walnut with brass disk finial opposite which is steel spiral worm.

This pistol's unusual features include vertically grooved steels in the Spanish manner and a hooked arm screwed to the left side of the breech. This arm hooks over the pan cover when the latter is closed and evidently served to prevent the pan cover from being pushed open when the pistol was removed hastily from its holster.

> Lewis Barbar, London, before 1733
> Overall length 16 in.; barrel 9 in.
> Caliber .58 (24 gauge). Weight 3 lb.
> Literature: Ricketts, *Firearms*, p. 81, pl. 88.

144. Officer's Double-barreled Over-and-under Flintlock Pistol (Bedford 702)

One of a pair. Barrels brazed together without central rib, in two stages, both round, engraved girdle between; upper barrel with steel blade front sight; breeches inscribed BARBAR and stamped with London proofmarks between which is mark LB (Lewis Barbar). Right-hand lock serves upper barrel, left-hand lock serves lower barrel; rounded lock plates with external main springs and "steel" springs situated underneath pans, as on Queen Anne turnoff pistols; two triggers, forward one for right-hand lock, rear one for left-hand lock. Walnut butt; steel spurred pommel with engraved borders, cap of silver chased with faun's mask; blank silver escutcheon with acanthus leaf at base; steel trigger guard; single ramrod pipe on right side; ramrod has steel tool with threaded end.

This pistol must be among the last made by Lewis Barbar, since his son took over the business and registered his own mark in 1741. Double-barreled over-and-under pistols of this type seem to have been a standard production of Lewis Barbar. Several pairs are known, all having in common a silver butt cap set on a steel pommel.

> Lewis Barbar, London, about 1740
> Overall length 15½ in.; barrel 9 in.
> Caliber .66 (16 gauge). Weight 2½ lb.

145. Double-barreled Turnoff Box-lock Flintlock Pistol (Bedford 703)

One of a pair. Side-by-side cylindrical cannon barrels in three stages, separated by molded rings, ending in raised muzzle rings; each barrel has its own pan and steel; barrels numbered 1 and 2 on underside, aligned with corresponding numbers on breech; London proofmarks between which are initials IG (Joseph Griffin) on underside of breech of each barrel. Box lock of brass with left- and right-hand cocks and two triggers; lock engraved on reverse with name GRIFFIN

within a rococo cartouche and on obverse LONDON; double-bolt safety with crescent grip operates on both cocks at same time at half cock. Walnut butt; silver furniture; spurred pommel with engraved borders surrounded by cartouche of shells and scrolls that frames cap chased in relief with grotesque mask; escutcheon of rococo form, surmounted by shell engraved with owner's dragon-head crest.

> Joseph Griffin, London, 1750–60
> Overall length 11½ in.; barrel 6 in.
> Caliber .47 (44 gauge). Weight 1½ lb.
> Literature: George, *English Pistols and Revolvers*, p. 54, nos. 1, 2, pl. VIII.

146. Converted Double-barreled Percussion Pistol (Bedford 1098)

One of a pair converted from flintlock to percussion and provided with a case by Blissett in the 19th century. Side-by-side cannon barrels in three stages separated by molded girdles and terminating in expanded muzzle rings, stamped with London proofmarks. Left- and right-hand locks, each serving its barrel; lock engraved HEYLIN CORNHILL on reverse and LONDON on obverse on ribbons within rococo scrolls; double-bolt safety engages both locks at half cock; two triggers, forward one serving right-hand lock. Walnut butt; silver spurred pommel engraved with flower trails and cartouche of shells and scrolls that frames cap chased in high relief with grotesque mask; pommel similar to that on no. 145; silver

escutcheon surmounted by classical helmet, with trophy of arms at base, and engraved with owner's initials WTH; steel trigger guard engraved with floral motifs.

Joseph Heylin was master of the Gunmakers' Company in 1777. He worked at Cornhill, London, from 1763 to 1799.

> Joseph Heylin, London, about 1760
> Overall length 11½ in.; barrel 6 in.
> Caliber .47 (44 gauge). Weight 1½ lb.

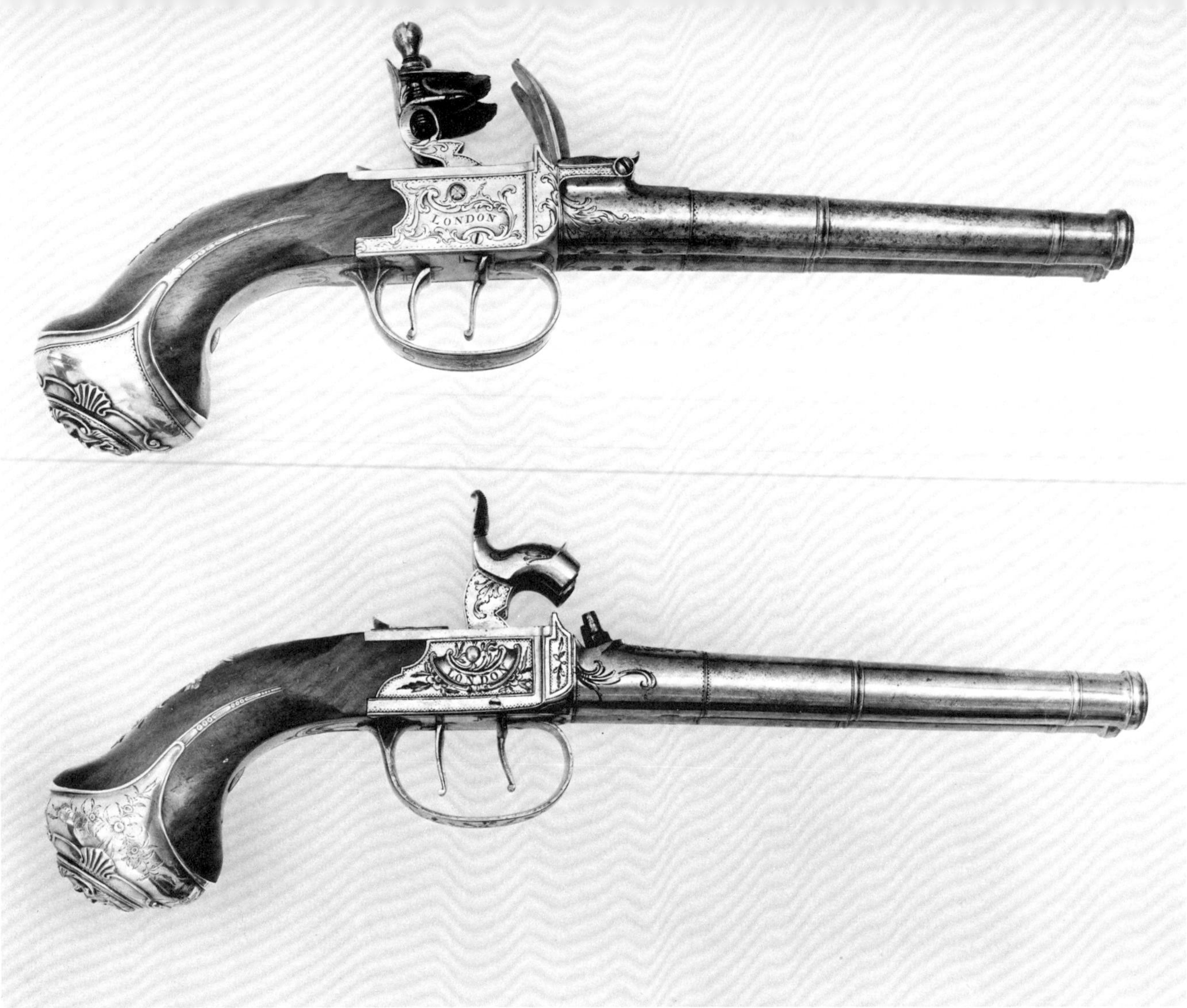

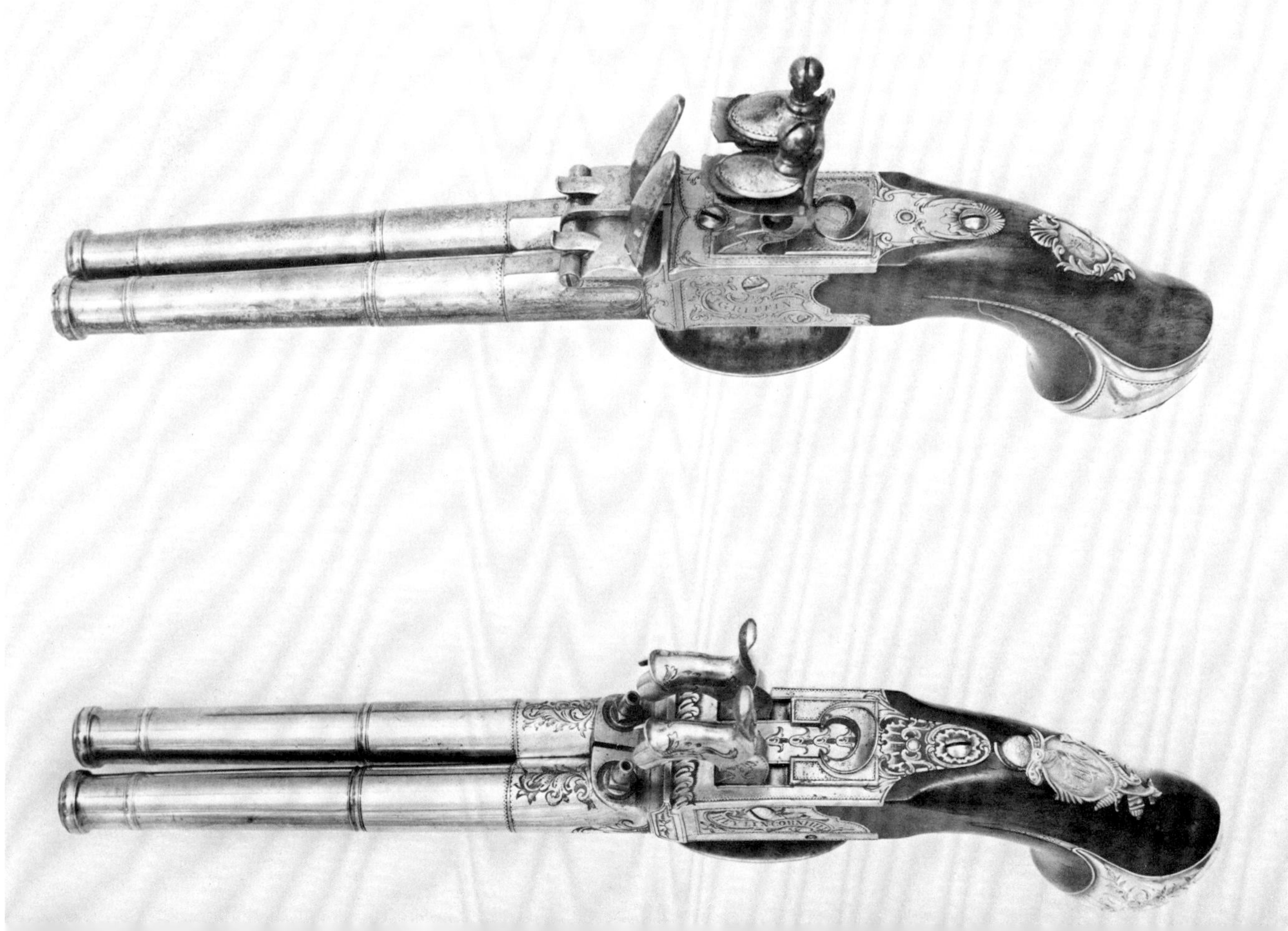

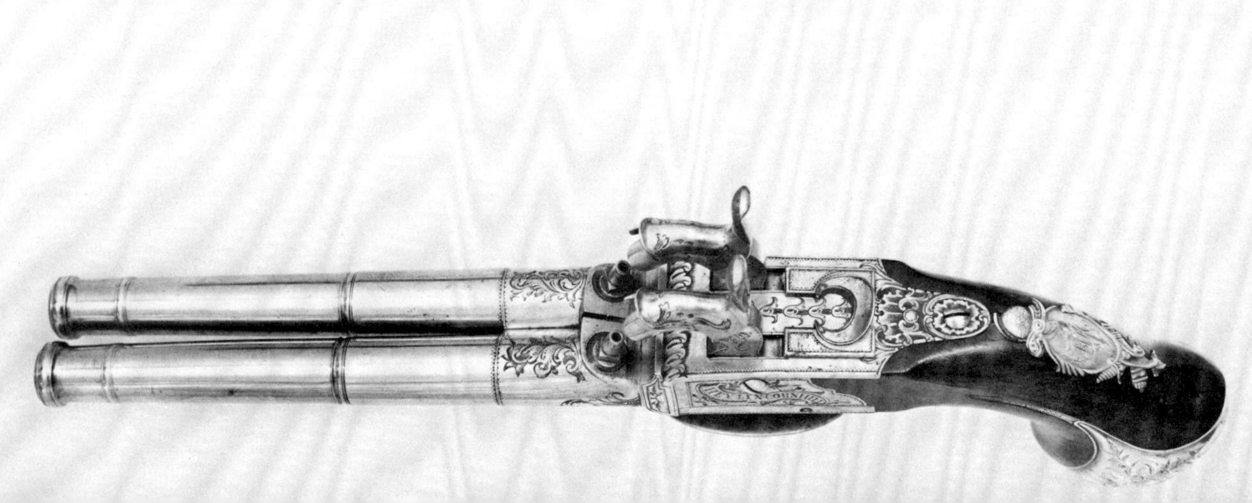

147. Double-barreled Rifled Turnoff Box-lock Flintlock Pistol (Bedford 413)

One of a pair. Side-by-side brass cannon barrels, rifled with twelve grooves, in three stages with molded girdles between, ending in expanded muzzle rings; brass box lock wrought integrally with octagonal breeches; undersides of barrels stamped 1 and 2, aligned with corresponding numbers on breech; on bottom of breech are stamped Birmingham private proofmarks between which is barrelsmith's mark TR in rectangle (Theophilus Richards). Box lock engraved on obverse with name T. RICHARDS within rococo scrollwork; two side-by-side pans with single flash fence are served by single steel and single cock; bolt controls sliding pan cover of left pan, so priming in right pan is fired first; brass bolt safety operates at half cock. Walnut butt inlaid with scrolling wire; silver butt cap, engraved with floral scrolls, secured by two iron screws.

Theophilus Richards, Birmingham, about 1760
Overall length 12½ in.; barrel 6½ in.
Caliber .53 (32 gauge). Weight 2 lb.

148. Double-barreled Turnoff Box-lock Flintlock Pistol (Bedford 1519)

One of a pair. Side-by-side barrels in three stages with moldings between, ending in expanded muzzle rings and grooved at breech for turnoff key; London private proofmarks. Box lock integral with octagonal breeches; side-by-side pans with single flash fence are served by single steel and single cock; on obverse of lock plate is bolt that controls sliding pan cover on right-hand side; (companion pistol has bolt for closing pan cover on left-hand side); priming pans fired separately, left-hand one first. Box lock, trigger guard, and outer face of steel are finely chased in low relief with floral designs against matted gold ground. Walnut butt profusely inlaid with scrolling silver wire ending in flower heads and enclosing oval escutcheon engraved with owner's initials GP; silver butt cap chased with flower surrounded by scrolls with Birmingham hallmark,

date letter for 1776, and silversmith's initials RB.

The butt-cap mark suggests that the silver mounts were purchased in Birmingham, the marks on the barrels that the pistol was finished in London.

Joseph Bunney, London, 1776
Overall length 11¼ in.; barrel 5⅜ in.
Caliber .45 (50 gauge). Weight 1¾ lb.

149. Officer's Double-barreled Flintlock Pistol (Bedford 1171)

One of a pair. Barrels set side by side, of browned stub twist with central rib; transverse engraved gold line at breech; sighting through groove in false breech and silver blade front sight; gold-lined vents. Lock plate with beveled edges, flat faced, engraved with flower sprays and name D. EGG; pan cover with roller bearings riding on elliptical ridge on feather spring; bolt safety locks cock at half cock; two triggers, forward one discharging right-hand lock. Walnut three-quarter stock with checkered grip carved with spray of flowers behind barrel tang; silver butt cap with borders centering on flower head; silver trigger guard

of French fashion, engraved with trophies of arms and flower sprays, and struck with silversmith's mark MB (Moses Brent), date letter for 1784, leopard's head, and lion passant.

Durs Egg, London, 1784
Overall length 15½ in.; barrel 10 in.
Caliber. 54 (30 gauge). Weight 2½ lb.

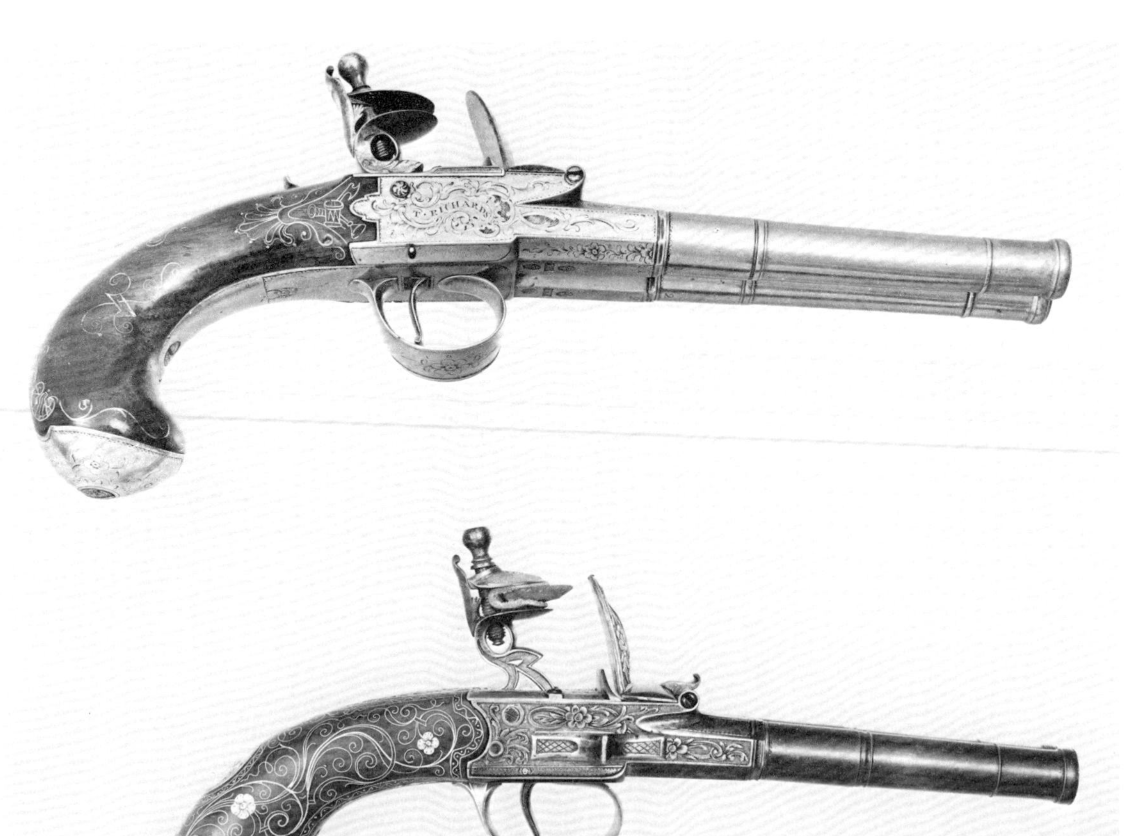

147
148

147
148

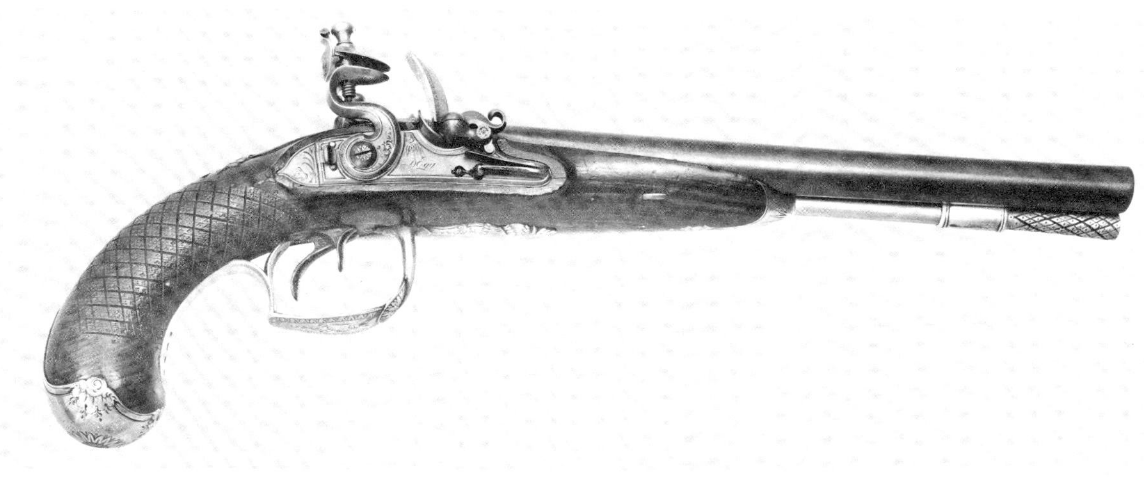

149

149

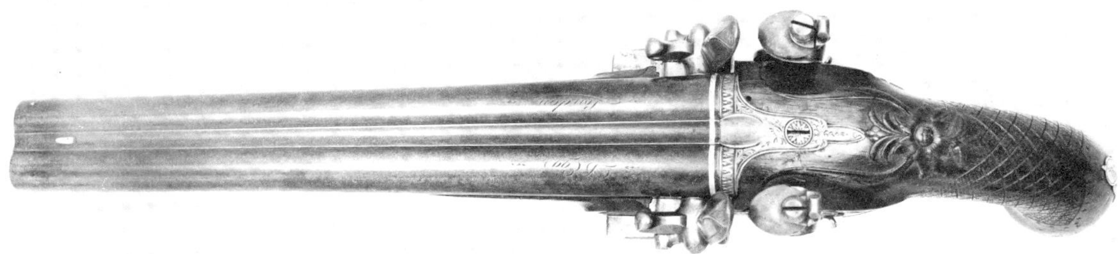

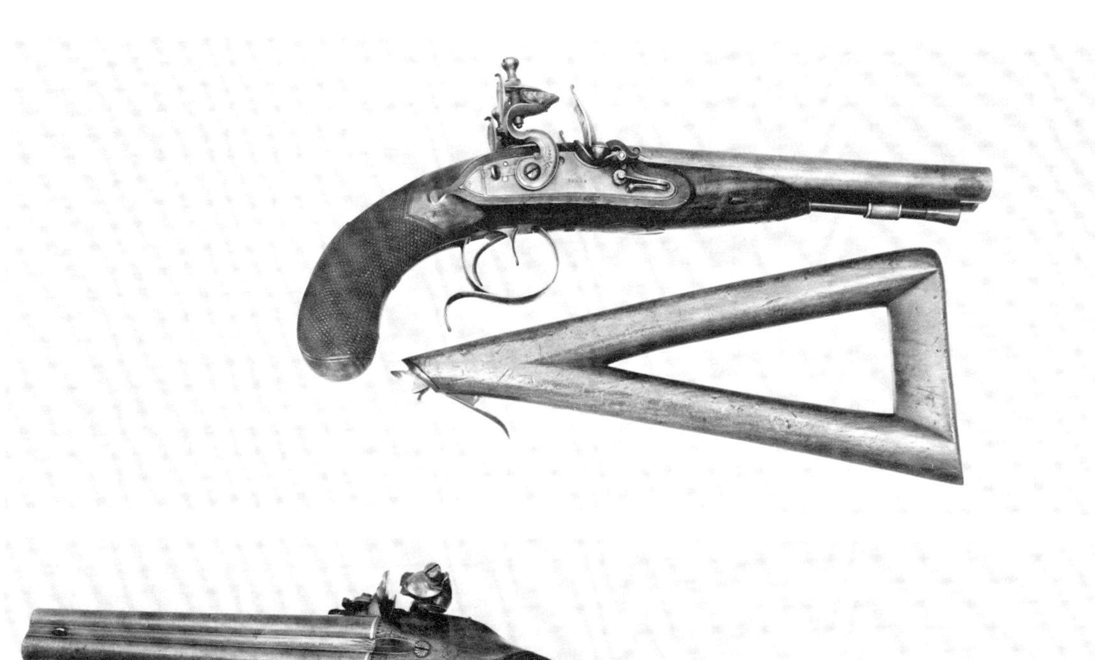

150

150

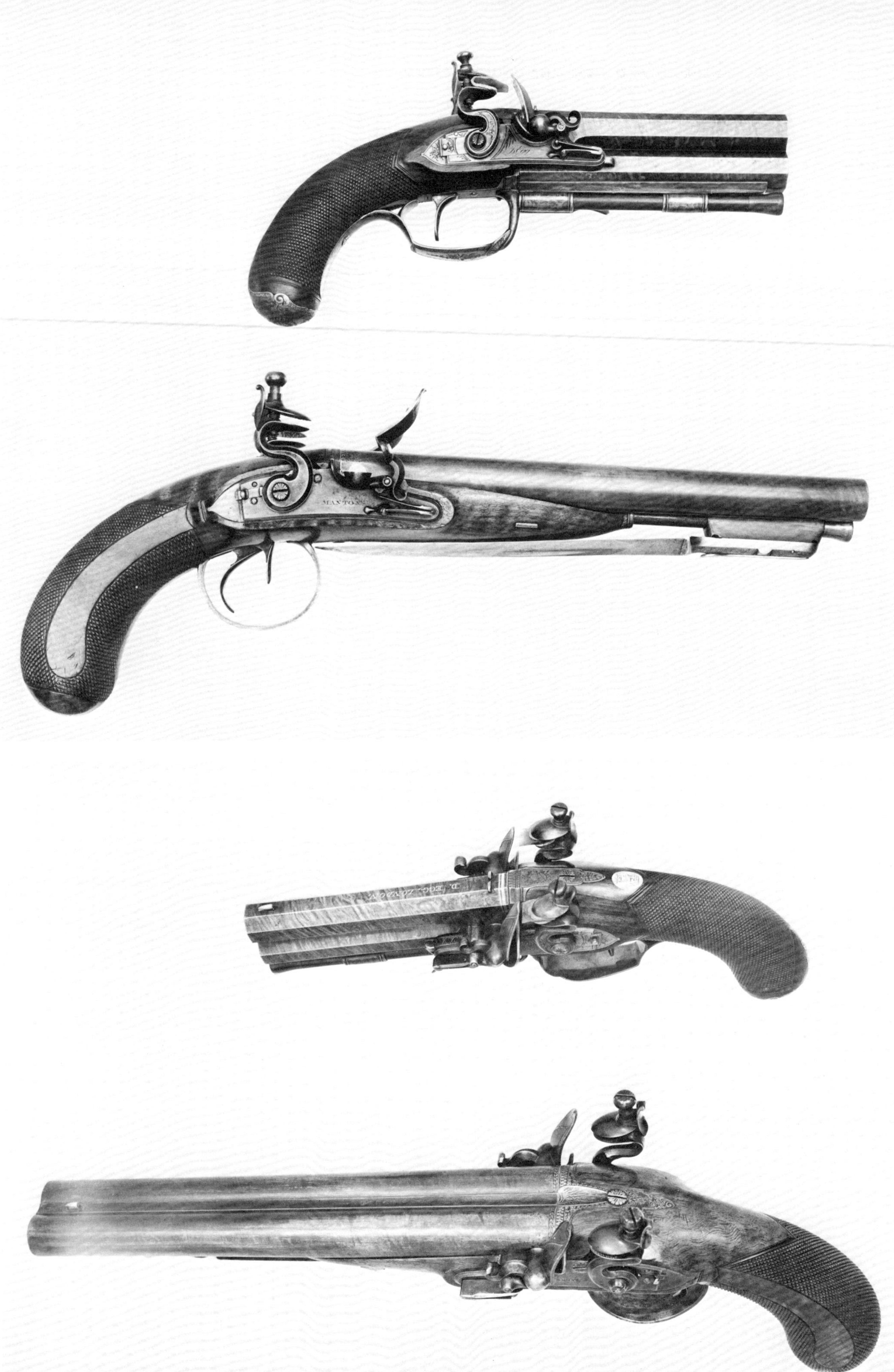

150. Double-barreled Flintlock Pistol with Removable Gunstock (Bedford 481)

One of a pair. Side-by-side browned twist barrels, cylindrical, with central rib, inscribed INNES *Maker to his MAJESTY Edinr* on rib; gold transverse line at breech on each barrel; false breech engraved with conventional foliage; sighting along central rib, steel blade front sight; gold-lined vents; single barrel slide. Flat-faced lock plates, cocks engraved with flower sprays; roller bearings on feather springs; bolt safety engages at half cock; two triggers, forward one operating right-hand lock. Walnut three-quarter stock with checkered butt; blued rear ramrod pipe and trigger guard with spur for third finger have pineapple finials; ramrod with horn finial and, on opposite end, steel spiral worm. Detachable walnut shoulder stock keyed into hollow in butt; shoulder stock is pierced to reduce weight, upper edge is reinforced with an iron strap.

Francis Innes was the leading Scottish gunmaker of his period. No. 150 and its mate were doubtless intended for an officer. An engraving of Sir Sidney Smith at the breach of Acre in 1799 shows him carrying a pistol with a shoulder stock of this type.

> Francis Innes, Edinburgh, about 1790
> Overall length 35 in.; shoulder stock 26 in.; barrel 8⅞ in.
> Caliber .45 (22 gauge). Weight 3½ lb.
> Literature: Blackmore, *Firearms*, p. 81.

151. Officer's Double-barreled Over-and-under Flintlock Pistol (Bedford 1089)

Browned twist barrels, two gold transverse lines on upper barrel; London proofmarks; stationary rear leaf sight and gold front sight; hooked breech, false breech engraved with flower sprays; on underside of lower barrel is grooved rib with two ramrod pipes; ramrod with horn finial and threaded worm; gold-lined vents and pans. Left- and right-hand locks; lock plates, with faceted borders, engraved with flower sprays and inscribed D. EGG; single trigger discharges right-hand lock first; roller bearing on feather spring; bolt safeties lock both cock and pan at half cock. Walnut half stock with checkered butt; blued steel furniture with repeated engraved borders; butt cap with tang secured by engraved screw; oval gold escutcheon engraved with royal crest beneath coronet of royal duke; French-pattern trigger guard. Blued steel belt hook attached on left-hand side of lower barrel.

This pistol belonged to Frederick Augustus (1763–1827), duke of York and Albany, second son of George III. He fought a duel with Lieutenant Colonel Lenox of the Coldstream Guards in 1789; the pistols they used are now in Windsor Castle.

> Durs Egg, London, about 1790
> Overall length 10¾ in.; barrel 5 in.
> Caliber .48 (42 gauge). Weight 1½ lb.
> Literature: Laking, *The Armoury of Windsor Castle: European Section*, cat. nos. 206–207; Christie's sale, March 30, 1827, lot 4.

152. Officer's Double-barreled Pistol with Bayonet (Bedford 1297)

Barrels, browned twist, side by side with central rib hooking into false breech; barrel rib inscribed MANTON LONDON; sighting along central rib, silver blade front sight; breech ends of barrels engraved with overlapping-leaf borders; gold-lined vents; single barrel slide. Lock plates, flat faced, with beveled edges, inscribed MANTON; steels with friction-reducing rollers; bolt safeties lock at half cock. Walnut three-quarter stock with checkered grip; blued steel trigger guard engraved with trophy of arms; ramrod has brass finial and, on opposite end, wad screw over which is screwed brass cap. Bayonet released by raising spring and swinging to right. Serial number 2728.

The bayonet appears to be an afterthought. It is attached to an enlarged ramrod pipe under the barrel.

> John Manton, London, about 1797
> Overall length 15¾ in.; with bayonet extended 22 in.; barrel 10 in.
> Caliber .65 (17 gauge). Weight 3½ lb.
> Literature: Neal and Back, *The Mantons: Gunmakers*, p. 73.

153. Officer's Double-barreled Flintlock Pistol (Bedford 715)

One of a cased pair. Barrels, browned twist, side-by-side cylindrical, with central rib inscribed I. PURDEY PRINCES STR LEICESTER SQUARE LONDON; London proofmarks; serial number 509; patent breech, each side with recessed platinum line; sighting along central rib; silver bead front sight; false breech engraved with scrolls; platinum-lined vents; single barrel slide with silver oval slots. Lock plates, flat faced, engraved with scrolls, repeated feather border motif, and gunmaker's name PURDEY within ribbon; waterproof pans; steels with friction-reducing rollers; bolt safeties engage at half cock; two triggers, forward trigger operating right-hand lock. Walnut three-quarter stock with checkered grip; blank rectangular silver escutcheon; engraved steel trigger guard has traces of bluing; trigger guard and ramrod socket have engraved pineapple finials.

> James Purdey, London, about 1818
> Overall length 12¾ in.; barrel 6½ in.
> Caliber .64 (18 gauge). Weight 2 lb.

153

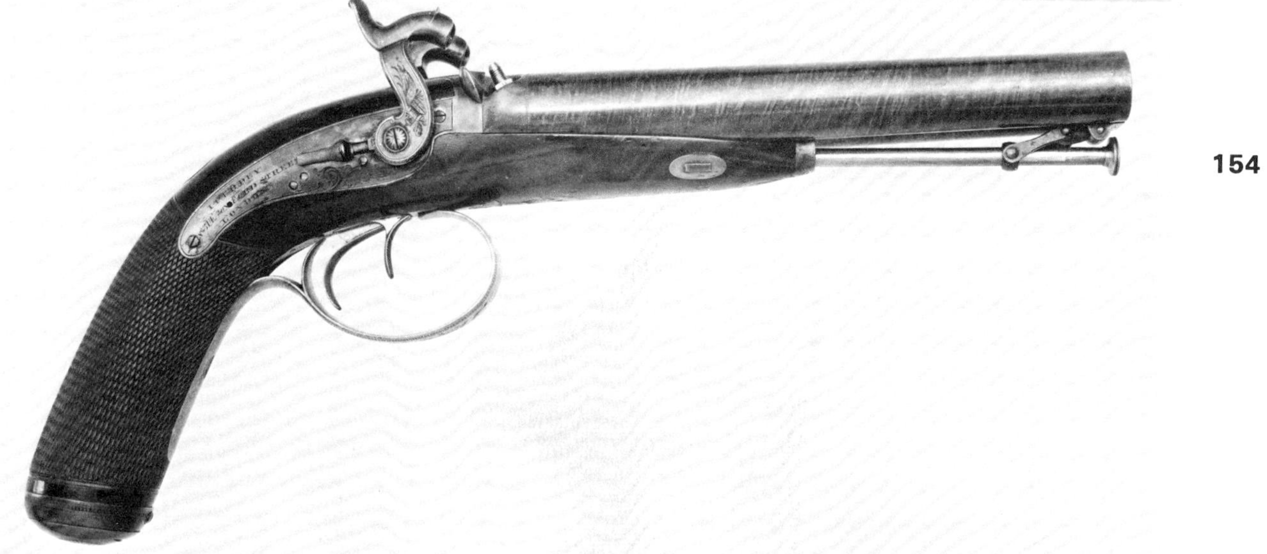

154

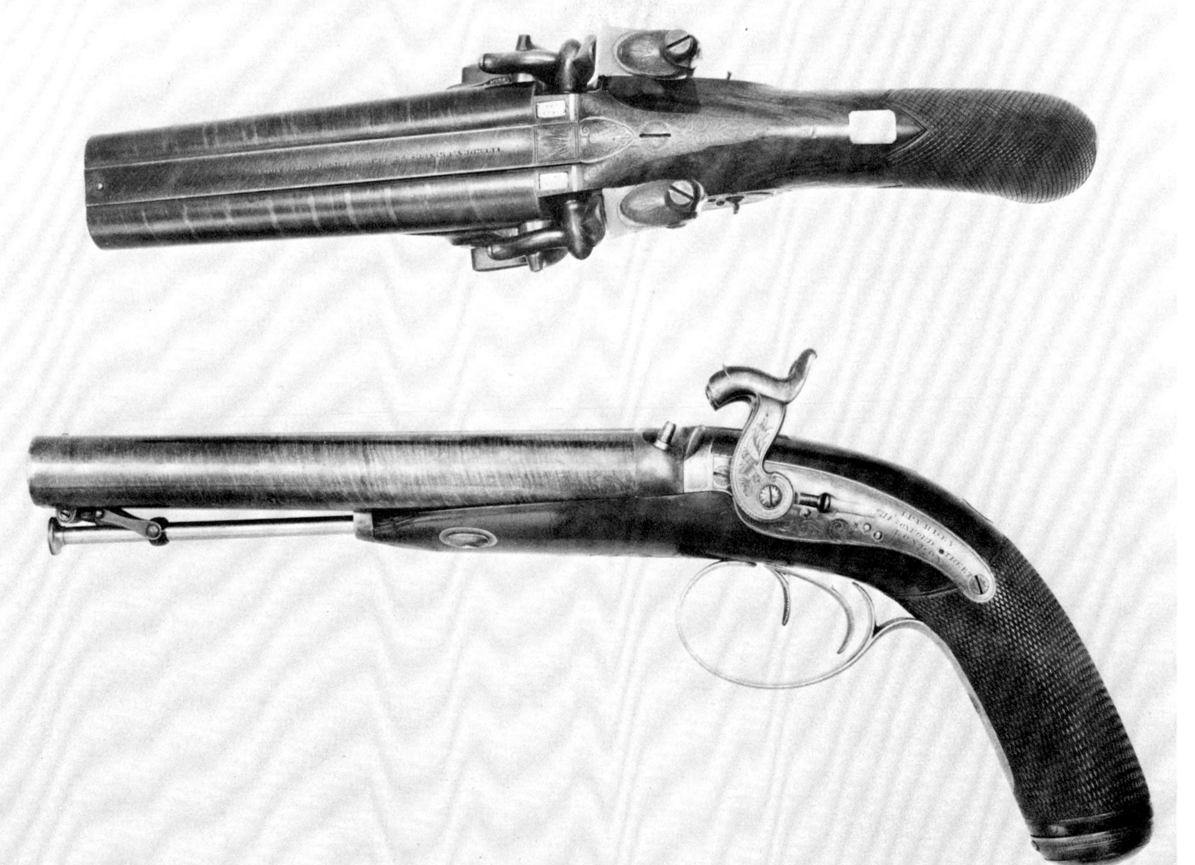

153

154

155

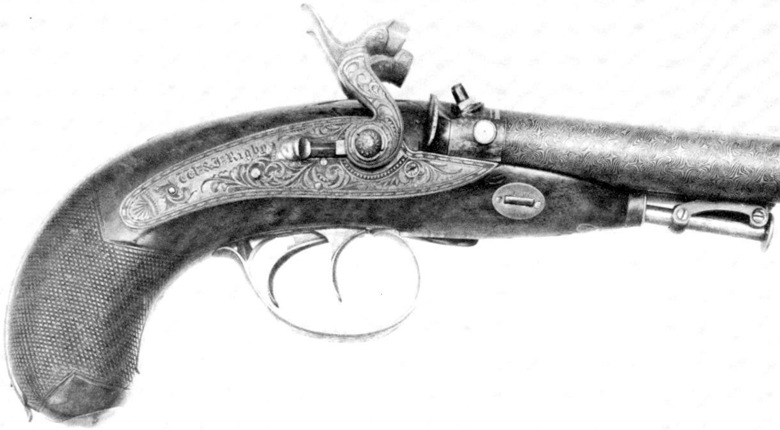

156

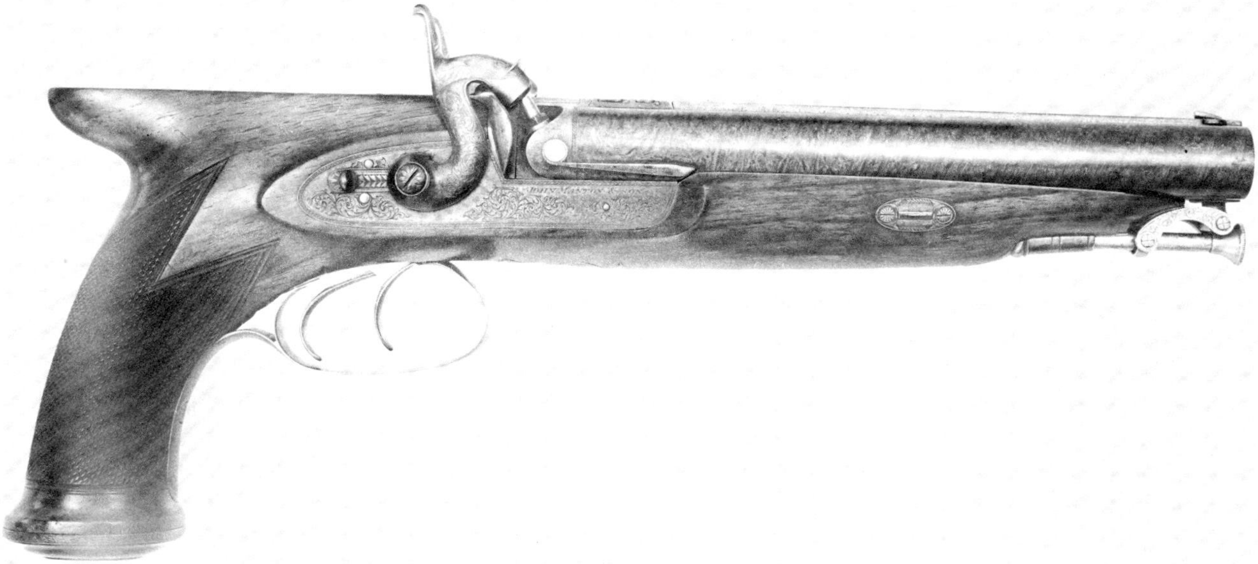

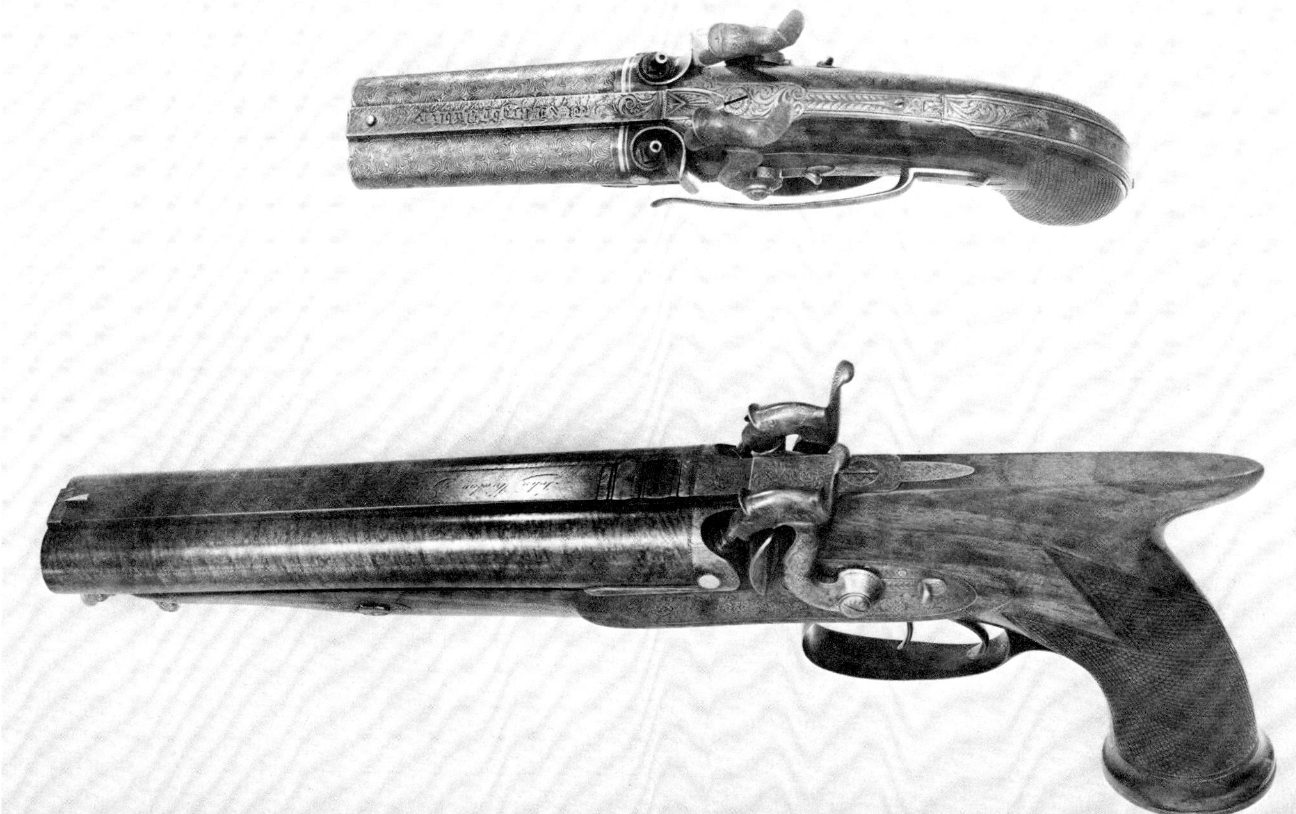

155

156

154. Officer's Double-barreled Percussion-cap Pistol (Bedford 1219)

Barrels, browned twist, side-by-side with central rib; patent breeches with platinum line, case hardened, as is the false breech; sighting along central rib, silver bead front sight; single barrel slide with oval slots. Lock plates, with case-hardened finish, inscribed I. PURDEY NO. 314 1/2 OXFORD STREET LONDON; back-action locks engraved with scrollwork; dolphin hammers; bolt safeties operating at half cock. Walnut three-quarter stock with checkered grip; steel furniture engraved with trophies of arms, and with traces of original bluing; butt has hollow receptacle with hinged and engraved steel cap; blank octagonal silver escutcheon; trigger guard and ramrod socket have pineapple finials; swivel ramrod of steel for loading on horseback. Serial number 2114.

This pistol has an unusual refinement in that the forward trigger, discharging the right-hand lock, is hatched to give the finger a surer grip. The pistol retains its original case.

James Purdey, London, about 1831
Overall length 14¾ in.; barrel 8 in.
Caliber .73 (12 gauge). Weight 3 lb.

155. Double-barreled Percussion-cap Pistol (Bedford 1064)

One of a pair. Barrels, Damascus twist, side-by-side, cylindrical, with patent breeches, two platinum lines, false breech engraved with scrollwork; sighting along central ridge, silver bead front sight; platinum-lined safety vents. Lock plates engraved with scrollwork and inscribed WM & JN RIGBY; back-action locks; dolphin hammers; bolt safeties engage at half cock. Walnut three-quarter stock with checkered butt; blued steel furniture engraved with scrollwork; silver butt cap; pineapple trigger-guard finial; belt hook attached to left-hand lock plate; swivel ramrod. Barrel tang

continued as hinged back strap extending to end of butt, which opens on spring revealing five empty receptacles: two for cartridges, two for spare nipples, separated by a rectangular one. Serial number 8712.

The first Rigby of Dublin was established in 1735. William Rigby succeeded to the business in 1819 and subsequently entered into partnership with his younger brother, John. They were pioneers in the forging of Damascus barrels. Their distinctive style, noticeable in no. 155, was a fine pattern deeply etched to bring the harder metal into relief.

William & John Rigby, Dublin, about 1842
Overall length 9 in.; barrel 3⅞ in.
Caliber .52 (32 gauge). Weight 1¼ lb.

156. Double-barreled Rifled Percussion Pistol (Bedford 1021)

One of a pair of the type sometimes known as the howdah pistol. Side-by-side heavy rifled barrels of browned twist with raised flat central rib; both barrels rifled with eight grooves; patent breeches with platinum-lined escape vents; sighting along central ridge with two hinged leaf V-sights and silver blade front sight. Lock plates, flat faced with engraved feather borders, scrollwork, and name JOHN MANTON & SON; dolphin hammers; bolt safeties engaged at half cock. Walnut full stock with horn finial, saw handle, checkered butt; pommel with engraved oval steel butt cap; trigger guard engraved with scrollwork and terminating in pineapple finial; serial number 12359 engraved on trigger-guard strap; stirrup swivel ramrod.

In 1814 or 1815 John Manton took his son, George Henry, into partnership; thereafter the firm was known as John Manton & Son. It produced about 250 firearms a year. On the death of John Manton (1834), George Henry made his son Gideon a partner. George Henry Manton died in 1854.

John Manton & Son, London, about 1852
Overall length 14½ in.; barrel 8⅛ in.
Caliber .61 (20 gauge). Weight 3¼ lb.

12

AIR AND BLUNDERBUSS PISTOLS AND GUNS

Air guns vary greatly in type. The compressed air firearm, with which we are concerned here, has been used in war and in the hunting of such game as stag, deer, chamois, and boar. It stores its energy in the form of air pumped into a reservoir located between the inner and outer barrel tubes, in the butt, or in a ball placed below the barrel. Two of our pistols (161, 162) and a gun (168) have a simulated flintlock, including cock and dummy steel, which gives them the appearance of conventional firearms. The cock is actually an essential part of the mechanism. With the fall of the cock a projecting lug on the cock itself or on the tumbler strikes the opening valve and releases sufficient air to propel the ball. In one of our pistols (161), dating about 1770, the barrel consists of two tubes, one inside the other. The inner tube is the barrel proper, while the space between the inner and outer tubes is the air reservoir. The other types of reservoir are more often found. In two of our examples (nos. 162 and 168) the air is held in a ball of brass or bronze, screwed to the gun under the breech end of the barrel. The neck of the ball is fitted with a pin valve, which, when struck by a lever of the lock, releases part of the air. A much more practical solution was to have the reservoir in the hollowed butt (no. 163), from which it was unscrewed and charged with a special pump. Our example is a repeating air pistol in which the bullets are contained in a tubular magazine alongside the barrel, a system that was invented in 1779 by Bartholme Girardoni, an Italian inventor in Austrian service. The Girardoni air gun was introduced into the Austrian Army as the Model 1780 and was used by some Jägers. The gunmaker Samuel Henry Staudenmayer, who signed our pistol, introduced the Austrian mechanism to England. Staudenmayer worked for the Prince of Wales and made for him a similar repeating air rifle that is today in the Windsor Castle Armoury.

Air guns were produced by several unusually able gunmakers. Marin Le Bourgeois, who is credited with the invention of the French flintlock early in the seventeenth century, is also known to have made an air gun. Johann Gottfried Kolbe, who came to England from Suhl in Thuringia, was in London between 1730 and 1737. At that time he made the splendid air gun, considered to be one of the finest silver-mounted firearms in existence, and now in the Victoria and Albert Museum. A strike-a-light with split barrel by Kolbe is in our group (no. 194). Johannes Samuel Pauly came to England in 1814 and took out a patent for an "Apparatus for Discharging Firearms by means of Compressed Air," an example of which is in the exhibition (no. 131).

The second type of firearm in this group is the blunderbuss, widely used in England from early in the seventeenth century. A characteristic feature is the expanded muzzle. This was primarily an aid in loading; contrary to popular belief, the wide muzzle had no effect on scattering the charge. The firearms were usually loaded with pistol balls or shot for use at close quarters. Blunderbusses were on occasion used in the army, mainly by the cavalry; they were more often used in the navy. The blunderbuss was widely used by civilians, by travelers against highwaymen, by householders against thieves. Barrels and mounts were often of brass, as may be seen on our earliest pistol (no. 157), dating about 1680, and on a carbine (no. 167), dating about 1785. Primarily a firearm of the flintlock period, the blunderbuss appeared in numerous forms. In the present group are four pistols dating from 1680 to 1800, the last a box-lock with spring bayonet. There is also a dog-lock carbine of the mid-seventeenth century and three flintlock carbines dating from about 1690 to 1785. The latest carbine also has a bayonet. These brass-barreled blunderbusses with folding bayonet were often carried as the personal arm of a mailcoach guard.

---

157. Blunderbuss Flintlock Pistol
(Bedford 1215)

Brass barrel in two stages separated by molded girdle around which is engraved conventional foliage; breech octagonal changing to polygonal, engraved with overlapping foliage; forward stage circular, expanding toward muzzle; London proofmarks and indecipherable barrelsmith's mark. Lock plate, rounded, engraved with strawberry foliage and inscribed G. FISHER; of early construction with no bridle between pan and pan-cover screw. Walnut full stock carved with shell behind barrel tang; brass furniture; butt cap with spurs, sides engraved with strawberry foliage; serpentine side plate; blank escutcheon surmounted by lion's mask; trigger guard with vase finial; ramrod has horn finial and, at opposite end, iron spiral worm. Barrel, lock, and furniture of about 1680; restocked probably about 1730.

George Fisher was master of the Gunmakers' Company in 1677.

George Fisher, London, about 1680
Overall length 14 in.; barrel 7 3/16 in.
Muzzle diameter 1¼ in. Weight 3¼ lb.

158. Blunderbuss Flintlock Pistol
(Bedford 1275)

One of a pair. Brass barrel in three stages separated by molded girdles, octagonal changing to polygonal at breech, two forward stages of circular section expanding to blunderbuss muzzle; left facet at breech

157

158

157

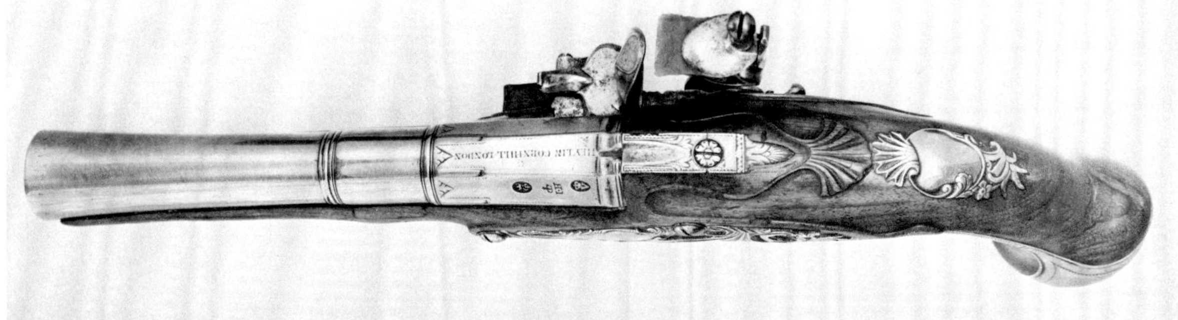

158

stamped with London proofmarks between which is mark IH crowned (Joseph Heylin). Lock plate, flat faced, with engraved borders and name HEYLIN; bolt safety engages at half cock. Walnut full stock has carved shell adjacent to barrel tang; brass furniture; spurred butt cap cast and chased in high relief with trophy of arms surrounded by cartouche composed of shell and scrolls; pierced and scrolled side plate includes rococo cartouche; blank escutcheon surmounted by shell, scrolls and flowers at base; trigger guard has pedestal-and-vase finial.

In spite of its relatively late date, this pistol has earlier features, including an octagonal breech, ramrod pipes of baluster form, and a symmetrical trigger-guard finial. This pistol and its mate were purchased from Heylin by the Danniell family of Colchester, in whose possession they remained until recently.

Joseph Heylin, London, about 1760–70
Overall length 14 in.; barrel 7¾ in.
Muzzle diameter 15/16 in. Weight 2 lb.

159. Blunderbuss Flintlock Pistol
(Bedford 706)

One of a pair. Barrel in two stages separated by molded girdle engraved with flowers; octagonal at breech, engraved with rococo scrolls; forward stage round, expanding to blunderbuss muzzle; London proofmarks stamped on three facets at breech. Lock plate, flat faced, with name BARKER engraved on ribbon within rococo scrolls; engraved borders; gold-lined vent; bolt safety engages at half cock; faceted steel. Walnut full stock carved with shell behind barrel tang; steel furniture; spurred pommel, sides engraved with sprays of flowers; flat side plate engraved with rococo scrollwork, inlaid in stock, and secured by two side nails; oval escutcheon, flower above and vase below, engraved with initial W; trigger guard with acorn finial; ramrod has iron worm.

W. Barker, London, about 1770–80
Overall length 14¼ in.; barrel 8 in.
Muzzle diameter 1⅛ in. Weight 1¾ lb.

160. Box-lock Blunderbuss Flintlock Pistol with Bayonet
(Bedford 730)

Cannon barrel in three stages separated by molded girdles, octagonal at breech, forward stages circular, muzzle ring; London proofmarks on exposed bottom facet of barrel; on right side of barrel are attached socket and pipe that house brass ramrod; under barrel is spring bayonet; when bayonet is folded, its tip fits into notch in trigger guard; when trigger guard is pressed back, bayonet is released. Box lock forged integrally with breech; engraved on reverse side with foliation and name W. BOND in scroll; on obverse are

engraved trophies of arms and address LOMBARD ST 59 LONDON in oval. Walnut butt, checkered; silver butt cap engraved with spiral ornament and conventional leaves; bolt safety engages at half cock; steel trigger guard; iron belt hook secured by two screws.

William Bond was master of the Gunmakers' Company in 1829. He died in 1836. He was the son of Edward Bond, who was admitted freeman of the Gunmakers' Company in 1799.

William Bond, London, about 1800
Overall length 9 in.; barrel 4¼ in.
Muzzle diameter ¾ in. Weight 1¼ lb.

161. Air Pistol with Simulated Flintlock
(Bedford 1214)

Brass barrel of circular section in two stages separated by molded girdle; at breech inscribed BATE LONDON; grooved rear sight on barrel tang; blade front sight; compressed-air chamber in cylinder surrounding barrel. Lock plate, flat faced, engraved with rococo scrolls and name BATE in ribbon; loop-neck cock; plunger that releases air valve is connected with cock; lock is provided with both pan and pan cover and spring, although these are not functional. Walnut full stock carved with shell behind engraved barrel tang; brass furniture; spurred butt cap, spandrels engraved with flower sprays and carved with shell on each side; on underside of butt cap is stud that when pressed opens oval cap and reveals valve attachment for air pump; side plate engraved with scrollwork and secured by two side nails; blank escutcheon surmounted by helmet and bordered with trophy of arms; trigger guard with flower-spray finial; ramrod with horn finial and, on opposite end, iron spiral worm.

Edward Bate, London, about 1770
Overall length 20⅜ in.; barrel 12⅜ in.
Caliber .42. Weight 4 lb.

162. Air Pistol with Simulated Flintlock
(Bedford 1011)

Barrel of gilt brass, octagonal, covered with brown lacquer; under barrel are spherical brass air reservoir and silver grooved rib for silver-headed ramrod; silver ramrod pipe; plunger release for air barrel is connected to descent of cock; rear V-sight on false breech; inset iron front sight. Lock plate, flat faced, filed with beveled edges engraved with overlapping leaves; sunburst engraved in front of cock, below this is name BATE; hair trigger and detent. Walnut three-quarter stock with silver fore-end engraved with sunburst; checkered butt with brass recess for attachment of shoulder stock; trigger guard engraved with trophies and struck with lion passant, crowned leopard's head, sovereign's head in pro-

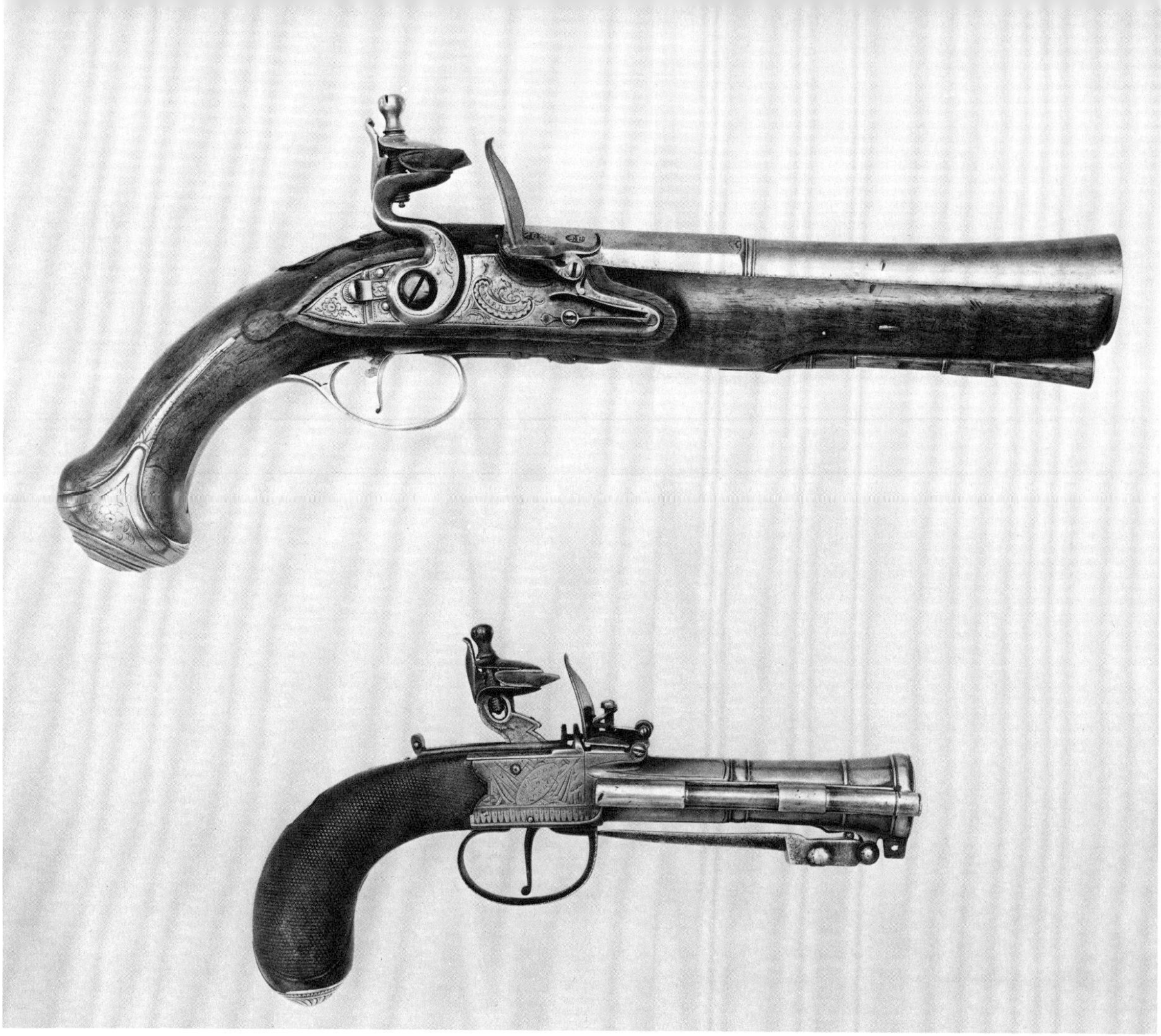

159

160

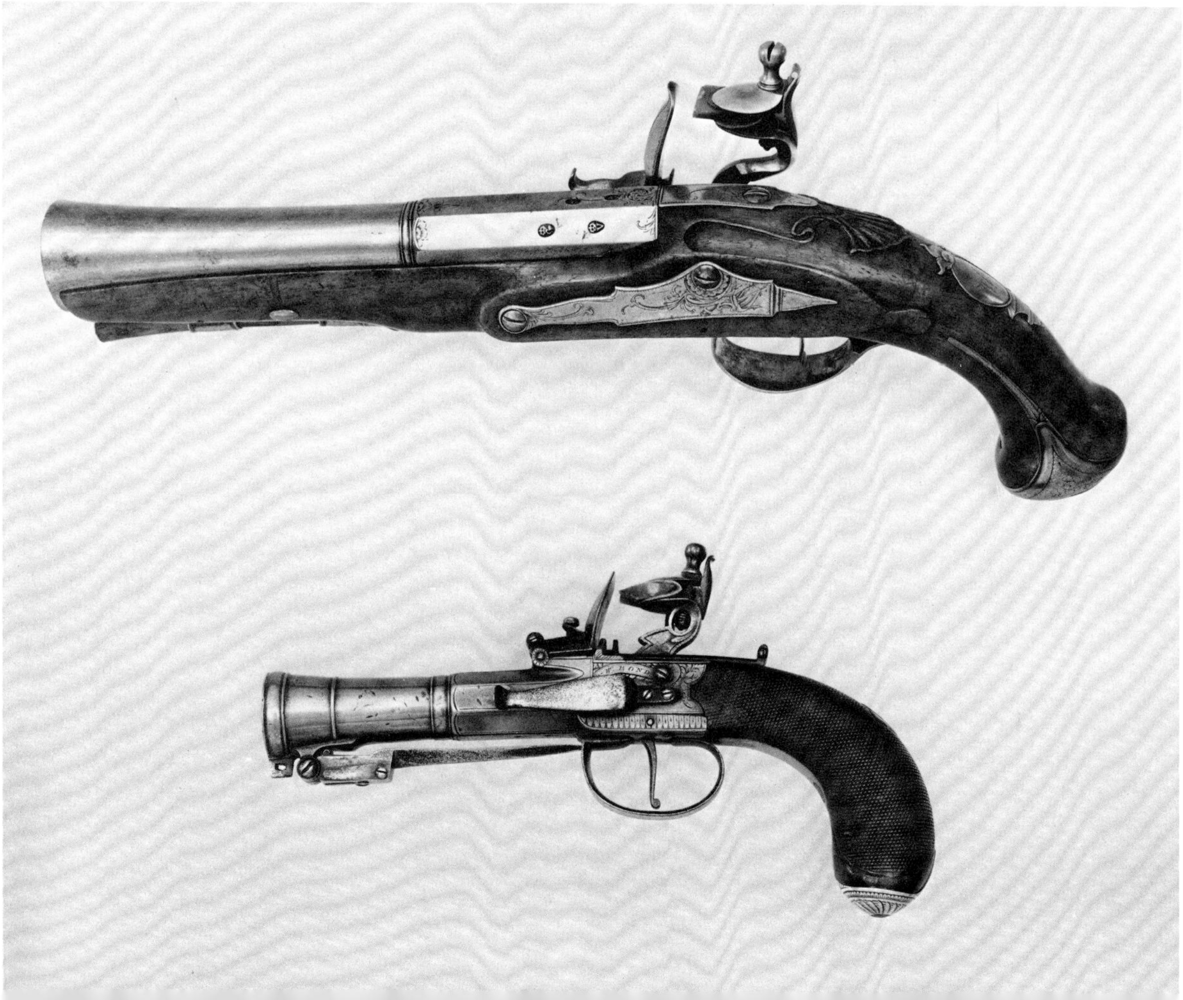

159

160

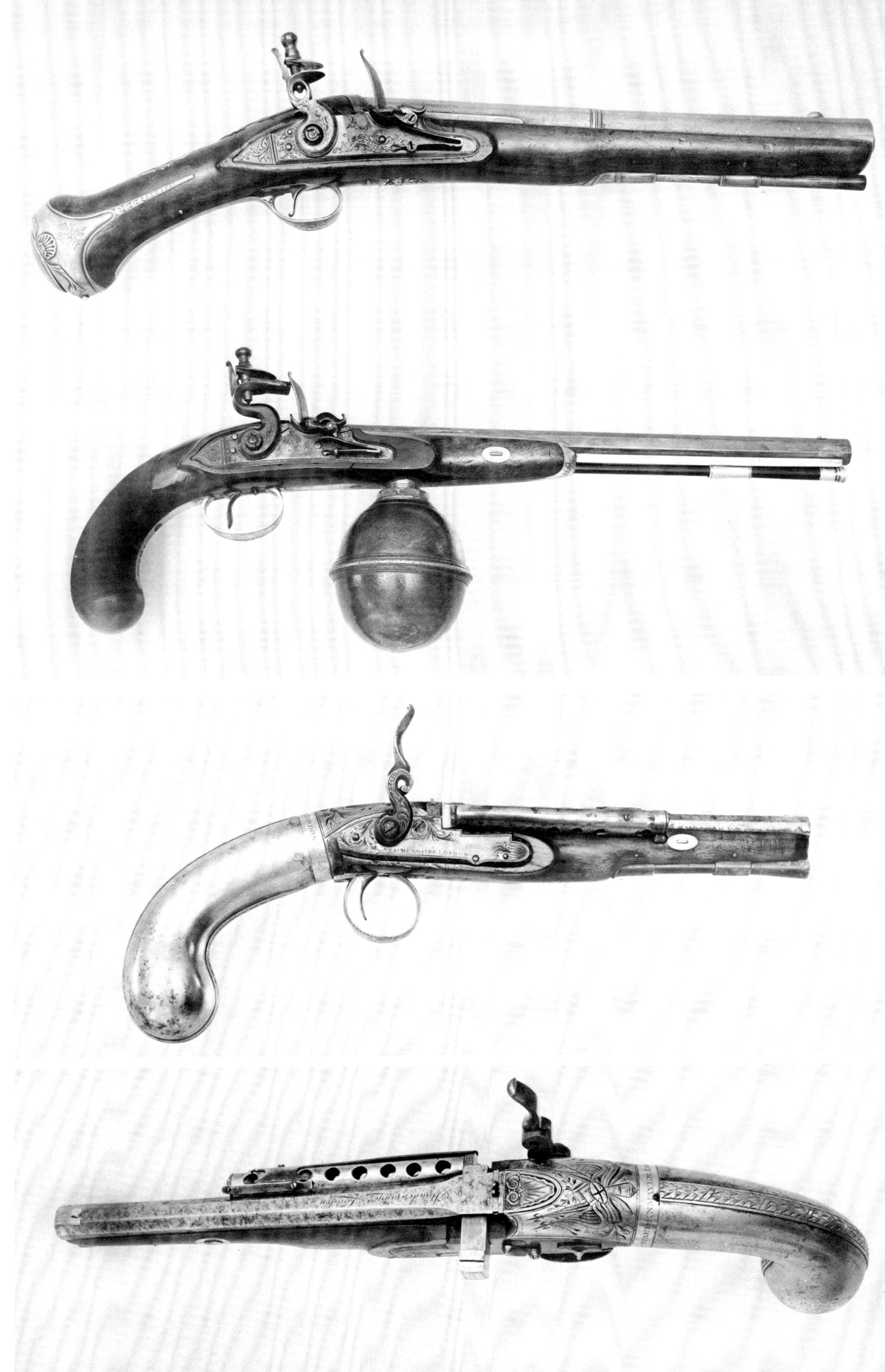

file, date letter for 1809, and initials MB (Moses Brent).
Thomas Bate, London, 1809
Overall length 19⅜ in.; barrel 14 in.
Caliber. 30. Weight 5 lb.

163. Air Pistol (Bedford 1293)

Barrel, octagonal, except square at breech, with traces of browning; on right side is tube with eight perforations serving as magazine; loading from magazine is accomplished by pushing to the right a transverse bolt situated at breech with aperture at its right end; bolt receives ball and, when spring is released, places it in breech; top facet of barrel inscribed *Staudenmayer London* (in script), same inscription in Roman letters appears on lock plate and on circular brass band bordering front end of grip; rear iron inset V-sight; silver inset front sight. Lock plate, flat faced, engraved with scrolls; specially designed lock does not simulate flintlock, as is often the case with air pistols; on reverse side of lock plate is sliding bolt for locking grip; in front of bolt is pivoted safety that prevents release of plunger. Walnut full forestock reaching to muzzle with horn fore-end; trigger guard with pineapple finial; stock engraved behind barrel with trophies of arms. The air reservoir is contained in the hollow polished steel butt, down the back of which is a central band chiseled with foliage. The reservoir has to be unscrewed and charged with air by a separate pump. The procedure for discharging is first to cock the hammer and release the safety; when the trigger is pressed and the hammer descends, a plunger opens the reservoir, releasing sufficient air to discharge the ball.

Samuel Henry Staudenmayer at first worked for John Manton and was considered one of the finest rifle borers of his time. Subsequently he worked in Cockspur Street until 1834. He was often employed by the Prince of Wales, later Prince Regent. His locks are very similar to those of John Manton. A repeating air rifle by Staudenmayer is in Windsor Castle (Blackmore, *Royal Sporting Guns at Windsor*, p. 50, pls. 38, 39).

Samuel Henry Staudenmayer, London, about 1800
Overall length 14½ in.; barrel 8⅜ in.
Caliber .44 (54 gauge). Weight 2½ lb.

164. Blunderbuss Dog-lock Carbine (Bedford 1000A)

Barrel in two stages, octagonal changing to polygonal and round, enlarging toward muzzle; London proofmarks; barrel secured by two transverse pins and barrel tang, which is secured by vertical screw from lower side of stock. Lock plate, flat faced, engraved with strawberry foliage and inscribed *W. Phippes* (in script); lock with horizontally acting sear, dog safety catch engaging between half and full cock, internal steel spring; cock engraved with monster; faceted steel. Walnut full stock, club-shaped butt with cow-horn butt plate and fore-end strap; iron trigger guard is replacement; brass ramrod pipes with stamped decoration.

A pair of dog-lock pistols by William Phippes is in the George F. Harding Museum in Chicago (inv. no. 2634). Phippes was an ironsmith and worked from about 1645 to 1660. He was the first to be prosecuted by the Gunmakers' Company for making firearms when not a member of the company.

William Phippes, London, about 1650–60
Overall length 30¼ in.; barrel 17½ in.
Muzzle diameter 1¼ in. Weight 6 lb.

165. Blunderbuss Flintlock Carbine (Bedford 999)

Blunderbuss barrel in two stages separated by molded girdle, at breech octagonal changing to polygonal, engraved at rear of breech with strawberry foliage and on alternate facets in polygonal section with overlapping leaves; front section round, expanding toward muzzle; on facet at breech are London proofmarks and gunmaker's mark, initials WN surmounted by star (William Nutt). Lock plate, rounded, engraved with strawberry foliage terminating in dragon heads and inscribed W. NUTT; engraved line borders. Walnut full stock carved to outline barrel tang; brass furniture; flat butt plate, its tang engraved with strawberry foliage terminating in monster's head, is secured by five iron nails; pierced serpentine side plate; movable iron suspension ring secured on reverse side of stock; escutcheon sur-

165

166

165

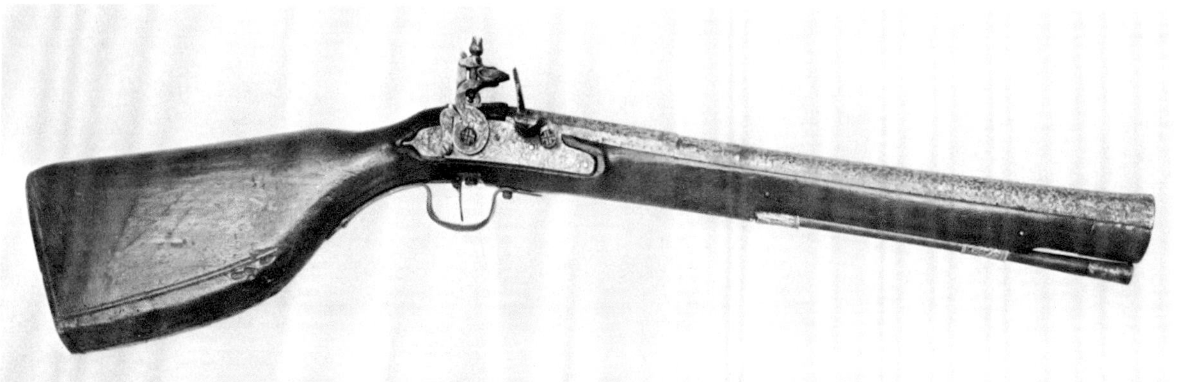

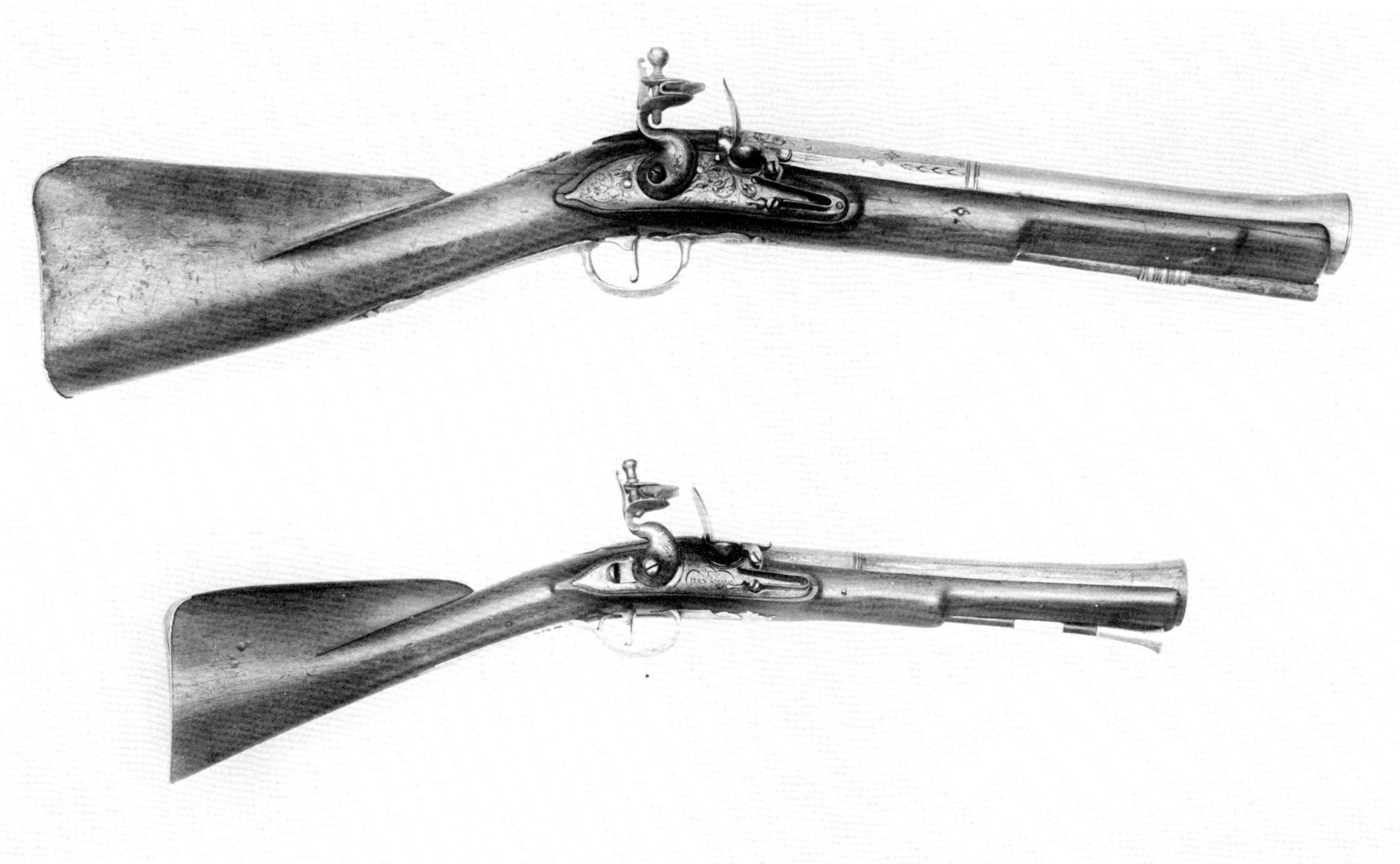

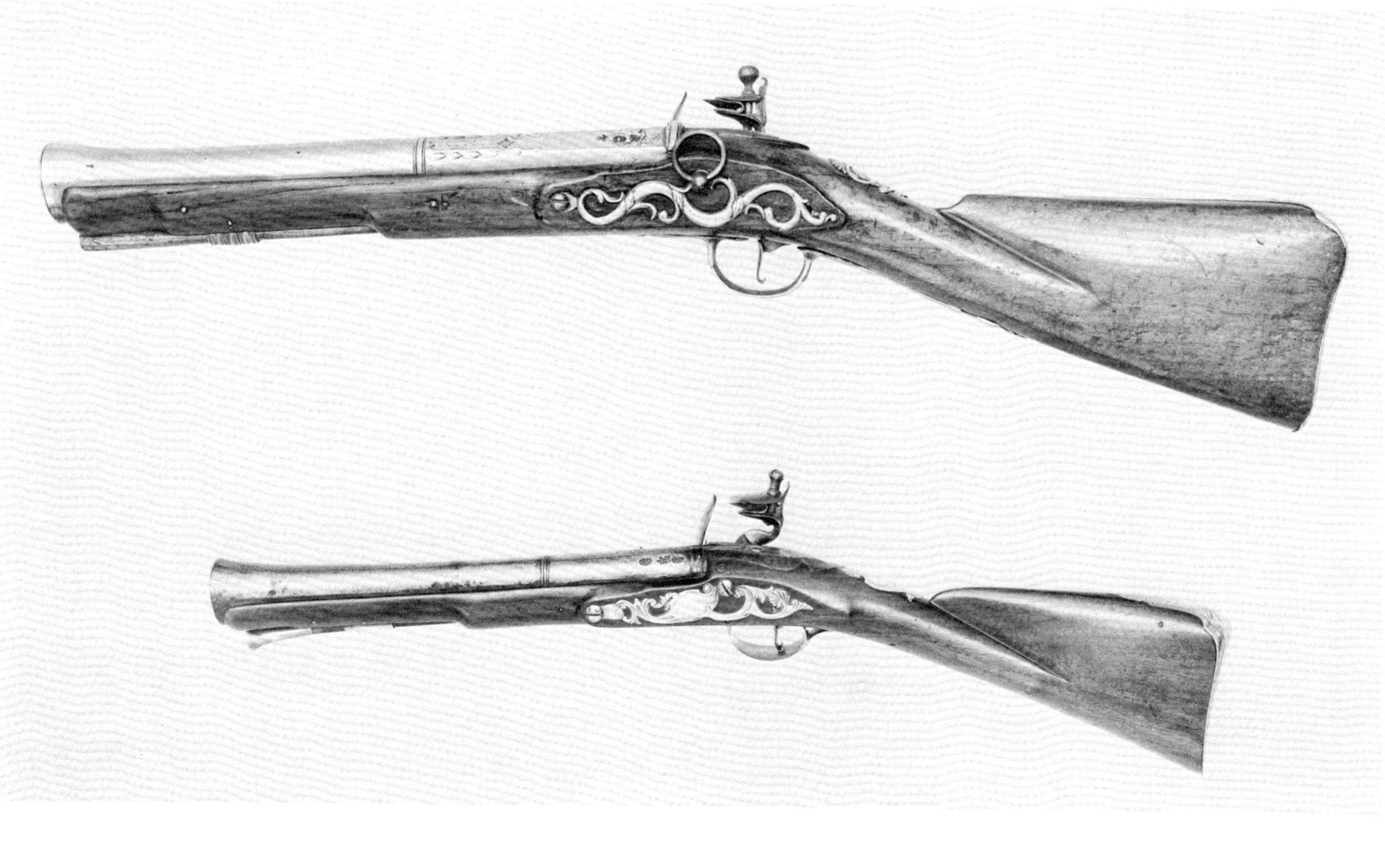

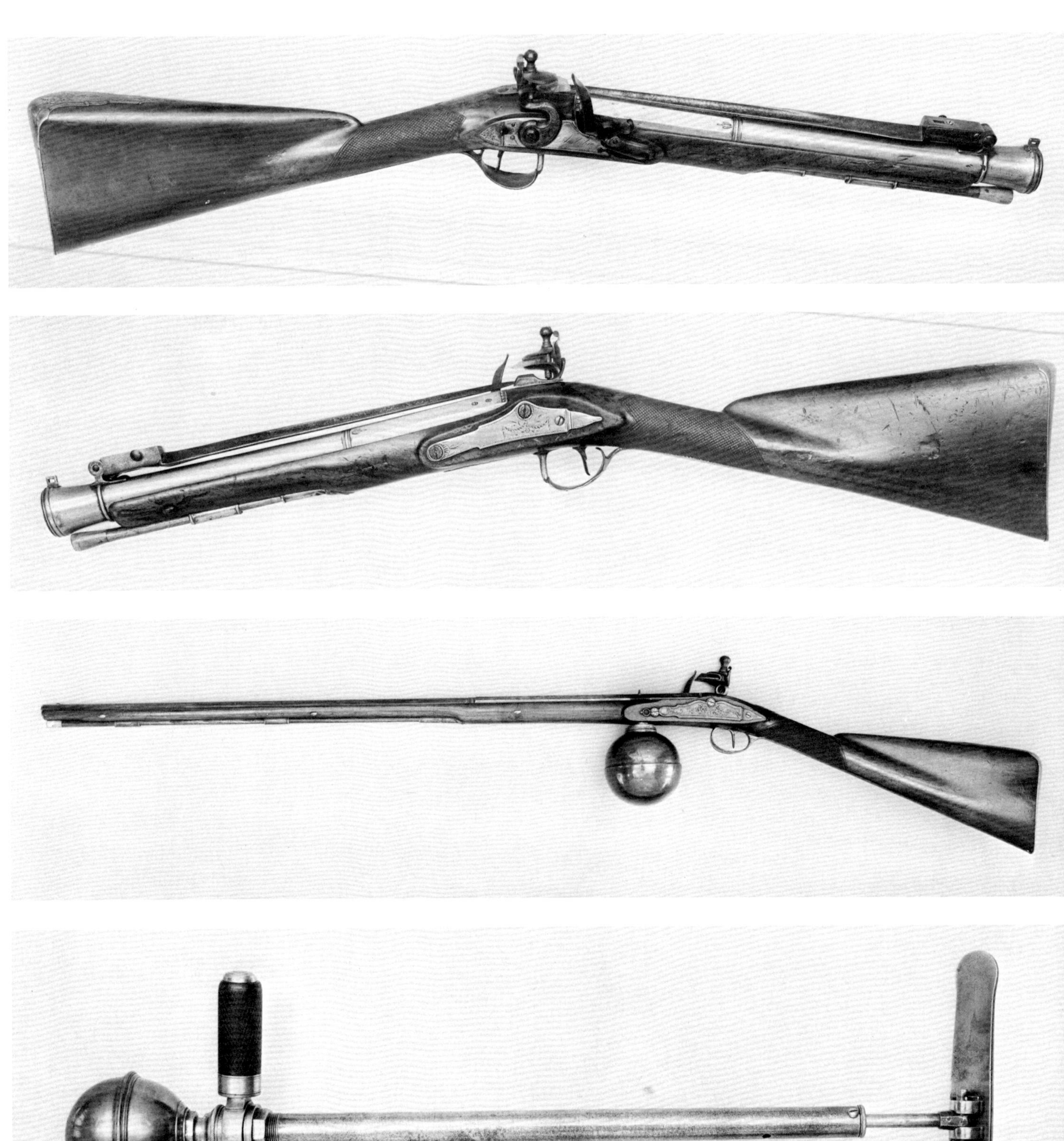

mounted by grotesque mask of baroque form engraved with owner's crest (superimposed initials AM, surmounted by three stars); trigger guard, engraved with warrior's head, has vase finial; ramrod has brass disk finial and, at opposite end, iron spiral worm.

William Nutt is recorded between 1689 and 1715 in the Board of Ordnance Ledger in the Admiralty Library, London. He was admitted freeman of the Gunmakers' Company in 1689 and was master in 1715–17.

William Nutt, London, about 1690
Overall length 27½ in.; barrel 13½ in.
Muzzle diameter 1⅜ in. Weight 6¼ lb.
Literature: May, "Some Board of Ordnance Gunmakers."

166. Blunderbuss Flintlock Carbine
(Bedford 998)

One of a pair. Barrel, circular, in two stages with three girdles, expanding toward blunderbuss muzzle; barrel inscribed LONDON; rococo scrollwork engraved over breech. Lock plate with rounded face, engraved border, inscribed T. HENSHAW within scroll; sliding safety. Walnut full stock engraved with leaf behind barrel tang; silver furniture; butt plate tang engraved with hunting trophy; pierced scrollwork side plate including asymmetrical cartouche; oval escutcheon surmounted by shell, flower at base; trigger guard and butt plate bear London hallmark and silversmith's mark, apparently JA (Jeremiah Ashley); ramrod has silver tubular finial and, on opposite end, iron spiral worm.

As a rule, blunderbusses are rather rugged and simply decorated firearms. No. 166 and its mate are exceptional in that the finely finished silver mounts include even the ramrod pipe and ramrod head. Thomas Henshaw was admitted freeman of the Gunmakers' Company in 1742.

Thomas Henshaw, London, 1750
Overall length 22 in.; barrel 10½ in.
Muzzle diameter 1¼₆ in. Weight 3 lb.

167. Blunderbuss Flintlock Carbine and Bayonet
(Bedford 984)

Barrel, brass, octagonal at breech changing to round, with ring at muzzle; hinged spring bayonet on top of barrel; at front of muzzle is iron stud with rectangular perforation for locking bayonet; tip of bayonet fits into socket at breech, and bayonet is locked and released by sliding bolt; private view mark and proofmark. Lock plate of brass, flat faced, with bolt safety, inscribed with name *Aislabie* (in script); roller on pan cover. Walnut full stock with checkered small; brass furniture; butt plate tang, side plate, and trigger guard engraved with floral design; side plate with three side nails; trigger

guard with pineapple finial; pinned brass ramrod pipes with two steel slides securing barrel.

Aislabie, about 1785
Overall length 29 in.; barrel 13¾ in.
Muzzle diameter 1¼₆ in. Weight 4¾ lb.

168. Air Gun with Simulated Flintlock and Pump
(Bedford 1359, 1359A)

Barrel, browned stubs, in two stages separated by molded girdle, octagonal at breech, remainder of circular section; on top facet at breech in inlaid silver ribbon inscribed H W MORTIMER LONDON; stationary rear leaf V-sight; iron front sight; two transverse gold beaded lines at end of breech; three barrel slides. Lock plate, flat faced, engraved with scroll, blued, and filed with beveled edges; on lock plate in inlaid silver ribbon is inscribed H. W. MORTIMER; head of cock pivot is square with engraved circular area in center. Walnut full stock with rococo shell carved behind barrel tang; blued steel furniture engraved with flower sprays; flat side plate engraved with foliate scrolls; beneath breech, bronze spherical air reservoir; plunger that releases air valve connected with cock.

The pump has an iron base. Cylindrical iron piston is moved in an iron tube; twin handles; screwed on top is brass air reservoir that, when charged, is removed and screwed into gun.

H. W. Mortimer, London, about 1775
Overall length 49¾ in.; barrel 33½ in.
Caliber. 42. Weight of air gun 7 lb.
Ex coll. First Earl of Minto, Minto House, Howick, Roxborough.

169. Seven-barreled Naval-service Volley Gun
(Bedford 399)

Six barrels grouped around seventh barrel with intercommunication vents so that all seven fire at once; Ordnance proof on each barrel. Lock plate, flat faced, stamped with crowned GR, TOWER, and broad arrow; flap loop-neck cock. Walnut half stock; brass furniture.

The volley gun was first submitted to Board of Ordnance in London by James Wilson in July 1779, and was described as a newly invented gun with seven barrels to fire at one time. It was decided by a committee of officers that it was not suitable for the army but might be useful on board ships for firing from the roundtops. Henry Nock, a large-scale supplier of military arms, was given a trial order for 20 pieces and was subsequently successful in obtaining a contract for 500, each weighing 13 lb. These he delivered in 1780. No further orders for seven-barreled guns were given until October 1787, when another 100 were ordered from Nock, this time at a reduced price. For this order, guns of the second model, of which no. 169 is an example, were supplied. The main difference between the two models is in the placing of the feather spring, which is in normal position in the first model, and reversed, with point toward the butt, in the second model. Nock was the sole maker of volley guns, and he produced in all 655 of them. They are described in his bills as "pieces with seven barrels, each with steel rammers, brass furniture and double bridled locks unrifled." The reference to double bridle applies to the bridle between the tumbler and end of the main spring inside the lock.

Henry Nock (1741-1804) became a freeman of the Gunmakers' Company in 1784 and set up a shop at 10 Ludgate Street near St. Paul's Cathedral. In 1787 he patented an improved forward breech in which there were two powder chambers, the smaller firing before the powder in the main chamber was burnt. He became master of the Gunmakers' Company in 1802, and in 1805 his business was taken over by James Wilkinson. The earliest reference to Nock dates from 1775, when he was described as a gun-lock-smith. His commission to provide seven-barreled volley guns in 1780 seems to have been his first success as an Ordnance contractor. Subsequently he not only supplied quality guns for the Prince of Wales and the aristocracy, but continued as a large-scale Ordnance contractor.

Henry Nock, London, about 1788
Overall length 37 in.; barrel 20 in.
Caliber .54 (30 gauge). Weight 12¼ lb.
Literature: Blackmore, "The Seven-Barrel Guns."

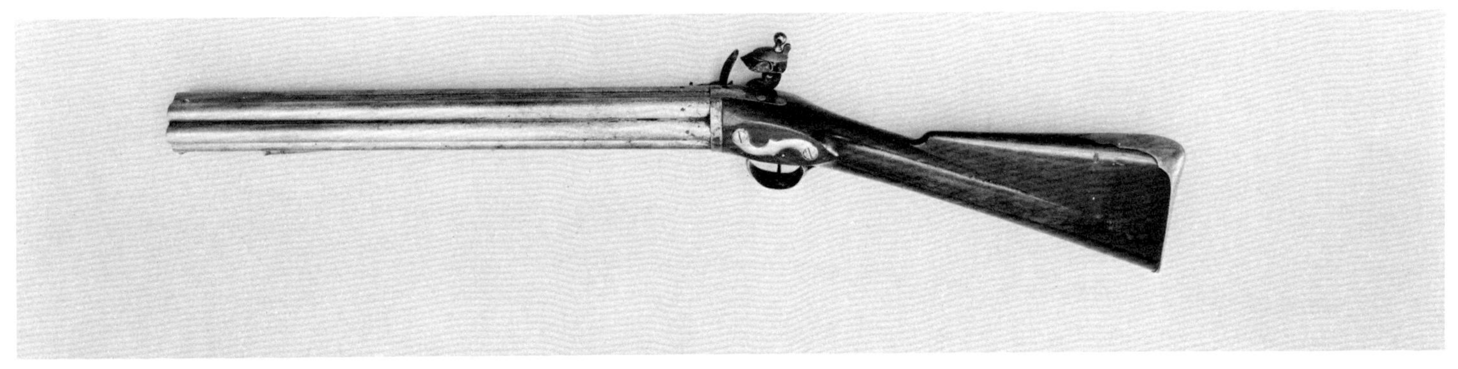

13

FORSYTH PISTOLS
AND GUNS

The flintlock gun, which lasted more than 250 years, had to be primed, wind or damp would cause it to misfire, and there was an interval between the flash of the priming and the explosion of the charge. The need for more rapidly detonating compounds was evident. Possible compositions had long been known to chemists (notably to Claude L. Berthollet), but no one had yet applied them satisfactorily to igniting gunpowder. Then, in 1807, Alexander John Forsyth (1768-1843), a Scotch clergyman and sportsman with an interest in both chemistry and mechanics, patented a device for firing a gun by the explosive qualities of fulminate of mercury. His invention, which gave instantaneous discharge and greatly improved the certainty of fire, opened up an entire new field of gunmaking.

The original patent model employed a magazine turning on a tube or roller (roller-primer) screwed into the breeching of the firearm; a small portion of the fulminating powder being deposited in the roller, the magazine was restored to its firing position, and the cock struck on a pin with a spiral spring attached to it, which action inflamed the gunpowder.

It was not long before all the principal gun-producing nations were making some form of detonating firearm. There were pill locks (the Forsyth slide-action magazine uses small pellets), tube locks (no. 85), patch locks (no. 177), and finally the percussion cap, which superseded all the others.

It should be pointed out that Forsyth did not invent the percussion cap. The cap-lock system of ignition was a two-stage invention consisting of nipple and detonating cap. The nipple was devised for patch-lock firearms soon after 1807. A detonating patch was pressed fast to the striking nose of the hammer and driven on the nipple by the falling hammer. The invention of the percussion cap has been credited to Joshua Shaw, a British landscape painter who established himself in Philadelphia, but there are several other claimants. One of the pistols in this exhibition (no. 211) is inscribed on the barrel "Joseph Egg Inventor of Copper Caps." The cap almost immediately superseded the loose detonating powder method of ignition, and existing firearms were altered to its use, which explains why original, unaltered Forsyth arms are so rare.

After his patent was granted, Forsyth established the gunmaking firm of Forsyth & Company. An excellent group of workmen under the master gunmaker James Purdey made the firearms, for the roller-primer, which contained a supply of about 25 charges of priming explosive, required the most exacting care and skill to insure safety. The first mechanical alteration was made by one of Forsyth's workmen, Joseph Vicars, who invented a self-acting magazine, sliding along a bar by means of a lever attached to the cock. Having kept his invention a secret from his employers, he was discharged, and entered the service of W. Beckwith, who soon produced it, only to be stopped by the patentee. Because the patent was for a new principle, rather than for any particular mechanical means, Forsyth was able to avail himself of all improvements and prevent others from competing with him.

An extraordinary group of Forsyth & Company firearms is exhibited in this group: four roller-primer examples (nos. 110, 171, 173, 182), two sliding-magazine pistols (nos. 174, 176), two flintlocks (nos. 172, 179), a patch-lock (no. 177), and four percussion-cap pistols (nos. 175, 178, 180, 181). No less than six of these firearms are one of a cased pair with accessories, although the case and other member of the pair are not shown.

170. Roller-primer Demonstration
Specimen (Bedford 656)

Primer has serial number 62R and screw on either side for adjusting tightness of felt pads on roller; stamped with initial F below which is word PATENT in scroll; roller primer shaft lined with platinum; no barrel. Lock plate squared at both ends, engraved with repeated feathers at edge and foliation, inscribed FORSYTH & CO. PATENT. Walnut stock with checkered grip; blued iron trigger guard, engraved with foliation, has pineapple finial; single side nail with engraved head.

This piece was used as a gunmaker's specimen to show the manner in which the lock works. The only earlier Forsyth serial number known is on the roller primer Forsyth rifle in the Smithsonian Institution.

Forsyth & Co., London, 1808
Overall length 9 in.
Weight ¾ lb.
Literature: Bedford, "The Forsyth Percussion System," ill.; George, *English Pistols and Revolvers*, pl. XV, 3; Neal and Back, *Forsyth & Co.: Patent Gunmakers*, p. 31.

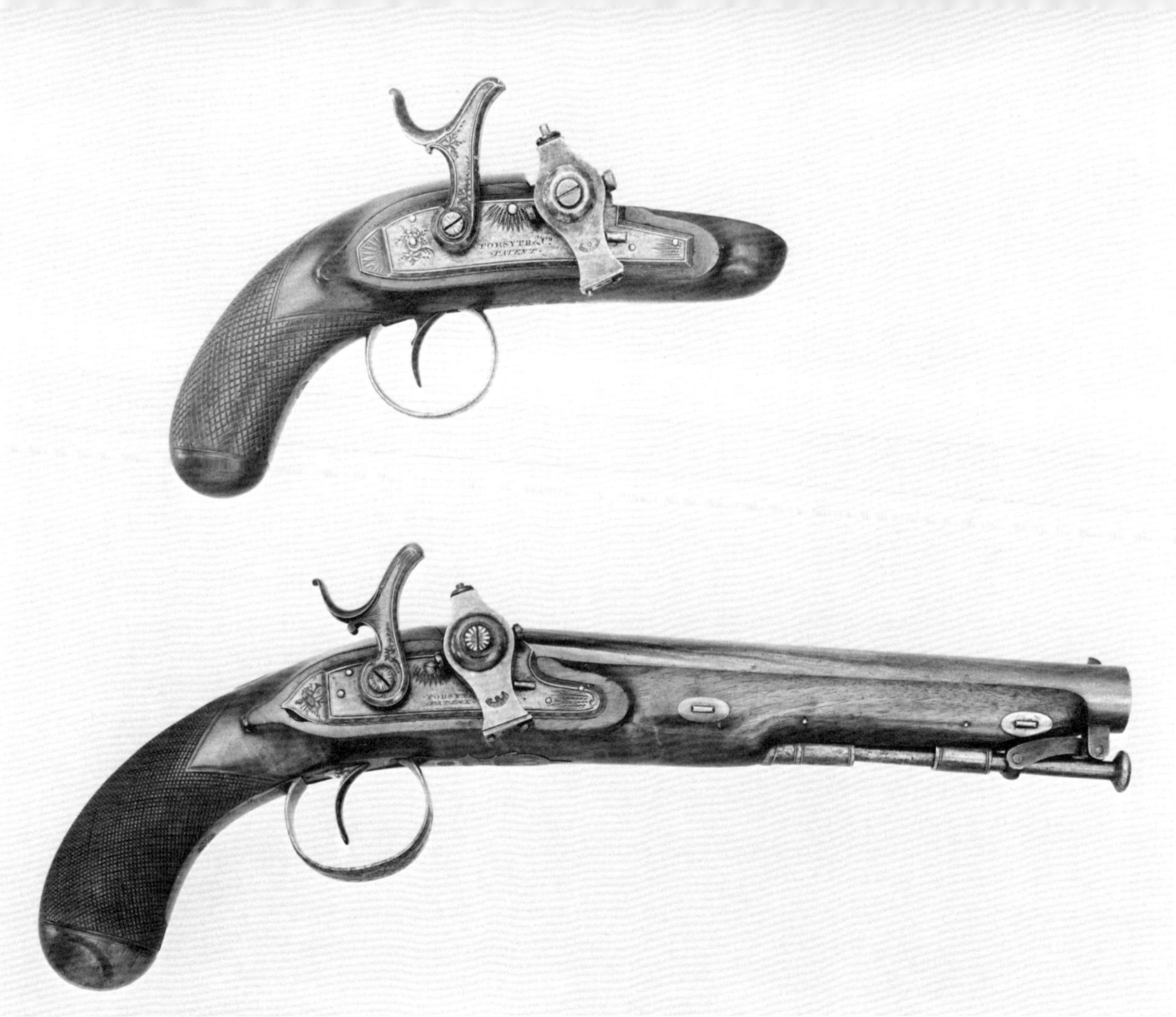

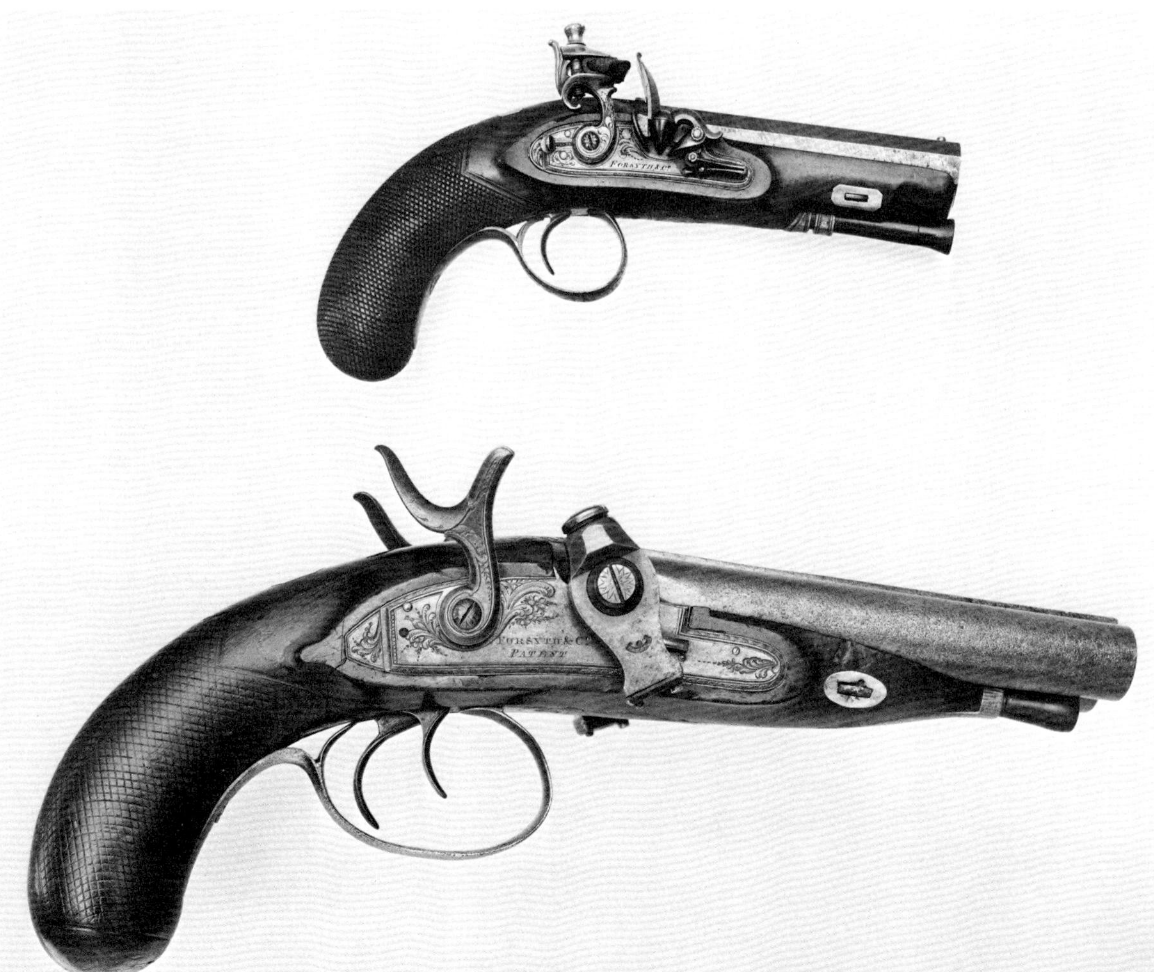

171. Roller-primer Pistol   (Bedford 1107)

Barrel, round, with top facet stamped FORSYTH PATENT GUN COMY. LONDON; iron blade front sight and stationary rear leaf sight; two barrel slides with silver slots. Lock plate, pointed and depressed at rear end, engraved with trophy and inscription FORSYTH PATENT; primer has screw on each side for adjusting tightness of cork inserts against shaft preventing detonation flash from firing fulminate in magazine; on front of primer, F PATENT engraved in a scroll; serial number 203 appears on primer, on top edge of lock plate, and under breech and barrel. Walnut full stock with checkered grip; blued iron furniture; single side nail; oval silver escutcheon; trigger guard, engraved with trophies, has pineapple finial; two iron ramrod pipes; iron ramrod, with swivel secured to barrel, has flattened finial and, on opposite end, transverse perforation for attaching swabbing cloth.

Forsyth & Co., London, 1809
Overall length 13¾ in.; barrel 9 in.
Caliber .67 (16 gauge). Weight 2¼ lb.
Literature: Bedford, "The Forsyth Percussion System," ill.; Neal and Back, *Forsyth & Co.: Patent Gunmakers*, pp. 33–34; Winant, *Early Percussion Firearms*, fig. 1, top.

172. Pocket Flintlock Pistol   (Bedford 1292)

Barrel, octagonal, top facet inscribed FORSYTH & CO. LONDON; barrel also marked ME 306, police regulation mark for Meath that was stamped on weapon under provisions of Arms Act of 1843; breech has two inlaid platinum lines; silver bead front sight and stationary iron rear V-sight; barrel tang engraved; single barrel slide with oval silver slots. Lock plate has French cock and bolt safety and is inscribed FORSYTH & CO.; platinum-lined vent; flash fence integral with pan, on each side of which is inclined water drain; feather spring with roller. Walnut full stock with checkered grip; steel furniture; octagonal silver escutcheon engraved with initial C surmounted by coronet; blued, engraved trigger guard with pineapple finial; steel ramrod pipes; ramrod has brass finial with iron worm and threads for screwing on brass cap.

Forsyth & Co., London, about 1810
Overall length 7 in.; barrel 3¾ in.
Caliber .49 (37 gauge). Weight ¾ lb.
Literature: Neal and Back, *Forsyth & Co.: Patent Gunmakers*, p. 40.

173. Double-barreled Pistol with Forsyth Roller-primer Locks   (Bedford 1166)

Barrels, round, with broad convex rib inscribed JOSEPH MANTON'S PATENT ELEVATION (partly obliterated); each barrel has two inlaid gold bands at breech; barrel tang and screw engraved with foliation; barrels have leadlike surface, apparently due to cleaning with acid; silver bead front sight; single barrel slide with oval silver slots. Lock plate engraved with foliation and inscribed FORSYTH & CO. PATENT; primers are plain, apart from screw head and F PATENT engraved in scroll. Walnut full stock with checkered butt; iron furniture; blank octagonal escutcheon; trigger guard and ramrod socket have pineapple finials; short ramrod with tubular iron finial.

This weapon was originally a shotgun, serial number 4942, made by Joseph Manton in 1809. In 1814 it was converted by Forsyth to roller-primer ignition, serial numbers 982 and 983.

Joseph Manton, London, 1809; converted by Forsyth & Co., London, 1814
Literature: Neal and Back, *Forsyth & Co.: Patent Gunmakers*, p. 42.

174. Rifled D-slide Pistol   (Bedford 1185)

Barrel, Damascus steel, blued, octagonal, rifled with twenty-four grooves; top strap marked FORSYTH & CO. PATENT GUN MAKERS LONDON; two gold inlaid lines on breech; serial number 1667 marked under barrel, on breech plug, inside lock, and on slide; engraved barrel tang and screw; iron front bead sight and stationary iron rear V-sight; single barrel slide with oval silver slots. Lock plate is engraved, has bolt safety, and is inscribed FORSYTH & CO. PATENT; roller slide. Walnut half stock with checkered grip and silver fore-end; iron furniture; engraved trigger guard with pineapple finial; two ramrod pipes; ramrod has brass finial and, on opposite end, iron worm, above which are threads for brass cap.

Forsyth & Co., London, 1818
Overall length 15¼ in.; barrel 10 in.
Caliber .50 (37 gauge). Weight 2¼ lb.
Literature: Bedford, "The Forsyth Percussion System," ill.

175. Percussion Pistol   (Bedford 1225)

One of a pair. Barrel, Damascus steel, browned, octagonal, inscribed on top facet EGG NO. 1 PICCADILLY LONDON; two inlaid platinum bands at breech; silver blade front slight and iron rear V-sight; engraved barrel tang and screw; single barrel slide has oval head with silver octagonal slots. Lock plate, rounded at both ends, engraved with foliation and with inscription JOSEPH EGG BY PERMISSION OF FORSYTH THE PATENTEE. Walnut full stock has checkered grip; engraved, blued iron furniture; single engraved side nail; octagonal silver escutcheon; trigger guard, engraved with foliation, has pineapple finial; iron

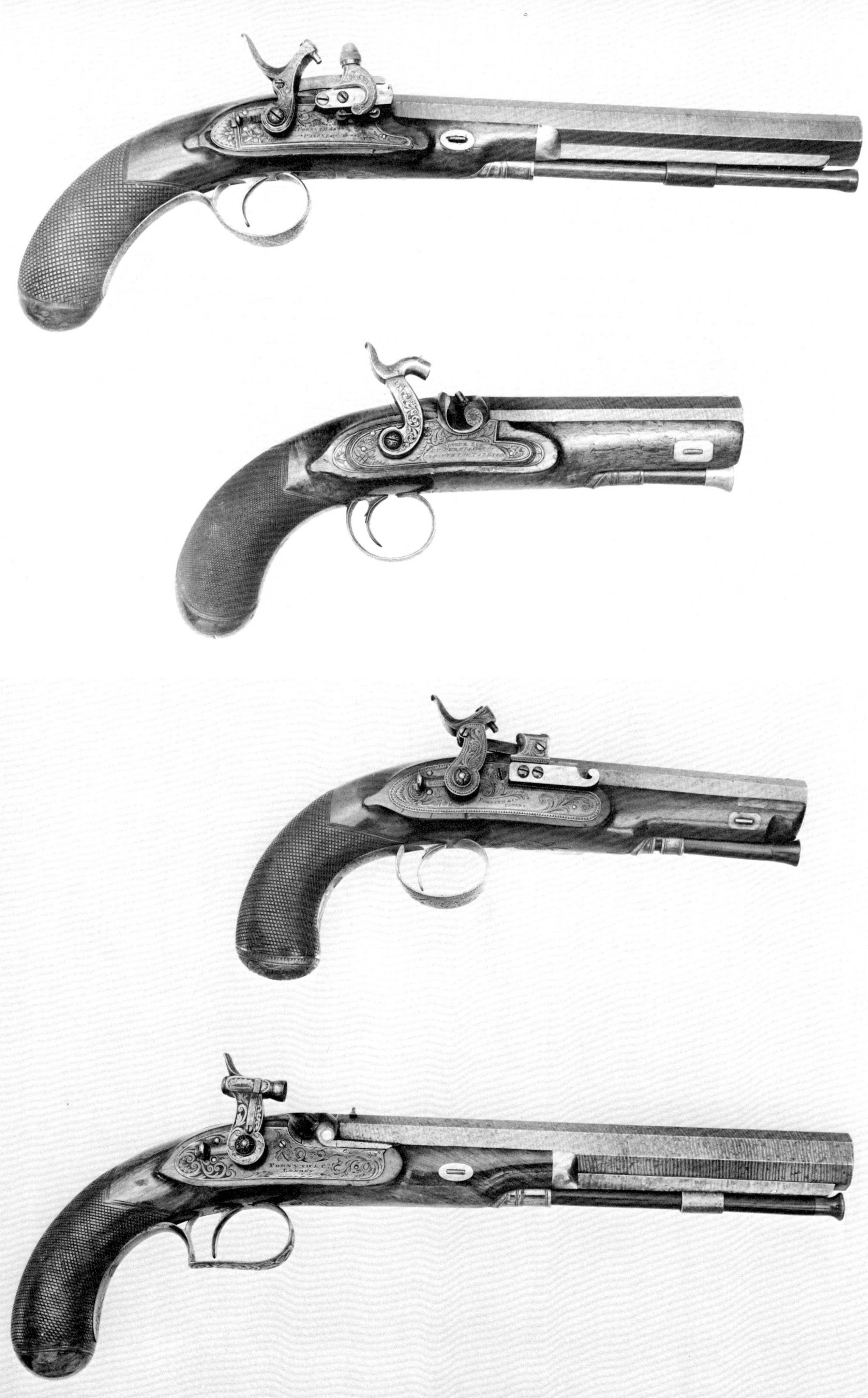

ramrod pipe; ramrod, with brass finial, has elongated brass tool at opposite end.

> Joseph Egg, London, about 1825
> Overall length 10¼ in.; barrel 5½ in.
> Caliber .78 (12 gauge). Weight 1¾ lb.
> Literature: Bedford, "The Forsyth Percussion System," ill.

176. Sliding-magazine Rifled Pistol
(Bedford 494)

One of a cased pair. Barrels, octagonal, rifled with twenty-four fine grooves, and inscribed FORSYTH & CO. PATENT GUNMAKERS LONDON; London proofmarks and barrelsmith's mark WF (William Fullerd); breeches have two platinum bands; single barrel slide. Lock plate has borders engraved with repeated dentate motif and foliation, has rounded ends and bolt safety, and is inscribed FORSYTH & CO. PATENT; priming magazine was connected with hammer by steel link, and moved with sliding motion backward and forward, in such a fashion that, when hammer was at full cock, primer was in position above flash pan, allowing supply of detonating powder to fall into pan, and that, as hammer fell, primer slid forward, uncovering pan; firing pin was screwed into head of hammer and fitted exactly into pan, sealing it and preventing any escape of gas through vent. Walnut full stock, checkered grip; silver butt cap. Serial number 3357 or 3358 of each pistol is placed on barrel, stock, primer, and inside of lock plate.

Fittings of mahogany case (not in exhibition), in addition to usual powder flask, bullet mold, loading mallet, and cleaning rod, include small box containing spare strikers and ivory priming flask for detonating powder, with which to fill magazines. In lower right compartment is a picker and combined blued steel wrench-screwdriver for dismounting pistol. Trade label in case shows operation of the roller-primer lock with address: No. 8 Leicester St. Leicester Square, London.

> Forsyth & Co., London, 1827
> Overall length 11 in.; barrel 5½ in.
> Caliber .52 (33 gauge). Weight 1½ lb.
> Literature: Bedford, "The Forsyth Percussion System," ill.; George, *English Pistols and Revolvers*, pp. 108–109, pl. XV, 1, 2; Neal and Back, *Forsyth & Co.: Patent Gunmakers*, pp. 64–65, pl. 83 (ill. of trade label).

177. Patch-lock Dueling Pistol
(Bedford 1514)

One of a cased pair. Barrel, Damascus steel, browned, octagonal, marked FORSYTH & CO. PATENT GUN MAKERS LONDON; breech inlaid with two platinum transverse bands; brass bead front sight, iron stationary rear V-sight; single barrel slide with silver slots. Lock plate engraved with scrolls and name FORSYTH & CO. LONDON (London, in place of Patent); locks have hammers of Joseph Manton type with detachable strikers; each of strikers has notch by means of which it is locked in place by spring, peg of which can be withdrawn and replaced with one that contains patch; bolt safety; platinum-lined vent. Walnut half stock has checkered grip and silver finial; engraved and blued steel furniture; silver octagonal escutcheon engraved with owner's initials WK (William Knight); trigger guard engraved with foliate scrolls and secured by two screws; two ramrod pipes; ramrod with horn finial and, on opposite end, tubular brass powder measure (ramrod of second pistol has brass terminal with iron worm above which are threads for screwing on cap). Serial numbers 3508 and 3509.

Mahogany case (not in exhibition) lined with lavender baize; inlaid brass circular plate inscribed TO WM KNIGHT ESQ. FROM P. K. Fittings include patch cutter, mallet, combined powder and bullet flask, bullet mold, funnel for pouring lead, nipple wrench, and oilcan stamped on base C. & J. W. HAWKSLEY.

> Forsyth & Co., London, 1828
> Overall length 15 in.; barrel 10 in.
> Caliber .54 (30 gauge). Weight 2½ lb.
> Literature: Neal and Back, *Forsyth & Co.: Patent Gunmakers*, p. 67, pl. 49.

178. Cap-lock Pistol
(Bedford 1209)

One of a cased pair. Barrel, Damascus steel, browned, octagonal, top facet marked FORSYTH & CO. PATENT GUNMAKERS LONDON; barrel forger's initials WF (William Fullerd), are partially covered by loop under barrel that receives slide; single barrel slide with oval slots; two platinum bands inlaid in breech, iron bead front sight and stationary iron leaf rear sight; barrel tang engraved with foliation. Lock plate engraved with foliation and inscribed FORSYTH & CO.; back-action locks; engraved screw at rear end of lock plate; flash fence integral with waterproof breech; platinum-lined vent. Walnut half stock with horn finial and checkered grip; small section on left side of forestock lacking; blued steel furniture; single engraved side nail; blank octagonal silver escutcheon; ramrod, with brass powder-measure finial, fits into two pipes and into stock socket; trigger guard engraved with foliate scrolls. Serial number 3671 or 3672 appears on breeches, barrels, and bullet mold.

Mahogany case (not in exhibition), lined with green velvet, has powder flask, bullet mold, screwdriver, and other fittings.

> Forsyth & Co., London, 1830
> Overall length 14⅞ in.; barrel 10 in.
> Caliber .50 (37 gauge). Weight 2½ lb.
> Literature: Bedford, "The Forsyth Percussion System," ill.; Neal and Back, *Forsyth & Co.: Patent Gunmakers*, pp. 68–69.

174
175
176
177

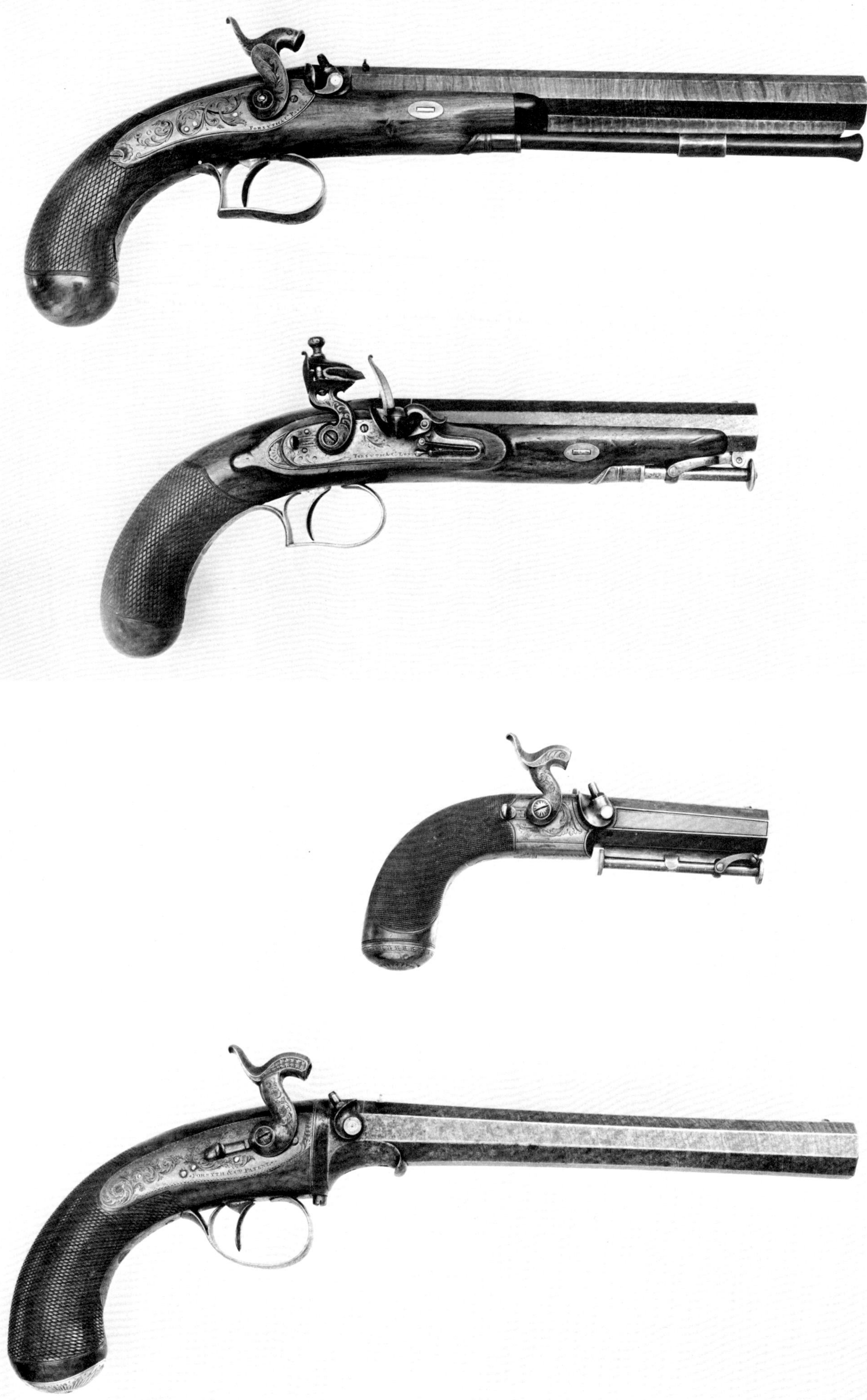

179. Officer's Flintlock Pistol (Bedford 776)

One of a cased pair. Barrel, Damascus steel, browned, octagonal, inscribed on top facet FORSYTH & CO. PATENT GUN MAKERS LONDON; London proofmarks; breech has platinum-lined vent and two platinum transverse bands; silver bead front sight; stationary iron rear V-sight; engraved barrel tang and screw; single barrel slide with oval silver slots. Lock plate inscribed FORSYTH & CO. LONDON (London rather than Patent because these pistols are flintlocks); bolt safety; flash fence; waterproof priming pan; feather spring with roller. Walnut full stock with checkered grip; steel furniture; single side nail; trigger guard engraved with braid motif; single ramrod pipe; iron swivel ramrod has discoid finial and, at opposite end, ball seater. Serial number 3699 or 3700 appears on barrels, breeches, and lock plates.

Mahogany case (not in exhibition), with trade label, contains pistols, rod with globular head, iron worm, brass jag, flask with compartments for balls and powder, screwdriver, oilcan, bullet mold stamped with number 25, patch cutter, and other fittings.

> Forsyth & Co., London, 1833
> Overall length 11⅜ in.; barrel 6¾ in.
> Caliber .56 (26 gauge). Weight ¾ lb.
> Literature: Bedford, "The Forsyth Percussion System," ill.; Neal and Back, *Forsyth & Co.: Patent Gunmakers*, p. 69, fig. 85 (ill. of trade label).

180. Pocket Percussion Pistol
(Bedford 1260)

One of a cased pair. Barrel, octagonal, inscribed FORSYTH & CO. LONDON; facets bordered by engraved lines; iron front sight, iron rear leaf sight; barrel tang engraved with foliation and secured by two screws. Percussion hammer checkered at top to aid in cocking; bolt safety; platinum-lined vent; folding trigger. Walnut checkered half stock; steel furniture; butt cap has hinged cover with engraved central flower; iron ramrod, with disk at each end, has swivel and is held in place by iron clamp.

Mahogany case (not in exhibition), lined with green baize, has label reading: Forsyth & Co. No. 8 Leicester St. Leicester Square, London. Case contains: jag with ebony handle; oilcan; bullet mold numbered 44; copper flask with compartments for balls, powder, and caps; iron box containing caps and labeled: Joyce's Anticorrosive Percussion Gunpowder. This powder was manufactured by me in the forms of Caps, Patches, Balls and Grain is warranted free from any rusting or corroding quality to be effective in every climate & not to misfire. Signed: Fredk Joyce Practical Chemist 57, Upper Thames Street London.

> Forsyth & Co., London, about 1834
> Overall length 6¾ in.; barrel 3¼ in.
> Caliber .52 (38 gauge). Weight ¾ lb.

181. Cap-lock Pistol   (Bedford 873)

One of a cased pair. Barrel, octagonal, marked FORSYTH & CO. PATENT LONDON; London proofmarks in shield-shaped area on underside of barrel at breech junction; two platinum inlaid bands on breech block; iron front bead sight; stationary rear leaf sight. Cap lock engraved with foliation; platinum-lined vent; bolt safety. Walnut checkered grip; butt cap of engraved silver; single engraved side nail; plain silver oval escutcheon; blued iron trigger guard numbered 4200 (mate has serial number 4201).

> Forsyth & Co., London, 1838
> Overall length 14¼ in.; barrel 9 in.
> Caliber .505 (36 gauge). Weight 2¼ lb.
> Literature: Neal and Back, *Forsyth & Co.: Patent Gunmakers*, p. 76.

182. Patent Roller-primer Shotgun
(Bedford 351)

Barrel, Damascus steel, tapered cylindrical, on top near breech inlaid in gold FORSYTH & CO. PATENT GUN MAKER'S LONDON; two gold bands at breech; serial number 381 appears under barrel; barrel tang and screw engraved; single barrel slide with oval silver slots. Lock plate has squared ends, rear end depressed, engraved with foliation and inscribed FORSYTH & CO. PATENT; original primer replaced during working life of gun, present one has no number and is not marked F Patent. Walnut half stock, checkered at grip, has silver fore-end; butt-plate of iron, its tang engraved with foliation and hunting dog, is secured by two engraved screws; trigger guard, engraved with foliation, has pineapple finial; two plain brown iron ramrod pipes and one polished iron baluster pipe at entrance of stock socket; ramrod has silver finial and, at opposite end, brass tube with iron worm above which are threads to receive brass tubular cap; under stock is slotted discoid button of iron for attaching shoulder sling.

> Forsyth & Co., London, 1810
> Overall length 43⅝ in.; barrel 28 in.
> Caliber .70 (14 gauge). Weight 5 lb.
> Literature: Neal and Back, *Forsyth & Co.: Patent Gunmakers*, p. 36.

183

183

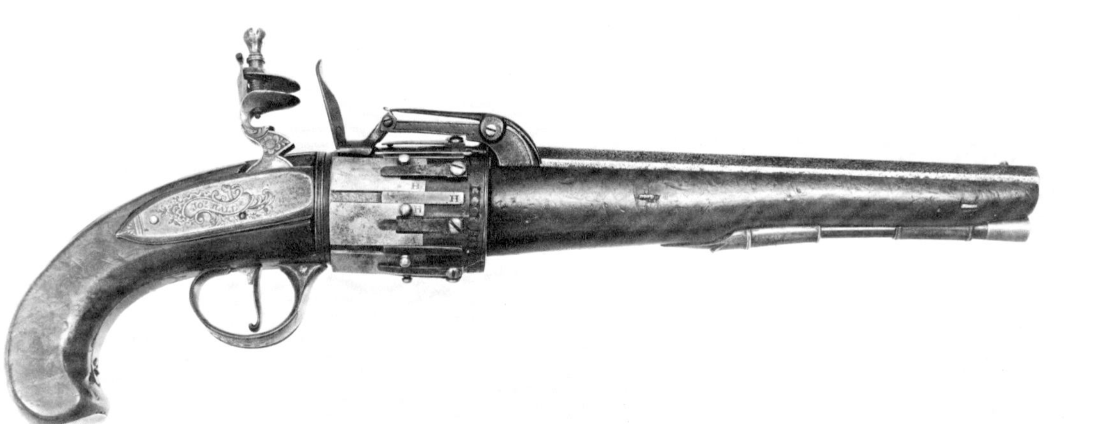

184

185

14

REVOLVERS

The principle of the revolver, like the principle of rifling, had been known for centuries before it could be put to practical use. One of the latest and best revolvers produced before the Colt, which incidentally was first patented in England in 1835, was the flintlock revolver patented in England in 1818 by Elisha Hayden Collier of Boston, Massachusetts. This was an improved version of the revolver patented in America in 1818 by Artemus Wheeler, Collier's collaborator. Collier's patent specifications illustrate the single action that used a spiral spring that was wound up like a clock by hand-turning the cylinder. Attempts to interest the British Ordnance in the weapon (1819 and 1824) were unsuccessful because it was considered to be too complicated. Collier simplified the revolver by omitting the cylinder-revolving mechanism. The altered Collier has a cylinder with five chambers chamfered at the muzzles. One after another the chambers were aligned with the tapered breech of the barrel by a spring. Ignition was supplied by a single flintlock with a magazine for powder in the back of the steel, so that the piece had only to be re-cocked for each shot without the trouble of priming. The cylinder was pulled back and turned by hand. The principal drawbacks of this firearm were the complexity and fragility of the mechanism, the cost of manufacture, and the necessarily cumbersome lock that was slow to operate and inconvenient to carry.

The Collier revolver, which was skillfully made, appeared in the transition period from flintlock to percussion and was an improvement over any multifiring arm that preceded. However, it was the percussion cap that facilitated the invention of a practical revolver. There apparently was no way to make a satisfactory revolver as long as it was necessary to ignite the main powder charge by sending the spark of flint on steel into a loose primary charge. Collier anticipated the two principal features of the Colt revolver. The first was the revolving of the cylinder by cocking the hammer, the second was the locking and alignment of the chamber with the barrel at the moment of firing. Not many of the mechanically rotated Collier arms were manufactured. Collier testified at the Colt versus Massachusetts Arms Company trial that he had made only between fifty and a hundred of the mechanically rotated arms for the Indian market.

The Collier first model has the flintlock with cock inside the lock plate, ratchet and pawl operated magazine primer, and smooth cylinders. The second model is a flintlock with outside cock, fluted cylinder, and link-connected magazine primer. The third model refers to the original percussion, with the fluted cylinder reduced at the breech end to better accommodate the nipples in the cylinder and reduce the distance from cap to powder charge. The Collier system was practical when fitted with the percussion cylinder.

In the exhibition the three models of Collier five-shot revolvers, shotguns, and rifles are represented thus: a first-model flintlock revolver (no. 185); a first-model revolver rifle (no. 192); two second-model revolvers, one (no. 187) a flintlock, the other (no. 186) a conversion from flintlock to percussion; and two early original third-model percussion revolvers, one of a pair of revolvers, serial nos. 106 and 107 (no. 188), and a revolver shotgun (no. 193). In this group are also two flintlock revolvers that show features that appear in the Collier revolver, one (no. 183) made by R. Wilson in 1738 the other (no. 184) made by Joseph Hall of Dublin about 1770. In addition to the Collier revolvers and the Collier related firearms, this group includes a flintlock revolver carbine (no. 191) by Powell of Dublin, made about 1780; a rare seven-chambered percussion-cap turret revolver (no. 189) made by James Wilkinson & Son about 1840–50; and a Deane, Adams & Deane double action percussion-cap revolver (no. 190), the competitor of the Colt.

The Collier Company addresses in London were: No. 6 Herberts Passage, Beaufort Building, Strand (from about 1819 to 1824); Collier & Co., Gunmakers, 54 Strand (London Directory for 1825); No. 3 N. Piazza, Royal Exchange, London (London Directory for 1828). The 54 Strand address appears on nos. 188 and 193.

The broadsheets issued by Collier indicate support by Samuel Nock, W. A. Beckwith, and Thomas Mortimer, all of whom are represented by firearms in this exhibition. It is reasonable to assume that these gunmakers made some, if not all, of the parts of the Collier revolver.

---

183. Flintlock Revolver   (Bedford 1113)

Cannon barrel in three stages with molded girdles between, ending in expanded muzzle; London proof-marks and barrelsmith's mark RW with diamond at top (R. Wilson); four-chambered cylinder, engraved with floral scrolls within silver band, is rotated by hand; each chamber when aligned with barrel is locked in position by pushing forward steel trigger guard, its front end thus engaging in slot cut in rear of chamber. Lock plate rounded, inscribed *Wilson* (in script), with engraved borders and floral scrollwork; inverted V-spring below pan; automatic primer attached to back of steel, operated by two gear wheels on cylinder side and recharged with priming powder through hinged spring cap on top. Stock in two parts, forestock restored; butt of walnut carved with shell behind barrel tang; silver furniture; spurred pommel, spandrels engraved with shells within scrollwork and chased with scrolled strapwork cartouche that frames pommel cap, which is chased with flower; spurs marked with date letter for 1738, initials IA (Jeremiah Ashley), lion passant, and leopard head crowned.

The mechanism of this revolver, particularly the priming magazine, is exceptionally advanced for the early date. Its mate is in another collection in the United States.

> R. Wilson, 1738
> Overall length 15¼ in.; barrel 6⅛ in.
> Caliber .50 (36 gauge). Weight 2¼ lb.

184. Eight-chambered Flintlock Revolver (Bedford 1016)

Barrel, octagonal, top facet inscribed JOS. HALL DUBLINI FECIT; rear V-sight on breech; iron blade front sight; two barrel slides. Cylinder has eight chambers, each aligned with barrel by manually turning cylinder; cylinder locked by pushing trigger guard forward; chambers are numbered 1 to 8 on end of cylinder, and eight pan covers are lettered A to H; each pan cover must be pushed open by hand when its chamber is aligned with barrel; steel pivoted at end of long arm and aligned with cock. Lock plate, flat faced, engraved with maker's name JOS. HALL on ribbon within rococo scrollwork. Walnut forestock and butt, latter with silver butt cap and blank oval silver escutcheon; steel trigger guard.

Joseph Hall apparently specialized in this type of revolver, as several have survived. It was necessary for Hall to devise a special form of pan-cover spring to hold the pan cover and steel in position over the touchhole.

> Joseph Hall, Dublin, about 1770
> Overall length 15½ in.; barrel 8 in.
> Caliber .40. Weight 2½ lb.

185. Collier First-model Five-shot Flintlock Revolver (Bedford 1059)

Barrel, cylindrical; top strap and cylinder spindle each attached by two screws, all four screws extending into barrel, an indication that revolver was never fired but was an early model; two additional screws at rear of top strap pass through top of box-lock plate. Priming magazine, pawl-and-ratchet operated, seated on bronze shroud progressively covering five cylinder touchholes; bronze pan is integral with bronze disk behind chamber; cylinder is bored with five tubes and stamped at rear with London proofmarks; flash shield is lacking. Lock plate inscribed *E. H. Collier* (in script) PATENT NO. 1 (roman letters). Flat-sided stock of cherry or American walnut without butt cap.

This pistol, similar to one in the Tower of London marked 23, appears to have been made by Elisha Hayden Collier prior to his departure from Boston for England in August 1818. On November 24, 1818, he was granted a patent (number 4315) for "a gun, pistol, or other fire-arm capable of being fired off several times in succession with only once loading."

Collier manufactured or had manufactured for him three principal types of revolvers, cylinder guns, and rifles. These are classed here as first model, second model, and third model. No. 185 represents the first model, though it does not include the automatic rotating spring or links that were specified in the patent. Only one known example, serial number 4, in the Tower of London, has any remnants of the automatic rotating device. Apparently Collier found the device too expensive to make and immediately began production without it.

Elisha Hayden Collier, London, 1818
Overall length 12⅛ in.; barrel 4 in.
Caliber .44 (54 gauge).
Literature: Bedford, "Collier and his Revolvers"; Grancsay and Lindsay, *Illustrated British Firearms Patents 1714-1853;* Taylerson, *The Revolver, 1818–1865*, pp. 23–31.

186. Collier Second-model Five-shot Converted Flintlock Revolver (Bedford 1020)

Cylinder, hand rotated, converted from flintlock to percussion cap by insertion of nipples in five cylinder touchholes, removal of priming magazine and shroud, and replacement of flintlock cock with percussion hammer. Barrel, browned, octagonal, smooth bore, inscribed E. H. COLLIER, 48 LONDON, with under-barrel rib and one ramrod pipe; ramrod with steel finial and, on opposite end, iron worm; stationary rear iron leaf V-sight, silver bead front sight. Lockplate, inscribed E. H. COLLIER, 48 PATENT, decorated with feather border, scrolling leaves, and trophy. Serial number 48 also appears on spindle, top edge of lock plate, and rear surface of cylinder. Walnut stock with checkered grip; flat butt cap without decoration; single side nail; eight-pointed elongated silver star inlaid on reverse of stock; blank silver escutcheon.

On Collier's second model the upper strap is held to the breech by a lock screw. To dismount the pistol, it is necessary to remove this screw and the screw pin located just forward of the trigger guard, which permits the cylinder, top strap, barrel, and spindle to be removed forward. The serial number sometimes also occurs on the cylinder back-up plate.

Elisha Hayden Collier, London, about 1824
Overall length 15 in.; barrel 6⅜ in.
Caliber .47 (44 gauge). Weight 2¼ lb.
Literature: See no. 185.

187. Collier Second-model Five-shot Flintlock Revolver (Bedford 1112)

Barrel, browned twist, octagonal, inscribed E. H. COLLIER, 89 LONDON; cylinder, browned, hand rotated, retains original flash shield. Lock plate and priming magazine inscribed E. H. COLLIER, 89 PATENT; priming magazine loaded from top, and aperture closed by a rotating gate; magazine was locked by tightening screw at base of gate; engraved scrolling foliation decorating top jaw, cock, and shroud around cylinder touchholes; single ramrod pipe; ramrod with brass cap and capped worm.

One feature of the patent present in all remaining examples of Colliers is the gas-tight seal between barrel and cylinder that is formed by a male step at the end of the breech mating in succession with the female recesses cut in the forward ends of the cylinder chambers. A helical spring thrusts cylinder and barrel into engagement at all times except when the cylinder was manually drawn back against the spring to permit rotation. During firing, a cam attached to the sear locked a plunger against the cylinder, preventing it from recoiling until the cock was raised. The cylinder could not be rotated, therefore, until the cock was placed on half or full cock. Priming powder was deposited in the flashpan by way of a linkage with the priming magazine, a slotted feed plug mounted transversely across the bottom of the steel being turned each time the pan cover was shut down for discharge.

Elisha Hayden Collier, London, 1825
Overall length 15 in.; barrel 6⅜ in.
Caliber .47 (44 gauge). Weight 2¼ lb.
Literature: See no. 185.

188. Collier Third-model Five-shot Percussion Revolver (Bedford 890)

Barrel inscribed COLLIER & CO. 54 STRAND, LONDON, rebrowned, octagonal, with under-barrel rib and one ramrod pipe; rib is rounded and checkered for rear three inches and has decurved front edge that prevents unintentional ramrod release; ramrod with brass fore-end and capped worm; upper barrel strap held to breech by lock screw; silver bead front sight and keyed leaf rear sight on top strap cut slightly concave fore and aft. Cylinder, originally browned but now cleaned, with neck at rear to accommodate nipples; original flash shield with snap attached to rear of ramrod socket. Lock plate inscribed COLLIER & CO. PATENT. Walnut stock has eight-pointed silver star inlaid on obverse; single side nail; steel furniture blued, all screw heads engraved. Serial number 107 appears on trigger-guard tang, rear of cylinder, and cylinder spindle; number 2 occurs on top edge of lock plate, rear of cylinder, and rear of flash shield.

This pistol is the second of a pair numbered consecutively.

Collier & Co., London, about 1827
Overall length 14½ in.; barrel 6¼ in.
Caliber .50 (36 gauge). Weight 2 lb.
Literature: See no. 185.

189. Seven-chambered Percussion-cap Turret Revolver (Bedford 1114)

Barrel, browned twist, octagonal, lower facet stamped with London proofmarks; silver bead front

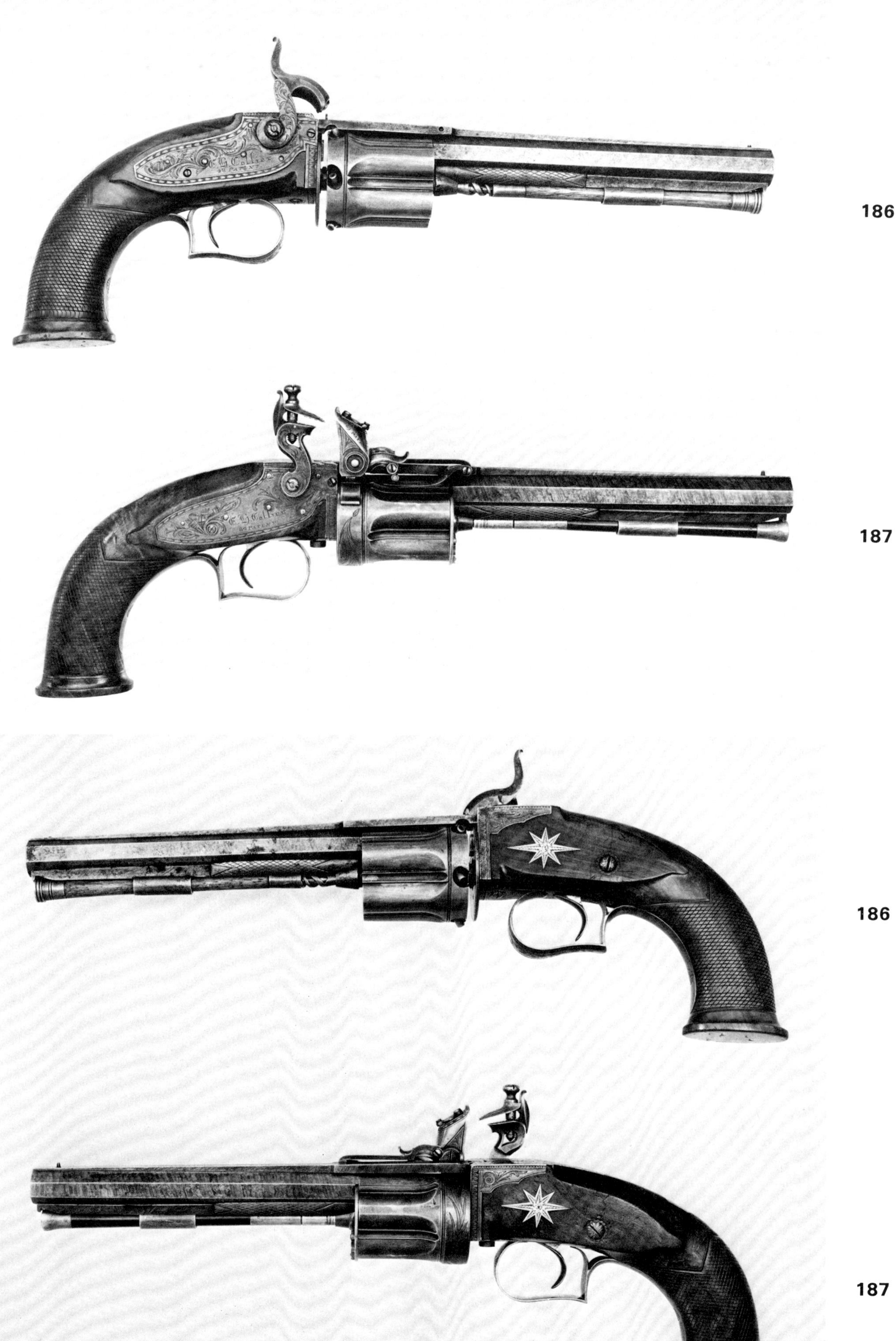

186

187

186

187

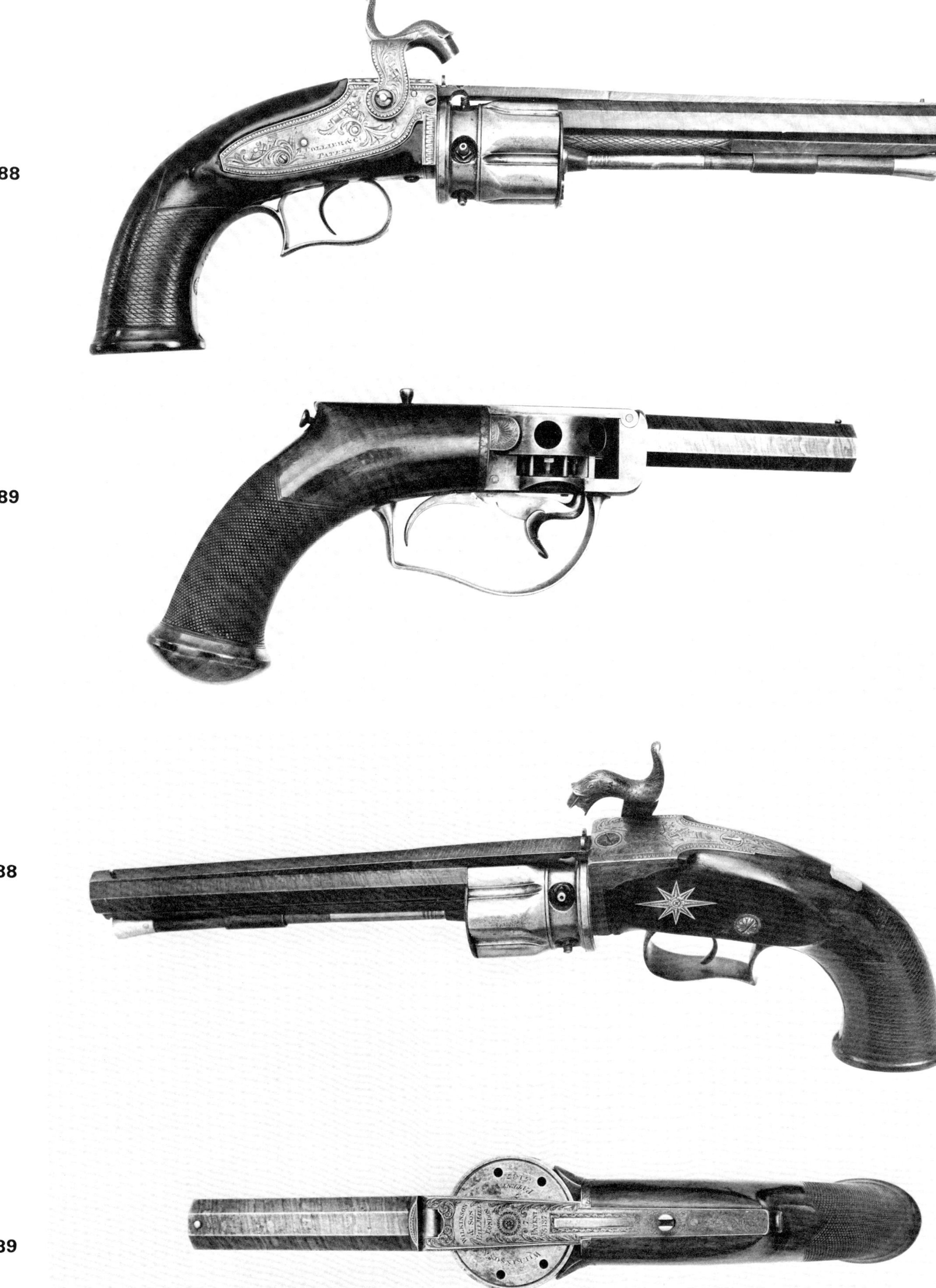
188
189
188
189

sight; rear sight cut in release stud of cylinder-revolving mechanism; cylinder with hand-rotated action set horizontally behind barrel; top of cylinder inscribed WILKINSON & SON 7 PATENT 5137; spring situated in top strap operates locating stud for cylinder; top strap finely engraved with foliate scrolls and inscribed WILKINSON & SON PALL MALL LONDON 7 PATENT 5137; under-barrel hammer adjacent to trigger; trigger and hammer guard blued and engraved with foliation. Walnut butt with checkered grip; at top of grip is small stud that, when pressed, allows top strap to hinge upward, permitting removal of cylinder for reloading.

This pistol was manufactured to M. Poole's English patent number 7286 of 1837 for a manually rotated under-hammer radial percussion pistol. It is possible, therefore, that 5137 is a Wilkinson serial number. Only three examples of firearms made to the Poole patent are known.

> James Wilkinson & Son, Pall Mall, London, about
> 1840–50
> Overall length 12 in.; barrel 4 in.
> Caliber .44 (53 gauge). Weight 2 lb.

190. Five-chambered Double-action Percussion-cap Revolver (Bedford 1232)

Barrel, frame, and cylinder blued; barrel, octagonal top facet inscribed J. PURDEY, 314½ OXFORD STREET LONDON, even though pistol actually made by Deane, Adams & Deane; on right-hand side of frame inscribed ADAMS PATENT NO. 11,479 R; inscribed on cylinder NO. 11,479 R; London view mark stamped three times and proofmark stamped twice on cylinder; iron blade front sight, stationary rear V-sight. Checkered walnut butt.

Adams's number 10,460 R was a pistol incorporating the hesitating lock mechanism first patented in November 1853. The example exhibited does not incorporate the new patent, but the serial number suggests a date about one year later. The Deane, Adams & Deane self-cocking percussion-cap revolver was the most popular pistol of the middle decades of the 19th century in England.

> Deane, Adams & Deane, about 1854
> Overall length 10½ in.; barrel 4⅜ in.
> Caliber .34 (120 gauge). Weight 1¼ lb.
> Literature: Taylerson, Andrews, and Frith, *The Revolver, 1818 to 1865*, pp. 92–93, pl. 8, lower ill.

191. Six-chambered Flintlock Revolver Carbine with Blunderbuss Muzzle
(Bedford 951)

Barrel, browned twist, cylindrical, expanded at muzzle; breech inscribed POWELL DUBLIN; barrel is set slightly to left in relation to stock, and cock has right-angle bend in order to position it in relation to each steel; each chamber of cylinder has individual brass pan and steel pan cover with spring; chamber block is released and turned by hand, trigger guard being pressed forward for aligning chamber with barrel; loading takes place on front of cylinder plate below barrel in circular opening aligned with barrel muzzle; circular opening has pivoted cover. Lock plate, flat faced, engraved with name POWELL in oval cartouche surmounted by eagle. Walnut butt with checkered grip; engraved steel furniture; hollow in butt has hinged door; steel butt plate has tang engraved with bird and flowers and partridge finial; steel trigger guard with brass tang.

> Powell, Dublin, about 1780
> Overall length 36 in.; barrel 15½ in.
> Muzzle diameter ⅞ in. Weight 8½ lb.

192. Collier First-model Flintlock Five-shot Revolver Rifle (Bedford 952)

Barrel, cylindrical, polished steel, rifled with seven grooves; silver blade front sight; top strap with

190

191

192   191

193

three screws and bottom strap with two screws attached to barrel at breech; rib with concave facet and two ramrod pipes on bottom of barrel; notch in fore-end of rib prevents ramrod from sliding out when rifle is tilted downward; replaced ramrod with brass finial and, at opposite end, brass tube with iron worm, the tube threaded for brass cap. Lock plate engraved *H. E. Collier* (in script; engraver reversed initials) and PATENT NO. 17 (roman letters); pawl-and-ratchet-operated priming magazine mounted on bronze shroud; rear of cylinder and ramrod socket numbered 5. Plain walnut stock; plain rounded butt plate with tang, all-steel loading rod embedded in toe of butt; strap swivels attached to barrel under rib and stock.

This rifle is similar to no. 185.

Elisha Hayden Collier, London, about 1820

Overall length 47 in.; barrel 27 in.; cylinder 3¼ in.

Caliber .64 (18 gauge). Weight 9¼ lb.

193. Collier Third-model Percussion Five-shot Revolver Shotgun (Bedford 1371)

Barrel, Damascus steel, browned, round in section; silver bead front sight; London proofmarks on left rear of barrel with numeral 21 stamped between view mark and proofmark; one other piece by Collier is known with this proof and number; barrel tang engraved with foliation; concave top rib inscribed COLLIER & CO. 54 STRAND LONDON; hollow rib under barrel is half its length (length of ramrod) and has notch near edge to fit ramrod finial; short wood ramrod with brass finial and, on opposite end, brass tube with iron worm, the tube threaded for brass cap. Lock plate inscribed COLLIER & CO. PATENT; feather borders and scrolling foliage engraved on lock-plate hammer, breech frame, and trigger guard; trigger-guard tang inscribed NO. 197; single percussion hammer pivoted on lock plate; five cylinders each separated by longitudinal groove and each with nipple; cylinder block unlocked by pushing it back and revolved by hand. Walnut stock checkered at grip; blued steel furniture; butt-plate, tang engraved with scrolling foliage, partridge finial; blank oval silver escutcheon. Gun dismounted in same way as no. 186.

Elisha Hayden Collier, London, about 1829

Overall length 45 in.; barrel 25 in.; cylinder 3¼ in.

Caliber .625 (20 gauge). Weight 6½ lb.

15

PEPPERBOXES, MULTIBARRELED PISTOLS, POCKET PISTOLS, AND OTHERS

This group of twenty-seven firearms, spanning the period 1690-1855, shows great variety in construction and demonstrates the versatility of the makers, twenty-four of whom are represented.

Four noteworthy pieces with fixed single barrel are exhibited: a combined ax and flintlock pistol (no. 219) by Edward Turvey, about 1690-1700, a boy's sporting flintlock gun (no. 220) by David Wynn, about 1720, a strike-a-light with split barrel (no. 194) by Johann Gottfried Kolbe, about 1735, and a steel percussion cap turnoff pocket pistol (no. 212) by William and John Rigby of Dublin, about 1825–30. The end of the butt of the Rigby pistol is bored and has a slot on one side to serve as a key in unscrewing the barrel of the companion pistol. Single-barrel pieces also, but of different construction, are five flintlock pistols with turn-off barrels, dating from about 1750 to about 1800 (nos. 195, 197, 200, 202, 204). The fifth one, a presentation piece, is engraved with the names of naval heroes.

Proceeding to double-barreled pieces, there are eight over-and-under pistols, dating from about 1790 to 1835, of which five are flintlocks and three percussion-cap. Represented among them are turnover and turnoff barrels and a combination of these systems (no. 218), as well as the tap action (nos. 201, 207, 208, 209). Unusual features appear on a pistol by Joseph Egg (no. 211), which has left- and right-hand percussion locks with external mainsprings, and on a percussion-cap pocket pistol by William and John Rigby (no. 213), which has a revolving hammer that is turned by hand above the appropriate nipple. The tap action is provided with a tap on the reverse side of the pistol by means of which the priming pan was revolved by hand so that the priming could reach vents on different levels.

Three of the pistols with four barrels are flintlocks, and two of these (nos. 196, 205), though differing in construction, have the same unusual feature that all barrels discharge simultaneously. The third is a turn-off pistol with box-lock (no. 198).

A pepperbox is defined as a hand firearm with three or more barrels encircling a central axis, firing shots successively with one striker. With a separate barrel for each shot, it is unlike the revolver, in which all shots pass successively from a revolving cylinder through a single barrel. Pepperboxes were used mainly in the protection of homes, though some travelers carried them. After 1850 the pepperbox gave way to the revolver. Of the five pepperboxes in the exhibition, two are flintlocks (nos. 198, 199) and three are percussion-cap (nos. 215, 216, 217).

The box-lock, described in the introduction to Group 11, appears on fifteen of the pistols in the present group. The pocket pistol, often fitted with a box-lock, is well represented. Pocket-size pistols usually have a turnoff barrel, the turnoff loading procedure providing great striking power in the small pistol (see introduction to Group 4).

194. Strike-a-light with Split Barrel
(Bedford 1500)

Similar to a Queen Anne pistol in general appearance. Brass cannon barrel in three stages with molded girdles between, and muzzle ring; engraved at breech with acanthus foliage; upper half of barrel hinged on left side; brass tube that held taper is hinged near muzzle inside barrel; when piece is discharged, upper half of barrel opens and taper is lit automatically; under lock, barrel inscribed KOLBE. Brass body forged in one with breech; brass pan; round-faced steel cock filed with raised edges. Walnut butt carved with shell behind barrel tang; silver furniture; grotesque-mask butt cap has London hallmark; side plate chased with trophy of arms; blank escutcheon with shell and scroll.

Johann Gottfried Kolbe, originally from Suhl in Thuringia, made many fine arms for the court of Saxony. Subsequently he came to England, where he must have been working between 1730 and 1737. At this time he made a splendid air gun for George II, now in the Victoria and Albert Museum (494-1894). He also made a pair of five-barreled flintlock pistols, now in the Royal Armoury at Windsor Castle (Laking, *The Armoury of Windsor Castle, European Section*, nos. 798, 807).

Johann Gottfried Kolbe, London, about 1735
Overall length 10¼ in.
Weight 1½ lb.
Literature: Hayward, *The Art of the Gunmaker*, vol. II, pp. 81–82, pl. 24

195. Turnoff Pocket Flintlock Pistol
(Bedford 1092)

One of a pair. Round cannon barrel in three stages, molded girdles between, ending in expanded muzzle rings; engraved over breech with trophy of arms and in

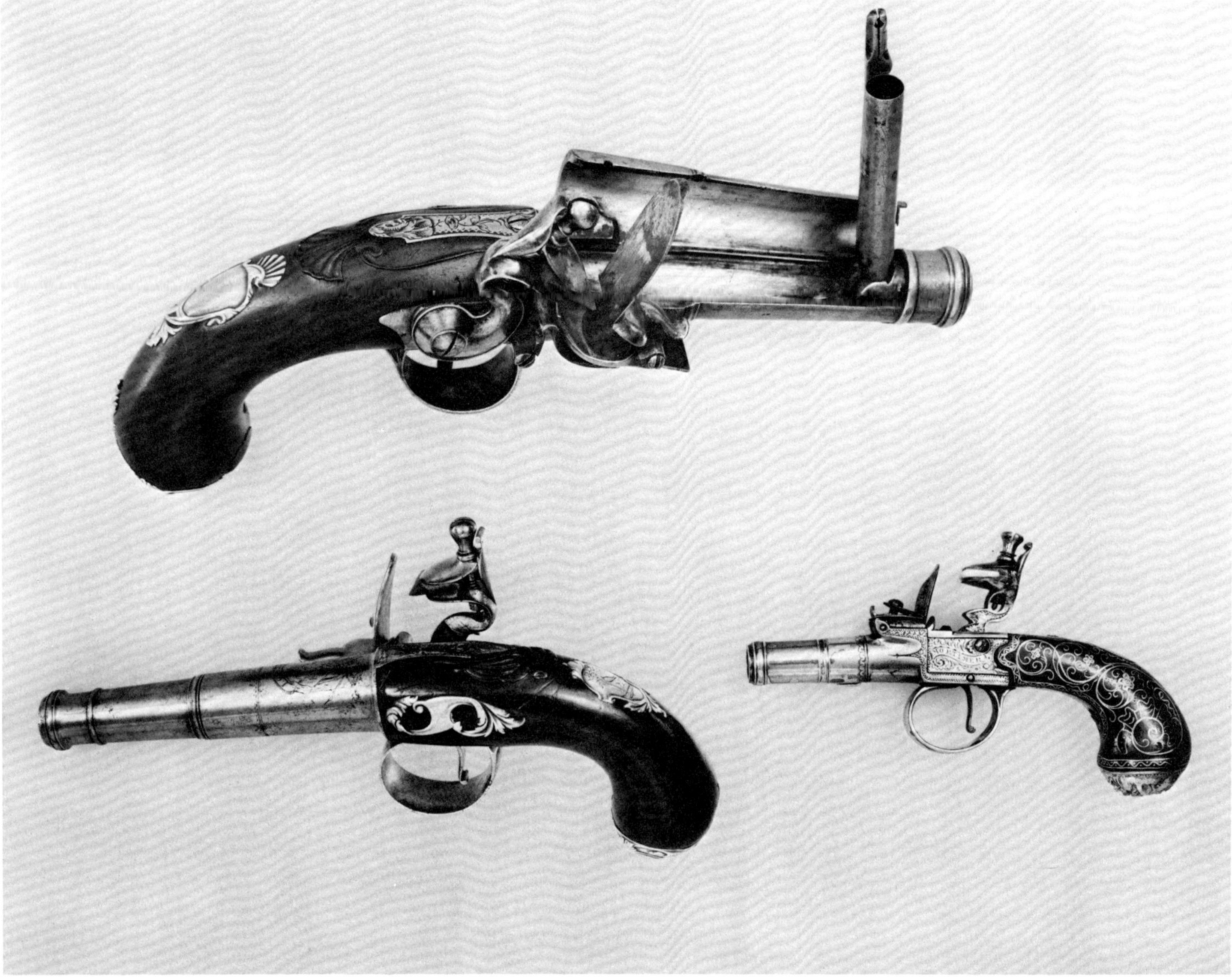

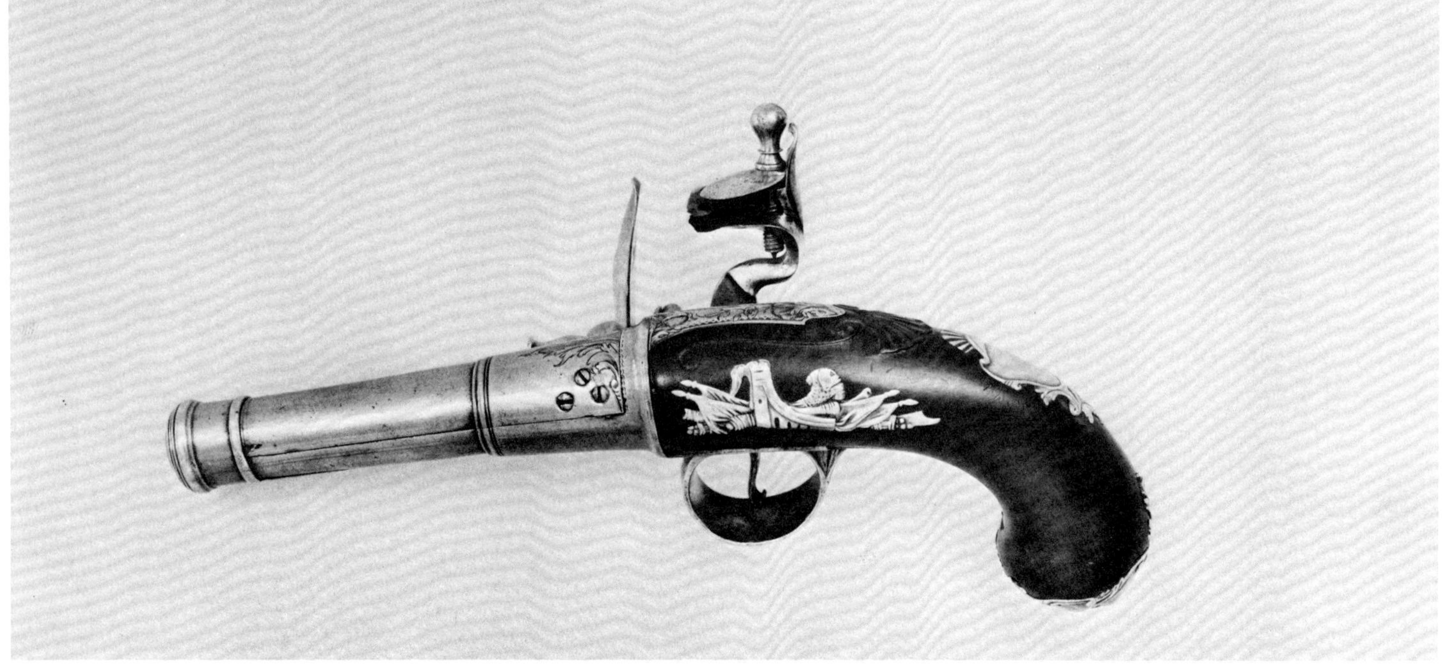

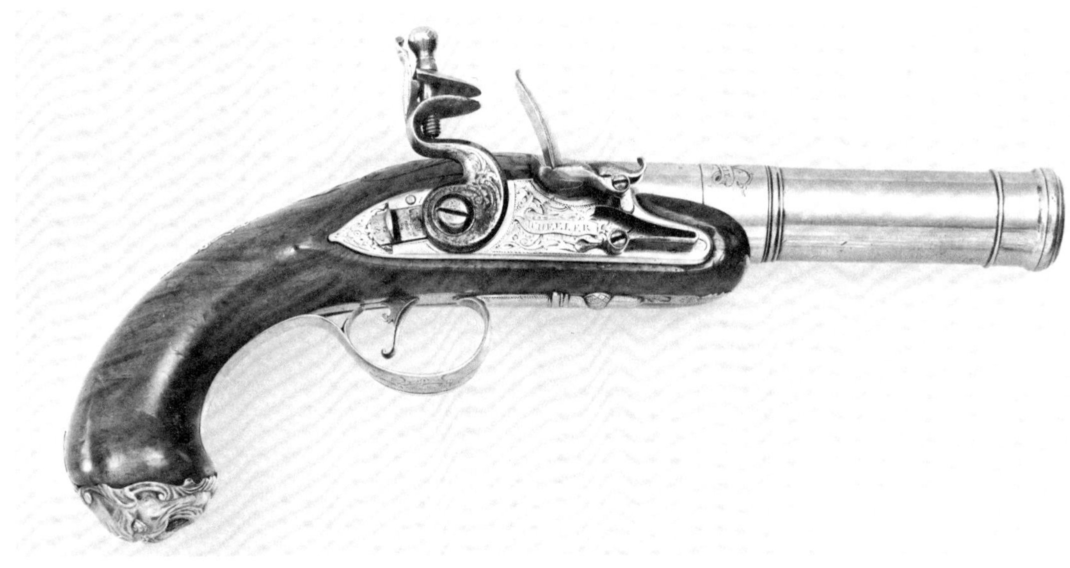

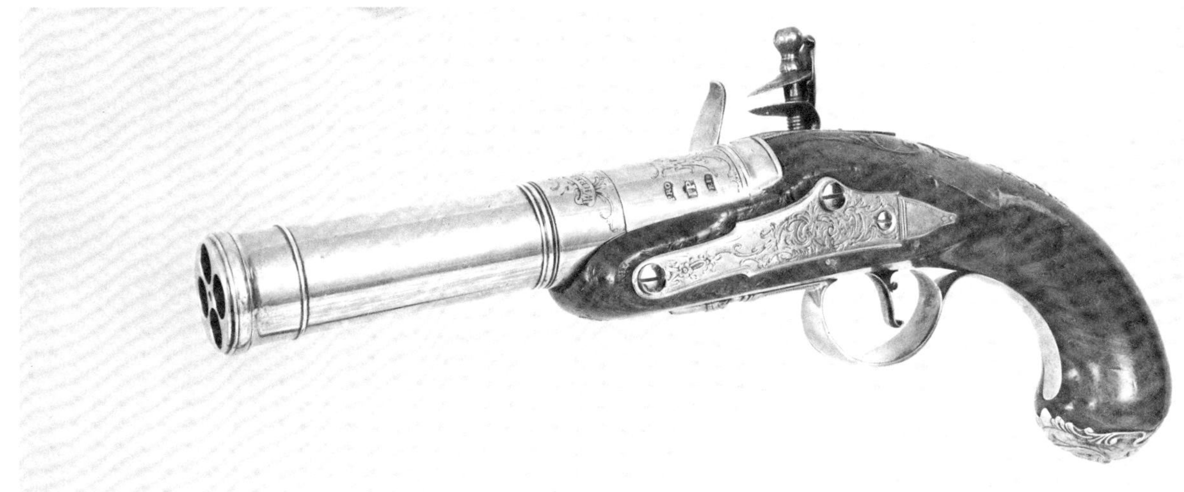

ribbon the place name LONDON; below lock, barrel is inscribed *Hirst* (in script); underside of barrel has elongated projection that fits barrel wrench; numeral 1 is stamped near junction of barrel and breech to aid in aligning. Lock plate forged integrally with breech; cock rounded and filed with raised edges; gold-lined pan; inverted-V steel spring. Walnut butt carved with trophy behind barrel tang; silver furniture; butt cap chased with shell and faun's mask; reverse-curved foliate side plate; asymmetrical escutcheon engraved with crest

(cap of maintenance surmounted by bird holding branch in beak).

The maker worked at Tower Hill from about 1745 to 1775.

John Hirst, London, about 1750
Overall length 8 in.; barrel 4⅛ in.
Caliber .52 (33 gauge). Weight ¾ lb.

194

196. Turnoff Belt Flintlock Pistol
(Bedford 889)

One of a pair. Barrel, lock plate, and mounts all of tutenag (nickel-silver alloy). Cannon barrel in three stages with molded rings between, ending in muzzle ring grooved for front sight; ribbon on front section of barrel inscribed WHEELER FECIT; breech engraved with rococo scrollwork and stamped with Birmingham proofs, PRO and VED (Proved), between which is barrelsmith's mark JP (John Probin); chamber is of unusual length, 2½ inches, and thickness, approximately ½ inches; forward part of barrel drilled with four small barrels,

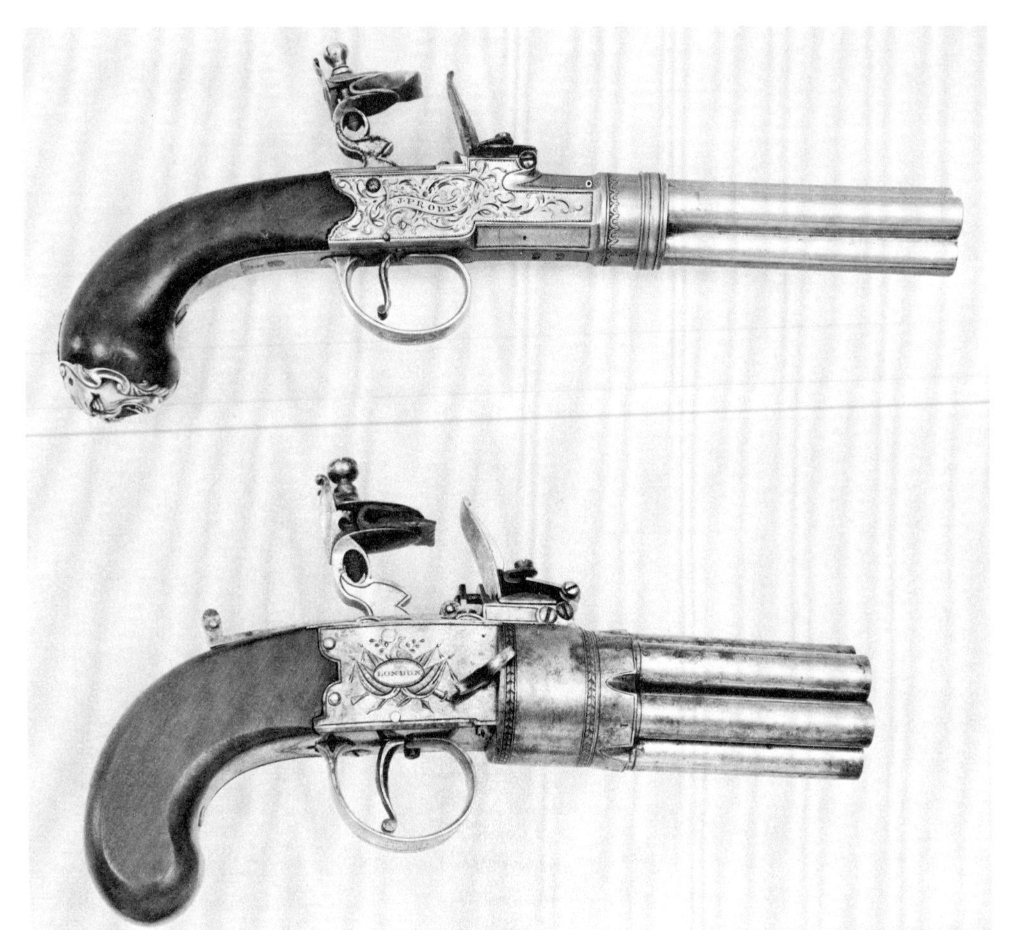

198

199

198

199

all fired simultaneously. Lock plate, flat faced, engraved with maker's name WHEELER on ribbon against rococo scrollwork; bolt safety operative at half cock; gold-lined vent and pan, some of gold lacking. Walnut three-quarter stock carved with shell behind barrel tang; silver butt cap chased with grotesque mask; flat side plate engraved with rococo scrolls; blank escutcheon framed by rococo scrolls; trigger guard with acorn finial.

> Robert Wheeler, Birmingham, about 1760
> Overall length 12½ in.; barrel 6½ in.
> Caliber .40 (71 gauge). Weight 2½ lb.

197. Turnoff Pocket Flintlock Pistol
(Bedford 1512)

Barrel and furniture of silver. Cannon barrel in two stages, engraved around breech; stamped on underside of breech are anchor (Birmingham), lion passant (sterling), date letter for 1774, and silversmith's initials CF (Charles Freeth); London private proof stamped twice on right side of breech. Box lock forged integrally with breech; on reverse side of lock is engraved in ribbon the name MORTIMER, on obverse LONDON. Walnut butt profusely inlaid with scrolling silver wire; butt cap chased with grotesque mask and stamped with Birmingham hallmark and lion passant; blank oval escutcheon.

The presence of a Birmingham hallmark on the breech indicates that this pistol must have been delivered to its London retailer already finished. It was, however, submitted for proof in London.

> Mortimer, London, 1774
> Overall length 5¼ in.; barrel 2 in.
> Caliber .35. Weight 5½ oz.

198. Four-barreled Turnoff Belt Flintlock Pistol
(Bedford 891)

Barrel body and trigger guard of tutenag (nickel-silver alloy); cluster of four barrels, each of circular section, joined by ring at breech; breech and lock plate forged together; Birmingham proofmark stamped on

lower facet of breech. Box lock is engraved on either side with rococo foliage and flowers, and on obverse in ribbon is inscribed J. PROBIN; ring-neck cock. Walnut butt; butt cap chased with mask and stamped with anchor, lion passant, and leopard's head; rococo

blank silver escutcheon is stamped with anchor, lion passant, Birmingham date letter for 1776, and silversmith's initials CF (Charles Freeth); trigger guard engraved with neoclassic urn.

> J. Probin, Birmingham, 1776
> Overall length 11¾ in.; barrel 6¼ in.
> Caliber .40 (71 gauge). Weight 1¾ lb.

199. Seven-barreled Turnoff Revolving Flintlock Pistol
(Bedford 1506)

The only known flintlock pepperbox by Twigg. Each barrel, plain, cylindrical, cut at muzzle to receive turnoff key; six barrels grouped around central seventh barrel; all seven screwed into cylindrical breech cut with six vents; behind vents is capstanlike central projection on end of which at right angles to axis of barrels is gear wheel; barrels are turned manually, and on either side of action is wing-headed screw; screw on right holds six barrels and cylindrical breech in position in outer cylinder; screw on left controls spring bearing on gear wheel; the tighter the screw, the more difficult it is to turn the barrel cylinder from one vent to the next. Breech fits within cylindrical member that is forged in one with box lock; trophies of arms engraved on either side of lock plate, and in oval on reverse is inscribed TWIGG and on obverse LONDON; ring-neck cock; bolt safety locks cock and pan. Walnut slab butt.

> John Twigg, London, about 1780
> Overall length 10 in.; barrel 4¾ in.
> Caliber .36 (97 gauge). Weight 3½ lb.

200. Steel Turnoff Pocket Flintlock Pistol
(Bedford 1557)

Barrel, plain, cylindrical, London proofmarks on underside of breech; breech forged integrally with box lock; on either side of lock plate are engraved trophies,

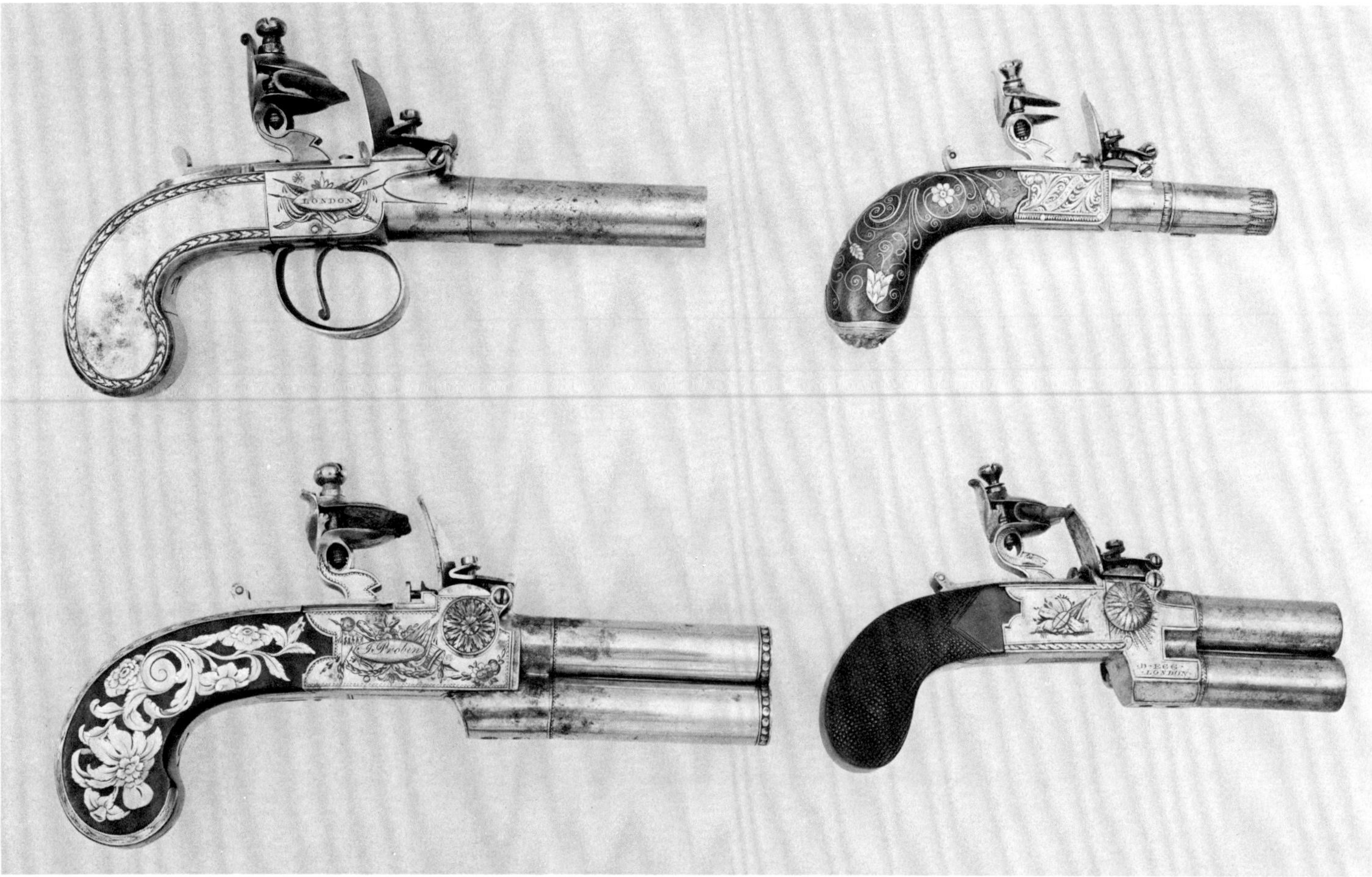

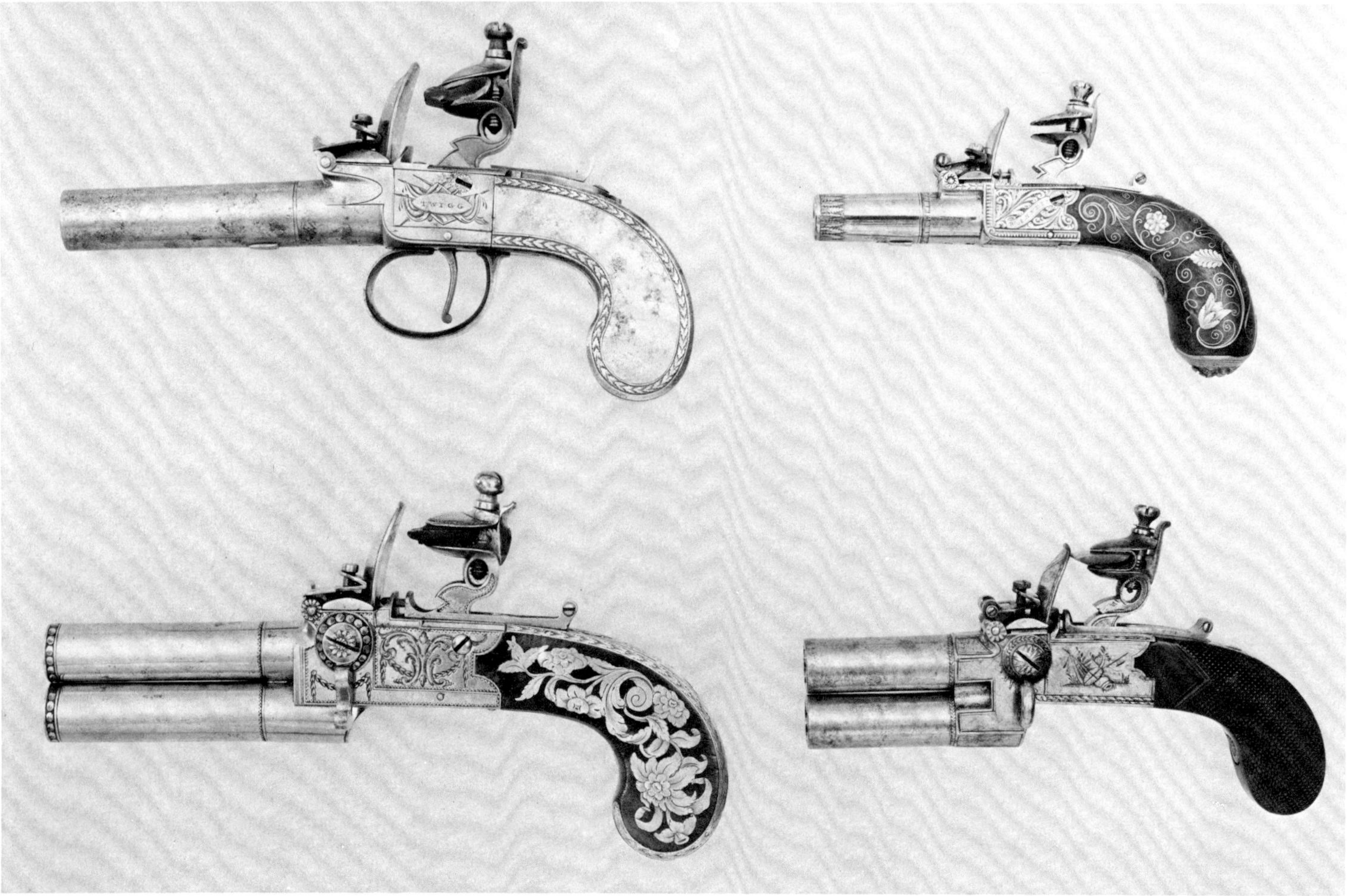

with TWIGG inscribed in oval on reverse and LONDON in oval on obverse; bolt safety engages at half cock. Edges of butt engraved with repeated overlapping foliage; blank oval escutcheon engraved on top of butt.

John Twigg, London, about 1785
Overall length 7 in.; barrel 3⅝ in.
Caliber .44 (52 gauge). Weight ½ lb.

201. Double-barreled Over-and-under Tap-action Flintlock Pistol (Bedford 1580)

Plain round barrels, ends of muzzles cut to receive turnoff key. Breeches forged integrally with box lock, which is finely engraved with neoclassic ornament on reverse side, and with maker's name *J. Probin* (in script) set against trophy of arms on obverse; folding trigger automatically opens when piece is cocked; ring-neck cock; bolt safety locks cock and pan at half cock; two-tiered pan with cutoff lever on reverse. Flat walnut butt inlaid with cut silver sheet finely engraved with floral ornament; edges of butt inlaid with silver strips engraved with overlapping leaves.

As the pistol illustrates, by the end of the 18th century the best gunmakers of Birmingham could equal those of London.

J. Probin, Birmingham, about 1790
Overall length 7½ in.; barrel 3½ in.
Caliber .40 (71 gauge). Weight ¾ lb.

202. Turnoff Pocket Flintlock Pistol (Bedford 1075)

One of a typical pair of best-quality Birmingham pocket pistols made for a Windsor retailer. Turnoff barrel engraved with ring of leaves at each end; Birmingham proofmark stamped three times on underside of barrel. Breech forged integrally with box lock, which is inscribed W. ABNETT; folding trigger opens at full cock. Walnut butt inlaid with scrolling silver wire terminating in flowers; silver butt cap chased with lion's head; diamond-shaped blank escutcheon.

W. Abnett, Windsor, about 1800
Overall length 4⅞ in.; barrel 1¾ in.
Caliber .32. Weight ¼ lb.

203. Double-barreled Over-and-under Tap-action Turnoff Pocket Pistol (Bedford 1277)

Plain round barrels with interior of muzzles cut to take key for unscrewing; on underside of lower breech is stamped twice the gunmaker's mark DE crowned (Durs Egg); breech end of lower barrel inscribed D. EGG LONDON: Breeches and box lock plate forged in one;

folding trigger; two-tiered pan with cutoff on left-hand side; bolt safety locks cock and pan at half cock; box lock is engraved with trophies of arms on each side. Checkered walnut butt.

Durs Egg, London, about 1800
Overall length 5⅝ in.; barrel 2½ in.
Caliber .40 (71 gauge). Weight ½ lb.

204. Presentation Turnoff Pocket Flintlock Pistol (Bedford 1579)

Short, plain barrel, blued, inlaid in gold with tree, branches of which bear plaques engraved with names: HOWE, NELSON, DUNCAN, SMITH, WARRAN, ST. VINCENT; gold muzzle and breech rings; breech forged integrally with box lock, which is signed in gold on reverse INNES and on obverse MAKER TO HIS MAJESTY. Flat-sided butt of steel with gold inlay, on one side scrolls and oval medallion enclosing figure of Britannia, on other side figure of Galatea seated in chariot drawn by two sea horses and, below, recumbent lion; top of butt inlaid with plain oval escutcheon supported by ribbon rail terminating in entwined dolphins; ring-neck cock; concealed trigger and bolt safety locking both cock and steel.

This pistol was evidently made to commemorate the victories won by British against the French and Dutch. Richard Howe, in command of the Channel fleet from 1793, blockaded the French until the battle of June 1, 1794, when he won a resounding victory; he resigned his commission in 1797. Viscount Horatio Nelson fought in the Battle of the Nile (1798) and at Copenhagen (1801), was made Commander in Chief of the Mediterranean fleet in 1803, and was killed at the Battle of Trafalgar (1805). Viscount Adam Duncan obtained flag rank in 1787, was made Admiral and Commander in Chief of the North Sea fleet in 1795, and won the victory of Camperdown against the Dutch (1797). Sir William Sidney Smith's most famous action was at the siege of Acre (1799). He was made Rear Admiral in 1805. Sir Samuel Warran was in command of the flagship *Glory* off Cape Finisterre in 1805. John Jarvis, earl of St. Vincent, was made Admiral in 1795. In 1797 he won a victory off Cape St. Vincent. In 1801 he became First Lord of the Admiralty, and in 1821 he was promoted to Admiral of the Fleet.

Francis Innes, Edinburgh, about 1800
Overall length 4½ in.
Literature: Sotheby's sale, March 22, 1971, lot 350, ill.

205. Four-barreled Turnoff Flintlock Pistol (Bedford 707)

One of the rarest of all known types of English flintlock pistols, used at close quarters against a crowd.

Maker to his
MAJESTY

204

GUN MAKERS
TO HIS
MAJESTY

205

H. MORTIMER &
FLEET ST

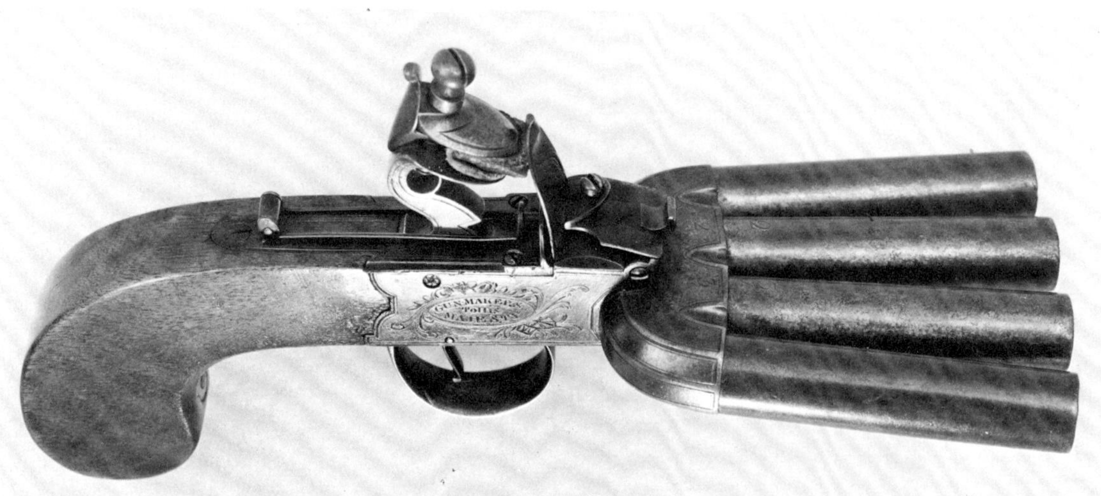

205

Four plain, splayed cylindrical barrels, numbered one to four, each cut at muzzle to receive turnoff key; London view mark and proofmark stamped twice on underside of breech. Breech forged integrally with box lock; barrels and lock are browned; both sides of lock plate engraved with foliation; in ribbon on reverse is inscribed H. W. MORTIMER & SON 89 FLEET ST.; on obverse, GUNMAKERS TO HIS MAJESTY; bolt safety engages at half cock and locks on both cock and pan; pan has four vents, one connecting with each barrel; all four barrels discharge at once. Walnut slab butt.

H. W. Mortimer & Son, London, about 1800
Overall length 9¼ in.; barrel 4 in.
Caliber .45 (50 gauge). Weight 1½ lb.

206. Double-barreled Over-and-under Pocket Flintlock Pistol   (Bedford 1073)

Octagonal barrels, browned, have silver bead front sight; at breech of each barrel is rectangular indentation stamped TATHAM . EGG; at breech two inlaid silver transverse bands; silver-lined vents. Lock plates, flat faced, with overlapping leaf borders engraved with sunburst in front of cock; signature on left lock plate is authentic; signature on right lock plate is copy and is misspelled TAITUM & EGG. Left- and right-hand locks, the right-hand lock communicating with upper barrel; bolt safeties engage at half cock; French-style cocks, waterproof pans, roller bearing on steel spring; single selective trigger discharges each barrel in turn. Checkered walnut butt; silver furniture; short-spurred pommel with engraved borders, hinged butt cap in center engraved with device of Shah Fath Ali of Persia; trigger guard has serial number 1217.

Originally made by Tatham & Egg in London, this appears to have been reworked in Persia. The barrels are replacements and the hinged butt cap is a Near Eastern addition. Small pocket pistols with double barrels, set over and under, were a specialty of the London gunmaker Joseph Egg (see also no. 211).

Tatham & Egg, London, about 1810
Overall length 8 in.; barrel 3⅛ in.
Caliber .45 (51 gauge). Weight 1¼ lb.

207. Three-barreled Tap-action Pocket Flintlock Pistol   (Bedford 1525)

Cylindrical barrels in vertical row, plain with ring at breech, muzzles filed to receive turnoff key; barrels numbered 4, 5, and 6, these numbers aligned with corresponding numbers on breech; breech forged integrally with box lock. Lock plate engraved on each side with trophy of arms, which on reverse includes name PROSSER and on obverse the address CHARING CROSS LONDON; bolt safety locks cock and pan at half cock; tiered pan has cutoff lever on reverse side. Walnut butt with blank oval silver escutcheon.

John Prosser, London, about 1810
Overall length 5⅝ in.; barrel 2¼ in.
Caliber .33. Weight ¾ lb.

208. Three-barreled Turnoff Tap-action Pocket Pistol with Bayonet   (Bedford 790)

Barrels, cylindrical, blued, and grouped two above, one below; stamped with Birmingham gunmakers'

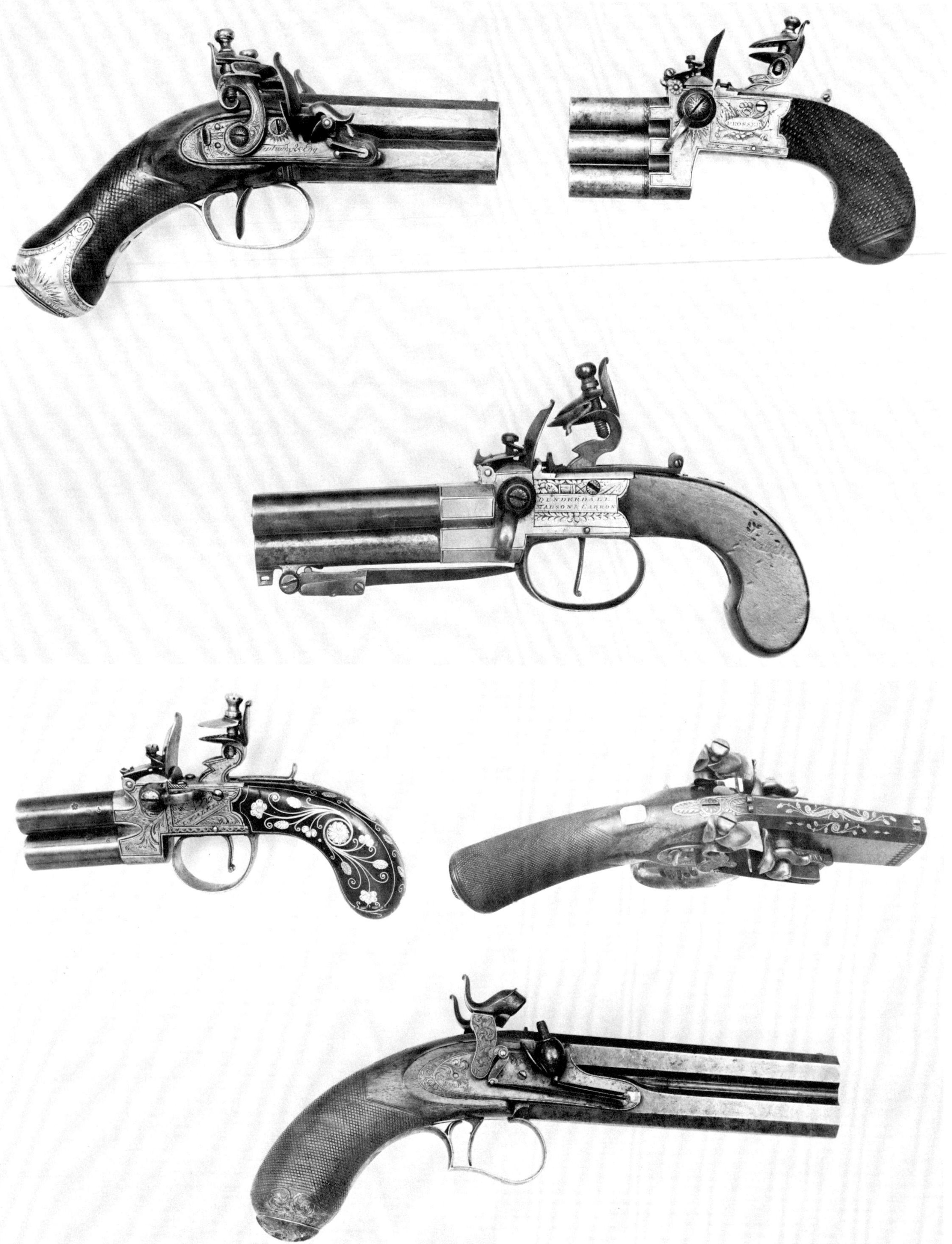

proof and barrelsmith's mark IR crowned; bayonet hinged under barrel. Brass breech forged integrally with box lock, the latter engraved on reverse with name DUNDERDALE, MABSON & LABRON, on obverse with trophy of arms; tiered pan with tap at side for revolving each tier in turn to appropriate barrel vent; bolt safety locks cock and pan at half cock. Walnut slab butt with octagonal silver escutcheon.

> Dunderdale, Mabson & Labron, Birmingham, about 1810
> Overall length 8½ in.; barrel 2¾ in.
> Caliber .40 (71 gauge). Weight 1¼ lb.

five marks including Birmingham hallmark, silversmith's mark FNJ, and date letter for 1820. Projecting from the center is head of ramrod, which is screwed through threaded aperture.

The locks of this pistol are of particularly sophisticated design, with their screws for increasing or releasing tension on the springs. Active from about 1805 to 1825, William Smith was gunmaker to the Prince Regent.

> William Smith, London, 1820
> Overall length 7¾ in.; barrel 3¼ in.
> Caliber .38 (83 gauge). Weight 15 oz.

209. Double-barreled Over-and-under Turnoff Tap-action Pocket Pistol
(Bedford 1013)

One of a pair made in Birmingham for retailing in London. Barrels, cylindrical, blued, muzzles filed to receive turnoff key; barrels numbered 5 and 6 and aligned with corresponding numbers on breech; underside of breech stamped with Birmingham proofmarks. Box lock forged integrally with breeches; both sides of lock plate engraved with foliation; in diagonal bands on reverse is inscribed name I. WALKER and on obverse LONDON; ring-neck cock; bolt safety engages at half cock; lever for tap action on reverse side of lock. Walnut butt, rounded, is inlaid overall with silver wire scrolls that terminate in leaves and flower heads; blank octagonal escutcheon.

> I. Walker, London, about 1820
> Overall length 6¼ in.; barrel 2½ in.
> Caliber .40 (71 gauge). Weight 11 oz.

210. Double-barreled Over-and-under Pocket Flintlock Pistol
(Bedford 1037)

Both barrels wrought in one piece, blued, of octagonal section with repeated leaf border engraved around muzzle; upper barrel inlaid with gold scrollwork and inscribed W. SMITH LONDON on ribbon. Left- and right-hand locks, right-hand lock serving upper barrel; lock plates, flat faced, with engraved leaf borders; platinum-lined vents; external main springs connected by swivel links to tails of cocks; cocks with loop necks; bolt safeties engage at half cock; waterproof pans; pan-cover arm has extension passing through lock plate, end of which has roller bearing that rides on steel spring inside lock plate; screw on lower edge of lock plate enables adjustment of tension of steel spring. Locks provided with detents; two triggers, forward trigger discharges the upper lock. Walnut half stock, checkered butt; oval butt cap engraved with flower and repeated leaf border; blank octagonal escutcheon; silver trigger guard struck on inside with

211. Double-barreled Over-and-under Percussion Pistol
(Bedford 1065)

Barrels of browned twist, octagonal, brazed together with central rib; top facet of upper barrel inscribed JOSEPH EGG INVENTOR OF COPPER CAPS; silver blade front sight; ramrod with brass finial at each end fits into polished steel pipe on reverse side; bottom facet of lower barrel inscribed NO. 1 PICCADILLY LONDON. Left- and right-hand percussion-cap locks have external mainsprings, with hook of spring attached by link to toe of cock; each lock plate inscribed JOSEPH EGG; single selective trigger discharges each barrel in turn. Walnut butt has checkered grip; blued and engraved steel furniture; butt cap finished with projecting ridge known as "skull splitter"; octagonal blank silver escutcheon.

Various gunmakers, including Joseph Manton, claimed to have invented the copper percussion cap, and Egg's claim should not perhaps be taken too seriously, despite the inscription.

> Joseph Egg, London, about 1825
> Overall length 10 in.; barrel 5 in.
> Caliber .47 (44 gauge). Weight 1½ lb.

212. Steel Percussion-cap Pocket Pistol
(Bedford 1143)

Plain cylindrical barrel; Birmingham proofmark stamped on bottom of breech; alignment number 2 stamped on both barrel and breech. Butt and breech forged in one piece; both sides of grip are engraved with scrolls; on reverse of grip is engraved name WM & JN RIGBY and on obverse DUBLIN; folding trigger; dolphin hammer, the tumbler with three indentations, one raising hammer just clear of nipple, the next to half cock, then full cock; end of butt is bored and has slot on one side to serve as key for unscrewing turnoff barrel of companion pistol.

William Rigby took over the Dublin business of his father, John Rigby, in 1819 and entered into partnership

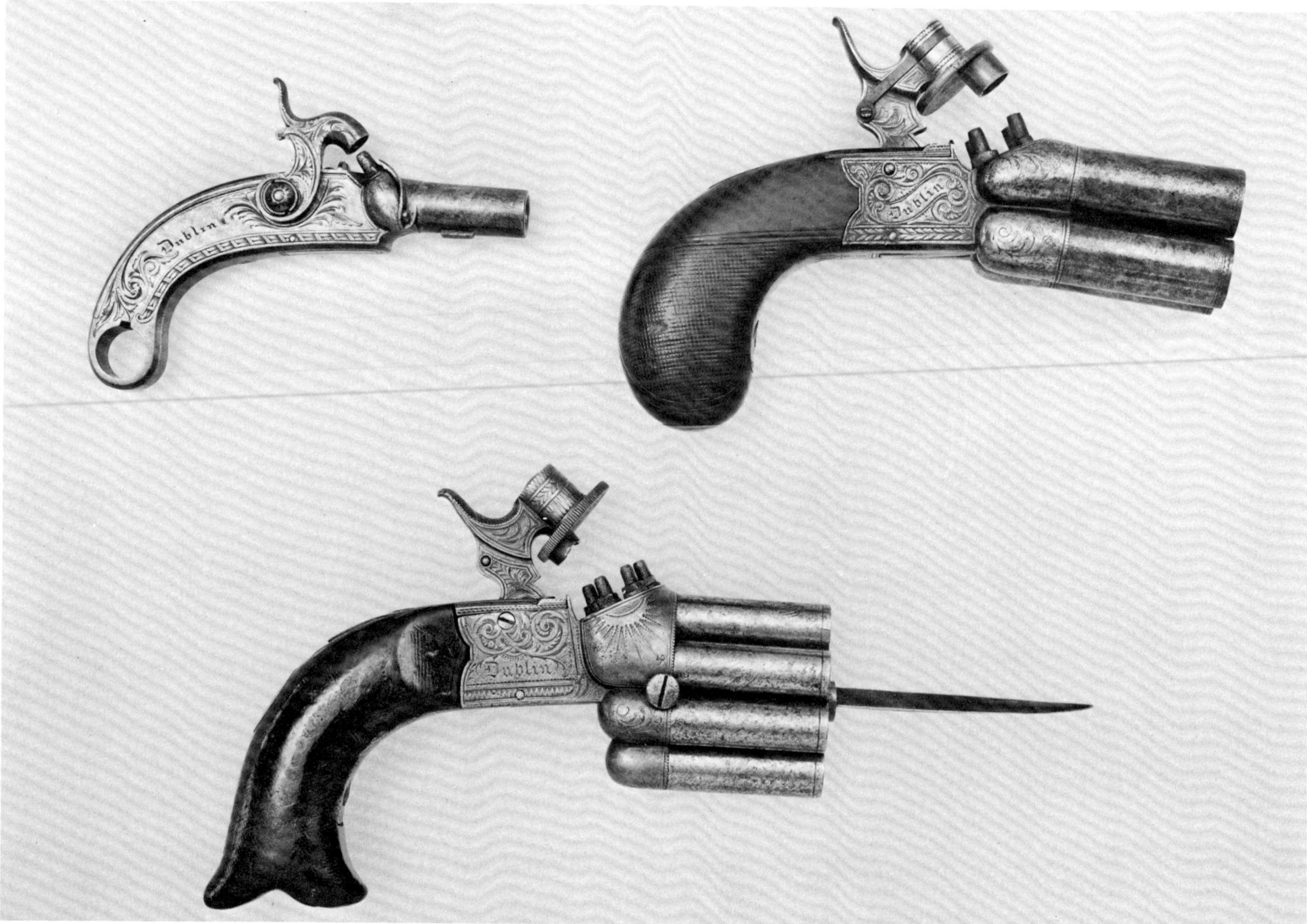

with his younger brother, also named John Rigby, shortly afterward.

> William & John Rigby, Dublin, about 1825–30
> Overall length 5½ in.; barrel 2 in.
> Caliber .33. Weight 7½ oz.

213. Four-barreled Turnoff Percussion-cap Pocket Pistol with Revolving Hammer
(Bedford 1014)

Plain cylindrical barrels, two above and two below; muzzles engraved with invected border and cut to accept turnoff tool. Breeches forged in one with box lock, which is engraved with foliation and inscribed on reverse in a ribbon WM & JN RIGBY and on obverse DUBLIN; barrels, each with its own nipple, numbered 1 to 4; hammer has revolving striker turned clockwise by hand before each discharge, and a spring that clips it automatically in place above appropriate nipple; folding trigger opens automatically at full cock. Walnut butt is checkered; silver oval cap; silver octagonal escutcheon.

> William & John Rigby, Dublin, about 1835
> Overall length 7 in.; barrel 3 in.
> Caliber .52 (33 gauge). Weight 1¼ lb.

214. Six-barreled Turnoff Percussion-cap Pistol with Fixed Bayonet and Rotating Hammer
(Bedford 712)

Six cylindrical barrels arranged in two groups of three, numbered 1 to 6, and cut to receive turnoff tool; six nipples, one for each barrel, arranged in circle; hammer with head rotated counterclockwise by hand is located in correct position over each nipple by notched spring. Breeches and box lock are forged in one, engraved with scrolling foliage and with sunburst on each side; on reverse of lock is inscribed M. & J. PATTISON, on obverse DUBLIN; folding trigger opens automatically at full cock. Walnut butt has fishtail finial; silver oval escutcheon. Bayonet has shaft inserted at central point between six barrels and is fixed by screw on obverse at breech.

Mark and John Pattison worked in Dublin from about 1835 to 1850.

> Mark & John Pattison, Dublin, about 1835
> Overall length including bayonet 10 in.; barrel 2¾ in.
> Caliber .33. Weight 1¼ lb.
> Literature: Winant, *Firearms Curiosa*, p. 89, pls. 82–83.

215. Percussion-cap Pepperbox Pistol
(Bedford 1029)

Seven barrels, each with silver bead front sight and percussion cap, revolve around central spindle;

alternate barrels have London proofmark and view mark, the latter appearing four times; barrels are hand-turned clockwise, but with automatic locating spring; behind breech is concave discoid plate that encloses nipples. Box lock with side dolphin hammer; bolt safety engages at half cock; on top of lock plate in chamfered rectangle is inscribed W. PARKER HOLBORN LONDON. Walnut butt is checkered and has carved pommel and cylindrical compartment; steel butt cap with hinged trap; barrels and lock are case hardened.

William Parker worked in Holborn from 1795 until his death in 1841.

> William Parker, London, about 1840
> Overall length 8¾ in.; barrel 3¼ in.
> Caliber .34. Weight 1½ lb.

216. Six-barreled Pepperbox Percussion-cap Revolver
(Bedford 1211)

Barrels, case hardened, revolve around central spindle; areas between barrels fluted, barrels faceted; Birmingham proofmarks stamped at breech in fluted areas; a number, 1 through 6, stamped on each barrel. Frame, engraved with scrollwork, is silver plated; trigger pressure has double action, both raising hammer and revolving cylinder; checkered walnut butt has cylindrical compartment and engraved, hinged circular trap; blued steel trigger guard and butt cap.

This pistol was apparently made in Birmingham for a Gloucester gunmaker.

> T. Fletcher, Gloucester, about 1840
> Overall length 8 in.; barrel 2⅞ in.
> Caliber .30. Weight ¾ lb.

217. Four-barreled Pepperbox Pistol
(Bedford 728)

Barrels with case-hardened finish revolve around central spindle; leaf border engraved around muzzle; separating each cylindrical barrel from the next is a wide channel; barrels are numbered 1 through 4 at breech, and London view mark and proofmark are stamped in alternate channels. Lock plate wrought in one piece with concave disk that shields nipples; lock plate engraved with scrollwork over and under signature; reverse of lock plate inscribed WITTON DAW & CO. 82 OLD BROAD ST. LONDON, obverse inscribed IMPROVED REVOLVING PISTOL; double action; safety bolt locks hammer. Checkered walnut butt with cylindrical compartment; flat oval butt cap with hinged trap. Lock plate and trigger guard have original case-hardened finish.

This pistol is in mint condition. John Witton and George Daw were in partnership at 82 Old Broad Street from 1851 to 1854.

> Witton Daw & Co., London, about 1850
> Overall length 9¾ in.; barrel 3⅞ in.
> Caliber .51 (36 gauge). Weight 1¾ lb.

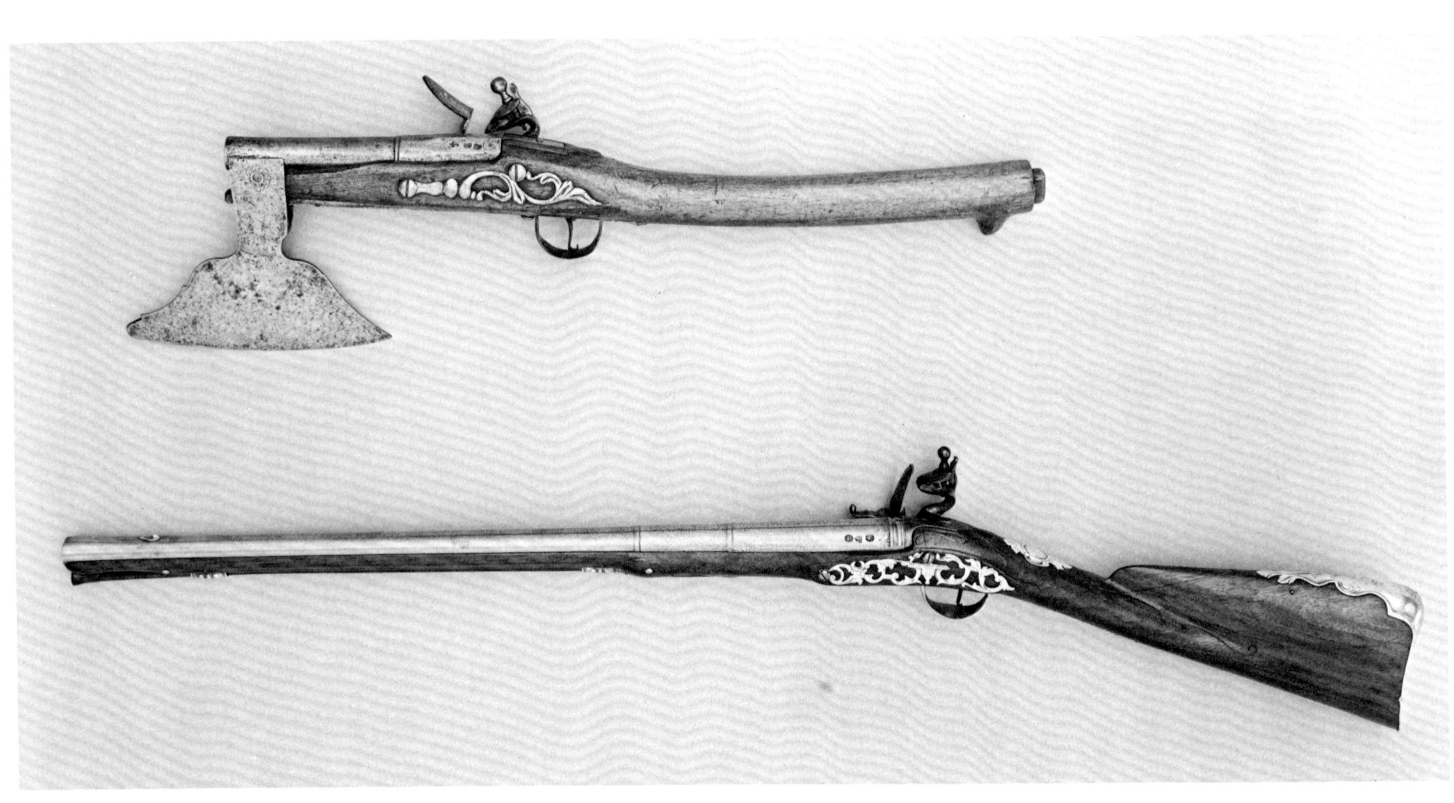

218. Double-barreled Turnover Turnoff Box-lock Percussion-cap Pocket Pistol
(Bedford 1080)

Cylindrical barrels engraved with border of foliage around muzzle and cut to receive key for unscrewing; London proofmarks; breech and box-lock action wrought integrally and engraved all over with scrolling foliage; on reverse, enclosed in ribbons, engraved J. LANG 22 COCKSPUR ST., and on obverse LONDON; dolphin cock with bolt safety operative at half cock. Walnut butt, checkered, has cylindrical compartment; convex steel butt cap, engraved with foliage, has hinged trap; oval silver escutcheon.

Joseph Lang worked for Alexander Wilson of 1 Vigo Street and from 1812 of 14 Tichbourne Street, Piccadilly. He established himself in business at 7 Hay Market in 1821. In 1826 he advertised the stock of Joseph Manton, who had gone bankrupt. Lang showed his work at the Great Exhibition, Hyde Park, 1851. In 1853 he moved to 22 Cockspur Street.

Joseph Lang, London, about 1855
Overall length 6¾ in.; barrel 2 in.
Caliber .46 (48 gauge). Weight ¾ lb.

219. Combined Ax and Flintlock Pistol
(Bedford 887)

Barrel in two stages, octagonal changing to polygonal at breech, remainder cylindrical, molded girdle between; on left facet at breech are stamped London view mark and proofmark, also fleur-de-lis, with initials (effaced, but presumably mark EW with fleur-de-lis of Edward Turvey); barrel tang engraved E. TURVEY (much effaced). Lock plate, rounded, with line edges, engraved with name E. TURVEY and strawberry foliage, also on cock; steel trigger guard, trigger-guard strap extends practically entire length of stock and beyond ax socket, its end flanged. Walnut stock of ax type, slightly curved; at muzzle and at right angles to barrel

is fixed an ax blade held in position by prongs on forward end of trigger-guard strap and by transverse iron peg; at rear of butt is cylindrical hollow in which fits wood ramrod with carved head (partly broken); pierced foliate side plate.

Ax pistols were usual in Hungary and Poland, where they were carried in processions. This is the only recorded English example. Edward Turvey was admitted freeman of the Gunmakers' Company in 1690 and was master in 1713.

Edward Turvey, London, about 1690–1700
Overall length 24¾ in.; barrel 7 in.
Caliber .77 (10 gauge). Weight 3½ lb.

220. Boy's Sporting Flintlock Gun
(Bedford 393)

Barrel, cylindrical, with hooked breech, in three stages with simple rings between and chased at breech with leaf decoration; barrel inscribed DAVID WYNN LONDINI; London proofmarks at breech between which are initials DW (David Wynn) surmounted by fleur-de-lis; two barrel slides slotted with limit pins; barrel slightly expanded at muzzle with silver sight chased as conventional lion's head and flowing mane; notched breech for rear sight. Lock plate, rounded, inscribed DAVID WYNN; lock plate, cock, and steel with raised

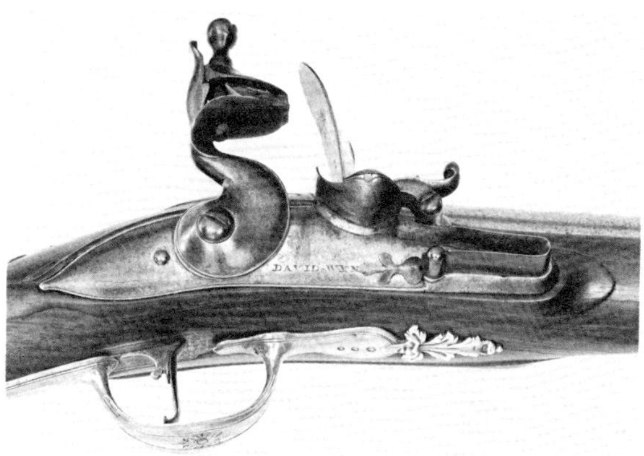

edge; no bridle on pan cover, inside bridle on tumbler; flash fence. Walnut full stock with carved raised edges to outline mounts and with foliage behind barrel tang; silver furniture; butt plate with tang ending in acanthus-leaf decoration; pierced foliate side plate with two side nails; escutcheon has acanthus-leaf decoration above and below and is engraved with initial D surmounted by crown; trigger guard, engraved with flower, has vase, plant, and mask finial; two baluster ramrod pipes; whalebone ramrod has steel worm and, at forward end, walnut finial with steel disk.

David Wynn, London, about 1720
Overall length 35¾ in.; barrel 22¼ in.
Caliber .62 (19 gauge). Weight 3½ lb.

GUNMAKERS AND SILVERSMITHS

The numbers below refer to catalogue numbers

Gunmakers

Abnett, W., Windsor, 202
Aislabie, 167
Bailes, William, 87
Barbar, James, 26
Barbar, Lewis, 16, 17, 24, 50, 60, 143, 144
Barker, W., 159
Barne, Harman, 2
Bass, John, 76
Bate, Edward, 161
Bate, Thomas, 162
Bennett, John, 33, 107
Bidet, S., 125
Bond, William, 160
Brooke, Robert, 115
Brunn, Samuel, 66
Bumford, John, 31
Bunney, Joseph, 148
Caddell, Thomas, Doune, 42, 45
Campbell, John, Doune, 43
Christi, 44
Clarkson, Joseph, 61, 86
Clinton, 108
Cole, Elias, 109
Collier, Elisha Hayden, 185-187, 192
Collier & Co., 188, 193
Collumbell, David, 29
Dafte, John, 7
Deane, Adams & Deane, 190
Delany, Henry, 53, 56
Dolep, Andrew, 9
Dunderdale, Mabson & Labron, Birmingham, 208
Egg, Durs, 36, 74, 78, 95, 111, 142, 149, 151, 203
Egg, Joseph, 83, 175, 211
Ellis, Henry, Doncaster, Yorkshire, 12, 49
Ermendinger, James, 10, 11
Fisher, George, 157
Fletcher, T., Gloucester, 216
Forsyth & Co., 170-182 inclusive
Freeman, James, 54, 57, 126
Glass, I., 127
Gorgo, Jacques, 134
Green, Thomas, 13
Grice, Joseph, 32

Griffin, Joseph, 30, 63, 145
Hall, John, 55
Hall, Joseph, Dublin, 184
Harvey, Robert, 19
Heath & Hurdd, Birmingham, 137
Henry, Alexander, 101
Henshaw, Thomas, 166
Heylin, Joseph, 146, 158
Hirst, John, 195
Innes, Francis, Edinburgh, 150, 204
Jover, William, 128, 139
Jover & Son, 35
Kolbe, Johann Gottfried, 194
Lambe, John, Salisbury, 136
Lang, Joseph, 218
Manton, John, 68, 75, 96, 152
Manton & Son, John, 156
Manton, Joseph, 77, 85, 91, 94, 173
Mathias, 8
Mills, William, 93
Moore, Daniel, 88
Mortimer, 197
Mortimer, H. W., 130, 168
Mortimer & Co., H. W., 79
Mortimer & Son, H. W., 205
Mortimer & Son, Thomas, 81
Murdoch, John, 46
Nicholes, J., Oxford, 15
Nicholson, Edward, 48
Nock, Henry, 169
Nock, Samuel, 70
North, Edward, 28
Nutt, William, 165
Osborne, Charles, 99
Palmer, Rochester, 38
Paris, Jr., Nicholas, Warwick, 58
Parker, William, 215
Pattison, Mark & John, Dublin, 214
Pauly, Samuel, 131
Peddell, James, 105
Peele, T., Whitehaven, 64
Phippes, William, 164
Powell, Dublin, 191
Probin, John, Birmingham, 34, 196, 198, 201
Prosser, John, 80, 207
Purdey, James, 69, 92, 97, 98, 100, 153, 154, 190
Ransford, Michael, Dublin, 27
Richards, John, 141

Richards, Theophilus, Birmingham, 147
Richards, Thomas, Birmingham, 65
Richards, Westley, Birmingham, 84
Rigby, John, Dublin, 82
Rigby, William & John, Dublin, 155, 212, 213
Rowland, Robert, 20, 23, 135
Segalas, Jr., Israel, 62
Seret, Isaac de, 133
Sibley, John, 118
Sinckler, Richard, 21, 22
Smith, Samuel & Charles, 39
Smith, William, 210
Staudenmayer, Samuel Henry, 163
Stvart, John, 41
Tatham & Egg, 206
Turvey, Edward, 53, 219
Turvey, William, 25
Twigg, John, 72, 76, 89, 90, 199, 200
Upton, William, Oxford, 47
Vernon, 122
Walker, I., 209
Warren, Charles, 6
Wheeler, Robert, 138, 196
White, John, 119
Wilkes, James, 124
Wilkinson, Henry, 37
Wilkinson & Son, James, 132, 189
Willmore, James, 52
Willowes, John, 18
Wilson, Robert, 140, 183
Witton Daw & Co., 217
Wogdon, Robert, 67, 71, 73
Wornall, Edward, 14
Wynn, David, 51, 59, 220

Silversmiths

Ashley, Jeremiah, 25, 29, 30, 166, 183
Brent, Moses, 32, 33, 35, 68, 149, 162
Brooker, James, 26
Bull, William 13, 14, 19, 21
FNJ, 210
Freeth, Charles, 129, 197, 198
IH, 22
King, John, 31, 64, 67, 87, 88, 89

SELECTIVE BIBLIOGRAPHY

Books

Akehurst, Richard
Sporting Guns. New York, 1968 // *Game Guns and Rifles from Percussion to Hammerless Ejector in Britain.* London, 1969.

Atkinson, John A.
Duelling Pistols, and Some of the Affairs They Settled. London, 1964.

Baker, Ezekiel
Remarks on Rifle Guns. London, 1800.

Baxter, D. R.
Superimposed Load Firearms, 1360-1860. Hong Kong, 1966.

Blackmore, Howard L.
British Military Firearms, 1650-1850. London, 1961 // Victoria and Albert Museum. *The Art of the Armourer. An Exhibition of Armour, Swords and Firearms.* London, 1963 // *Firearms.* London, 1964 // *Guns and Rifles of the World.* London, 1965 // *Royal Sporting Guns at Windsor.* London, 1968.

Blair, Claude
Pistols of the World. London, 1968.

Cottesloe, Lord
The Englishman and the Rifle. London, 1945.

Cruso, John
Militarie Instructions for the Cavallerie. Cambridge, 1632.

Davies, Edward
The Art of War. London, 1618-1619.

Ferguson, J.
Two Scottish Soldiers. Aberdeen, 1888.

George, J. N.
English Pistols and Revolvers. Onslow County, North Carolina, 1938 // *English Guns and Rifles.* Plantersville, South Carolina, 1947.

Glendenning, Ian
British Pistols and Guns, 1640-1840. New York, 1967.

Grancsay, Stephen V.
The Metropolitan Museum of Art. *Loan Exhibition of European Arms and Armor.* August 3–September 27, 1931. New York, 1931.

Grancsay, Stephen V., and
Lindsay, Merrill
Illustrated British Firearms Patents, 1714-1853. New York, 1969.

Grose, Francis
Military Antiquities, Representing a History of the English Army from the Conquest to the Present Time. 2 vols. London, 1801.

Harris, Clive
The History of the Birmingham Gun-Barrel Proof House. Birmingham and London, 1946.

Hastings, Macdonald
English Sporting Guns and Accessories. London and Sydney, 1969.

Hawker, Peter
Instructions to Young Sportsmen in All That Relates to Guns and Shooting. London, 1824. (Ninth edition, London, 1844.)

Hayward, J. F.
The Art of the Gunmaker. 2 vols. New York, 1962-1963.

Laking, Guy Francis
The Armoury of Windsor Castle: European Section. London, 1904.

Lenk, Torsten
The Flintlock: Its Origin and Development. London, 1965.

Lindsay, Merrill
One Hundred Great Guns. New York, 1967.

Mann, James G.
Exhibition of Arms, Armour and Militaria Lent by H.R.H. The Duke of Brunswick at the Tower of London. April 10–October 31, 1952. London, 1952.

Markland, George
Pteryplegia: Or, The Art of Shooting Flying. London, 1727.

Neal, W. Keith, and Back, D. H. L.
The Mantons: Gunmakers. London, 1967 // *Forsyth & Co.: Patent Gunmakers.* London, 1969.

Pollard, H. B. C.
A History of Firearms. London, 1927.

Reid, A. J. F.
The Reverend Alexander John Forsyth and his Invention of the Percussion Lock. Aberdeen, 1909. (Reprinted, 1955.)

Ricketts, Howard
Firearms. London, 1962.

Roads, C. H.
The British Soldier's Firearm, 1850-1864. London, 1964.

Robins, Benjamin
New Principles of Gunnery. 2 vols. London, 1742.

Taylor, Leslie B.
A Brief History of the Westley Richards Firm, 1812-1913. Stratford-upon-Avon, 1913.

Taylerson, A. W. F., Andrews, R. A. N., and Frith, J.
The Revolver, 1818-1865. New York, 1968.

Thomas, Bruno, and Boccia, Lionello G.
Oesterreichische Florenzhilfe. Historische Prunkwaffen aus dem Museo Nazionale (Palazzo del Bargello) zu Florenz, restauriert in den Werkstätten der Wiener Waffensammlung. Vienna, 1970.

Whitelaw, Charles E.
"A Treatise on Scottish Hand Firearms," in *European Hand Firearms of the Sixteenth, Seventeenth & Eighteenth Centuries,* by Herbert J. Jackson. London, 1923. Pp. 53-108, 8 pls., 2 diagrams.

Winant, Lewis
    Firearms Curiosa. New York, 1955 // *Early Percussion Firearms.* New York, 1959.

Wilkinson, Henry
    Engines of War. London, 1841.

Periodical Articles

Bedford, Clay P.
    "Admiral Nelson's Guns—The Seven Barrel Volley Guns—Fact or Fancy?," *The Gun Report,* October 1967, pp. 8-13, 18 figs. // "The Forsyth Percussion System," *American Society of Arms Collectors, 15th Anniversary Bulletin,* Spring 1969, 24 figs. // "Collier and his Revolvers," *American Society of Arms Collectors, Bulletin,* Fall 1971.

Blackmore, Howard L.
    "The Mark Plate of the Gunmakers' Company," *Journal of the Arms & Armour Society,* London, September 1954, pp. 115-129, 2 ill. // "The Seven-Barrel Guns," *Journal of the Arms & Armour Society,* London, June 1955, pp. 165-182, 4 pls. // "The Experimental Firearms of Henry Nock," *Journal of the Arms & Armour Society,* London, December 1956, pp. 69-109 // "Henry Hadley, 'Foreigner,' and four pairs of his pistols," *Connoisseur,* October 1957, pp. 82-87, 20 figs. // "An Early Pellet-Lock Gun," *American Rifleman,* July 1960, pp. 24-25, 6 figs.

Blair, Claude
    "The Eggs and their Origins," *Journal of the Arms & Armour Society,* London, December 1966, pp. 353-357 // "Joseph Egg's Inverted Flintlock," *Antique Arms Annual,* 1971, p. 174, ill.

Eaves, Ian
    "Some Notes on the Pistol in Early 17th Century England," *Journal of the Arms & Armour Society,* London, September 1970, pp. 277-344, 20 pls.

Fox, Robert
    "The Fire Piston and its Origins in Europe," *Technology and Culture,* July 1969, pp. 355-370, 2 pls.

Harrison, Jr., G. Charter
    "The J. C. Lowe Collection of Cylinder Guns," *The Gun Collector,* 1951, pp. 497-556, 100 figs. (Includes "The Collier Revolver," pp. 500-506, 3 figs.)

Hayward, J. F.
    "English Pistols of the XVII Century," *Apollo,* October 1947, pp. 94-96, ill.; January 1948, pp. 5-9, ill. // "The Firearms Collection of the Armeria Reale, Turin," *Apollo,* February 1951, pp. 50-53, 5 ill.; May 1951, pp. 126-128, 4 ill. // "English Firearms of the 16th Century," *Journal of the Arms & Armour Society,* London, March 1960, pp. 117-141, 15 pls. // "Silver Mounts on Firearms," *Proceedings of the Society of Silver Collectors,* Summer 1966, pp. 13-18, 4 figs. // "The Huguenot Gunmakers of London," *Journal of the Arms & Armour Society,* London, December 1968, pp. 117-143, 14 pls.

Hewitt, John
    "Notice of the Combined Use of the Match-lock and the Flint-lock in the Progressive Improvements in Firearms," *Archaeological Journal,* 1860, pp. 225-226, ill.

Hoff, Arne
    "Scottish Pistols in Scandinavian Collections," *Journal of the Arms & Armour Society,* London, December 1955, pp. 199-214, 6 pls.

Hollaender, A. E. J.
    "The Archives of the Worshipful Company of Gunmakers of the City of London," *Archives,* 1952, pp. 8-19.

Latham, John
    "Early Breech-Loaders," reprinted London, 1968, from *Journal of the Royal United Service Institution.*

May, W. E.
    "Some Board of Ordnance Gunmakers," *Journal of the Arms & Armour Society,* London, September 1969, pp. 201-204.

Mayer, Joseph R.
    Flintlocks of the Iroquois, 1620-1687, Research Records of the Rochester Museum of Arts and Sciences, No. 6. Rochester, New York, 1943.

Neal, W. Keith
    "Pistols for Two," in *The Saturday Book,* edited by John Hadfield. London, 1970. Pp. 157-170, 16 figs. // "The Ferguson Rifle," *American Society of Arms Collectors, Bulletin,* Fall 1971.

Reid, William
    "Pauly, Gun-Designer," *Journal of the Arms & Armour Society,* London, March 1958, pp. 181-210, 9 pls.; 254-258 // "The Present of Spain. A Seventeenth-Century Royal Gift," *Connoisseur,* August 1960, pp. 21-26, ill.

Scurfield, R.
    "British Military Smoothbore Firearms," *Journal of the Society for Army Historical Research,* Summer 1955, pp. 63-79.

Sherlock, Herbert A.
    "Early British Grenade Launchers," *Military Collector and Historian,* June 1951, pp. 44-46.

Stern, Walter M.
    "Gunmaking in Seventeenth-Century London," *Journal of the Arms & Armour Society,* London, March 1954, pp. 55-100.

Suydam, C. R.
    "A Queen Anne Flintlock Pistol by Israel Segalas," *The Gun Report,* January 1965, pp. 58-59.

Tylden, G.
    "The Use of Firearms by Cavalry," *Journal of the Society for Army Historical Research,* Spring 1940, pp. 9-15.

Westropp, M. S. Dudley
    "Irish Gunsmiths and Sword Cutlers," *Journal of the Arms & Armour Society,* London, March 1956, pp. 13-18.

Williams, H. W.
    "An Eighteenth-Century Gunsmith's Pattern Book by Robert Wilson," *Connoisseur,* July 1938, pp. 29-31, 3 figs.